COMMENTS OF THE PRESS.

Comments of the press on the first edition of Synthetic Bible Studies : —

The *Homiletic Review* says the method of Bible study it exemplifies is "the best that has been presented to the public."

The Pittsburgh Christian Advocate: "We know of no other way in which one can so easily and satisfactorily get a comprehensive view of the Bible as in this way."

The *Quarterly Review* (United Brethren) : We know of nothing better of its kind for the use of higher classes in the Sunday School, and for Theological Seminary's Bible study in English, and for the minister's private study."

The *Record of Christian Work :* "It is many years since a Bible study help has been given to the world of which so many commendatory things may be said."

The *Baltimore Methodist :* "This is an age of Bible study, and the many 'helps' published to make this study interesting and profitable are numerous. We venture to affirm, however, that none equal the present method, both for practical and exegetical work. Dr. Gray has given us a book which every student, teacher and preacher of the Bible ought to possess. Such books cannot be measured by money value, bnt only by the impetus given to Bible study and the solid character built up thereby."

Watchword and Truth : "Anyone wishing help in scripture study can do no better than purchase this book. It is admirable, evangelical, accurate and helpful. No wonder the first edition is completely exhausted before the newspapers of the land have had a chance to review the book. We predict for it an enormous sale of many thousands."

Herald and Presbyter : "This is a very attractive book. Any one who wishes to study the Bible systematically will find it invaluable. It would be an excellent guide for a series of Sabbath evening lectures. It gives a bird's-eye view of the whole Bible, and enables one to see it to be a beautiful whole. It should certainly be a very welcome book to every minister and Bible student."

Christian Endeavor World : "A study of the Bible by books so as to gain a definite, comprehensive knowledge of the special contents of each is something that many are seeking. Dr. James M. Gray has been doing much for the past few years in promoting systematic reading and study of the Bible, and has aroused great interest in the matter. His course, 'Synthetic Bible Studies,' will receive and deserve a hearty welcome as it now appears in a book form."

SYNTHETIC BIBLE STUDIES

SYNTHETIC BIBLE STUDIES

CONTAINING AN OUTLINE STUDY OF EVERY BOOK
OF THE BIBLE, WITH SUGGESTIONS FOR
SERMONS, ADDRESSES AND
BIBLE EXPOSITIONS

BY JAMES M. GRAY, D. D.

Minister in the Reformed Episcopal Church, Dean of the Moody
Bible Institute, and author of "How to Master the English
Bible," "The History of the Holy Dead,"
"Primers of the Faith," Etc.

91392

NEW EDITION. REVISED AND ENLARGED

BS591
.G77

NEW YORK   CHICAGO   TORONTO

FLEMING H. REVELL COMPANY

LONDON AND EDINBURGH

New York: 158 Fifth Avenue
Chicago: 80 Wabash Avenue
Toronto: 27 Richmond St., W.
London: 21 Paternoster Square
Edinbnrgh: 100 Princes Street

PUBLISHER'S NOTE.

The first edition of Synthetic Bible Studies covered but twenty-two books of the Old Testament and twenty-one of the New, but the present edition includes every book of the Bible. The first was published without the author's revision, but this has had the advantage of his oversight. The studies originally appeared in a religious weekly, and were so widely used and blessed to ministers and Bible students generally, that they have been gathered together in this more permanent form; the matter still retaining however the personal and familiar style of a teacher addressing a class of other teachers, which had been adopted in the newspaper articles.

The design is not that readers should study this book, but study the Bible by its aid. To that end it was hoped to be found useful in the organization and conduct of Bible Classes in churches, Endeavor societies and Young Men and Young Women's Christian Associations, but especially in frontier towns and other places where facilities for Bible study are meagre, and people are hungering for the Word of God. As a matter of fact, however, pastors even in our largest cities, have borne witness to its value in their pulpit preparation, and in awakening an interest in Bible Study among their people that has told in the deepening of their spiritual life, the increase of church attendance, and the revival of the work of God in other lines. In some instances congregations have supplied themselves with copies for general study.

It had not been thought necessary or desirable to treat all the books of the Bible in this volume with the same relative uniformity of length. The poetical books for example, do not lend themselves so readily to the synthetic method, and in the case of some of the minor prophets their lesser importance suggested a briefer treatment to admit of a less bulky and expensive volume. The somewhat extended outlines of the first and fourth gospels seemed also to justify the narrower limits of the second and third. Further explanations where necessary will be found in the text.

INTRODUCTION.

We are to engage in what is called the synthetic study of the Bible, which means, as we use the term, the study of the Bible as a whole, and each book of the Bible as a whole, and as seen in its relation to the other books. The word "Synthesis" has the opposite meaning to "Analysis." When we analyze a subject we take it apart and consider it in its various elements, but when we synthesize it we put it together and consider it as a whole, which is what we are now about to do in a certain sense with the Word of God.

THE VALUE OF THE PLAN.

The value of the plan may be illustrated in different ways. Suppose you were about to study history, you would find it desirable to read first an outline of the world's history, a single volume, say, a small book, but one which would give you almost at a single glance a comprehensive survey of the whole field. The impression might be dim, but you would feel a satisfaction, a sense of power in knowing that your eye had swept the horizon, and that afterwards everything you saw would be within those limits. Then you would take up in their order each of the three great divisions of history, ancient, medieval and modern, and study or read them more particularly. Following this you would concentrate your attention on one division, multiplying the books read, but limiting the range of thought and focusing the mind upon some special period or nation. It is thus you would become a master of the subject.

Suppose it were geeography instead of history. You would first look at a globe, or map of the world, and after that single, all-including glimpse, you could more intelligently consider the hemispheres, con⁺inents and states, and ultimately the mountain ranges, rivers and lakes. It would be abstruse, tedious and difficult were you to begin the other way and work backwards, and yet that is the method many employ in Bible study, accounting in great measure for their lukewarmness in it and the paucity of results.

I have read of an English mountain climber who, whenever exploring a new region, always ascends the highest summit first. He thus gathers a bird's eye view of the whole section, and can pursue the investigation of the lower leve s with an un erstand ng of their relativity that strengthens his grasp of the situation with every movement he makes. That plan needs to be applied for successful Bible study. Let us use the telescope first and the microscope afterwards.

WHAT IT HAS DONE.

Just to interest you a little more and get you lovingly wedded to the idea, let me tell you some of the results this plan of Bible study has wrought. You will forgive a personal allusion, I trust. It is about twelve or fifteen years since the Holy Spirit impressed it upon my attention in answer to long continued

Introduction.

prayer for light upon the subject. The whole story would not be uninteresting were there time to tell it, but I can only say that from that day to this the blessing that has followed me has been like the mountain stream that increases as it flows towards the great ocean. First there came a strengthening of conviction as to the infallibility of the Bible—every part of it, and this was followed by a deepening of my own inner spiritual life, then a broadening of my mental vision so that I came to have an interest in the pursuit of related studies such as never before, and finally a lightening of my labors in the ministry that made previous drudgery a present delight. Oh, how easy it is to get sermons, and how rich, and helpful and attractive they are to both sinners and saints when you know how to find them in the Bible! Here is a hint surely not only to pastors and evangelists, but Christian workers of all classes who have religious talks and addresses to make, and public meetings to conduct. How glad you are to do it, but how difficult and unsatisfactory the work seems! How you long to get hold of the Word of God in such a way as to put yourself and others at ease in engaging in such service!

Shortly after applying this method of Bible study in my own case I began to experiment on others, some theological students who were under my care, with like blessed results. Then the plan became introduced to different Bible institutes and at least one theological seminary in the land. Here two classes of minds were met; those with a university training and others with scarcely more than a common school education, but the effect was just the same in either case, and now not only hundreds but thousands of such students, some of them in the uttermost parts of the earth, are praising God for having revealed to them His Word in this simple way.

Out of these Institute classes gradually grew popular evening classes in different parts of our country and Great Britain. In several instances these have reached a membership of 1,000 to 2,000 or even more, and are held weekly both summer and winter, with a sustained interest and enthusiasm. As I am not the only teacher of these classes by any means, I can speak of them with the greater freedom.

HOW TO DO THE WORK.

The first thing expected of you is that you will read the lesson assigned to you each week. Little can be gained in any kind of Bible study without this, and especially under the present plan. Its great advantage lies in getting the people to read the Bible for themselves. You are not asked to memorize what you read, or tax your energies in any other way than by the simple reading. Let the task be made in that respect just as easy and pleasant as possible.

The second rule is, read the lesson continuously. By this I mean two things. In the first place, always read the lesson through at a single sitting. Do not read part of it now, and part some other time, but if it be possible read it all at once. In the second place, do not be influenced by the chapters and verses when you read. They are valuable for reference, but often hinder in other respects in getting at the mind of the writer. This rule is necessary to be observed with great particularity, since it is only by the continuous

Introduction.

reading of a given book that we can grasp the central line of thought, the pivotal idea, which is so essential to the understanding of the others related to it.

The third rule is, read the lesson repeatedly. Even if it is needful to read it more rapidly than you would otherwise wish to do, for the present purpose I should prefer you to read it several times rapidly than only once very slowly. You will appreciate the reason for this better as we proceed, but just now please take it on faith. The first time you go over the lesson in this way you may see nothing in it that your mind takes hold of, but the next time you will see a little, and the next more, and so on till the complete outline stands out clearly before you. This is what I desire to accomplish in you, and for you. By God's blessing you shall see what you can yourselves do in mastering His Word, and it will greatly increase your sense of spiritual power and joy.

The fourth rule is, read the lesson independently. Do not fly to the commentary and Bible "help" for assistance till after you have finished the lesson yourself. This is not to depreciate such assistance, which is invaluable in its place, neither is it to inspire an inflated idea of what you are going to get here, but to emphasize what was said above. To master the English Bible you must begin by getting your own individual impression of the contents or outline of each book. This, even if far out of the way, is better for a learner than the impression of some one else who is nearer correct. The drill of changing and qualifying what you think you have obtained is of great value in the end. Moreover, you will not fall so wide of the mark as some of you may in your modesty imagine. You will be delightfully disappointed at your success. And then too, what you get will be your own, and no matter how it may be altered afterward by subsequent study, it will still be your own and you will always be the stronger for it. You will have the consciousness of walking on your feet and not on stilts.

The last rule, but not the least by any means, is to read the lesson prayerfully. There are two reasons for this: In the first place, the Bible can not be studied "just like any other book," because it is unlike every other book in the world. It is God's own Book. The Holy Spirit wrote it through holy men of old (2 Peter 1:21), and its Author is its only true and safe interpreter. Coleridge said: "The Bible without the Holy Spirit is a sun-dial by moonlight," and a greater than he said: "We have received, not the spirit of the world, but the Spirit which is of God, that we might know the things that are freely given to us of God." (1 Corinthians 2:12).

But then the other reason is this: Do we not want our Bible study to be something more than a feast of intellect? Do we not want Him whom our soul loveth to tell us where He feeds His flock, where He maketh them to rest at noon? (Solomon's Song 1:7). Do we not want to be caused to lie down in the green pastures and led beside the still waters? Do we not desire a rich blessing in our souls? But how can this be without the power of the Holy Ghost through the Word, and how shall we obtain this power except as we ask? (Luke 11:13). Cultivate prayer, I beseech you. Punctuate the reading of every book, and chapter and verse with it if you want this study to be a real delight.

JAMES M. GRAY.

CHAPTER I.

The Book of Genesis (1-11).

The object now before us is to get hold of the facts of these chapters of Genesis. We shall not do much in the way of their interpretation, indeed, that is not our thought in any of these lessons. The facts must come first and interpretation afterwards. To a great extent if we get the facts the interpretation will take care of itself, for the Bible is wonderfully self-interpretative. Moreover, until the facts are clearly seen, we are not ready for interpretation. This latter also can be gathered from books which will be suggested as we go along perhaps, but the facts, the basis of all Bible study, can only be obtained by the synthetic reading of the Bible itself.

And it is only the great outline facts we are seeking. To have too many of them in our minds would defeat one of the purposes in view which is not only to obtain, but to retain what we get. And then, too, it will be found that if the reading be done as requested in the introduction, the great facts will easily suggest and bring to mind the lesser ones related to them. Of this we shall be persuaded as we advance.

The Word Outline.—What then is the first great fact in the book of Genesis? At once, you respond, "The creation of the world." What are its chapters? 1 and 2. Now give the next great fact. "The fall," chapter 3. The next? "The deluge," chapters 5-9. And the last, so far as this lesson is concerned? "The dispersion of the nations," chapters 10-11.

The following then is our word outline of the lesson:
Creation, 1-2. Fall, 3. Deluge, 5-9. Nations, 10-11.

Only four words, but if we have done the reading asked they will suggest to us the general details that group themselves under each one. Let us see if this is not true.

The First Great Fact.—What does the word "Creation" suggest? Can you state the events of the six days in their order? Here they are:

Light. Firmament. The Dry Land. Light-holders. Fish and Fowl. Cattle and Man.

Notice, that light was created four days before the sun. Objectors to the Mosaic record used to laugh at that, and say there could have been no light before the sun, since the sun was the source of light. But later scientific discoveries indicate that there is a light separate from the sun—that the earth itself is luminous. This gives authority for the use of the word "Light-holders" as applied to the creation of the fourth day.

Notice, that the word "Firmament" means the expanse or atmosphere that is around the earth supporting the clouds.

Notice, that in the case of "The Dry Land" the herb and the tree came first and the seed in each case afterwards, different from what we observe now, and yet as science shows inevitable at the beginning. Here again we have a comparatively recent confirmation of the authority and inspiration of the Mosaic record.

The Law of Recurrence.—But this does not exhaust the word "Creation." What have we in chapter 2 different from chapter 1? After referring to the hallowing of the seventh day, the writer describes more in detail one of the acts of creation spoken of only in a general way before. What act is it? "The creation of man." Here then we meet for the first time a peculiarity of the rhetoric of the Holy Spirit with which it is necessary for us to become acquainted at once. We shall need to recognize it many times in the course of our work, especially in the more difficult books of the prophets, and to understand it is vital either to get at their facts or the interpretation of them. This peculiarity is defined as the Law of Recurrence. Look at the name well, and get it fastened on your mind. What is the law of recurrence? It is that peculiarity of the Holy Spirit as an author by which he gives first the outlines of a subject, and then recurs to it again for the purpose of adding details. To quote the language of a great authority on Bible exegesis, "Many have quite overlooked this, and read Scripture as if the order of narration were always the order of accomplishment, and as if consecutive chapters were necessarily consecutive as to time. But if Scripture be read so, confusion and mistakes are certain."

9

In the first chapter then, we have the account of creation in outline, and in the second part of the same account in detail. The part thus given in detail concerns the creation of man. There is a reason for this detail about man in all that follows, for the Bible is not a history of the world, but a history of man, especially the redemption of man. But what are these details about the creation of man? There are at least four, (a), the nature of his being, verse 7, (b), the location in which he was placed, verses 8-14, (c), the moral test laid upon him, verses 15-17, and (d), the help-meet given him, verses 18-25.

Notice, that the nature of man seems to be three-fold. There was first his body made of the dust of the ground, then the breath or spirit of life put into it, and finally the combining of these two forming a third, so that "the man became a living soul." (Compare I Thessalonians 5:23.) It is said chapter 1, verse 26, that God made "man in His own image," and morally that is explained in part by such a passage as Colossians 3:10, but constructively, if one may use such a word in this connection, it is explained by the fact that God Himself is a Trinity in unity, and has given us this reflection and proof of Himself in our own nature.

Notice, that the whole description of the location of man in Eden carries on the face of it the idea of historicity. Eden and the story associated with it can hardly be a myth when we see the Holy Spirit laboring so to speak, to identify its whereabouts not only by the names of the rivers flowing out of it, and the countries they watered, but even the very nature of the soil of those countries.

Notice, that Adam was a highly intelligent man to be able to name every living creature brought before him, and that this fact has a bearing upon the assumption of some that man is a development from a lower animal.

The Second Great Fact.—As we have thus divided the word "creation" into its lesser facts, let us do the same for the word "fall." Can you recall the details of the chapter for which it stands?

Name the events in their order, thus:—

The temptation of the serpent, 1-5.

The fall of the woman and the man, 6-8.

The appearance of the Lord God, 9-13.

The pronouncement of the curse, 14-19.

The provision of a covering, 21.

The exclusion from the garden, 22-24.

Notice verse 15 especially, and familiarize yourself with the language of the first promise of hope and redemption for fallen man, because that promise is historically the source of all the other promises of Christ in type and prophecy with which the Old Testament abounds.

Notice, that the "serpent" represented more than a mere "beast of the field," judging by his reasoning faculties as well as power of speech, and compare that conclusion with Revelation 12:9, and 20:2, where the Holy Spirit plainly identifies him with Satan.

Notice, the plan adopted in the temptation of the woman as outlined in verse six, and compare it with 1 John 2:16, which indicates it to be the representative plan by which Satan tempts every man; and then examine the record of Christ's temptation in the wilderness (Luke 4), to discover that it signally failed in the case of the Second Adam.

Notice, that verse 21 contains a suggestion in miniature of the whole plan of redemption through the shed blood of a substitutionary victim. The "coats of skins" could not have been obtained without the death of an innocent animal, while the covering of our first parents with them naturally suggests such a passage as Isaiah 61:10, or Romans 3:22, or 2 Corinthians 5:21. May not such an interpretation of this verse throw light on Hebrews 11.4? What was that as to which Abel had "faith," if not this previous revelation of the necessity of a sacrificial victim and a mediator through whom to approach God? Was it not Cain's rejection of God's way of access that led to his own rejection?

Notice, that the expulsion of the guilty pair from Eden was not an act of judgment unmitigated by mercy, for as they had now "obtained the knowledge of good and evil without the power of resisting evil," it would have added to their calamity if, by eating of "the tree of life," they had rendered that state everlasting.

The Third Great Fact.—The third word in our word outline suggesting the third fact is the "Deluge," chapters 5-9. It may be asked, Why include chapter 5? But only those who have not read as they were requested to do will be likely to ask that question, for it will be seen that on the principle of "the law of recurrence" that chapter was written for the purpose of calling particular attention to

CHAPTER III.

The Book of Genesis (28-40).

If "Isaac" is the sixth great fact in Genesis what is the seventh? Jacob? And the eighth? Joseph? Just add then these two names to the word outline of the last lesson, and you will discover that the whole of this long book can be easily kept in mind in eight words. I mean as to its great leading facts, of course. How this simplifies Bible study, and stimulates us to go on from book to book!

The History of Jacob.—Now please recall the great facts in the life of the patriarch Jacob as in the previous cases, and put them down somewhat like this:

Birth, 25.
Purchase of the birthright, 25.
Deception of his father, 27.
Flight to Haran, 28.
Marriage and prosperity, 29-30.
Return to Canaan, 31-35.

It will not be difficult to hold these six details in memory, and if you have read the chapters as requested the minor matters can also be recalled. For example, ask yourself these questions:—Who, besides Jacob, was responsible for fact number three? What was the chief event in fact number four? How was Jacob himself wronged in fact number five? What four events give the chief interest to fact number six?

What We May Learn from Jacob.— Jacob is not the least interesting of the patriarchs. While not so grand as Abraham or docile as Isaac, he is more like the average man, and that makes his life-story full of peculiar meaning to us.

Notice how it illustrates the sovereignty of God. Compare Malachi 1: 1-4, and Romans 9: 10-13. But let us not charge God foolishly in this case. Remember that the choice as between Jacob and Esau did not necessarily terminate on their Heavenly life, but earthly life. It was a question simply of the earthly birthright. Both may be in Heaven for aught we know. Nor did Esau suffer anything serious so far as temporalities were concerned. He was also blessed and led the kind of life he doubtless enjoyed. Nor was God merely arbitrary in His choice and acting without moral reasons. On the contrary what He did greatly magnified His grace, and when rightly viewed, contributes to the hope and comfort of poor lost sinners such as we all are. The word "hate" as applied to Esau in the passages compared, must not be taken in the common sense of that term, but only as a Hebrew idiom intensifying the idea of choice. We shall have occasion to look into this farther when we reach the Scriptures referred to.

Notice how it illustrates the grace of God. Here is rich material for a Bible reading. Think of the love that chose such a man, bore with him, prospered, protected, and guided him, revealed God to him, and sanctified him. The Almighty sometimes speaks of Himself as "The God of Jacob," and is there any title that goes very much deeper in sounding the depths of His condescension and willingness to bless! And His grace is brought out all the stronger by Jacob's plotting and scheming to get that which God had promised him, and would have given Him without it.

Notice how it illustrates prevailing prayer. Its secret is not strength but weakness. Jacob was not wrestling with some one, but Some One was wrestling with him. God was bringing him to see what a poor, worthless creature he was in himself. As C. H. M. says, it was not until the seat of his strength was touched, his thigh put out of joint, that he learned to say, "I will not let Thee go."

The new era in his history began then. Up until that time he had held fast by his own plans and schemes, but after that he was ready to hold fast by God. Now he receives the name "Israel," one who has prevailed with God.

Joseph a Type of Christ.—There are many points of similarity between Joseph and Christ, and as in the previous lesson it will be found fruitful to trace the parallel. Consider the meaning of his name as indicated in the margin references of your Bible, 30: 24, i. e., "Adding," or increase, or fruitfulness, and compare Isaiah 9: 6-7, Luke 1: 31-33, John 3: 30. Consider the effect of his birth upon Rachel, taking away her reproach, 30: 24, and ask yourself in what particulars Christ hath taken away reproach? He took away the reproach of sin, did He not? See Colossians 2: 13-15, Romans 8: 1.

And also the reproach of the law, see Isaiah 42 : 21, for He fulfilled it and kept it, and in so doing showed it to be holy, and good and true, notwithstanding that men, through sin, had condemned and trampled it under foot. What is the next great fact in Joseph's life suggesting a likeness to Christ? The peculiar love of his father for him, suggesting Proverbs 8 : 30, Isaiah 42 : 1, Matthew 3 : 17. And the next fact? The sufferings endured through the hatred of his brethren, including the sale into slavery, imprisonment in Egypt, etc., bringing into mind Psalm 69 : 4, and John 15 : 25. And the next fact? His deliverance from prison and exaltation to the throne of Pharoah, as foreshadowing in some degree Christ's resurrection and ascension into glory, compare Acts 2 : 22-24. And the next fact? His marriage to a stranger, as indicating Christ taking to Himself the church to be His bride, composed of both Jews and Gentiles, and sharing with Him at once both His rejection and His glory, compare Ephesians 1 : 3-4, 2 : 4-7, 3 : 1-6, 5 : 24, 32. And the last fact? His interview with, and revelation of himself to his brethren beautifully typical of Christ's dealings with Israel in the latter day, see Zechariah 12 : 10, 13 : 1.

Gather these facts into orderly shape, and a most helpful and stimulating Bible reading will spring into life under your hands.

The Prophecies of Christ.—Having now finished the word outline of the book, let us go over it again for the purpose of bringing into one view its Messianic references, and at the same time fastening the details still firmer in mind. What prophecies of Christ does Genesis contain? In answering the question, you are not called upon to read the book again, but only mentally review the facts already emphasized. Recall the eight words of the outline. Dwell on each one sufficiently long to refresh your recollection as to its details. Take the word "Creation", which covers chapters 1 and 2. As you think over the work of the six days in chapter 1, and the fuller account of the creation of man in chapter 2, no prophecy occurs to you. But when you come to the next word, "Fall", instantly "the seed of the woman," chapter 3 : 15, flashes into your mind. Pursue the thread through the other words, "Deluge," "Nations," "Abraham," and there again you meet such a prophecy in chapters 12 : 7, and 17 : 7, compared with Galatians 3 : 16. In the same way, "Isaac" yields nothing, but "Jacob" in the blessing on his sons, refers to the Coming One in chapter 49 : 10. Observe in this connection the development of Messianic truth. At first He is the seed of the woman simply, rather indefinite and undetermined; in the second place, the range is narrowed to a particular race of the woman, the line of Abraham; and in the third place, the line is drawn still closer to include only the tribe of Judah. Thus will it be found as we proceed, that the features of the Saviour's personality become more and more clearly indicated and defined by the various prophets, not only stimulating expectation with every generation, but increasing the means by which He may be identified when He comes.

The Human Types of Christ.—I would now suggest that we again run over the eight words of the outline in order to gather together the human types of Christ. Under the word "Creation", Adam suggests himself, for whose typical relation to Christ see such places as Romans 5 : 12-21, and 1 Corinthians 15 : 21-22, 45-49. Under the word "Deluge" we think of Noah, whose typical relation is somewhat weaker, except as we think of him in the light of a preacher of righteousness to a gainsaying generation. Under the word "Abraham" we have already spoken of Melchisedec. Add to these Isaac and Joseph, whose histories have been treated somewhat at length, and we have the principal characters who are referred to in this typical connection, although their number might be multiplied.

The General Types of Christ.—I would ask you to go over the eight words a third time in the same way, to ascertain the general types of Christ as distinguished from the human. For example, under the word "Creation," we at once think of Light as such a type, compare John 9 : 5. Under the "Fall", we think of the coats of skins previously spoken of. "Deluge" suggests the ark as a type of Christ in whom we are saved, Acts 4 : 12. The word "Abraham" brings to mind the ram caught in the thicket. "Jacob", the ladder to which Christ Himself refers, John 1 : 51. These then are the chief Messianic references :—

Prophecies.—The seed of the woman.
           The seed of Abraham.
           The seed of Judah.

Human Types.	General Types.
Adam.	Light.
Noah.	Coat of skins.
Melchisedec.	Ark.
Isaac.	Ram.
Jacob.	Ladder.

CHAPTER IV.

The Book of Exodus (1-19).

Genesis has sometimes been called the Book of Beginnings, which is the real meaning of the word, because of the nature of its contents, which give the origin of things. We have in it the beginning of the world, of man, of the Sabbath, marriage, sin, prophecy, and sacrifice, as well as the beginning of the nations and Israel. This brings us down to the twelfth chapter, but after that practically there are no beginnings, but only a recurrence of what has gone before.

Exodus in the same way has sometimes been called the Book of the Departure or the Going Out, from the etymology of the word, and also because it gives the history of the departure of the Israelites from Egypt.

The Israelites entered Egypt when Joseph was in power, seventy souls in all, (Genesis 46: 27). They left there 215 years afterward, according to the chronology in the margin of our Bibles, when their men of war alone numbered 603,550, not counting women and children, not counting men under 20, and also leaving out of consideration the whole tribe of Levi (Numbers 1: 44-50). During this period their experiences had varied. While Joseph lived and the Pharoahs of that period, they were happy and prosperous in the land of Goshen. But by-and-by a change of dynasty occurred, and political revolution took place, and the new government viewed their increasing numbers and influence with alarm and jealousy. In consequence they began to subject them in every possible way, and it is at this point in their history the book of Exodus begins (chapter 1: 7-10.)

Proof from Recent Explorations.— Allusion was made in an earlier chapter to the way in which recent explorations in Bible lands throw light upon these historical statements in the Word of God, and this is particularly true of the present period. "It would be easy," says an authority on the subject, "to multiply illustrations from the ancient records of Egypt of many circumstances in the life of Joseph." The situation and limits of the land of Goshen are now known, as well as the history of the dynastic changes that resulted in the exodus of the Hebrews. It is ascertained that Rameses II., the Pharoah of Moses' time, was like his predecessor, a great builder, corroborating chapter 1: 11. His mummy has recently been discovered, as well as that of his daughter, the Princess who saved the infant Moses from perishing in the river Nile, and brought him up as her own son. How near these circumstances seem to bring the history of that time, and how real it is made to appear!

In like manner, careful examinations have now "put the route of the exodus beyond all reasonable doubt." We know also the real character of the desert through which the Hebrews passed. Shur is a rolling plain where shrubs and herbs give pasturage to cattle. Water courses cross it. Charming spots like Elim are found here and there, indicating how they found sustenance during that period. There is a plain at the foot of Sinai now called Er-Rahah, two miles long, and half a mile wide, where a multitude of 2,-000,000 souls could easily have assembled, and the sights and sounds described could easily have been seen and heard by all. The site of Kadesh-Barnea too, is now definitely settled. Thus, without going further into detail, is the accuracy of the story we are about to consider wonderfully confirmed.

The Facts of the Chapters.—We are now ready to consider the facts of the chapters, which will be brought before us in a series of questions. The first great fact is clearly suggested by the one word, "Bondage." But what were the sub-facts that entered into this bondage, what are its elements referred to in the text? Were there not chiefly two, their rigorous service under the hard task-masters, and the decree for the destruction of male issue?

What is the next fact? The birth of Moses. But that naturally includes the further facts of his life to the time when he has fled from Egypt and Pharoah's palace.

The third fact? His call, including the story of the burning bush, the revelation to him of Jehovah, his hesitancy to respond, and the collaboration of Aaron.

The fourth fact is the story of the plagues, including what led up to them in the return to Egypt, the demand on Pharoah, and his obduracy.

The fifth fact is the Passover, growing out really from the last plague, the sixth is the crossing of the Red Sea, the seventh, the entrance upon the wilderness journey.

This last fact might be subdivided for convenience by the number of places at which they stopped. Try to recall them, and the circumstances occurring at each. You will be aided here as in the instance of the dispersion of the nations, by consulting the map in the back of your Bible. It is described as the "Peninsula of Sinai." Observe Marah, and why it was so called. Elim. Rephidim. What great miracle occurred after leaving Elim, and in the neighborhood of Rephidim? What miracle at the last-named locality? What battle was fought there? Who commanded the forces? What was done to relieve Moses of care? At whose suggestion?

Perhaps we had better make a separate fact of their arrival at Sinai. Whither is Moses now called? What distinction does Jehovah bestow on Israel? (19:5-6). Describe what was seen and heard on and about the mount.

Things to be Explained.—The class understands that interpretation and explanation are not among the things promised in these lessons for many reasons, but that does not exclude all allusion thereto if necessity seems to compel and space permit. For example, 4:24, and the following verses, may puzzle many who have no commentary at hand to examine. The idea there seems to be that some great mental distress or physical illness came upon Moses which he recognized as a chastisement for the neglect of the circumcision of his son. This neglect perhaps was occasioned by his wife's aversion to the act, who now overcame her maternal feelings sufficiently to perform it herself, and thus bring relief to her husband. This critical experience was doubtless not only of value to Moses' own inner life, but had its influence upon him as the leader of and legislator for Israel in after years. Especially would it stir him to enforce the law of circumcision which was so peculiarly the mark of distinction for that people.

The hardening of Pharaoh's heart, 4:21, and other places, is apt to be a stumbling-block to some, but it must be remembered that the Divine messages and judgments were not the cause but only the occasion of that hardening. Such passages must be interpreted in the light of the Divine character and the Holy Scriptures

taken as a whole, and we know therefrom that God never deals unjustly or arbitrarily with His creatures, whose own free actings are always the cause of their downfall and punishment. (Compare 2 Thessalonians 2:11-12).

The borrowing of the Egyptian jewels by the Israelites has given rise to questioning, but the word "borrow" in that instance means to demand or require. The Israelites who had been kept in great poverty and denied their just wages by their persecutors, now insisted upon full remuneration for their labor which was thus paid in silver articles adapted for convenient carriage. The dread of them inspired in the Egyptians by Jehovah made it comparatively easy to obtain what they asked. Compare Genesis 15:13-14; Psalm 105:37; Ezekiel 39:10.

Chapter 12:40 present a difficulty where the period of their sojourn is given as 430 years, while as we have seen the Bible chronology calls for only 215 years spent in Egypt. Galatians 3:16-17, throws some light upon it as showing that the period began to be reckoned from the date of the promise to Abraham, which makes precisely 430 years. As bearing upon this the Septuagint (Greek) translation of the Old Testament, makes that verse read, "The sojourning of the children and of their fathers, which they sojourned in the land of Canaan and in the land of Egypt."

Things to be Noticed.—In all our studies thus far the attention of the reader has been called to certain special features which it were well to particularly notice by way of suggestion, even though their explanation were not called for. In the present instance the promptings of faith on the part of Moses' parents as well as himself should be dwelt upon. Compare Hebrews 11:23-29. There was nothing hap-hazard either in the hiding of the babe in the Nile nor in his own renunciation of Egypt afterward. The whole thing was profoundly religious and born of the same undoubting belief in God that justified Abraham.

Notice again the command for Moses to write certain things in a book, 17:14, 34:27. This has an important application to the theory of some that Moses is not the author of the Pentateuch or the first five books of the Bible. If you carefully observe the number of times in which he is said to write this or that, or in which the statement is made that the Lord spoke directly to him, you will perceive that to remove those passages from the Pentateuch would be to leave little as a remainder. The inference is very plain—to plain people.

Notice too the typical character of the Passover. The Passover itself is a remarkable type of redemption through Christ, while the central feature of the Passover, the lamb, is equally impressive as symbolizing Christ Himself (1 Corinthians 5 : 7-8). We shall enlarge from this later.

Notice finally, certain important particulars about the miraculous plagues. There are two kinds of miracles, absolute and providential. The latter are those which are not miraculous in themselves, but in the circumstances attending their performance. Such were the plagues of Egypt. They were the natural phenomena of that land, only in this instance they came at an unusual season and in an unusual degree of intensity, as well as in immediate response to the prophet's command. The Nile which was turned into blood was the patron God of the Egyptians, a fact which greatly added to their humiliation in that circumstance. The same thing was true in some measure of several of the other plagues, one of their gods, for example, was represented with a frog's head, they also worshipped flies, reared temples in honor of the ox and the cow, and idolized the sun which was turned into darkness. Observe the reference to the magicians in this case, found in 2 Timothy 3 : 8. That they represented Satan as Moses represented God, there can be little doubt. Their defeat under the circumstances was an impressive illustration of the supremacy of the latter, which they themselves acknowledged, 8 : 16-19. While they appeared by their enchantments to be able to reproduce two of the plagues on a small scale, it is notable that they attempted to go no further, and that even in those instances they could not undo what they had done as in the case of Moses.

The Passover a Type of Redemption. —The next chapter will deal with the types more particularly, but we shall avail ourselves of the present opportunity to dwell on the one most distinctive and comprehensive type of redemption found in the Old Testament. What are the points of similarity that suggest themselves? Be careful to begin at the beginning, and school yourself to think orderly and logically throughout. We may differ as to what constitutes the beginning here, but it strikes me that the need of the Passover is the first thing. What was its need? The condition of the people, their bondage and suffering. The analogy between their condition and that of the sinner in bondage to sin, Satan and death, and the suffering entailed, is not difficult to trace. What then is the next thought? The origin of the Passover. It originated in God, in His mercy and purpose to deliver. Its revelation as well as inception was Divine, bringing to mind the fact that we are not only indebted to God's grace for our deliverance from sin, but for the inspired Word and authenticated messengers through which the same has been ministered to us. The next thought might be the means of the Passover with all the suggestiveness of the slaying of the lamb and the sprinkling of its blood, as brought before us in New Testament teaching in 1 Corinthians 5 : 7-8, Romans 3 : 24-26, 1 Peter 1 : 18-20, and other places. Another thought might be the effects of the Passover, seen to be at least three-fold, e. g., salvation from death, deliverance from bondage, and entrance into Canaan, symbolizing at once salvation both from the guilt and power of sin, and rest in the fullness of Christ. And then there is a final thought in the application of the matter, since the effects or blessings of the Passover were for all who believed and obeyed God in making the necessary provisions in the slain lamb and sprinkled blood, without reference either to the question of character or the degree or quality of faith. The New Testament Scriptures which form the parallel to this are of course very numerous and familiar. "Whosoever believeth," "Whosoever will may come," "Not by works of righteousness which we have done," etc. For such places as these consult the marginal references in your Bibles or Cruden's Complete Concordance

CHAPTER V.

The Book of Exodus (20-40).

There were two further observations on the subject-matter of the last lesson I should like to have made had it not been already somewhat extended. The first was the "difference" which God put between the Egyptians and Israel, 11:7. Notice that it was the difference between "life" and "death," and its determining point was the sprinkled blood of the lamb. Teachers who are conducting classes will, it is hoped, seize upon such opportunities to illustrate and emphasize the distinction between the saved and the unsaved as based on faith in the atonement of Jesus Christ.

The second observation refers to "the beginning of months," 12:1-2. This is interesting not only as bearing on the fact that the Jews have a religious as well as a civil year, the one beginning in the spring (March-April), and the other in the autumn (September-October), but also as showing that their deliverance from Egypt marked a new era in their history. Henceforth in their relations to Jehovah, the past was to be regarded as a blank. The suggestion is obvious that "redemption is the first step in real life."

Our New Work.—You have already recalled that the last word in the Word Outline of the previous lesson was "Sinai." Now what occurred at Sinai? It is easy to reply that there the Israelites received the revelation of the law, the tabernacle and the priest-hood. There were two other events, for example, the idolatry of the golden calf, and the building of the tabernacle, after its pattern had been shown to Moses in the Mount. Nevertheless, the first three mentioned constitute the outline, which might read thus:

8. Sinai.
   a. law, 20-24.
   b. tabernacle, 25-27, 30-31.
   c. priesthood, 28-29.

Let us analyze a little what is found under the word "Law." Observe that we have here a remote application of "the law of recurrence" hitherto explained. That is, we have first, the law in general as set forth in the ten commandments, 20:1-17, and then in detail in what follows to the close of chapter 24. In the first, God lays down certain fundamental principles, so to speak, and in the second, shows certain applications of those principles to ordinary, everyday life. It might be illustrated, perhaps, by the distinction between the constitution of a state, and the enactments of its legislators from year to year, the latter in a sense growing out of the former.

Notice, the frequent allusions to the fourth commandment. Since the original institution of the Sabbath, which means "rest", Genesis 2, it has been referred to at least five or six times. Observe the reason for the keeping of this day as stated, 23:12.

Notice the revelation of the character of God afforded in the law. His condescension is seen in occupying Himself with the details of daily life, the death of an ox, the loan of a garment, the loss of a tooth. What a motive for holiness, what a source of comfort this affords! His justice is seen in the even balance held between the rich and the poor, the punishment for bribery, defalcation, etc., penalty on the guilty and protection for the innocent. Remember in the same connection that this is the law which will maintain in the Millennium about which we are to study later on. God has doubtless given this law to be obeyed by all men on the earth, and His purpose in that matter will not ultimately be defeated.

Notice the revelation of the character of man afforded in the law. The fact that such law must be enacted shows that such crimes will be committed. He is right who says that the most refined member of the human family carries about in his bosom the seeds of the darkest and most horrifying abominations. Compare Romans 2:1; 3:23, Mark 14:18-19.

Notice particularly the place the law is said to occupy in the scheme of redemption, Galatians 3:24. It brings us to Christ in the sense that it shows us what sin is in God's sight, how far off we are from being what God requires, and how absolutely essential is a Saviour of God's providing.

The Tabernacle.—The Divine sense of the importance of the revelation of the tabernacle is seen in the preparation for it, 24:15-18. Let the subject receive the most prayerful attention. Carefully note each article referred to.

Beginning with chapter 24, what four articles of furniture are mentioned in succession? At chapter 26 the framework of the building is spoken of. What was the material and predominating colors of the curtains (1-6)? How many coverings were to be made and of what materials (7-14)? How were the two parts of the building proper separated, and by what names were they distinguished (31-33)? What articles were placed in the Most-Holy Place? What in the Holy Place? What part of the tabernacle is spoken of in chapter 27:9-19? What specific article for the outer court is mentioned in the preceding verses of that chapter? What subject interrupts the revelation of the details of the tabernacle in chapters 28-29? In returning to the tabernacle what is its next article of furniture mentioned? In which of the three places, the Most Holy, the Holy, or the outer court, was it to be placed? What precise position was it to occupy? What was the last article named, and in which of the three places was it to stand (30:17-21)? What provision was made for the financial support of the tabernacle service (30:11-16)? What prohibition was laid upon the people with reference to the composition of the ointments and perfume (30:22-38)? What provision did God make for the execution of His plans in the erection of the tabernacle (31:1-11)? What chapters contain the account of their execution? When were they completed (40:17)? How did God show His approval of the work (40:34)? What was to be offered on the brazen altar twice every day (29:38-39)? What kind of offering was this to be (verse 42)? How in this same verse does God indicate that He will bless the people? How is the same idea expressed in verses 45-46? Indicate the divisions of the building thus:

The outer court.
The holy place.
The most holy place.
The furniture of the outer court:
The brazen altar.
The laver.
The furniture of the holy place:
The table of shew bread.
The golden candlestick.
The altar of incense.
The furniture of the most holy place:
The ark of the testimony.
The mercy seat.

It will greatly aid the student if he can examine a drawing or picture of the tabernacle and its contents. Such will be found in a good Bible dictionary, such as Smith's which ought to be in every well-equipped private library. Then there are special books on

the tabernacle treating of its typical character which are highly useful from a spiritual point of view. Some are large and expensive, but I here mention others within easy reach, such as, "The Tabernacle and Priesthood," by H. W. Soltau, "All of Blue," by Frank White, "Mosaic Institutions," by W. G. Moorehead, and "Shadow and Substance," by George C. Needham.

The Tabernacle—A Type.—The deep significance of the revelation of the tabernacle doubtless lies in these two mysterious facts, (1) it was a pattern of things in the heavens, and (2) it was to be the dwelling-place of God on earth. As to the first fact little can be known at present, but the Christian should dwell upon it in the light of the epistle to the Hebrews, especially such passages as 8:1-5, 9:11-12, 22-28, 10:11-14.

As to the second fact, God made the tabernacle His dwelling-place in the sense that His visible glory abode there (Exodus 40:34-38), and there He met the people and communed with them in the person of the high priest (25:22). But in this particular it becomes a wonderful type of the Person and work of the Lord Jesus Christ (John 1:14), in whom God dwelt among us. And not only is the tabernacle itself such a type, but every article in it, and every part of it points to Him in some particular way. For example, take the ark and mercy-seat together, the latter resting upon the former, in the one we have Christ in His life fulfilling the law on our behalf, and in the other we have Christ in His death becoming a propitiation for our sins. Here mercy and truth meet together, righteousness and peace kiss each other. It is a beautiful thought that in I John 2:2, the word "propitiation" is precisely the same in its meaning as the word "mercy-seat." If you will read that precious verse in that way it may reveal Jesus to you in a new light.

Coming out of the most holy into the holy place, we have the altar of incense symbolizing Christ's intercession, the table of shewbread, representing Him as our food, and the golden candle-stick as our light. In the outer court He is in the brazen altar our sacrifice for sin, and in the laver our cleanser or regenerator.

Even the difficult parts of the sacred building suggest Him. The "fine twined linen" of the curtains expresses His spotless manhood, the "blue," His heavenly character, "purple," His royal position, "scarlet," His human sufferings upon the cross. Their measurements, number, couplings, loops and taches all find a significance in Him. The coverings of goats' hair, rams' skin, and badgers' skins are not without their meaning also, as will be seen by a perusal of some of the books referred to above. At first it may seem to some as if these points of suggestion were somewhat strained, but as one grows "in grace and in the knowledge of our Lord and Saviour Jesus Christ," he comes to recognize Him more frequently in the Word, and to rejoice in Him as the One ever in His Father's eye, and the alpha and omega of all that He has to reveal to man. One needs to be very careful, however, not to be led astray here by fanciful and unwarranted interpretations of some of these things, the only safeguard against which is constant dependence upon the teaching and guidance of the Holy Ghost.

Nor should we forget either, that the tabernacle foreshadows in some sense that blessed truth to the true believer, of God's indwelling in him, 1 Cor. 6:19, John 14:15-23. And then what shall we say of Revelation 21:2-5? Is it possible that the original Moses saw in the Mount, whose pattern he set up in the wilderness, is that which God hath prepared aforetime to be His habitation in the new earth throughout the age of eternity? Such hints as these should quicken our interest in the study of the subject of the tabernacle.

The Priesthood.—When we approach the revelation of the priesthood, perhaps the first thing that strikes us is its position, cutting in two as it does the revelation of the tabernacle. But remember that the Holy Spirit is the Author of the Word, and that He makes no blunders. Even though we do not always understand the meaning of such things, it is our duty to regard them as Divine and seek light. A very probable reason for this proceeding is suggested in C. H. M.'s "Notes on Exodus," referred to before, pages 263-265, and 289-291.

You will observe that the two chapters containing the revelation of the priesthood are naturally divided by the subjects of which they treat. What is the subject of each? Be careful to identify each of the garments, remembering that the high-priest especially is a type of Christ, and that each has a significance in its teaching concerning His work for us. After the general statement (28:4-5), the details follow to the end of that chapter. Take time to write them down.

The ephod is named first. The material, coloring, shoulder-pieces and breastplate are all significant, and particularly, of course, the names of the tribes of Israel engraven on the precious stones. "The strength of the priest's shoulder and the affection of his heart were wholly devoted to the interests of those he represented. This typified in Aaron, is actualized in Christ." The girdle is the symbol ot service. "Urim and Thummim" which mean "lights and perfections," is peculiarly mysterious, but seems to be "connected with the communication of the mind of God on various questions of detail in Israel's history," see the marginal references or concordance for other places where the words are used. The application to Christ is clear who, by His Word and Holy Spirit, communicates the counsels of God to us, John 12:49-50, Acts 2:32-33. Observe the bells on the hem of the ephod and the reason for them, (verse 35). Our High Priest has passed into the heavens, but those whose ears are chastened to the sound, have daily evidence that He ever liveth. Observe the engraving on the plate resting upon Aaron's forehead and the meaning assigned to it, (verse 38), "It shall be always upon his forehead, that they may be accepted before the Lord." Wonderful demonstration in type that Christ's holiness is ours, and that because of it God looks on us with complacency. Do not fail to observe that Aaron's sons are not forgotten, and that coats, and bonnets, and girdles and breeches are ordained for them in their particular ministry (verses 40-43). If the high priest (Aaron) typifies Christ, his sons, the priests, are regarded as typifying, first, Israel itself (19:6), and afterwards the church, (1 Peter 2:9), and, of course, every individual member of the church. These garments, therefore, may represent those qualities and graces with which the true people of God and members of Christ are endued in their own sphere for worship and service.

Reaching chapter 29, observe the preparation for the consecration of Aaron and his sons. The washing (verse 4), the anointing (verse 7), the sacrificial offerings (verses 10-18), the consecrating act (verses 19-21), etc., all of which, of course, illustrate the fundamental truths of the Gospel concerning our standing in, and relationship to Christ.

The Types in Exodus.—Exodus, unlike Genesis, contains no distinct prophecies of Christ, but its typology in that respect as already seen, is very abundant. And there are other types than those which apply only to the Person of Christ. As in the case of Genesis, so here, I would ask you to recall the words of the outline of the book, with the sub-divisions under them, for such suggestions as may come to you. For example, "Bondage" contains no type of primary importance, nor "Birth of Moses." But when we come to "Call of Moses," the burning bush comes into view. Here we are furnished with a type of Israel, which, although in the furnace of Egypt, was not consumed because God was there. It becomes in the same way, and for the same reason, the type of the church, and of the individual believer in Christ. Material for a Bible reading will be found in the treatment of such a theme. The word "Plagues" suggests no type, but the next word, "Passover," brings before us the great type of redemption already treated of, and in the paschal lamb a remarkable type of the Redeemer Himself. "Red Sea," we need not dwell upon, but the word "Wilderness," and especially "Rephidim," one of the stopping-places therein, produces at least two types of Christ, the manna and the smitten rock. When we reach the last word, "Sinai," we have the tabernacle itself, and for that matter every part of it, and every article of furniture it contains, the daily lamb spoken of in chapter 29, and the priesthood of Aaron. It is not assumed that these are all the types by any means, but the principal ones, and those upon which the church at large is generally agreed.

CHAPTER VI.

The Book of Leviticus.

We have found a secondary name for each of the other books already studied, one which more plainly suggests to English readers the general character of its contents, and we may do the same for Leviticus. It might be called the Book of the Laws. Not Law, but Laws. The Book of the Law is a title frequently ascribed to the Pentateuch, but "The Book of the Laws" well describes the third division of the Pentateuch, because it is a Divine revelation of the laws which were to govern the priests chiefly, in their administration of the tabernacle service, and their care of the people both materially and spiritually. Remember that the latter are still at Sinai, that Leviticus was given to Moses at that place, and that it is in its nature a supplement to, really a part of, the preceding book of Exodus.

Regarding it, therefore, as a book of laws, what is the first great fact, or law, it contains? No difficulty is experienced in answering, "The Law of the Offerings." How many chapters are taken up with the consideration of this law? 1-7 inclusive. What is the law of the offerings? In other words, how many distinct kinds of offerings are enumerated? Five: Burnt, meal, peace, sin, trespass.

You will observe that I have written the name of the second "meal," instead of meat, as being the designation given in the Revised Version, the more correct rendering of the word, and the more befitting the nature of the offering itself, which contains no meat in the sense of flesh as we now use that term.

The Significance of the Offerings.— Many offerings and sacrifices are referred to in the history of Israel, but it will simplify matters very much and save confusion, if we remember that they all fall under this law, they are always one of these five. It does not matter whether they are offered for the priest himself, the nation, a ruler of the nation, or a common person; it does not matter whether the offering is a bullock, a sheep, a goat, a turtledove or a pigeon, in any case it is one of these five. In chapter 7, reference is made to offerings for vows, and thanksgiving, and voluntary offerings, but they are simply different aspects of the one trespass offering.

It must not be supposed, of course, that these offerings in themselves satisfied God. See Hebrews 10 : 4. Their importance lay in what they symbolized, viz.: the Person and the work of the Lord Jesus Christ. The careful study of the offerings will do more to exalt Him in our eyes, and teach us the real character of His vicarious life and death, than any other part of the Bible. C. H. M.'s "Notes on Leviticus" will afford help, and also "Mosaic Institutions," by Moorehead, spoken of in a previous chapter. The best book, however, is entitled, "The Law of the Offerings," by Andrew Jukes. It is small and inexpensive, but fuller than any of the others. A good volume, or commentary, on the whole book of Leviticus is found in the Expositor's series, written by the late Professor S. H. Kellogg, D.D.

These offerings do not represent in every case the same aspect of Christ's Person and work, but different aspects. In the burnt and meal offerings we see His consecration, in the peace offering His communion and fellowship with God, in the sin and trespass offerings His atoning sacrifice. In all these particulars, however, it is not Christ alone who is thus seen, but we (who are believers), in Christ. Nothing will strengthen our assurance of salvation, or melt our hearts in love toward Him, or awaken our adoration of His character and grace, like an understanding of our position in Him as set before us in this wonderful revelation.

The Second of the Laws.—After passing from the law of the offerings, what is the next great fact in Leviticus? The consecration of Aaron and his sons, chapters 8-10. The law about this consecration was really given in Exodus as we saw, and in the present instance we have the first execution of that law; but to accommodate ourselves to the secondary name of the book, let us call it "The Law of Consecration." It will be observed that the details of the consecration occupy chapters 8-9, and are in accordance with the previous commands received. But when we reach chapter 10, whose contents really belong to the present division of the book, an exception occurs.

To understand what follows in the death of Aaron's sons, notice carefully the last verse of chapter 9, which speaks of the sacrifice on the brazen altar in the outer court, and holy fire from the Lord consuming it. It was this fire, the same that consumed the sacrifice, that should have been employed in the censers to burn the incense before the Lord. Nadab and Abihu neglected this, and offered "strange fire," and were instantly slain. This looks like a terrible punishment for a slight offence. But the offence was not slight. It was a flagrant disobedience of a plain command, several commands, in short. Not only did they disobey in the matter of the fire (see 16:12), but also it would seem, in performing an office which belonged only to their father, the high priest, for, as some think, they went into the holy of holies. Moreover, two went in where only one was permitted. Furthermore, the offence was committed at a very critical moment in the history of the people, at the very beginning of their covenant relationship to God. It suggests a somewhat similar occurrence in the opening era of the Christian church, Acts 5:1-2. In both cases a signal manifestation of the Divine displeasure was necessary for the sake of impressing the lesson upon the whole nation in the one case, and the whole church in the other. It need not be supposed, however, that this punishment involved the eternal loss of the souls of these men. That question need not be raised in this connection at all. It was a case of God's judging in the midst of His people, not a case of His actings among "them that are without." It affords a solemn warning, however, to any within the visible church who would depart in their worship from the plain revelation of God, and to any without, who would seek to approach Him in some other way than the prescribed one. John 14:6, Acts 4:12.

The Third of the Laws.—The next law will be found to include the contents of several chapters, 11-22 inclusive, omitting perhaps 16, which treats of a separate subject of much importance. The name usually given to this law (11-22), is that of "The Clean and the Unclean," and will be found to include such subjects as the creatures that may, or may not, be eaten (11), the ceremonial purification of women (12), the detection and purification of leprosy (13-14), personal uncleanness (15), the prohibition concerning blood (17), incestuous connections (18), purification of the priests (21-22), while chapters 19-20 repeat certain laws given before, doubtless for the purpose of emphasizing them, and the specific punishments attached to them. The three main subjects of the law may be characterized as follows:

a. Food. b. Disease. c. Personal habits.

Of course, one reason for the enunciation of these laws concerned the health and the morals of the people, and to this day, notwithstanding their imperfect obedience thereto, the Hebrews remain the healthiest and most moral of all races. But a broader reason points to the design of God to keep the nation separate from every other (20:25-26). This applies to all the laws of this book, and has a bearing on what was said in an earlier lesson as to God's purposes in calling Israel to be His special people. They were to be peculiar for the world's sake, as a source of blessing to the whole earth. Nor should it be overlooked that there is a deep spiritual and special significance to many, if not all, of these distinctions and prohibitions. Of those concerning leprosy is this particularly so. It is a striking representation of sin, and will well repay a careful study as the basis of a Bible reading on that subject.

Amid so many things to be specifically noticed, it is difficult to distinguish. But notice the allusion to these laws in Acts 10: 11-16, and see how God raises the thoughts of the apostle, and through him the whole church, far above their Levitical application. See how he teaches that the true cleanness these things typified, was that accomplished through being washed in the blood of the Lamb.

Notice that class of laws which brings us the thought of God's tenderness and care, 19: 9-10, compared with Ruth 2: 14-16, also 19: 13, compared with James 5: 4. What live topics these furnish for the times in which we live, and how they indicate that the Bible is the source of the true sociology as well as soteriology! This is the book for the modern social and political reformers as well as the preacher.

Notice the teaching in chapters 21-22 concerning the priestly position, which has such a practical bearing on the standing of believers in Christ in the light of the last lesson. The sons of Aaron were priests by birth, and nothing could break that relationship. There were many things which might interfere with the full enjoyment of their privileges, but the relationship remained. The spiritually-minded student will easily see the application of this to the doctrine of assurance on the one hand, and the distinction between salvation and fellowship or communion on the other.

The Fourth of the Laws.—To return to chapter 16, what is its subject? Shall we identify it as "The Law of the Day of Atonement?" Observe when it was given, (verse 1). It seems to be recorded out of its due order, and yet there must have been some reason for it. Observe that this was the only occasion when the high priest entered the holy of holies (verse 2). What change took place in his customary garments (verse 4)? Were these simple garments more in accord with the character of the day as one of sorrow, penitence and humiliation, or since the offerings of that day were entirely expiatory did the garments better typify the holiness of Him who became our atonement? For whom did the high priest present a sin-offering as well as for the nation (verse 5)? What peculiar offering was presented for the people on this day (verses 5-

10)? What special act of the high priest conveyed the idea of the transfer of Israel's sin to the scape-goat (20-22)? At what time of the year did this day come (29-30)? (corresponding pretty nearly to the close of our September or beginning of October). The chief features of this law might be thus specified:
a. Once a year. b. Two goats. c. Holy of holies. d. Complete expiation.

Notice in regard to "d," that the design of the day of atonement was the putting away of all the sins of the people from the highest to the lowest, that they may have committed through the whole year. Incidental and occasional sin-offerings during the year, had, it may be, overlooked much of which the people were ignorant, but on this day there was a general clearing-up of everything so that nothing remained to be atoned for. Blessed be God for a Saviour thus typified, whose blood cleanseth us from all sin (1 John 1, 7).

Notice the word for scape-goat in the Revised Version (Azazel), one which gives great difficulty to expositors. Some think that as the slain goat represented Christ satisfying Divine justice by laying down His life, the scape-goat represented Him burdened with our sin, deserted by His Father for a season, and delivered for His "bruising" into the hand of the prince of darkness. The goat led into the wilderness brings to mind Matthew 4: 1. Others ignoring the difficulty about Azazel, speak of the slain goat typifying Christ's death as glorifying God with respect to sin in general, vindicating His character and meeting all the claims of His law, even though no sinner were saved (Isaiah 49: 1-3, John 12: 27-31, 13: 31-32). While the scape-goat gives us the application of His death to the sins of the people. Where are our sins who believe in Christ? God is glorified in putting them away forever through the sacrifice of His Son, "as far as the east is from the west."

Notice the distinction pertaining to the people of God under the Gospel as compared with the law, in Hebrews 7: 26-28; 9: 6-14, 24-26; 10: 1-4, 19-22.

The Fifth of the Laws.—What is the theme of chapter 23? Read carefully, and write down the names of the various feasts:

Sabbath, 3; Passover, 5; Unleavened bread, 6-8; First-fruits, 9-14; Pentecost 15-22; Trumpets, 24-25; (Day of Atonement), 27-32; Tabernacles, 33-44.

As the "day of atonement" was a fast rather than a feast, it is not enumerated in the above list, though its chronological place is indicated.

Notice that the Sabbath was always a holy convocation, suggesting that meetings for public worship are an essential feature of the observance of one rest day in seven.

Notice that the passover (1 day) immediately followed by the feast of unleavened bread (7 days), made a single feast of 8 days coming in the spring. The first-fruits followed in early summer, the waving of the sheaf signifying the presentation to the Lord of the whole harvest as His, a beautiful type of Christ in the resurrection, 1 Corinthians 15:20. The Pentecost, from a Greek word meaning 50, was sometimes called "the feast of weeks" (Exodus 34:32), occurring as it did 7 weeks after the feast of unleavened bread, and "the feast of harvest" (Exodus 23:16), since it celebrated the ingathering in the autumn. The feast of trumpets was really the New Year feast (about the last of September or first of October), reminding them that all their times were in God's hands, while that of the tabernacles following it so closely, and lasting 8 days, was to commemorate the wilderness journey and the dwelling in booths.

Notice, that some of these feasts must have been ordained only with reference to their observance in the land of Israel after the people had become settled in their national abode.

Notice also that they involved the gathering together of the people, at least the males, in some central place, and for the same object, at least three times a year, and while they were in the nature of joyous excursions, they also contributed to the maintenance of a spirit of fellowship, patriotism and worship. Surely God is a wise Legislator, a benevolent Ruler, and a loving Father!

Notice that the typical and spiritual significance of these feasts must be very rich, though we can not dwell upon it. One who has given particular thought to it speaks of the Passover, the first of the autumnal feasts, as typifying redemption, the tabernacle, the last in the list, millennial glory, while between the two we have the resurrection of Christ in the first-fruits, the calling out of the church in the Pentecost, and the ultimate conversion and restoration of Israel in the trumpets, and day of atonement.

The Law of the Sabbatic Year.— The next great law is found in chapter 25, the name of which is at the head of this paragraph. How often did the Sabbatic year come (verse 4)? What was to rest in that year (verse 5)?

What use might be made of the natural increase of that year (6-7)? What provision was made for their support the following year (20-22)?

If it be asked what was the object of this law, two or three thoughts suggest themselves. It would be a good thing for the land to lie fallow a year. It would remind the people of God's ownership of everything, and their stewardship only. It would also quicken their trust in and thanksgiving to God for His benefits. It is well to observe, however, that the law was neglected and proved a contributing cause to their subsequent captivity in Babylon, see 2 Chronicles 36:21, in the light of the immediate context.

The Law of the Jubilee Year.— How often did the jubilee year come (verse 8)? How and when announced (verse 9)? Who and what was set free in that year? (Individuals that had come into bondage and land that had been sold, verses 10, 13-17, 23-28, 39-42, 47-55). On what principle of equity were these transfers to be made (verses 14-17, 25-27, 50-52)? On what ground were they to be jealous of oppressing one another (verse 17)? What reward promised to obedience (verses 18-19)? Why could not the land be sold out-right (verse 23)? What does this suggest as to the probable future return of Israel to that land? (see Isaiah 11:10-16, Jeremiah 32:36-42, Ezekiel 34:11-15). What exceptions are made to the return of property in the Jubilee (verses 29-30, 32-33)? It has been suggested that this provision was made to encourage strangers to settle among them. They could not purchase land, but might purchase houses in walled cities as convenient for purposes of trade, etc. What prohibition is laid in the matter of slavery (verses 39-42)?

It is unnecessary to point out that the Jubilee must have been "the most soul-stirring and enrapturing" of all the Jewish solemnities. It was connected with the day of atonement and based upon what it affected. Redemptive joy comes through the shed blood of the Great Substitute. The feast bore witness to the glad day spoken of for Israel by all the prophets.

The Types of Christ.— Leviticus is so full of precious suggestions of the Person and work of Christ, that to enumerate them would be to repeat a large part of what has been said. But the three most conspicuous types are:

The offerings.
The priesthood.
The two goats.

CHAPTER VII.

The Book of Numbers (1-19).

A secondary name for Numbers might be "The Book of the Journeyings," since it gives the story of Israel from the departure from Sinai to the arrival at Moab on the border of Canaan. If you examine the chronological hints in the margin of your Bibles, you will see that the period covered by Exodus and Leviticus was not more than a year or two, while that of Numbers was about 38 years. Map No. 2 in the back of your Bible will be an aid in mastering this book. You will see the course of the journey was first northwest as far as Kadesh, then south again to a fork of the Red Sea, and finally northwest as before, around the land of Edom to Moab. The outline is not unlike the form of a somewhat irregular "W." We shall study the book in accordance with a geographical outline, considering first the principal events or facts at Sinai before they started, then what occurred between Sinai and Kadesh, and then between Kadesh and Moab.

This book might almost be called the book of the murmurings, as well as the "journeyings," for from beginning to end it is pervaded with the spirit of rebellion against God, justifying a sort of abstract given of the period in Psalm 95:10, "Forty years long was I grieved with this generation." Let us not forget also that while the annals of many powerful nations of that same period are entirely lost to the world, these of a comparative handful of people are preserved, because of the relation they bear to the redemption of the world through Jesus Christ. This, as well, accounts for the Divine long-suffering towards them, and for all the exhibitions of Divine love which the book contains. In 1 Corinthians 10, we learn that the things that happened to them were "examples" unto us, in other words, their history throughout was a sort of object lesson illustrating God's dealings with us to-day in a spiritual sense, and in no part of their history is this more true than in Numbers.

I. At Sinai, I-X.—What are the chief facts or events associated in this book with Sinai? The reading in accordance with the prescribed rules will make it easy to reply:

1. Numbering and arranging the tribes, 1-2.

2. Choosing and assigning the Levites, 3-4.

3. Special laws and regulations, 5-10.

What was the value or necessity of fact one? Doubtless that every Israelite might know his own tribe or family, especially that the genealogy of the promised Messiah might be ascertained. And then, too, for convenience on the march, and the better preparation for conflict with enemies.

Which tribe was omitted from the numbering, and why (1:47-53; 3:5-13)? Which tribe was multiplied by two to thus fill the vacancy in the original number (1:32-35)?

In how many divisions were the Levites classified, and what general duties of the tabernacle were assigned to each (3:17, 25-26, 29, 31, 33, 36-37)? What relative position in the camp was occupied by the Levites (2:17)? Who encamped closest to the tabernacle on the east (3:38)? What special instructions were given for the sons of Kohath (4:1-15)? What was the law for the cleansing and subsequent consecration of the Levites (8:5-22)? By what symbolic act did Israel identify itself with the Levites as a substitute (8:10-11)? Compare also the following verse. What did God do with the Levites which Israel gave Him, and how does His action illustrate the way in which He still uses His people's gifts (8:18-19)?

Things to be Noticed.—Notice the illustration of God's power and wisdom in sustaining such a host for 40 years, in a country where there was neither bread nor water to be obtained—no transports, no supply trains, no friendly nations to contribute anything. God was in the midst of them. He was all, but He was enough (Deuteronomy 2:7; 8:4).

Notice the typical position of the Levites. Their calling for such a special and elevated service was not of debt but of grace, if we consider their ancestry (Genesis 34 and 49). But observe their preparation for it (8:5-8, 12)—"the blood of atonement, the water of cleansing, the razor of self-judgment." And if we ask whether there were anything antecedent to this which marked them for this selection, perhaps we find the answer in the surrender of their wills to God as indicated in Exodus 32:25-29, with which compare Deuteronomy 33:8-11, and Malachi 2:4-6.

The Minor Regulations.—Under the head of fact number three, attention should be called to the exclusion of the unclean from the camp as bearing on our obligation to put away sin from our individual lives not only, but also the exercise of discipline in the church. Compare Joshua 7:11-12, and 1 Corinthians 5.

Attention should be called as well to the further allusion to the trespass offering, originally spoken of in Leviticus, to emphasize the two features of confession and restitution, since it is only thus the believer can enjoy Paul's experience, Acts 24:16.

Nor is the law about jealousy without its significance to us. See the Divine care to maintain the integrity of the innocent as well as to punish the guilty (5:14, 28). Typically, Jehovah Himself is the husband, Israel the wife proven unfaithful, alas! The application can be made to Christ and the church, or the individual believer in place of the church. Sin is spiritual adultery.

The law of the Nazarite is full of interest. Here one sets himself apart to God in a special manner, temporarily or permanently. He separates himself from things lawful in themselves, but calculated to interfere with his deeper communion and blessing. He is peculiarly a type of Christ as suggested in such words as John 17:16-19, but an example to every believer who desires to come into the place of spiritual power. Study such New Testament passages as, "Mortify therefore your members which are upon the earth," "Ye are bought with a price, therefore glorify God in your body," "Come out from among them and be ye separate."

II. From Sinai to Kadesh, X-XIX.—The outline of this part of their journey may be marked by the various "murmurings" or rebellions recorded of them, for example:

Taberah, 11:3; Kibroth, 11:34; Hazeroth, 12:15-16; Kadesh, 13:26.

When did they start (10:11)? Who accompanied them, and why invited (29-32)? What form of prayer was associated with each stage of the journey (35-36)? Is the cause of their first complaint mentioned (11:1)? What was the punishment in this case? As to the precise nature of this "burning" nothing is known, some regarding it as external, and analogous to that which destroyed Nadab and Abihu, while others regard it as internal, i. e., some kind of "a wasting effect of the Lord's displeasure." It is also proper to say here, that the exact localities of these places referred to can not be defined with certainty.

We call the next stopping-place Kibroth, although the proper word as you perceive is somewhat longer. The shorter term, however, will answer our purpose better, as easier to remember. To what was this "murmuring," in part attributable (11:4)? To what Divine appointment or institution did it lead (16-17, 24-30)? What is the name of the New Testament council of which it may have been the origin? With what particular ceremony were they set apart (17)? What was the immediate result of this anointing (25)? What was the special cause of murmuring in this case (18)? Does the faith of Moses seem to have been equal to this emergency? What explanation of verse 31 is given in the Revised Version? (Showing that the quails flew that high, but were not so thick on the ground). How did this gratification of their desire become a judgment on them?

Spiritual Lessons.—Notice the impressive warnings this affords about worldliness. We long for its gratifications, forgetting its slavery. We are led astray in that direction through our association with false professors or "people of mixed principles."

Notice God's dealings with Moses. How gently He passes by his exhibition of infirmity, and notwithstanding this lapse, bears testimony to his faithfulness (12:7). And yet how impartial in chronicling his faults, thus giving us another incidental proof of the truth of this record!

Notice the secret of a ministry of power. The appointment of the rulers in Exodus as compared with the elders here, illustrates the contrast between a ministry exercised in human strength and in the Divine strength (Zechariah 4:6, Luke 4:18, Acts 2).

Notice the meaning of the word "prophesied," (11:25). Its importance for this particular lesson is not so great, but for other reasons it is well to know that the usual Hebrew word for "prophet" is of passive import, and implies not so much a speaker as one spoken through. Nor is it restricted in meaning to the foretelling of events, but implies any kind of utterance prompted by Divine influence, without reference to time. All this has a very important bearing on the doctrine of inspiration, especially the interpretation of such a passage as 2 Peter 1:20-21, showing that the historical as well as the prophetical books so called, are equally inspired.

What is the event at Hazeroth as given in chapter 12? What gave rise to this spirit of rebellion? What punishment fell on Miriam? Why not on Aaron (verse 11)? How is the greatness of the character of Moses shown in this incident? Of course, the practical lesson from this is the seriousness of speaking against God's servants (see such a passage as 1 Thessalonians 5 : 12-13); but there is also a typical light in which some have viewed it. Moses is regarded as representing Christ in being rejected by his people, who thrust him out of Egypt into Midian. His Ethiopian bride, is the church (composed chiefly of Gentiles). Aaron and Miriam are the Jews opposing this union. The leprosy is the Divine judgments on the Jews, who are nevertheless interceded for by those they oppose, the Christian church. But as Miriam was shut out from the camp only for a season, so when the "seven days" of Israel's rejection are run out, she will be restored again to her land and her God in Jesus Christ.

What is the great event at Kadesh, chapters 13-14? How many spies were sent out? How many reports brought back? What difference is seen between the majority and minority reports? In what did they agree or disagree? To which report gave the people heed? What two men protested against their conduct? How is Moses' jealousy for God exhibited? His love for the people? His own greatness of soul (verse 12, last clause)? What is the great hope set before us in verse 21? What punishment was visited on the rebellious? What happened to the men who brought the false report? How does verse 30 illustrate 11 Peter 2 : 9? What showed the impenitence of the nation (40-44)? What further punishment overtook them? With whom did this whole plan of the spies originate (Deuteronomy 1 : 19-24)? Does Numbers 13 : 3 necessarily contradict this? May not God have permitted it merely, when He saw them bent on the purpose? May not the commandment, in other words, have been based on the moral condition of the people? (Compare 1 Samuel 8 : 22).

Notice that the great lesson of this section is one of warning about unbelief. When at Kadesh there were but a few leagues to travel and they would be in Canaan. Why did they fail? Take God's answer for it (Hebrews 3 : 19).

The Rebellion of Korah.—Chapter 15, which we will not dwell on particularly, is an impressive illustration of Divine grace in the light of the previous conduct of the nation. Its re-

newed reference to offerings and sacrifices when they came into the land, shows God's purpose still to make good to them, (i. e., to their children who should actually possess Canaan), all His previous promises. Particularly touching is the allusion to sins of ignorance in verses 22 and 28, with which should be contrasted, however, the warning about presumptuous sins (30-31), of which an illustration is afforded in the verses immediately following. How strange the happenings of the next chapter in the light of all this!

What two tribes were chiefly represented in this rebellion (verse 1)? How numerous the ring-leaders (verse 2)? What their animus (verse 3)? To whom does Moses first address himself, and why (6-11)? What made Korah's conduct particularly reprehensible? Of what base falsehood were the sons of Eliah guilty (12-13)? What suggests the possible extent of this rebellion (19)? How once more is the magnanimity and mercy of Moses exhibited (20-22)? What punishment fell upon the ring-leaders (32-35)? What illustrates the blind passion of the people at this time (41)? What punishment befell them?

What further miraculous evidence does God give as to the authority of Moses and Aaron in chapter 17? How does He offset any tendency to conceit in Aaron by the commands of chapter 18 : 1-7?

The recent death of so many Israelites had put a large part of the nation in a state of legal uncleanness, which greatly alarmed them (17 : 12-13). What standing ceremony is now enacted for the purification of such uncleanness, in chapter 18? What evidence have we that this sacrifice, like all the others, pointed towards our Lord Jesus Christ (Hebrews 9 : 11-13)? Why so much should be said about uncleanness from contact with the dead is not clear, except as natural death shadows forth spiritual death and the deadly pollution of sin which occasions it. There may also have been sanitary reasons, however, although in the nature of the case they could not have been the more supreme.

Notice the many deep lessons of this section. For example, the wonderful mercy of God towards men who have forfeited all claim upon it. The nation had no right to Canaan, but God brings them in, and this for his own glory's sake.

Notice how much is said about the "stranger" in chapter 15, and compare it with Paul's teaching about the Gentiles, Romans 9-11.

Notice that sins of ignorance cannot

be passed over. "While grace has made provision for them in Christ, holiness demands that they be judged and confessed." Notice in what presumptuous sin consist (15:31), and be warned against it. "As the study of the Word is the safeguard against the former, subjection to the Word is the safeguard against the latter."

Notice the folly and peril of envy, jealousy and pride, and familiarize yourselves with such teachings and exhortations as Romans 12:3-8, 1 Corinthians 3:3, Philippians 2:3-8, etc.

Notice the provision, ample and royal, which God makes for His own, as illustrated in His care for Aaron and his house, chapter 18:8-32. Who loses anything when he relinquishes the world for Christ?

CHAPTER VIII.

The Book of Numbers (20-36).

In beginning this chapter we reach the third and last of the geographical divisions of Numbers. But a question may be raised here about the locality. In chapter 14:45, the people were driven by the Canaanites from Kadesh unto Hormah, after they had presumptuously tried to enter their land without the approval of God. How then do we find them at the former place again? The theory of some is that about 38 years have elapsed since that occurrence, during which time they have been dwelling at different places, of which no record has been kept, and that now for some peculiar reason they have returned to Kadesh. Others would solve the difficulty by saying there were two places of that name. But perhaps the most likely solution is that chapter 20 really follows chapter 14 chronologically, and that up to this time they had not left the immediate neighborhood of Kadesh. To go into particulars would not be a wise disposition of our time just now, and we will proceed to divide up and consider the following events without further reference to this question. From any point of view it seems proper to say they were now starting from Kadesh, and with that understanding we may map out the events of the itinerary thus:

Kadesh.
Mount Hor.
Moab.

What notable event is mentioned in verse 1? What further ground for "murmuring" is referred to? What was Moses directed to do in this case as distinguished from a somewhat similar action at Rephidim, recorded in Exodus? How did he and Aaron fail to sanctify God in this case? What punishment was inflicted on them therefore? How is their offense spoken of, Psalms 106:32-33? How does the New Testament refer to this rock

(or that at Rephidim), 1 Corinthians 10:4?

It is worth while to observe that since this rock symbolized Christ, the offense of Moses was of a deeper and more serious nature than even appears. This can be said even though Moses may have been ignorant of that fact. The two rocks indeed, like the two goats in Leviticus, are taken together to symbolize two aspects of His work. The smitten rock at Rephidim is representative of His sacrifice for us, the rock to be spoken to at Kadesh, of His intercession on our behalf. "Speak ye unto the rock," brings to mind such a passage as 1 John 1:9, which appeals to Christians rather than the unconverted, and on the basis of their previous acceptance of the atoning work of Christ. To smite the rock the second time, instead of simply speaking to it, would seem, (in type), to deny to Christ the full efficacy of His work, and rob the believer of the joy and comfort of it.

At Mount Hor.—What event seems to have made it necessary for the people to journey in this direction (see intervening verses)? What notable event occurred here (28)? What occasioned the "murmuring" here (21:4)? What punishment followed? What was the means of their deliverance therefrom? How did our Lord speak of its typical significance (John 3:14-15)?

If any one desires material for a discourse on the very heart of the Gospel, they will surely find it here. The whole human family have felt the serpent's sting (Romans 3:23). The very image of that which did the mischief was the channel through which deliverance came (Romans 8:3-4). Faith is the instrument, look and live (Isaiah 45:22). Look not to ordinances, or churches, or men, or angels, or even your own character, or penitence or prayers, but to Jesus Christ (John 3:16). Each one had to look for himself. Salvation is a personal matter.

But let us not leave Mount Hor without speaking further of the cause of the people's discouragement. Observe that the Edomites descended from Esau (Genesis 36), illustrating that he that is born after the flesh still persecutes him that is born after the Spirit. It affords a good figure of the hostility of the world to the church. Observe, too, that the main judgments of the prophet Obadiah are denounced against Edom, and because of this very treatment of his brother Israel in his emergency. And further, that although God could easily have made a way for them through Edom, He tried the patience of the one people, and delayed His vengeance on the other, by leading Israel a circuitous way. What an illustration it affords, furnished by the Divine hand itself, as to what the right path may be even though it has many windings, and is encumbered by numerous conflicts!

At Moab.—If the book of Numbers has been read carefully, you will recall that this section of our lesson practically includes all the rest of its contents. Please locate the country on the map, and see how close it is to Canaan on the east, since from that point the entrance upon the land was ultimately undertaken.

It might be interesting to notice the number of stopping-places spoken of in chapter 21, and the particular record of the conquest of the Amorites, and the possession of their land. Now begin those exterminating wars which Israel undertook at God's command, and as the expression of His wrath against the guilty nations of Canaan, till all should be cut off. Observe that the victory is ascribed to God. Compare Genesis 15:16, Deuteronomy 2:32-33, Judges 11:21, Psalm 135:10-11, and Amos 2:9.

What prophet comes prominently before us at chapter 22? So conspicuous is he, and so much space is given him, that we may attach his name to the next great fact in the book. By what nation were his services engaged? What other people seem to have been affiliated in the scheme? Does it appear that Balaam had any knowledge of the true God? How would you harmonize the fact that God permitted him to go, and was nevertheless angered at his going? What supernatural event occurred on the journey? What peculiar prophecy of Balaam about Israel has been strikingly fulfilled before our eyes (23:9)? How

many distinct efforts were vainly made to curse the people? How does the first part of verse 21 illustrate the believer's position through the righteousness of Christ? How does verse 23 illustrate the Christian doctrine of assurance? Name the verses in chapter 23 that refer to Christ, and, apparently, His millennial reign? How does the conduct of Moab in this case fulfill Deuteronomy 2:25?

The Story of Balaam.—Curiosity may be aroused concerning Balaam. A stranger to the commonwealth of Israel as he was, suggests questions as to the source of his knowledge of Jehovah, and the meaning of God's dealings with him. But it must be remembered—elation of Himself to that people. Such characters as Melchisedec and Job in the Old Testament and Cornelius in the New Testament, are a kind of parallel. Recall how God made Himself known to the heathen kings through the prophets Jeremiah or Daniel. The story of Jonah's special mission to Ninevah is also in point.

If any one is troubled at the apparent contradiction between God's permission to Balaam, and his subsequent punishment for what he was permitted to do, remember that God looketh at the heart. A careful study of these chapters is hardly necessary to show that he was a double-minded man, hoping against hope always that God would give him his own way. Use your concordance here to see what the Holy Spirit says about Balaam and "Balaamism" in other places of the Bible.

Minor Events.—If what follows in the book is classed as "minor events," it does not mean that they are less important in themselves necessarily, but only that they take up less room comparatively.

It will be seen from chapter 25, that what the Moabites could not accomplish against Israel by war or magical incantation, they came very near doing by more insidious means. What is the name of the idol mentioned in verse 3?

Baal was a general name for "Lord," and Peor for a "Mount" in Moab. Another name for this "Lord of the Mount" was Chemosh, whose rites were accompanied by the grossest obscenity. These lessons can not do much in the way of explaining such matters, but the Bible Dictionary heretofore recommended will come in place here. Which seems to have been chief in the trespass in this case, the people of God or the heathen (16-18)? And yet observe from the preceding verses that the one was punished as well as the other. Compare carefully chapter 31: 1-20. What warnings these lessons give about sin!

What. in a word, is the subject of chapter 26? What qualification of an earlier supposition is found in verse 11? On what basis was the land to be divided (53-54)? What word of God had been fulfilled prior to this numbering (64-65)?

If one has a taste for figures, it will be seen that the people had multiplied greatly, notwithstanding the devastating judgments on them. It will be seen, too, that the more sinful tribes diminished, while the others increased, so that the division of the land on the basis of populousness was a direct reward to some and punishment to others. To him that hath shall be given, but in the grace and providence of God the one that hath is the one who obeys and pleases Him. While the land was divided by lot, what shows that the matter was still under the control of God (Proverbs 16:33)? How were the rights and privileges of the female sex to be regarded in the distribution (chapter 27)?

Who is chosen to succeed Moses? What expression (verse 16) indicates God's ability to discriminate among men in assigning them their tasks? How is Joshua differentiated from others (verse 18)? What shows his need nevertheless, of special direction from the word of the Lord (21)?

It will not be especially needful to dwell on the repetition of the several laws about offerings and vows, chapters 28-30. This was made necessary, no doubt, by the fact of their approaching entrance into the land where those laws could be observed more strictly than in the wilderness, and because a new generation had sprung up since their first enactment. But let us pass on to the closing events which culminate in the appointment of the cities for the Levites, and especially, from among them, the

Six Cities of the Refuge, 35.—For whom were these cities appointed (verse 6)? What qualification of this appointment is contained in verse 11? And in verse 12? How were these cities located with reference to the Jordan? How comprehensive was this appointment (verse 15)? For how long a period was the confinement necessary in order to safety (25)? What were the names of these cities when subsequently selected (Joshua 20)? The subject of the cities of refuge affords suggestive material for a Bible reading. They may be considered a type of Christ in the following particulars:

Origin (Divine); Necessity; Accessibility; Sufficiency; Security; Applicability.

In working out the details it might be well to show that like our salvation in Christ, their value was limited to those that remained in them. "Abide in me." Also, point the contrast, that whereas they were restricted to the innocent man-slayer, Christ receives the guilty. The man-slayer had to be judged first, we believers are already judged, condemned, and yet free in Christ.

The Types in Numbers.—1. Types of the church.

a. The priests typify the church in worship.

b. The Levites typify the church in service.

2. Human type of Christ—Joshua.

3. Ideal type of Christ—the Nazarite.

4. General types of Christ.

a. Rock.

b. Brazen serpent,

c. Cities of Refuge.

The great prophecy of Christ in this book is that of the star spoken of by Balaam.

CHAPTER IX.

The Book of Deuteronomy.

A book has been written by Canon Bernard, entitled, "The Progress of Doctrine in the New Testament," in which he shows not only that the contents of those books are inspired, but that their present arrangement and order are also of the Holy Ghost. The same thing might be said of the Old Testament, especially of the Pentateuch which we are at present considering. It has been pointed out that the purpose of the Bible is, to give us the history of redemption through a special seed. In Genesis, therefore, we have the election of that seed (Abraham), in Exodus their redemption, in Leviticus their worship, in Numbers their walk and warfare, and in Deuteronomy their final preparation for the experience towards which all has been directed. (C. H. M.)

The Book of Review.—A secondary name for Deuteronomy might be "The Book of Review." The word comes from two other Greek words, deuter, which means "the second," and nomos, "law," the second law, or the repetition of the law. And yet your reading of the book has made it clear that it is more than a repetition of the law. In the first place, it repeats, or reviews, the history of the previous journeyings, and when it comes to renewing the law it adds certain things not mentioned previously, see 29:1. Compared with the other books also, it is characterized by a rather warm and oratorical style, and is more spiritual and ethical in its tone. The one great lesson it contains is that of obedience grounded on a known and recognized relationship to God through redemption. We will study it in four great divisions.

I. The Journeyings Reviewed, 1-4.—Mark the locality, 1:1-5, compared with the Revised Version. This will show that the contents of the book were given to Moses at the place where we left him in Numbers. Mark the time, 1:3, just at the close of the wanderings, so-called, and before Moses is removed, and Joshua prepares to lead the people across the Jordan. At what point does the review begin (6)? To what appointment does Moses refer in verses 9-18? To what does he allude at verse 37? What nations were they to omit from their conquests, and why (2:9-19)? Whose history illustrates that God sometimes punishes by letting men go their own way (24-30)? What other king does Sihon recall? What allusion is contained in chapter 4:10-13? What motive is ascribed to God in His dealings with Israel, verses 37-38?

Notice as you pass along, some of the many expressions illustrative of the spiritual glow of this book, such as 1:11, 31, 2:7; 3:24; 4:7, etc. Preachers will find rich as well as fresh material in this precious book for texts and themes of sermons. The "Homiletic and Practical" part of Lange's commentary will be found very helpful here (pp. 79-84).

II. The Laws Reviewed, 5-26.—At what point does Moses begin this review (verse 2)? With what reverence was this law to be regarded (6:6-9)? What caution is emphasized, 10-12? What secret of blessing, 18-19? How does 7:1-6 illustrate II Corinthians, 6:

14-18? Compare in the same way 7, 8, with Titus 3:5-7, and 8:3, with Romans 8:28. By whom, and under what circumstances, do we find 8:3 quoted in the New Testament? The same question may be asked with reference to verse 5. What summary of the Divine requirements is recorded in chapter 10:12-13? What points to a central place of worship to be established in Canaan (12:5-14)? Compare 14:23-26. What instruction is given with reference to false prophets and lying wonders (13:1-4)? What teachings of Christ about discipleship is based apparently on 13:6-8? What promise looks towards the national supremacy of Israel (15:6)? How were they taught benevolence (15:7-11)? What words of 1 John does this recall? What directions are given about a king (17:14-20)?

Spiritualism.—We have seen that this book contains several matters relatively new, but nothing yet touched on possesses a more "live" relationship to current religious events than the contents of chapter 18, beginning at verse 9. Observe the "abominations" they were to avoid, verses 10-11. Observe what they cost the Canaanites (12). The commission of these wickednesses was not the only cause of their extermination as was seen previously, but it was one of them, and a serious one. It is not within the province of our present work to examine the different shades of meaning in the words, "divination," "observer of times," "enchanter," "consulter with familiar spirits," etc., but one is not far wrong who describes them as identical in spirit with what we call fortune-telling, clairvoyance, lucky and unlucky days, mesmerism, and perhaps certain forms of hypnotism, and especially all that class of phenomena known as spiritualism. How God hates it! How plainly He warns against it! Let teachers not fail to emphasize what He says. A book recommended in an earlier lesson will be a valuable aid here, "Earth's Earliest Ages," by Pember. The author shows the connection between these things now being done, and those for which the Canaanites were dispossessed, and the antediluvians swept away. "Demon Possession," by John L. Nevius, D.D., is also to the point, and for pamphlets on the subject, cheap of price and easy to read, write the Scriptural Tract Repository, (H. L. Hastings), 47 Cornhill, Boston. Christians should be fortified on such subjects.

The Prophecy of Christ.—It is not a little strange, and worthy of careful thought, that the chapter which contains these allusions to the "lying wonders" of a false Christ, should also contain the clearest prediction of the true Christ we have yet met. It has always seemed to me like this:—The Israelites might be afraid that when Moses left them, they would be driven by the necessity of the case to do what the Canaanites did in the matter of worship. They would have no leader such as he, what else then could they do? The answer to meet their case is in verse 15. To whom does Moses refer approximately? To whom ultimately? For the answer to this last question consult the marginal references to John 1:45 and Acts 3:22-23. This clear and definite prophecy of Christ affords an opportunity to speak of another law of the rhetoric of the Holy Spirit of importance to be understood. The first law thus emphasized was called the law of recurrence, but this will be known as

The Law of Double Reference.—Now, what is "the law of double reference? It is that peculiarity of the writings of the Holy Spirit, by which a passage applying primarily to a person or event near at hand, is used by Him at a later time as applying to the Person of Christ or the affairs of His kingdom. It is not claimed that the human writers had this two-fold sense in mind always, even if at all, but that this was the mind of the Holy Ghost, in inspiring their words. As one of the ancient commentators puts it, "God, as the original Author of both Testaments, shaped the Old in relation to the New." Or, as Alford says, "No word prompted by the Holy Ghost had reference to the utterer only. All Israel was a type. * * * Christ is everywhere involved in the Old Testament, as He is everywhere evolved in the New." To get hold of this principle of interpretation is vital, especially in the study of the psalms and prophetical books. In the present instance, the primary reference to Joshua, and the ultimate to Jesus Christ is only a representation of what will be found to occur again and again as we proceed.

Do not leave this prophetic allusion to Christ, without observing the marked advance it indicates in the clearness of the conception of the Coming One. Compare the previous allusions to Him, and see how the material for His identification grows. He is not only to be of the seed of Abraham, and the tribe of Judah, but He is to be a Prophet like unto Moses.

III. The Future History of Israel, 27: 30.—The next general division of the book is peculiarly fascinating as containing one of the most notable prophecies in the whole Bible. It will be seen to give a forecast of the early history of Israel almost from the time they entered Canaan until the present period. Let us observe how the subject is approached.

What was one of the first things to be done on crossing the Jordan (1-8)? What else is commanded (11-13)? What outline of the curses is given (14-26)? Observe the number and character of the blessings to be bestowed on the ground of obedience (28:1-14). Observe particularly in what these blessings would eventuate (verse 13.) Compare the previous allusion to their national supremacy, as all these intimations in that direction have an important bearing on our later study of the prophetical books.

At what verse are the curses on disobedience renewed? Follow them along as far as verse 36, and there pause a moment. From your general knowledge of Israel's later history, when would you say this prediction, at least the first part of it, was fulfilled? Does it not seem to point very unmistakably to what we call their Babylonian captivity, say about 600 B. C.? Compare 11 Kings 25.

Now follow your eye along the succeeding curses until you reach verse 49. What still later incident in their history does it recall? Was not the "nation from far, whose tongue they did not understand," the Latin nation? Does not this point to the destruction of Jerusalem by Titus, the Roman general, A. D. 70? Read carefully the horrible details of the siege in the verses that immediately succeed, and compare them with Josephus' "History of the Jews." This last-named book should be owned and read by every Christian, if for no other reason than the demonstration it affords of the literal fulfillment of prophecy, and especially this prophecy.

But read further still until your eye rests, let us say, at verse 64. What have we here and in the following verses? Is not this a sad, but true forecast of the condition of the Jews in our own time? We only need to read the current newspapers to answer that question.

But is there no gleam of hope for this people, so beloved and blessed of God? Read chapter 30, especially verses 1-10. In the light of such promises should not we Gentiles be more sincere and importunate in prayer for the Jews than many of us are? Read Psalm 122, particularly verse 6, to see what blessing we may expect if we do so.

I am led to close the consideration of this section with an extract from Dr.

Gosman, the translator of Lange's commentary on this book. It is a little out of the line of the particular work before us, but its merit and timeliness are its justification. He says: "This chapter, in its prophetic declarations, which have been so strikingly fulfilled, contains clear proof of the Divine foreknowledge, and of the inspiration of Moses. This is all the more clear since the prophecies relate mainly and in their extreme and awful particularity, to the curses which should rest upon the unfaithful people. Moses does not spare his own people, but holds before them the glass of their future defection and sufferings, as he foresaw them. There might have been a motive for dwelling particularly upon their prosperity, but there is no assignable motive for the character of this discourse, unless it is found in the clear foresight given to him of what was to occur."

IV. The Close of Moses' Life, 31:34.
—The general title at the head of this paragraph will answer for the fourth and last division of the book. It may be subdivided thus:

The charge to Joshua, 31.
The song of remembrance, 32.
The blessing on the tribes, 33.
The burial on Mount Nebo, 34.

Why was Moses as a leader, not absolutely essential to Israel (31:3)? To what virtue are they exhorted (6-7)? What authority attached to the words of this book (9-13)? What was done with it (24-26)?

Why was the song written (19-21)? Observe its spirit of adoration, so different from many of our songs and prayers (32:1-4). Observe the touching and poetic allusion to God's providential care (9-14). Observe the allusion to their position of privilege (29-31). While it speaks clearly of awful judgments on account of sin, what gleam of hope does it contain (43)? How tersely are they taught the value of obedience (47)?

Observe the precious promises in chapter 33, verses 3, 12, 23, 25, 27. How these have comforted the saints in all ages! How they enhance the value of this book! How we should praise God for them!

Who wrote the account of Moses' death, chapter 34? Some think he did himself write it by inspiration, prior to the event. Some ascribe it to a successor, perhaps Joshua. It is hardly necessary to the maintenance of the Mosaic authorship of the Pentateuch to suppose that Moses wrote it himself. See the interest taken in the body of Moses, Jude 9. See the honor put upon Moses, Luke 9:28-36, also Revelation 15:1-3. Some students of prophecy regard him as one of the two witnesses of Revelation 11, and think that in company with Elijah, he will appear in the flesh in Jerusalem in the culminating days of the present age. He is a striking type of Christ, whose personal history will well repay prayerful study from that point of view. We part from him with sadness, but shall see him face to face one of these days, when with ourselves he shall be found casting his crowns at the feet of Christ, who loved him and gave Himself for him.

CHAPTER X.

The Book of Joshua.

Joshua might be called "The Book of Conquest and Division," with reference to the events in Canaan it records. According to the marginal chronology it covers a period of how many years? Its character is that of a military campaign, and I have read a criticism of it from that point of view, which places Joshua in the very first rank of military commanders, classing him with the Cæsars, and Hannibals, and Napoleons, and Wellingtons, and Grants of all ages. We know, of course, whence he secured his wonderful equipment, and are not surprised at this estimate of him, but it is interesting to have it come to us from another source. The first great fact in the book might be described as

I. The Command to Joshua, I.—Observe the renewal of the gift of the land, verse 4, and compare the marginal references to the same matter; for this is not a dead issue, but a very live one, and one that is coming up again in the settlement of "the Eastern question." Observe the promise, 5-6, and the conditions of blessing, 7-8. Also the promptness and leadership of Joshua, 9:15. Suppose we call the second great fact

II. The Spying of the Land, 2.—As this was not disapproved of God, we may assume it had His sanction, and shows that, notwithstanding His promise to Joshua, the latter was to use the ordinary methods of warfare except where specially instructed otherwise. The use of means is not dishonoring to God, nor does it discount faith in any way, sometimes indeed the very opposite is true. It may exhibit weaker faith to be straining after the marvelous always, than to be willing to carry on the work of God with the common agencies at hand.

It need not be supposed that God commended Rahab's falsehood by what we read in Hebrews 11:31, or James 2:25, any more than that He commended her other sins. Those allusions are to call attention to her faith, a living faith which took hold of God and saved her, sinner as she was. Indeed this story of Rahab is in several points a suggestive type of redemption, and can be employed as a sermon or Bible reading. Observe:

Her abode (a condemned city); her character; her faith; the promise she received; the token she displayed; her deliverance (chapter 6); her interest in saving others.

All these particulars can easily be wrought out into a most helpful and soul-stirring discourse.

III. The Crossing of Jordan, 3-4.—Let the title at the head of this paragraph identify the third great fact. See the preparation for it, 1-5, observe the particulars, 14-17, and memorials of the event, 4:8-9. Dwell especially on verse 15 of chapter 3, which shows it to have been all the more extraordinary because of the time it took place. The locality named in verse 16 was about 30 miles from their encampment.

This event has always seemed to me an impressive type of the mediatorial or intercessory work of Christ on behalf of His people. The priests standing in the river-bed until every member of the host had passed over in safety, strangely yet blessedly, brings to mind Hebrews 7:25. F. B. Meyer, in "Joshua, and the Land of Promise," suggests many spiritual analogies of this kind, helpful not only to the quiet reader, but also to one who is teaching the contents of the book to others.

IV. The Conquest of Jericho, 5-7.—As usual, locate the facts, beginning with those immediately preceding the event itself, the circumcision, the passover, the appearance of the Captain of the Lord's host. Observe that the act of circumcision indicated a gracious renewal on the part of God of His covenant with the children whose fathers had sinned against Him, and perished in the wilderness. In this sense verse 9 may be explained. What indicates the Captain of the Lord's host to be a Divine Person? How do His name and equipment indicate His interest in and approval of the invasion taking place? With what other Christophanies have we met previously?

There must have been a strategic reason for first attacking Jericho, and the plan seems to have been by its destruction to effectually separate the Northern foes in Canaan from those in the South, and thus prevent a military coalition. Observe the particular directions to Israel. No battlements, but a promenade! How foolish it must have seemed not only to their enemies, but even to some of themselves! Compare such a passage as 1 Corinthians 1:17-31. To what is this victory ascribed, Hebrews 11:30? Dwell on the marked illustration it affords of saving faith. The Israelites did nothing, and yet they did everything. They did the most they could do in the fact that they absolutely surrendered themselves to God, obeying Him to the last degree. Does not the man who truly accepts Jesus Christ do this? Dwell on the illustration it affords of conquering faith. Hearts are shut up like Jericho (6:1), but God gives them to His servants who obey Him.

The utter destruction referred to verse 21, seems horrible in our eyes, but two or three things are to be kept in mind in judging of it. In the first place, it is the teaching of the Bible itself that has made such an act horrible to us. In the second place, it was in perfect accord with the usual methods of warfare in those times. In the third place, and this is the all important thought, it was God's judgment on sin. Sin is unspeakably awful, and we must not minimize it. All through the Old Testament these object lessons are given us, which in the goodness of God, are intended to be deterrent both for nations and individuals, and which in the opposite event, only become types of the universal judgments or judgment to come. The death of the Son of God to put away the consequences of sin must have been vitally necessary to men. Let these Old Testament facts be used to impress this truth on those we teach, and lead them to the Saviour.

The Defeat at Ai, 7-8, which is the next great fact, will be found to emphasize what has just been said about sin, and to bring out one or two new thoughts about it. The former illustration applied to sin in the world, but this to sin in the church, or in the individual believer. Here "the children of Israel committed a trespass" (verse 1). See the consequences which befell all for the folly of one (2-5). Compare James 2 : 10, for an individual application. Joshua's ignorance of the cause of defeat (6 : 15) has a deep lesson likewise, which may bring to mind II Corinthians 6 : 14; 7 : 1, and kindred passages. Mr. Beecher once said that half of our troubles were just God dragging us; they would depart if we stood on our feet and went whither He desired. This story of Joshua's discouragement is in that line. Let verses 16-21 be used as an illustration of the deep principle in Numbers 32 : 23, last clause. Let it be remembered in Achan's case as in that of Nadab and Abihu, that it is not a question of the eternal damnation of his soul, but of God's earthly judgments among His people. Let the victory recorded in chapter 8 illustrate the power over spiritual enemies which becomes theirs who are living in obedience to God's commands.

VI. The Rescue of Gibeon, 9-10.—
This fact brings us to the most interesting part of the book, as it is also the most critical moment in the present history of Israel. Observe the wiles of the Gibeonites (3-13), and the failure of Israel to ask counsel of God before entering into a covenant with them (14-15). Observe, too, the relation which the Gibeonites ever after sustained towards Israel (22-27). Observe the confederation of the five kings against Gibeon, and the reason for it (10 : 1-5). Study the location of the kingdoms or cities represented by these kings, and observe that they were all in the southern part of Canaan. Their destruction, therefore, in a bunch meant the conquest practically, of the whole of that region. Observe the supernatural phenomena associated with the battle, e. g., the Lord's special encouragement to Joshua (8), the visitation of hail-stones (11), the remarkable prayer (12), and more remarkable answer (13-14), and finally, the issue of the contest (42).

Did the Sun and Moon Stand Still?—
This miracle shares with that in the book of Jonah, the distinction of being more "spoken against" than any other in the Old Testament. Joshua speaks in verse 12, and the historian in verse 13 in the popular language of men referring to the heavenly bodies. It seems to a spectator on the earth's surface as though they moved, while in reality the earth moves with reference to them. This miracle, therefore, lit-

erally construed, was the cessation of the earth's revolution on its axis by the space of a day. Men say this could not be, but they forget who God is, and what He has done. Given a God who can create the earth and set it rolling on its axis, and it can not be too hard for Him to stop it twenty-four hours without allowing it, or the universe of which it is an important part, to get out of order.

All the supernatural phenomena attendant on this battle, and its prime importance to Israel at that particular juncture, and hence to the plans and purposes of God in the earth, prepare us to accept this view of the case. In addition to this there is other corroborative evidence which may, or may not, be regarded as having value. For example, Professor C. A. Totten, a mathematician, and at one time professor of military science in Yale College, has made and published calculations to show that one day in the earth's history was 48 hours long. A tradition to the same effect is held by the Egyptians and Chinese.

These things are not stated for the purpose of maintaining a theory, or defending a principle of exegesis, or opposing Christians who take another view of the matter, but simply to express a personal opinion. Men whom we all love and respect hold differently. For example, F. B. Meyer, in the book previously referred to, speaks of this incident thus : "God could make the clock of the universe stop if it were necessary. But it is not necessary to believe that He did this. By some process, the laws of which are at present unknown to us, but of which we get glimpses, in refraction, in the afterglow of sunset, God was able to prolong the daylight until Israel had made an end of slaying their foes."

VII. The Close of the War, 11.—
The seventh great fact in the book may be stated in the words at the head of this paragraph, and requires the briefest treatment. Examine the map, and observe that the names of the places mentioned in the text bear out the general statement as to locality, in verse 2. Locate the particular field of battle, verse 5. Observe the vastness of the combination against Israel, (1-4), and the thoroughness of the victory (8, 10, 12). Observe that this did for the northern part of Canaan what the previous victory secured for the South. Observe the reference to the conclusion of the campaign (23), to which allusion will be made again in the study of the next book.

Verse 20 may trouble some, but it must be remembered that when such "hardening" is spoken of, it always pre-supposes conduct on the part of the people obstinately opposed to God's will. This was dwelt on in the case of Pharoah. Such hardening is a Divine judgment on men for wicked actions freely indulged in on their part. Compare 11 Thessalonians 2, especially verses 10-12. Is there any evil of the present day, of a religious character, which these verses bring to mind? What of Christian Science, for example? Let us beware of it.

VIII. The Division of the Land, 12-21.—In the consideration of this event there are certain especially interesting features to be observed. In the first place, the conclusion of the campaign noticed in the last chapter must be qualified to our understanding (13:1). The land was conquered in a general sense, but not in detail. The first settlers in this country conquered the land when New England was settled, but there was a great deal of conquering done afterwards before the Pacific coast was reached. The land was ours in one sense, and it had to become ours in another sense. Observe that the separate tribes were not as eager for this conquest as might have been expected, and that personal ease and advantage soon began to supersede zeal for God (16:10, 18:3, etc.). Observe the fulfillment of earlier instructions concerning Caleb and Joshua (14:6-14, 19:49-50), the setting up of the tabernacle (18:1), and the assignment of the cities of refuge (20).

IX. The Altar of Witness, 22.—Observe the commendable fidelity of the two and a half tribes (1-6), and the commendable action of patient inquiry and investigation (11-33) on the part of the other tribes. Individuals have sustained "strained" relations with one another for years, and nations have gone to war for the lack of observance of such an example. See Matthew 18:15. Observe the value of public memorials of great men and great events. How often have such memorials been referred to thus far in our studies! What statues, or monuments or tablets of this kind are in your town? What are you yourself doing personally, to instruct and benefit later generations in this way? Especially, how is the memory of God's great goodness being perpetuated in a public way? Is the Sabbath observed, Thanksgiving day, or Fast day? Is God publicly recognized and honored among us as He ought to be? Do our children thus hear us rehearse His wondrous acts of old time? Should not Washington's birthday, and the Fourth of July be holy days before the Lord, for His sake and our children's sake? What great memorial or "altar of witness" has God Himself set up for us in His church to keep perpetually before us and our children the wonderful sacrifice of His Son? All this is aside somewhat, but may be suggestive in the use of this chapter in preaching and teaching.

X. The Renewal of the Covenant, 23-24.—In what solemn and important act does Joshua now engage before his death? What commandment does he lay upon the people (23:6-8)? With what promise does he assure them (10)? What warning does he give them (12-13)? What seems to be his feeling as to their future conduct, as expressed in the general tenor of his words? What choice does he set before them (24:15)? What obligation do the people lay upon themselves in the verses that follow? What testimony to the authenticity of this book is contained in verse 26? At what age did Joshua die? Point out in these two chapters the ways in which he kept his own merit in the background and exalted God.

CHAPTER XI.

The Books of Judges and Ruth.

The story of the book of Judges is something like this:—While Joshua and the elders of that generation lived, (those who had personally known the wonders of Jehovah), the people continued in measurable obedience to the Divine law. But when they died, and another generation came on the scene, there was a steady decline. They had made the way easy for this, by failing to drive out all the Canaanites from amongst them, as we saw in the last chapter. The proximity of these corrupt heathen people began to act like leaven in the dough. Israel intermarried with them, and by degrees was led into idolatry by them. This weakened their power so that from conquerors they became the conquered. They turned their back upon God, who, in a sense, turned His back upon them, allowing them to be taken captive by their enemies, and sorely oppressed.

In their distress they would repent, and cry out unto Him, when He would deliver them through the instrumentality of some man, miraculously endued, called a judge. As long as this man lived they would be held in obedience, but on his decease a relapse into sin would follow, and the same round of experience be repeated.

The Preface to the Book.—The story as told above is outlined for us very distinctly in chapter 2:6-19, which takes the place of a preface to the whole book, and suggests that a spiritual outline of its contents might be held in mind in four words:

Sin, punishment, repentance, deliverance.

If you will look at the chronology suggested in the margin at chapter 1, and again at chapter 16, you will perceive it to be estimated that about 300 years was the period covered by the judges; to which should be added, however, the years of Eli and Samuel in the following book, (who were also judges), and which increases the time to 330 years, more or less. And yet this does not agree with Paul's words in Acts 13:20. A perfectly satisfactory explanation of this can not as yet be given, but it should content for the present to know that the data in Judges are somewhat obscure, and that the calculations of our commentators as indicated in the marginal chronology may have to be changed. This matter of Bible chronology will be referred to more particularly later on.

The Number of Judges.—How many judges are named in the book? At first you may reply 13, but the usurped rule of Abimelech, the fratricide, chapter 9, is not usually counted, thus limiting the number to 12. Take a sheet of paper, and write down for yourself the name of each judge and the name of the people from whom he delivered Israel, and also some peculiarity in his history that will differentiate him from the others in your thought, and aid you to recall him.

Familiarize yourself especially with the names of the leading judges, those to whose doings the largest space is given, i. e., Othniel, Deborah, Gideon, Jephthah and Samson. And, in addition, acquaint yourself thoroughly with the names of the heathen nations referred to—Mesopotamia, Moab, Philistia, Canaan, Midian.

Now look on the map, or examine a Bible dictionary, and see where these peoples were located with reference to Israel—on the north, east, south and west. This raises one or two questions: Was the whole of Israel in captivity to each of these peoples at different times, or only those tribes of Israel in closest proximity to each? And if the latter be our conclusion, as seems likely, did each judge rule over the whole of Israel at any one time, or only over so many of the tribes as were by him delivered from bondage? The latter seems the more probable idea, and gives a different conception to the period altogether. It indicates that the periods of these judges were not necessarily successive, and two or more may have been ruling at the same time in different parts of the land. It was this unsatisfactory state of things, as we shall see, that was instrumental finally, in moving the people to demand a king.

The Divisions of the Book.—The peculiar nature of this book does not lend itself easily to divisions as in the other cases, but your reading may have led you to recognize an outline not unlike the following:

1. Introductory, 1-3:4.
2. History of the judges, 3:5-16.
3. Particular details of evil, 17-21.

In the introductory portion, which tribe is given the distinction after the death of Joshua? What statement in chapter 1 repeatedly illustrates the lack of faith and obedience on Israel's part? What punishment fell on them for this (2:23)?

Under the second general division there are several things to dwell upon. For example, the deed of Ehud. It makes the blood run cold to read of it, but remember he was not a murderer, but a warrior. The whole world, and always, has made a distinction between these two. Was it an act of personal revenge, or patriotic and religious fervor? Is the deed approved in Scripture? This question brings up an important qualification that should be applied in countless instances in the Bible, of a similar character. A distinguished commentator justly calls attention to the fact that there hangs a shadow over the official career of this man. His name is not praised in Israel, nor is it said the Spirit of the Lord was upon him, nor that he judged Israel. These omissions may be without significance, but are they not noticeable? It has been stated that while his cause was pure, the same cannot be said of any other such assassination in history.

To a certain extent these qualifying remarks in the case of Ehud's act may be applied to that of Jael under the judgeship of Deborah. I can not but agree with others that while she acted under a Divine commission, and is, in fact, commended, yet she appears to have transcended proper limits in the means employed. These are questions, however, too deep for my soul to fathom, and I would be careful not to be found replying against God.

Material for a Bible Reading.—Pursuant to our custom, when opportunity offers we want to indicate good material for young preachers and others to use in the conduct of religious meetings. The history of the next judge, Gideon, furnishes such material. The theme might be styled "The Gospel in the History of Gideon's Judgeship." Carefully review the facts, and observe how they illustrate the following points:

1. Punishment follows sin, 6:1-6.
2. Repentance precedes deliverance. 6:7-10.

In this case note that a prophet was sent to Israel before a deliverer, and that the whole tone of his message was intended to convince of sin.

3. Deliverance is wholly through faith, as indicated, (a) in the selection of an obscure and uninfluential leader, 6:14-16; (b), in the insignificant army, 7:1-7; (c), in the foolish weapons, 7:16-23.

4. Faith rests upon evidence, as indicated in the signs and tokens given to Gideon: (a), the fire out of the rock, 6:21-22; (b), the dew and the fleece, 36-40; (c), the dream of the Midianite, 7:9-15. It will be easy to show how under the Gospel, God does not call on men to accept Jesus Christ for salvation without affording abundant evidence on which their faith may rest. Let us get hold of these facts in Israel's history in order to use them for God's glory and the good of souls in this way.

Did Jephthah Slay His Daughter?— The chief interest for us in the history of the next most prominent judge is perhaps stated in the preceding question, which presents another of the exceptional occasions when we might step aside from the main purpose of these lessons to explain a difficulty, or interpret an expression. It is to be wished that the turning aside in this case could settle anything, but it can not. Opinions about Jephthah's act have always differed, and always will, and the circumstance only affords another illustration of the wisdom of concentrating attention upon more profitable things. On the face of it, the record gives justification to the belief that he actually

sacrificed his daughter, "impelled by the dictates of a pious but unenlightened conscience," and so many commentators believe. And yet, happily, there is another view to be taken, which, without serious violence to the text, puts all concerned in a very different light, and supposes that the fulfillment of the vow consisted in the consignment of the maiden to a life of perpetual maidenhood. Those who have access to Lange's commentary, or the Schaff-Herzog Encyclopedia (article "Jephthah"), will find in either a very satisfactory treatment of the case. Perhaps the wish is father to the thought, but so far as the opinion of the writer is worth anything, it seems inclined towards this latter view.

Was Samson a Suicide?—The question about Jephthah is nearly matched by this concerning the succeeding judge, which, however, is capable of a more satisfying answer. That he was not a suicide is evident from his penitent and prayerful spirit at the last, from the fact that he was acting as a public magistrate in what he did, dying for his country and his God, and yet not seeking death except as it was the inevitable consequence of duty done. Hebrews 11:32, honors him in the ranks of the noble witnesses to faith.

The history of Samson, like that of Gideon, is very rich in spiritual teaching, and material for Bible readings and addresses. The fact that he himself was a Nazarite brings forward a typical relation to Christ (Matthew 2:23). His history identifies another of the manifestations of Jehovah-Jesus in the Old Testament (13:3-23). Verse 23, just referred to, is a text full of meat for a good sermon on such a theme as "God's love for man demonstrated by His acts." Verse 25 of the same chapter illustrates the anointing of the Holy Spirit for service as distinguished perhaps from the infilling of the same Spirit for holiness. Of course the remarkable physical power of Samson is only to be accounted for in this way. It was not in his hair, else there would have been no need that the "Spirit of Jehovah" should come upon him. The growth of his hair was only a token of his consecration, not the consecration itself, and when he failed to withstand Delilah, it was the surrender of the latter rather than the former that brought evil upon him.

Particular Details of Evil, 17-21.— This division will require no particular explanation further than the statement that it traces the evils of the time incident to the absence of a fixed and strong government, or more truly, the absence of obedience to God, (21:25). We see the decay of the priesthood, the growth of the spirit of individualism, and the spread of licentiousness and passion. The two events are (1), the history of Micah's idolatry, chapter 17-18, and (2), the history of the crime at Gibeah, 19-21.

The Book of Ruth.—The contents of this book are very simple, and tell their own story. During what period did the event occur (1:1)? The authorship is supposed to be the same as Judges, and attributed to Samuel. The chief interest in the book for us, outside of its own intrinsic beauty, is found in the genealogical table at the end, quoted by Matthew, and showing Ruth to have been an ancestress of Christ. As without this little book that fact would have remained unrevealed, we see a sufficient reason why the Holy Spirit should have caused it to be placed in the sacred canon.

CHAPTER XII.

The First Book of Samuel.

There are five leading characters in First Samuel, see if you can name them without assistance. What shall we call the first fact? The birth and call of Samuel? This may be said to cover chapters 1-3. Give the names of his parents. Give the meaning of his name. How did Hannah celebrate his birth (2)? Of what New Testament song does this remind you? What beautiful promise of guidance and preservation is found in verse 9? How was Hannah rewarded for her gift to the Lord (20-21)? How does this illustrate verse 30, last clause? What New Testament promises does it illustrate? How are Eli's sons described, and on what ground? Who is held responsible for them, and what judgment is pronounced against him? With whom might he be contrasted (Genesis 18: 19)? Compare also 1 Kings 2:27. What shows that God can teach His will to a little child? How does 3:19, 20 illustrate Isaiah, 44:26, first clause? It is to be observed that Samuel is the true founder of the Old Testament prophetic order, see Acts 3:24. Soon after his call, as our next great fact discloses, the ark was lost to Israel for a while, the tabernacle, therefore, ceased to have its significance as a center of worship, the high-priests' functions were suspended, and the mediatorship between God and the people rested altogether in the prophet. Let us call the next great fact

The Loss of the Ark, 4-7.—What nation is Israel's particular enemy at this time? What mistake was made in bringing the ark into the battle? How can this error of trusting in the symbol instead of the One symbolized, be shown to be paralleled by any in our day? What prophecy was fulfilled in 4:1:? What is the meaning of Ichabod? Was the possession of the ark a curse or blessing to its captors? How were their idols put to ridicule? How does 6:10-12 attest the supernatural? What judgment befell the Bethshemites, and why? Where, and for how long a period did the ark subsequently rest? How would you account for the changed condition of affairs in chapter 7? Examine prayerfully verses 4, 6 and 12. What was Samuel's "circuit" (16)?

Note that Israel's conduct about the ark was not justified by such passages as Numbers 10:35, 14:44, or Joshua 6:4, because they had not sought counsel of God through His prophet. It is more likely they were following the example of their heathen enemies, who carried their idol, or its symbols, with them to battle, believing power to be inseparably associated with it. By permitting the capture of the ark, therefore, God sought two ends, the discipline of Israel, and the vindication of His supremacy over the gods of the nations.

In this connection a question may be raised about the great number slain, 6:19, as being too many for the probable size of the place. All the authorities consulted seem to regard it as an error of the copyist in some way, but are unable to remove the difficulty. The literal rendering is "70 men, 50,000 men," and the problem is how to connect the two expressions to make good sense.

In referring above to the time of the ark's abode in Kirjath-jearim, attention should have been called to 11 Samuel 6, and 1 Chronicles 13, which indicate that a much longer period elapsed before its removal. But the explanation probably is that the twenty years passed before the people "lamented after the Lord," and the revival sprang up.

The Call of Saul, 8-12.—Although it had been clearly predicted in Deuteronomy (17:14-20), that they would have a king, yet observe how naturally it came about that the prophecy should be fulfilled. There was no collusion on the part of any of God's agents to bring it about, but the free acting of the people themselves. Thus has it been always under such circumstances, furnishing one of the incontrovertible evidences of the Divinity of the Word. How does 8:7 show the identity of God with His servants? What parallel do we find in Acts 9:4? What lesson about making requests of God may we learn from verse 9? Who originally chose Saul to be king (9:15-17)? By what Divine ceremony was he set apart for the office (9:1)? What Divine testimony was given to confirm his faith (10:10-13)? Of which of the judges does this experience remind us? Who now chooses Saul to be king (17:25)? How does this illustrate the relation between Divine foreknowledge and human free agency? What beautiful text for a discourse on the church does verse 26 contain? What parallel as between Saul's experience and that of Christ, is furnished in the next verse? (Compare the parable of the nobleman, Luke 19:14). Under what circumstances was the kingdom finally established to Saul (chapter 11, especially 14-15)? What illustration of God's merciful kindness is found in chapter 12, especially 12-15? On what ground was this kindness shown (verse 22)? Have you ever noticed what it is that God does for His own sake? (Look at Psalm 23:3, Isaiah 43:25, Ephesians 1:6, etc.). How does verse 23 impress Christians with the obligation of intercessory prayer? (See Ephesians 6:18).

The Rejection of Saul, 13-15.—Of what presumptuous sin was Saul guilty (13:9)? Did he show a penitent spirit, or a self-justifying one? What striking text for a discourse on the world-spirit in the church is found in verse 12? How is Saul's successor described, verse 14? It might be well to pause here long enough to inquire how a sinner like David could be so described. One part of the answer is found in a comparison between the two men, Saul and David. Both were sinners indeed, but while the latter was a regenerated, converted sinner, the former apparently was not. The pres-

ent instance affords such a point of comparison, for David, when rebuked for sin, as we shall see further on, is always humble and penitent, while Saul never is. (Compare Isaiah 66:2).

Under what circumstances was the rejection of Saul subsequently confirmed (chapter 15)? How does he justify himself in this case (verses 15 and 21)? What fundamental and universal principle is enunciated by Samuel in verse 22? How does verse 30 indicate the superficiality of Saul's humility? If you will carefully peruse the preceding chapter again, verses 47-52, it will probably appear that several years had passed in successful, military operations before this second test of Saul's character Godward was applied to him. It may be that an opportunity was thus given to retrieve his former error by an exact obedience. Who can tell how different it may have been with him had he improved it? It will be well for us to notice as we pass along, how frequently this occurs in the history of God's dealings with men and nations. He gives them tests now and then, not surely, that He may discover what kind they are, for He knoweth all things, but that they may be discovered to themselves, and in the presence of His judgments stand self-condemned. (See Psalm 51:4, Romans 3:19, Revelation 15:3). How much we need the aid of the Holy Spirit to endure what God may thus send upon us! James 1:12.

Observe that all through this business Saul follows his own ideas and wishes rather than God's decree, showing a selfish, arbitrary temper, and, as another expresses it, "An utter unfitness to perform the duties of a delegated king in Israel." Steps are now taken to indicate his successor, and as David is kept prominently before us in most of the following chapters, and especially in connection with Saul's treatment of him, let us designate the fifth great fact in the book as

The Persecution of David, 16-26.— What gave rise to Saul's jealousy (18:6-9)? Who comes prominently into view as David's friend (19:1-7)? Who else stands by him (18-24)? Also chapter 21:1-9? How does Ahimelech suffer for his kindness (22:6-23)? Where is David's hiding-place at this time, and who are with him (verses 1 and 2)? What city of Judah does he deliver (chapter 23)? How does God interpose on his behalf? Under what circumstances does David spare Saul's life (24:4-7)? And again (26:5-25)?

David Compared with Saul.—It might be well to pause again at this point for a further comparison between these two men. Does not Saul know that David has been chosen of God as his successor (20:30-31)? And yet observe how he seeks in every way to destroy his life and thwart God's purposes. How different in the case of David! Twice is Saul in his power, and though strongly and plausibly urged to slay him (24:4), yet does he refuse to do it. And why does he refuse? Is he afraid of Saul, or his bodyguard, or the anger of the nation? Is his hand restrained by the fear of man, or the fear of God (5-7)? What further light this sheds on that expression, "A man after God's own heart!" David knew he was to receive the kingdom, but his choice was to receive it in God's own way and time (26:7-11).

To what alien people does David finally flee for refuge (chapter 27)? What city is given him to dwell in (6)?

Some Things Hard to Understand.— In Peter's second epistle he speaks of some things in Paul's writings as "hard to be understood," and there are things of that kind here also. But it is a great thing for a teacher to have courage enough to say to his class that he "doesn't know," sometimes. Do not be afraid to say that to those whom you teach, when it is true. It will not weaken but rather increase their respect for you. And yet on the other hand, let it not put a premium on laziness. Do your best to find out, but when your best fails, own it frankly.

One of the things in the present case hard to understand is the apparent irreconciliableness of 16:14-23, and 17:55-58. Must not Saul have known David in the first instance? How then had he forgotten him in the second? Let us remember that David doubtless had been at home a good while, and grown from a boy to a man, that Saul had rarely seen him before except in moments of madness, and that possibly Abner had been absent from court when David was there. Let us remember also that these old narratives give very brief and partial views of certain occurrences, making it necessary sometimes for us to suspend judgment in the absence of more light.

Another "hard thing" is the allusion to the Spirit of the Lord departing from Saul, and an evil spirit from the Lord troubling him (16:14, etc.). As to the first, it must be kept in mind that there is a difference between the Spirit of the Lord coming into a man in the sense of regenerating him, as we have it expressed in the New Testament, and that same Spirit coming on a man in the sense of enduing or equipping him for some special service. The former transaction would seem to be an enduring one, and when the Holy Spirit comes to us at regeneration, He comes to abide forever (John 14:16); but the latter may be a changing experience, and as true of a man who is not a child of God as of one who is. You can easily recall men already treated of, who received the Spirit of the Lord in this sense. Balaam, for example. May we not believe that He came and went on him the same as on Saul?

But what about the evil spirit from the Lord? Well, that is deep and mysterious surely. But this is not the only place where such allusions occur. (See Job 1:6, and 1 Kings 22:19-23). Some would resolve this whole circumstance into an experience of melancholy on Saul's part, but the narrative clearly speaks of an objective spiritual wicked power that had control over him. But how did this come from the Lord? Only in the same sense that Pharoah's heart was hardened by the Lord. "The Lord gave him over to the power and might of this spirit as punishment for his disobedience and defiant self-will."

The Close of Saul's Life, 28-31.—We may now return directly to the consideration of Saul's history again. David's persecution at his hands is over, but his persecution of himself continues. What is the great fact in chapter 28? How is Saul's spirit of rebellion still evinced in this act? What chapter in Deuteronomy contains a solemn warning against it? As you read the text, do you think Samuel was actually brought up? May not the witch have been deceived (verse 12)? May not Saul have been deceived (verse 14)? But what about the words of the inspired historian (verses 15, 16)? Do not these make for a belief in the actual appearance of the prophet?

Did Samuel Appear?—Suppose we admit this, what then? Will it stultify God's teachings in Deuteronomy (18)? Will it give countenance to spiritualism? I think not. First, it may be lawful for God to do a thing, which He will not permit man to attempt to do. We can not deny God the right or the power to bring back the spirits of the dead if He shall so please. But this is not to say that spiritualistic mediums possess either the right or the power to do this. How, then, shall we explain the phenomena in their case? Is spiritualism all fraud? Have mediums no communication with spirits? It is possible, and quite probable that at times they have such communication; but we must bear in mind that there is an important distinction between evil spirits as such and the spirits of the dead. The first are demons, angelic beings, wicked in nature, like their head, Satan; but the second are still human beings, separate and distinct from them, always have been, and always will be. These demons may sometimes personate the dead, deceiving the mediums as well as their clients, it may be, and furnishing another argument why we should have nothing to do with them, but they are not the dead whom we knew and loved.

Was Saul Regenerated?—We now come to the last act in Saul's life (chapter 31). What kind of death did he die? Poor fellow! we instinctively say. What a contrast his life shows between the first time he appears before us, and the last! His life-story furnishes suggestive, if sad, material for a strong sermon to young men. Picture how favored he was. Favored in his personal appearance, his family influence, his selection as the first king of Israel; favored in his counsellors; favored in his association with Samuel; favored in his acceptance by the people, and in his earlier victories at arms. Favored all the way along in one grand career of triumph, till when? Show what was the turning point in his life, and how he then began to go down hill, almost without stopping, till he reached the foot of it, and ended his life practically by his own hand!

It is this that suggests the question at the head of this section. Some will answer, "Yes, Saul was what we call 'Converted,' as we may judge from such a passage as 10:9; but then, there was his disobedient and unholy life, and finally his awful death. How can these things be harmonized?" For one, I do not think chapter 10:9 is conclusive as to Saul's regeneration. The language is peculiar. "God gave him another heart," not a "new heart," or a "clean" heart, but another heart. That is, He qualified him for his work or office as king. I think Matthew Henry is about right, whose comment is, "He has no longer the heart of a husbandman, but that of a statesman, a general, a prince." But what about Samuel's words (chapter 28:19), "To-morrow shalt thou and thy sons be with me?" "Was not Samuel in heaven," some one may say, "and do not his words indicate that he expected Saul soon to be there?" It is doubtful if God's people went to heaven prior to the resurrection and ascension of Christ. They went to "Sheol," a Hebrew term for the place of the dead considered generally. A place this, apparently of two compartments, one for the righteous, and one for the unrighteous dead. Saul might have been with Samuel in Sheol, but not in that particular part of Shoel where Samuel was. The writer has a little booklet on this general subject, published by Revell, entitled, "The History of the Holy Dead," (15 cents), which some may be interested to read.

CHAPTER XIII.

The Second Book of Samuel.

In the Jewish canon, First and Second Samuel were regarded as one book; but it is obvious that Samuel was not its author beyond chapter 25. The remainder has been ascribed to different authors, but common consent, I believe, has fastened on Nathan or Gad, 1 Chronicles 29:29. Do not leave the consideration of Samuel altogether, without engaging in a character study of that wonderful man. One of the greatest in the Bible is he. See how God Himself estimated him in Jeremiah 15:1.

The book now under contemplation is chiefly concerned, as you have discovered, with the history of David;

the facts of whose life need to be gotten well in mind for two reasons. First, because of the large place he occupies in sacred story as the great ancestor and type of Christ, and secondly, in order to understand and utilize the Psalms. One half of the book of Psalms at least, was written by David; and written with reference to various occasions and experiences in his life. To understand many of their allusions, therefore, how needful to understand the circumstances giving rise to them? Moreover, unless we understand those allusions how can we extract the real comfort from the psalms either for ourselves or others? The titles of some of the psalms tell us when they were written, and this, of course, is a great aid; but in many cases the origin or connection only can be grasped by carefully reading the psalm in the light of the whole story of David's life. As a single illustration of the latter circumstance, read over again the story of David's connection with the city of Keilah in 1 Samuel, and then compare Psalm 31, for a possible likeness.

For the above reasons, it would be advisable to review 1 Samuel, especially chapters 16 to 26, which treat so largely of David's early history. For example, become familiar with his genealogy and connected topics. What was his father's name? The name of his tribe? His birth-place? What were the facts or incidents of his anointing? Go over again the larger events under the head of his persecution. Recall Goliath, Jonathan, Ahimelech, Adullam, Keilah, Saul's deliverances at his hands, Ziklag, etc.

The Exaltation of David, 1-5.—The persecutions of David at the hands of Saul are over, and now what follows? What shall we call the first great fact in book two? Over which tribe is David first anointed as king? How long does he reign over this tribe alone, and in what place? Who leads the struggle of the house of Saul against David? How does Abner meet his death? How long is David said to have reigned over the united tribes (5:4)? What was the capital of Israel (5)? What other name was given it (9)?

Notice the principle on which David still continued to act, as shown in the execution of the murderers, chapters 1 and 4. He will take no step towards the attainment of dominion except as led by God. A further illustration this, of the sense in which he might be called "a man after God's own heart."

The Messianic Covenant, 6-7.—There are certain chapters in the Bible that might be called the Alpine heights of revelation. Get hold of their facts, and see their relation one to another, and you have come into possession of the whole range of Divine truth. We have noticed some of them, e. g., Genesis 3, which gives the account of the fall, Genesis 12, the call of Abraham, Exodus 12, and 20, Leviticus 16, Deuteronomy 18, etc. Among these should be counted 11 Samuel 7, of which we are now to treat.

But let us see what leads up to it. Where had the ark been deposited, (see marginal note to chapter 6:2)? What circumstances led to its being there? According to the book of Numbers, chapters 3 and 7, what tribe should have carried the ark? Which division of that tribe? How should it have been carried? What mistake did David make in the matter? How was that mistake corrected on the second attempt? (Compare 6, 12, etc., with 1 Chronicles 15). Does the dancing of David on this occasion give precedent for the modern amusement of that name? Where did David dance, in a ball-room, or the open air? Did he dance with a companion, or alone? What was the motive or spirit actuating him, physical pleasure or the Divine glory?

Let not this circumstance of the mistake in bringing up the ark be entirely passed over, without calling attention to the lesson it teaches about service. David's motive in the matter was right—the ark should have been brought up. But his method was wrong—the ark should not have been brought up on a cart. God desires us to serve Him not only in the right spirit, but in the right way. This principle observed, would keep many individual Christians and churches from being led astray in the execution of questionable plans for the carrying on of the Lord's work. Its violation now and again, may explain the absence of Divine approval and blessing on some of those plans which were nevertheless entered into apparently with an honest purpose and a good heart.

The Prophecy of Christ.—This brings us to the center of this event. Now that the ark is safely in Jerusalem, what further Godward thought comes into David's mind? What specific reason is assigned against his execution of this purpose (1 Chronicles 22:8, 9)? What new blessing does God promise him however (7:11, last sentence)? To whom immediately did the promise in verse 12 apply? What expression in verse 13 points to the law of double reference hitherto explained? How does verse 10 also point to a time perhaps still future? What is the first sentence in verse 14? How is this shown definitely to apply not to Solomon but Christ (compare Hebrews 1:5)? In this last-named passage. (Hebrews 1:5), the apostle is comparing Christ with angels, showing his superiority thereto; and in the course of his argument exclaims, "To which of the angels said God at any time, 'I will be to him a Father, and he shall be to me a Son?'" The inference is (1) that God never said this to any angel, but (2) that He did say it to, or of, His Son. And yet the place in which the expression is used in the Bible is this at 11 Samuel 7 : 14. Therefore putting this fact together with others, it seems to place these words in Samuel in the category of distinct Messianic prophecies. It is thus evident that when God tells David He will build him a house, He is referring not to a material building, such as David contemplated for the ark, but a dynasty, a kingdom, and one that should be set up not in Solomon indeed, but in Christ.

Before leaving verse 14, I want to call attention to another rendering of the latter part of it, not only beautiful in itself, but adding very much to the proof of the Messianic character of the whole. It is that of Bishop Horsley, an English prelate of an earlier generation, and a Hebraist of acknowledged ability, who translates it thus :— "When iniquity is laid upon Him I will chasten Him with the rod of men." Thus is it not only made to apply to Christ, but to emphasize that particular feature of His work for man, His substitutionary sufferings, which gives the power and value to all the rest. It is of additional interest to know that this translation is corroborated by that of the great Methodist divine, Adam Clarke, who renders it much in the same language.

Did David Foresee Christ?—Our present chapter contributes something also to answer this question. For example, what was the effect of Nathan's message on David? As we read verses 18 and 19, it seems that he was overwhelmed with the feeling of God's wonderful purpose of honor and grace toward him, and compares the Divine dealing with that of man to the disparagement of the latter. But the two Hebrew scholars already quoted give a different rendering of verse 19, which will be appreciated, I feel sure. It is this :—"O Lord God, Thou hast spoken of Thy servants' house for a great while to come, and hast regarded me in the arrangement about the MAN that is to be from above, O God Jehovah !" According to this, David clearly apprehended Christ's day, as the latter said Abraham did, and was glad (John 8 : 56). This view of the case is corroborated to a certain extent by Romans 4 : 5-8. It may seem strange at first that such a different combination of words could be gotten out of verse 19, but if you will turn to the corresponding passage in 1 Chronicles 17 : 17, you will discover how much more nearly it agrees with the English in that case. The Hebrew of 11 Samuel 7 : 19, is evidently peculiar, affording some justification, even in its English dress, for

a different rendering, and in so far preparing us for that thus given. It is these considerations, among others, that led to the reference to this chapter as one of the more important in the Old Testament, and which will plead excuse for the space thus given to it.

The Great Down-Fall, 11-12.—The intervening chapters between the last great fact and this tell of David's many victories in the extension of his kingdom, illustrating God's interest in him (8 : 6-14), his own appreciation of it all (11), and his righteous standards of government (15), and natural goodness of heart (chapter 9). But this only serves to deepen the shadow that now falls upon his history. Who will dare trust himself in the light of what follows? There is very little here that needs to be explained to hearts that are naturally corrupt such as ours, but there is much that needs to be impressed in the way of spiritual instruction. See such passages as James 1 : 13-15, and 4 : 7. Contrast the dalliance of David with the brave flight of Joseph in Potiphar's house. Observe how one sin leads to another in the attempt to cover up adultery with murder. Verse 6 and the following leave David without excuse. No wonder the chapter ends in the way it does.

But see the kindness of God towards them whose hearts are right toward Him, even though they fall into sin, and black sin ! What endeavor is now made to bring David under conviction for this sin (12 : 1-12)? How does verse 13 illustrate the contrast already spoken of between David and Saul? What shows that though our iniquity may be put away so far as eternal condemnation is concerned, yet earthly chastisement may follow (verses 10-12, 15-18)? Compare also 1 Corinthians 11 : 32. What suggestion is found in verses 12 and 14 (of the lesson) as to a possible reason for God's acting in such a way? How does verse 25 show the perfect reconciliation which may take place with God on the ground of removal of sin? Read this verse in the Revised Version, but look in the margin of the King James for the meaning of Jedidiah. Does verse 23 indicate that David believed in the immortality of the soul, and the re-union of beloved ones in the future life? How may the last phrase in that verse be qualified by 1 Thessalonians 4 : 14?

Almost all Christians know that the 51st Psalm was written by David as expressive of his penitence at this time and it should be re-read and analyzed in connection with this part of our lesson. The 32d Psalm also is supposed to have been written at the same time, to show forth his gratitude for sin forgiven and joy restored. Let it be read as well, noting the psalmist's experience under conviction (3, 4), the effect of confession (5), the testimony to others (6), the joy and peace expressed (7), and the comfort and counsel of Jehovah in reply to him (8, 9). This will make a helpful Bible reading in connection with the story of the psalmist's sin.

The Rebellion of Absalom, 15-20.—

The words of chapter 12:10-12, now begin to be fulfilled, and sadness and trial follow David to the end of his life. There had been a triumphant note in the first part of his career notwithstanding his persecution by Saul, but the minor chords predominate after this. Baseness and beauty have often been combined in the same person since the days of Absalom, but his ingratitude and treachery will never be forgotten. Read the story of David's escape from Jerusalem (15:10-16, 30), in connection with the 3d Psalm. This will afford a good illustration of the way to really learn David's character. The psalms show us his heart. The feelings expressed in this psalm doubtless arose at the point indicated in 11 Samuel 15:12-13. See where the source of his comfort lay, his confidence in God, his hope and courage as brought out in the psalm. How helpful is such a revelation of his inner life to us at similar crises! Observe how trial enables one to test people. Read chapter 16 carefully with a view to character study—Ziba's meanness, Shimei's cowardice, Abishai's courage, David's humility, Hushai's friendship. What an interesting personality is Joab! Separate what is said about him from all the rest, that you may obtain the real picture of the man.

After Absalom's death what steps lead up to David's return (chapter 19)? What interesting text in verse 10 might be used for a discourse on the second coming of Christ? Whose character most impresses you in chapter 19? Which tribe takes the initiative for the king's return? To what feeling does this give rise (41-43)? Can you give the details of Sheba's rebellion? How all these burdens falling on David corroborated the saying in Proverbs 13:15!

The Conclusion of David's Life, 22-23.

—While the record of David's last days and death is found in the next book, yet all will agree that the song of thanksgiving, chapter 22, and the postscript following in chapter 23 really bring the story of his life to a climax. Amid so much that is beautiful and uplifting in the highest degree consider especially the declaration in 22:36: "Thy gentleness hath made me great." Are not these words fit for the song of the redeemed around the throne? And the words in 23:2: "The Spirit of the Lord spake by me, and His Word was in my tongue." Where in all Scripture can be found a clearer definition of verbal inspiration?

CHAPTER XIV.

The First Book of Kings.

In studying Kings it is recommended that after the first general reading of the book, you make a rough diagram of the rulers of the two kingdoms after the time of Solomon. Beginning with him as practically the last king of the united tribes, place in parallel columns under his name, and facing one another chronologically, the names of his successors in Judah and Israel, somewhat like this:

Solomon.

Rehoboam, 17.	Jeroboam, 22.
Abijam, 3.	
Asa, 41.	Nadab, 2.
	Baasha, 24.
	Elah, 2.
	Zimri, 7 days.
	Omri, 12.
Jehoshaphat, 25.	Ahab, 22.
Jehoram, 8.	Ahaziah, 2.

The figures in the above diagram indicate the period of each reign. It would be well if, in addition, you were to write the names of the corresponding prophets. For example, the prophet of Jeroboam's time was Ahijah. He was followed by Jehu in Baasha's reign, and he by Elijah in Ahab's time. This is not to say that there were no other prophets than they, but that they were the ones chiefly mentioned. It will be noticed that scarcely any mention is made of prophets in Judah, but this is not to say that there were none. As a matter of fact, there were many, as the books of Chronicles, and the books of the Prophets themselves indicate. The fact, however, that God did not forget Israel in this matter, notwithstanding their great unfaithfulness, and notwithstanding that He did not have the same covenant obligation to them as to Judah, is an impressive demonstration of His character of goodness and long-suffering patience. To get the line of the prophets in mind as well as that of the kings, will be a practical help to us by-and-by, in conceiving the place of the different prophets whose books we are soon to study.

Besides writing the names of the prophets on your diagram, write also some catchword or phrase that will stamp the history of each king on your mind, and help to bring before you the prevailing characteristics or predominating feature of his period. In this connection it might be further observed that a table or diagram of these kings is doubtless to be found somewhere in the back of your Bible; but you are urged not to examine it till after you have completed your own. This is in accordance with the fourth rule laid down at the very beginning of our work, viz.: to read independently. It is hoped you examine these rules once in a while, or more properly, examine yourselves to see if you are faithfully complying with them. Much of your interest and success depend on it.

After this general introduction to our book, let us spend a little time together in considering some of the more important characters or events brought before us by the Holy Spirit in its pages.

Solomon, 1-11.—Of which wife of David was Solomon the offspring? Considering the large place he occupies in history, God's peculiar favor toward him, and his typical relation to Christ (72d Psalm), does it not seem remarkable that he should have been born of that union? But look back again at 11 Samuel 12 : 25, and the note upon it in the last lesson, and see the reconciled relation in which David was now living with God. Oh, He is a God of mercy and grace! Read the 103d Psalm again, and consider whether David had not just cause to write it.

Was Solomon crowned before or after the death of David, and what circumstance necessitated it? How does this further illustrate the sorrowful character of the latter half of David's life? How many visions of Himself does God vouchsafe to Solomon? How does this fact add to Solomon's later culpability (11 : 9)? Note in this verse a striking text for a discourse on "Responsibility Proportioned to Privilege." What do you understand to be the character of that "wisdom" for which Solomon asked (3)? Judging by his career was it what we know as spiritual wisdom, or that which he required for the conduct and administration of the earthly kingdom only? What does this teach young people as to the way in which they should improve their great opportunity to make their requests known unto God (Philippians 4 : 6, 7)? What particular illustrations can you mention of Solomon's great wisdom and prosperity (4)? How does 4 : 32 prepare us to accept the hypothesis that he wrote Proverbs, Ecclesiastes, and the Canticles?

How long was he in building the temple? His own house? What chapter contains his wonderful prayer? How does Jesus utilize the visit of the Queen of Sheba (see marginal reference)? What was the nature of Solomon's guilt? What previous folly led him into it? What earthly judgments made his life unhappy toward the last? Who predicted the division of the kingdom after his death?

The Division of the Kingdom 12-14.— What do you recall in Solomon's reign that added to the taxation of the people? Wherein did his successor exhibit foolishness? While Rehoboam and his counsellors acted with perfect freedom, what shows God's hand to have been in the whole matter (12 : 22-24)? What event does this recall in 1 Samuel? Compare also Acts 2 : 23. Does this diminish the culpability of the wrong doing in any case? What comfort, nevertheless, may God's people draw from it (Romans 8 : 28)?

What was Jeroboam's motive in setting up the golden calves, religious or political? Wherein did he show an utter lack of faith (11 : 37-38)? Did he intend to throw off the worship of Jehovah altogether, or was it his thought still to have Him worshipped through a different medium? Which of the first two commandments, therefore, did he break? But did not the violation of the second involve that of the first? Compare the marginal reference to 13 : 2, and observe the literal fulfillment of that prediction. Such solemn facts are good to store away for illustrative purposes in your teaching and preaching, and have more power usually than others gathered outside of the Bible. How does the beguilement of the man of God (chapter 13) illustrate or intensify the warning of Matthew 24:24? Does Jeroboam profit by the advice received (33-34)? What punishment followed (compare 14:14-16, with 15:25-30)? Notice the prophecy of the captivity of Israel (14:15), 300 years before the event.

The Wickedness of Ahab, 16-22.—The next matter of supreme importance to be noticed is that indicated at the head of this paragraph or section. We have seen Jeroboam's house cut off in the death of Nadab by the usurper Baasha. Although a usurper in one sense, yet was he the executioner of God in another (16:1-4). But he learned nothing from the history of his predecessors, nor did any of the kings that followed him. Their continuance in evil, notwithstanding the object-lessons before their eyes is a moving demonstration that "it is not in man that walketh to direct his steps" (Jeremiah 10:23), and that "except a man be born again he can not see the kingdom of God." It is not evidence or education that men want, but life from above (John 5:40). Hence Baasha's line is cut off in Elah who reigns but 2 years, and at length, after the brief interregnum of the traitor and suicide Zimri, the house of Ahab comes into power in the person of his father Omri.

The Nature of His Sin.—Read carefully 16:30-33, and observe the feature in which Ahab's evil exceeded that of Jeroboam. The last-named broke the second commandment, and the first only indirectly, but Ahab broke the first of set purpose. It was his determination, under the domination of his wicked wife, to dethrone Jehovah in Israel altogether. Even His name was not to be mentioned. Baal, Bel, or Belus, as we may learn from a Bible dictionary, means lord, or master, the three names being merely as many forms of the one name of the supreme male divinity of the Phoenicians and Canaanites, as Ashtoreth was that of their supreme female divinity. The common opinion is that they represent the sun and moon, though some say Jupiter and Venus. The licentiousness demanded by their worship gave it attractiveness to poor lost and ignorant people. The word Baal is sometimes used in its plural form, Baalim, which indicates the idol to have been worshipped under different modifications. Baal-Berith means covenant lord (Judges 8:33), Baal-Peor, the lord of the opening (Numbers 25:3, etc.), Baal-Zebub, the lord of the fly (2 Kings 1:2, etc.). Human victims were sometimes offered to Baal (Jeremiah 19:5), and elevated places selected for the worship. An acquaintance with these few facts may illuminate the pages of Ahab's history, justifying God's dealings with him and the nation at this time, and explain some of the otherwise difficult features in Elijah's ministry.

Be careful to identify Syria on the map. This nation with which Israel is in conflict so much just now, becomes her wicked ally later on, and plays an important part in bringing about her captivity for that very reason. Moreover, we need to clearly identify her from Assyria, a greater nation on the east which became in time not only her mistress but that of Israel too. Do not miss these geographical and historical data if you wish to steer a clear course when we come into the study of the prophets.

The Story of Elijah.—The wonderful record of Elijah will make a grand subject for a Bible reading or address. Eliminate the facts, and make them stand out by themselves. A single catchword here and there ought to bring the details to mind with sufficient clearness if you have read the book properly. For example: Cherith; Zarephath; Obadiah; Mt. Carmel; Horeb; Elisha; chariot of fire. You observe I have gone into the second book of Kings for some of the facts in order to group the events of his whole life together. These few words carried in your mind, or on a card in your pocket to refresh your memory occasionally during the day, are enough to start you off on a train of thought of great value in preaching or leading a religious meeting. They may be dwelt on from two points of view, (a), what they teach of the character of Elijah, or (b), what they reveal of the character and power of God. Each fact suggests a separate idea or more, and all taken together will supply a rich feast. All of us can not be eloquent orators in the pulpit or elsewhere, but we can thus learn to bring things new and old out of the storehouse (Matthew 13:52), and be useful ministers of God saving and building up souls in the truth. "Elijah the Tishbite," by F. W. Krummacher, is an old book as they are counted now-a-days, but will never be surpassed either for exegetical or devotional purposes. It is to be obtained only in second-hand stores, but will prove a valuable aid. F. B. Meyer's work on the same prophet is of a somewhat similar character, and as more recent, can be purchased at any bookstore. It is published by Revell, and is inexpensive.

Jehoshaphat the Worldling.—This general view of 1 Kings should not conclude without some reference to this king of Judah, who from primitive times has been seized upon by teachers and preachers as an Old Testament type of the Christian worldling. A good king you found him to be, and yet the friendship and flattery of Ahab were too much for him. Study chapter 22 in connection with the record found in 11 Chronicles. See the king's thoughtlessness (4), his compunctions of conscience nevertheless (5-8), his narrow escape (30-32), etc. A good text might be found in verse 44. There is a sense in which he should not have made peace with Israel, as there is also one in which Christians should not make peace with the world (Genesis 3:15, John 15:19, 11 Corinthians 6:14-18, Galatians 4:28-29).

Observe the literal fulfillment of prophecy in the death of Ahab, as mentioned in this chapter, 37, 38.

CHAPTER XV.

The Second Book of Kings.

I would recommend in this case as in that of the book just studied that you make a careful diagram of the kings of both kingdoms. Leaving you to fill in the period of each reign, and such catch-words as may seem useful to recall the predominating characteristics. I will place the names of the kings before you in parallel columns, and as nearly as possible in chronological order. They run thus:

Kings of Judah, Kings of Israel.

Kings of Judah	Kings of Israel
Ahaziah.	Jeroboam.
Athaliah.	Jehu.
Joash.	
Amaziah.	Jehoahaz.
Azariah, (or Uzziah).	Joash.
	Jeroboam II.
	Zechariah.
	Shallum.
	Menahem.
	Pekahiah.
Jotham.	Pekah.
Ahaz.	Hoshea.
Hezekiah.	
Manasseh.	
Amon.	
Josiah.	
Jehoahaz.	
Jehoiakim.	
Jehoiachin.	
Zedekiah.	

An examination of the above will reveal one or two things to be especially noted. In the first place, your reading of the details has shown that while many changes of dynasty have occurred in the kingdom of Israel absolutely none have taken place in Judah. While the history of the first-named presents a constant succession of usurpations, revolutions and the like, that of the second is comparatively peaceful, and the kingly line has been kept intact in the tribe of Judah and the family of David to the end. Indeed, after the captivity also, as we shall see later on, the genealogical records were carefully examined and purged with the same intent. The reason for this is very clear when we remember the early promises touching the coming of the Messiah in the line of Judah and David. It was vital to His identification and acceptance that the descent be demonstrated unmistakably.

Another fact to be noticed is the longer life granted to the kingdom of Judah before the period of captivity. Examine the marginal chronology and satisfy yourselves as to the length of time that elapsed between the removal of Israel by Assyria, and that of Judah by Babylon. Locate each of these heathen nations on the map, and observe that the one conquered and succeeded the other in power between the two captivities.

The Kings of Israel.—Of the kings of Israel there are three it might be well especially to notice—Jehu, Jeroboam II., and Menahem. The first-named was the executioner of Divine punishment on the wicked house of Ahab and the Baal-worshippers, whose zeal for himself, however, exceeded that for God. This is evident from 10:29. Observe God's readiness to commend him for what had been done and reward him for it (30)—a verse one can scarcely read without wishing in his heart that Jehu had gone further and gained more. Why should not his children have sat on the throne of Israel forever instead of the fourth generation only? Would it not have been so, if Jehu had been out and out for God? Teachers of classes have here an excellent opportunity to impress the lesson of what we all miss in the way of blessing through our own selfishness. Like many another great man before and after him, in Israel and out of it, Jehu put politics before God, and was the loser by it.

The reign of Jeroboam II. is especially notable for its prosperity (14: 23-29). He enjoyed the longest reign of any of the kings of the ten tribes; his arms were successful, his coasts enlarged, and he had the further encouragement of seeing prophecy fulfilled in his day, as a further evidence of Jehovah's favor and willingness to bless. It was a golden age for Israel but, as in the days of Egypt under the Ptolemies, Rome, under Augustus, France, under Louis XIV., and England, under Elizabeth, it was an age of great profligacy, as we shall see in the study of Amos the prophet of the period, and was the time which marks the beginning of the rapid decline of the nation culminating in its captivity 60 or 70 years later.

Menahem's reign is of importance as that in which the great nation of Western-Asia, Assyria, first came against the land (15:19, 20). This nation was reaching out for the world-dominion, the great rival of Egypt, eager to command the Mediterranean Sea. At this time she got her first "grip" on Israel, which she never slackened until the end. As she followed up her success in the case of Israel with attacks on Judah we shall have more to do with her at a later period.

The Samaritans.—The captivity of Israel is another way of referring to the deportation of that people into foreign countries, which was part of the military and governmental policy of Assyria at that time, as well as her successor in power (Babylon). This was regarded as the easiest and cheapest way of controlling a subjugated people, since in a strange land and under new surroundings insurrections against authority could not be so successful. Observe that the same treatment was meted out to other captives who were brought to fill up the vacated cities of Israel (17:6, 24). These people came to be known as the Samaritans. Samaria was originally the name of the capital of Israel. When, and by whom was it thus founded (1 Kings 16:23, 24)? But subsequently the name came to be taken by a large province of Israel of which it was the center. Read carefully in the present lesson, 17:25-41, to obtain an idea of the religious history and character of these people, since it explains in part such later allusions as Ezra 4:1-6, John 4:9, etc. Another item of interest in this connection is the further fact, that the cities of Israel thus occupied by another people could not have been re-occupied by Israel if they had as a nation returned to their land. Not so in the case of Judah, however. No mention is made that the Babylonian government filled up their cities with other people. Hence, after a time, it was possible for Judah to return as it was not for Israel. In all this how plainly is seen the hand of God! The prophets Isaiah and Jeremiah had distinctly prophesied the national restoration of Judah, giving the very time and other detailed circumstances of the event (Isaiah 44:28, Jeremiah 29:10), but no such prediction had gone forth distinctively for Israel (the ten tribes as such).

The Kings of Judah.—Which would you single out as the particularly good or wicked kings in this list? Of the first-named, the story of Joash is interesting because of the conspiracy against him at his birth (chapter 11). What do you know of the history of Athaliah, the wicked grandmother of this king? Of what stock did she come? How long did she unlawfully reign over Judah? To what two persons did Joash owe his accession to the throne? How old was he at this time? What great religious event characterized his reign?

What would you say of Ahaz, was he good or wicked? What two people besieged Judah in his time (16:5)? To what great nation did he turn for aid? Please remember this incident, as it will throw much light on Isaiah 7 to 9. It was as unfortunate in the end for Judah herself, as it now was for her enemies that she thus entered into confederacy with that heathen people. Assyria thus obtained a hold upon her which threatened her life. In whose reign, and by what miracle was Judah subsequently delivered from her power (chapter 19)? Speaking of Hezekiah, what great prophet comes into view in his day? Wherein does he fail to honor God, and what prediction grows out of the event (20)? Note, that Babylon was a comparatively insignificant power at this time, which made the prediction all the more remarkable.

What later king compares favorably with Hezekiah? What notable discovery helped forward the revival in his reign? What irrevocable purpose of

God is made known to the nation at this time (22:16, 17)? By what king was Josiah slain (23:29, 30)? This brings us to a historical event of much importance. Egypt which comes prominently into view here after so long an interval, is contending with Assyria for the world-dominion. Judah lies between the combatants geographically, and is, in a sense, their battleground. This seems to account, in part, for the conflict recorded in this chapter, which in its consequences brings Judah for a while under the sway of Egypt. Whom does Pharoah now put on the throne (23:31-33)? To what nation, however does he afterward become a vassal (24:1)? Observe his rebellion against Nebuchadnezzar, resulting as we see from Daniel I. in a preliminary captivity of the people. Notice a second captivity in the following reign, at which time, doubtless, another great prophet was removed, see Ezekiel I. Zedekiah, however, who is now placed in authority by Nebuchadnezzar, manifests the same spirit of insubordination both to the will of Nebuchadnezzar and the will of God, and brings upon his nation what had been foretold by all the prophets from Moses to Jeremiah.

The Prophets of the Period.—I would like the class to give some attention at this point to the succession of the prophets. Who was the last great prophet in Israel, and who was his immediate successor? Following Elisha comes the list of those whose deeds and discourses have been recorded and transmitted to us in books separate from the record of the kings. The earliest of these seems to be Jonah. See II Kings 14:25. He was followed by Amos, who perhaps was contemporaneous with him for a time.

See Amos 1:1. The successor of Amos was Hosea who may also have been partially contemporaneous with him. See Hosea 1:1. The last named continued from the time of Jeroboam II. to the captivity, a period of between 60 and 70 years, the longest in the annals of the prophets.

To return to Judah, the first named of the prophets whose separate book has been handed down to us is possibly Joel and the nIsaiah, who entered on his office in the reign of Azariah or Uzziah, and was contemporaneous therefore with Hosea in Israel. See Isaiah 1:1. He was followed by Jeremiah, who began to prophecy in the reign of Josiah and continued to the captivity of Judah. See Jeremiah 1:1-3. These last two prophets were doubtless of great aid to Hezekiah and Josiah in the carrying out of their plans of political and moral reform. The great mission of Jeremiah, especially in the latter part of his ministry, was to instruct and exhort Judah to submit to the Babylonian yoke as conforming to the will of God. The explanation of this comes out clearly in Daniel. The people and their rulers were unwilling to comply, however, and the hatred which, in consequence, was entertained for Jeremiah caused him the great suffering which makes his life-story so full of touching interest. It was the unwillingness of the nation to yield compliance, however, that brought upon them all their distress at the hands of Babylon. A diagram of the prophets of 11 Kings might be arranged thus:

Kingdom of Judah,	Kingdom of Israel.
	Elisha.
	Jonah.
Joel.	Amos.
Isaiah.	Hosea.
Jeremiah.	

CHAPTER XVI.

The Books of I. and II. Chronicles and Esther

There seems to be no particular necessity to present an outline of the two books of Chronicles, because although they record certain facts not found in the Kings, yet to a certain extent they cover the same ground.

In the Jewish arrangement of the Old Testament certain books were grouped together like i and ii Samuel, and i and ii Kings, and known as one book, instead of two as with us, a fact

true of Chronicles which originally went by the name of the "Diaries" or "Journals," because composed, as it was thought, from the diaries or court records of the different kings. They are of a date later than the captivity, and although their author is unknown, yet their object seems to have been to show the division of families and possessions before that critical event in order to restore the same after the return. Emphasis, as you will find, is laid on the history of Judah rather than Israel, because of the Messianic expectations in that line. Certain apparent discrepancies between Chronicles and Kings may be accounted for in at least two ways: (1), the former omits what the latter gives in sufficient detail and vice versa; and (2), the former being written much later doubtless than the latter, the names of certain localities, etc., may have undergone a change.

It will have been observed that these books dwell particularly on the more glorious periods of the theocracy, depicting its bright scenes, and treating as briefly as possible those of the opposite character. For this reason the reign of David, Solomon, Asa, Jehoshaphat, Joash, Hezekiah and Josiah occupy more space relatively than others; and for this reason also it will be found that these books contain more spiritual nourishment for the downcast and the fearful than perhaps any other of the historical books of the Old Testament. I look back to testing times in my own Christian life when the Holy Spirit was pleased to use the two books of Chronicles to encourage me in disappointment and guide me in perplexity, with something of that restful delight one finds in recalling the picturesque scenery associated with the first visit to a new land. No books in the Bible I was using devotionally at that time are more marked than these, and with that recollection in mind I would call my readers' attention to such nuggets of gold as are found in the following verses:—I Chronicles 4:10, 5:20, 9:13, 20, 11:9, 12:32, 14:14, 15, 15:13, 19:13, 28:20; II Chronicles 14:11, 15:1-15, 25:9, 31:10, 32:8, 31, and many more.

The Book of Esther.—At this point we deviate a little from the arrangement of the books as found in the Bible, in order to defer our treatment of Ezra and Nehemiah until we reach the later or "post", Babylon prophets to which period those books belong.

The second of the poetical books, excluding Ruth, of which we treated earlier, is Esther, which belongs to the period of the exile, and which tells its own simple and yet thrilling story of God's providential care for His people Israel at that time. It requires little or no analysis or explanation, but a paragraph or two as to its authorship or authenticity may be profitable. Its authorship is unknown, though variously ascribed to Ezra, Nehemiah and Mordecai, with the preponderance of opinion, I believe, in favor of the last-named. It bears evidence also of being taken from the records of the Persian king of that period, Ahasuerus, a fact which does not necessarily militate against its inspiration and authority since the writer or compiler may have had as direct guidance in the selection of the materials from that source as if they were immediately revealed from heaven.

As others have pointed out, its historical character is undoubted, since, "besides many internal evidences, its authenticity is proved by the strong testimony of the feast of Purim, the celebration of which can be traced up to the events described in the book." The history of the Jewish nation and the Christian church in all the centuries confirms its claim, as does also the purpose of the book itself, which is to show the superintending care of God over His chosen people at a very critical period in their history.

CHAPTER XVII.

The Book of Job.

All questions concerning the historicity and antiquity of the book of Job, will have to be passed over in our present work for the want of space, but the reader may be referred for them to the author's, "A Primer of the Faith." (Revell Co.)

While some ascribe the authorship to Job himself, and some to Elihu, others, and their number is large, think it was written by Moses. But the question is indeterminable. The book is poetical in literary form, with the exception of what might be called the prologue, chapters 1 and 2, and the epilogue, chapter 42:7-17, which are prose.

The theme of the book seems to be the meaning and object of evil and suffering under the government of a holy, wise and merciful God, and may be outlined thus:
The prologue, ...1-2.
The dialogue, ...3-31.

The words of Elihu, ...32-37.
The words of the Almighty, ...38-41.
The response of Job, ...42 : 1-6.
The epilogue, ...42 : 7-17.

The Key to the Book.—The key to the book is found, I think, in the first chapter, which, after an introductory testimony to the character of Job, translates the reader to heavenly scenes (verse 6). The "sons of God" referred to in this verse are angelic beings who are represented as bringing in their reports to God, the mystery being that Satan is found "also among them." How, or in what sense, or on what ground, the prince of darkness is thus granted access to God is a question these lessons cannot take the space to discuss; but we accept the fact and draw certain inferences therefrom. He is seen here in his Scriptural attitude of the accuser of the brethren (Rev. 12 : 10) ; and when God taunts him, if one may so say, with the uprightness of Job whom he has been unable to corrupt, he at once charges him with a mercenary spirit, and declares that if God were to take his temporal blessings away from him he would be as bad as the rest. God accepts the implied challenge in these words, and puts His servant into the hands of Satan for a limited period, and the exercise of a terrible but limited power on Satan's part, that it may be seen if the charge be true. In other words, it is not Job so much who is on trial here, as God. It is not a question of Job's loyalty so much as it is one of God's power. Is the grace of God able to keep one of His servants loyal and faithful to Him, even though he be stripped of everything which men count dear on this earth? The outcome was victory for God and discomfiture for Satan under circumstances calculated to prove a great comfort and blessing to God's people in every generation. It is this thought that is suggested to me by the prologue, and which kept in mind, lightens up the meaning of the whole book.

The Discussion.—The dialogue proceeds on the determination of the question as to whether great suffering such as Job's be not an evidence of great sin on his part, Eliphaz, Bildad and Zophar affirming and Job denying. The dispute is carried on in a series of three acts, each act containing three arguments of the "friends" and as many defenses by Job, until the last when Zophar is silenced, and Job triumphs.

Job's defense would seem to be based on two grounds, (1), the admitted prosperity of the wicked, chapter 21, and (2), his own personal righteousness, chapters 29 and 31. It would seem at first that his friends sincerely intended to comfort him, but were finally driven to accusation by the caustic character of his replies, caused in part, no doubt, by his intense suffering. Whether his friends were sincere or insincere at the beginning of the dialogue must be determined by the view taken of chapter 4. It can be so read as to suggest either view.

The words of Elihu also suggest a series of three acts, out of which we gather that he rebuked both parties to the debate, 32 : 1-3, the friends for their accusations which were unwarranted in great measure, and Job for his self-righteousness, equally unwarranted. His philosophy of the sufferings differs from that of the others in that he believes they were sent for the good of the sufferer, see chapter 33 : 28-30. The first part of his speech is addressed to Job, chapters 32 and 33, the second to the three friends, 34, and the last again to Job, 35-37. As he closes he perceives a thunder storm gathering, whose description forms a grand and fitting climax to his address, and out of which the voice of the Almighty is now heard. The discussion thus far had been one-sided, confined to the mystery of evil, and the balance is now restored by considering the mystery of good which the Almighty reveals. It is notable that He gives no explanation of Job's suffering, renders no decision on the subject in debate, and offers no hint of compensation to His servant for what he has endured. The pervading idea of His wonderful revelation is that of power, absolute sovereignity, as though His design were to overwhelm Job and effect his unconditional surrender. The crisis in Job's life was something like that of Moses as he stood in the cleft of the rock, Exodus 33-34, or Elijah at Horeb, 1 Kings 19, or Paul on his way to Damascus, Acts 9, and the result in Job's case is not unlike that in their cases.

Sober meditation on the book leads to the inevitable conclusion that such experiences as those of Job, and they come in kind, only in a lesser degree, to about every true child of God, may be for discipline indeed, and to teach the lesson of submission so vital to be learned, but also to serve a divine purpose far exceeding human knowledge, in the superhuman world. Compare such passages as John 9 : 3, 1 Corinthians 4 : 9, Ephesians 3 : 10, and 1 Peter 1 : 12. What a dignity such a thought adds to the suffering for righteousness' sake !

CHAPTER XVIII.

The Book of Psalms (in General).

The book of Psalms has sometimes been classified according to authors. As, for example, the titles indicate that seventy-three were written by David, fifty are anonymous, twelve have the name of Asaph, and ten that of Korah, or the sons of Korah, attached to them, two are associated with the name of Solomon, one Moses, one Heman, one Ethan. A comparison of Acts 4:25 and Hebrews 4:7 shows that Psalms 2 and 95 respectively, were also written by David, though not ascribed to him by title in the book, and the question naturally arises whether he may not have been the author as well of a still larger number of the anonymous psalms. As some of those with the name of the sons of Korah were evidently written for them, may he have been their author as well? The same query arises about the 72d Psalm, which is one of the two to which Solomon's name is attached. I might add here that the titles of the psalms are regarded by many expositors as of equal authority with the text itself, and hence if we can ascertain what the title really is we may venture to build conclusions upon it.

The Subjects of the Psalms.—The book of Psalms again, has been classified sometimes according to the subject of the psalms. Angus, in his Bible hand-book, has a convenient classification of this character which I copy in part, giving the subject and in each case the numbers of a few psalms illustrating it. For example there are psalms of:
Instruction, like 1, 19, 39; Trust, 3, 27, 31, 46, 56, 62, 86; Praise, 8, 29, 93, 100; Distress and sorrow, 4, 13, 55, 64, 88; Thanksgiving, 30, 65, 103, 107, 116; Aspiration, 42, 63, 80, 84, 137; Penitence, 6, 32, 38, 51, 143; History, 78, 105, 106; Prophecy (Messianic) 2, 16, 22, 24, 40, 45, 68, 69, 72, 97, 110, 118.

The Books of the Psalms.—It may see strange to some to speak of the "Books" of the Psalms, but that expresses another kind of classification sometimes made. The whole book has been divided into five books, each ending with a similar doxology, as follows:

Book I, psalms 1-41.
Book II, psalms 42-72.
Book III, psalms 73-89.
Book IV, psalms 90-106.
Book V, psalms 107-150.
Notice the close of each of these books for the doxology spoken of.

There are those who question the truth or value of this division, however, on the ground, first, that the title of the book itself in the Hebrew, (Sepher Tehillim), is singular rather than plural. It is not the "books" but the book of Psalms. Second, the numbers of the psalms continue unbroken from the beginning to the end of the book. Third, there are other doxologies than those especially referred to, e. g., psalms 117 and 134.

The view of these others, therefore, is that the psalms comprise but one book with an order and unity throughout, the key to which is found in its final application to the Millennial age and establishment of the kingdom of God on the earth. According to these expositors, and I am strongly of their feeling in the matter, this explains what are known as the imprecatory or cursing psalms. These psalms have greatly puzzled many, but when we come to consider them as terminating on that period when the era of mercy for the Gentile nations closes, and the time of their judgment begins, it lightens their problem very much. In the same connection we want to remember that the author is speaking in the prophetic spirit, and that the enemies are conceived of as enemies of God Himself, whose permanent rejection of Him is implied. This view of the psalms in their ultimate and millennial application, moreover, explains those like the 91st, which promise exemption from such things as pestilence and war. This 91st Psalm was written doubtless on the occasion of Israel's deliverance from Egypt, but its language seems to indicate that it is a type of their greater and permanent deliverance in the time to come. This view of the 91st Psalm is strengthened if we conceive of the preceding psalm as giving a picture of Israel to-day, as many do conceive of it. I may add further, that the opinion which sees the key to the interpretation of the psalms in their ultimate millennial application furnishes further, an explanation of the frequent New Testament references to Christ which are found in the psalms where we would least expect them. It will come in the way of our later studies to point these out.

Analysis of Particular Psalms.— What we now propose is to analyze a few particular psalms as samples of their class. We shall begin with the Davidic psalms, by which we mean specifically, those in which the human author is very evidently speaking of himself and his experiences. Our object in this particular case is simply to assist in the understanding of such psalms for our own personal comfort and the use we may make of them in teaching others in the way of Bible readings, etc.

The 3d Psalm is the first of this kind that comes before us. What does the title say as to the occasion in David's life when it was written? Examine the marginal reference for the chapters in 11 Samuel where the story of Absalom's rebellion is told. It has always seemed to me that the psalm belongs at about the place indicated at chapter 15:10. Keeping these two passages of Scripture before you, 11 Samuel 15:10-30, and Psalm 3, ask yourself such questions as these, finding the answers in the psalm: To whom does David appeal from his conspirators (11 Samuel 15:12, 13, with the first verse of the psalm)? What insinuation did they raise against David, (2d verse of the psalm)? What great sin had David committed previously giving the thoughtless some

reason to feel that Absalom's rebellion was thus a judgment of God upon him? What does Psalm 51 testify as to David's repentance for this sin? What does Psalm 32 testify as to his forgiveness? On the ground, therefore, of that known forgiveness, how does David express his faith and confidence in God in the present crisis (see Psalm 3, verse 3)? In what was his strong assurance based (same, verse 4)? Do you suppose he was here referring to his experiences in Psalms 51 and 32? The story in 11 Samuel shows us David and his few faithful followers travelling over the Mount of Olives pursued by Absalom and the other conspirators; how does his faith in God effect his nervous and physical condition (Psalm 3:4)? Does he attribute his rest to natural or supernatural causes (same verse last clause)? How did he feel in the morning, with what courage did he awake (verse 6)? How does he express his confidence as to the outcome of the present rebellion (9)? With what general declaration and counsel to us does he conclude his psalm?

We thus see how easy it is to draw intelligent comfort and aid from the psalms of David when we understand their historical connection. We see also how necessary it is to understand the psalms in the light of their history in order to understand David himself. In 1 and 11 Samuel we have the outside of the man, but in the psalms we have the inside, and it is necessary to put the two together to appreciate how he could have been "a man after God's own heart."

CHAPTER XIX.

The Messianic and Millennial Psalms.

We closed our last lesson in the Psalms with an analysis of one of the psalms of David—an instance in which the title indicated its occasion. But the question arises whether any of the other Davidic psalms can be traced by their contents to their occasion in the same way? I think this is possible in many cases to those who make a careful study both of them and of the history of David, diligently comparing the two. Take the 31st Psalm as an illustration. This indeed is ascribed to David, but there is no intimation in the title as to when he wrote it. I

have always thought, however, that it was penned with reference to his experience at Keilah, for which you are referred to 1 Samuel 23. Read the first half of that chapter carefully and then observe such likely references to it as are found in verses 4, 7, 8, 11, 13, 14, 15, and 21, of the psalm. Such an exercise as this will be highly beneficial intellectually and spiritually.

We hasten on to consider the psalms of prophecy and especially those described as the Messianic Psalms. These latter are psalms in which not only is the Messiah referred to, but in which

He Himself in the Spirit is heard to speak. It is His feelings and experiences that are being expressed rather than those of the human author. We have said previously, that to know David it is necessary to study the psalms as well as the historical books that refer to him, but this is even more necessary in the case of Jesus. In the Gospels we read what He said and did and what was said and done to Him; in other words, we obtain a view of the outside of His life, but in the psalms we see the inner side, and learn how He felt and how He lived in the presence of His God and Father. To quote the language of M. E. Guers, a French writer on the subject: "Elsewhere the sacred authors speak to us of Jesus—of His vicarious sufferings and His bitter agony; but here it is Himself whom we hear. It is He who complains, who sighs and groans beneath the hand of the 'prince of the power of the air,' and of his instruments; it is He who trembles beneath the weight of God's anger; it is He, Himself, who initiates us into all His fears, all His alarms, all His terrors, and all His moral and physical tortures. In the New Testament we see only glimpses of the terrible combats of His soul; in the psalms we see all His anguish."

The Psalm of the Lord's Anointed.— We begin with the second Psalm, which is shown to be Messianic by a reference to Acts 4 : 23-28. That reference might lead some to suppose that the psalm found its complete fulfillment in the rejection and crucifixion of Christ at His first coming. But such is not the case. It belongs still more to His second coming, as a further consideration of its contents shows. The application to His first coming is a sort of adumbration of what will take place at His second coming. The prophets will teach us by-and-by that the nations will be gathered together against Jerusalem at that time and taking counsel against the Lord and His anointed (Christ) with the Anti-Christ at their head, and that the Lord will then "vex them in His sore displeasure." In fact, this psalm is one of the many Millennial psalms spoken of at the beginning.

What does Jehovah do in that day notwithstanding the tumult and opposition of the nations? See verse 6. Observe now how the Messiah Himself speaks in the verses following. What decree hath Jehovah made unto Him (7)? A reference to the New Testament passages indicated in the margin (Acts 13 : 33, Hebrews 1 : 5), will show the "begetting" of the Son

herein mentioned to apply to His resurrection. "He was declared to be the Son of God with power by the resurrection from the dead." (Romans 1 : 4). He was the Son of God eternally; He was the Son of God again as conceived by the Holy Ghost of the virgin Mary, the Son incarnate and Saviour of the world; but in the resurrection from the dead He is set before us as the Son of God in a new light, and with reference to His mediatorial Kingship, as the God-man. How is this thought expressed in verse 8 of the psalm? The word "heathen", you will observe, is translated "nations" in the revised versions, as meaning not only the heathen nations so-called, but the nations of Christendom as well if not especially. But how does the next verse show that the beginning of this reign at least will be signalized with awful judgment on those nations because of infidelity and sin? This agrees perfectly again with what the prophets will have to teach us later on, and shows that the ultimate fulfillment of the psalm is neither past nor present, but future. With what advice to the kings and judges of the earth does the psalm conclude?

The Psalm of the Resurrection.— The next of the Messianic Psalms I will call your attention to is the 16th, sometimes called the Resurrection Psalm from the nature of a part of its contents. It will be found quite different in its analysis from the preceding one.

But first, how do we show its Messianic character? By comparing verses 8-11 with the New Testament passages indicated in the margin, viz.: Acts 2 : 22-36, especially 25-28. Having established these last verses as the words of the Messiah rather than David, many expositors are of the opinion that we are justified in regarding the whole psalm in that light. If so, then the psalm presents itself to our understanding as one of the prayers of Jesus. Often it is recorded of Him in the Gospels that He prayed to His Father—spent whole nights in prayer, but no intimation is given of the substance of His prayers. Here in the psalms, however, some of these secret prayers are, as it were, published in advance! The psalms, indeed, have been called the prayer-book of Jesus. This is deeply interesting surely, and full of spiritual suggestion and comfort for us.

Let us then, considering this psalm as one of the prayers of the man Christ Jesus, observe:

Its spirit of confidence in God, verse 1.

Loyalty to God, verse 2.
Love toward the saints, verse 3.
Separation from the world, verse 4.
Contentment with His lot, verses 5, 6.
Obedience, verses 7, 8.
Hope, verses 9, 10.
Expectation, verse 11.
Those who are on the lookout for themes for Bible readings will find such a psalm as this prolific in suggestion. To fully appreciate the sense in verses 2 and 3 it will be needful to read them in the Revised Version.

The Psalm of the Cross.—I feel a strong desire before leaving this branch of our subject to speak of the 22d Psalm, sometimes called the Psalm of the Cross or the Crucifixion Psalm. That it is Messianic is not only assured by the first verse, whose words were repeated by Christ on the Cross, but by the whole of its contents, which describe the experiences of no man on earth except Jesus Christ, and which perfectly describe His at Golgotha.

Looking at the psalm in this light, we observe (1), our Saviour's cry of distress 1:2; (2) His trust and appeal to His Father's goodness, 3-5; (3) His description of His tormentors as He hung upon the Cross, 6-8; (4) His plea for help, 9-11; (5) His renewed description of His persecution and sufferings, 12-18; (6) His renewed plea for help, 19-21; (7) the answer which has come to Him from His Father's throne, bringing hope, 21, last clause, and 22; (8) His testimony to all the saints of God as based on the experiences He has passed through, 23, 24; (9) His prophecy concerning the future, 25-31. In this last division we behold His conviction of His resurrection from the dead (25), the ultimate conversion of the world (27), and the Millennial kingdom (28-31). The closing words of the last verse have a special interest attaching to them. The last word "this", being in italics, indicates that it is not in the original text, but added by the translators to better express the sense of the original in English. If we omit it altogether everyone will be struck with the similarity of the ending with the words "It is finished," which were the last words heard from Jesus on the Cross. The thought goes to sustain the idea that the words of this psalm throughout were repeated by Jesus during the agony of His crucifixion. It shows us His tried but trusting heart at that crisis, and comforts us very much in the conviction it begets that however the Father's face may have been averted from Him at the beginning, it shone upon Him again at the end, and that His life went out in victory.

The Millennial Psalms.—Before concluding our consideration of the psalms, I should like to speak further of their Millennial character. Take for example, the first Psalm: It announces judgment, a gathering together of the righteous in which no sinner shall be found. The reference is evidently to the resurrection, and to that called in Revelation 20, the First Resurrection, the one which will take place when Jesus comes for His saints (1 Thessalonians 4:13-18). Verse 6 of the psalm, for example, should read, "The ungodly shall not 'rise' in the judgment." Moreover, the word "judgment" is emphatic in the Hebrew as if it were preceded by the definite article in capitals, "THE judgment," associating it with that period spoken of by all the prophets as the time of Messiah's manifested power.

We have already considered the 2d Psalm from the Millennial point of view, and may now pass to the 8th, which from the use made of it by the Holy Spirit in the New Testament we gather that "stupendous volumes of glory for Christ underlie its beautiful but simple language." Verses 5 and 6, for example, are quoted three times in the New Testament and applied to Christ, Hebrews 2:6-8, Ephesians 1:22, and 1 Corinthians 15:24, 25. In these verses we may trace the four stages of our Lord's marvelous career as Man: (1), "Thou madest him a little lower than the angels," referring to His earthly birth and life of suffering. (2), "Thou crownedst him with glory and honour," referring to His present personal exaltation. (3), "Thou didst set him over the work of thy hands," referring to His coming kingdom in Israel on the earth. (4), "Thou didst put all things in subjection under his feet," referring to His universal reign in the post-millennial new heavens and new earth—George F. Trench, in "After the Thousand Years."

The 9th Psalm is very suggestive along the lines of Millennial interpretation. It is a "Psalm of David," and yet the language fits perfectly only on the lips of the nation of Israel in the day when the words of the prophets that we shall soon study shall be fulfilled, and Israel shall be redeemed and have become the earthly center of the Millennial power of Christ. The psalm opens with rejoicing, verses 1 and 2; this rejoicing is for deliverance from enemies, 3, 4; but these enemies are not individuals but nations, which are not only overcome for the time being, but practically for all time. Their name is blotted out forever, 5, 6. The word "heathen" is translated "nations" in the Revised Version, and indeed may be used interchangebly with that word or with the word "Gentiles." It does not always and necessarily mean the heathen, but as we shall discover later, it includes so-called Christian nations. These have persecuted Israel more or less for nineteen hundred years, and at the end will be gathered against her with more violence than ever before. These are the nations as well as the distinctively heathen that are to be overcome. That the Millennial period is meant seems clear from verse 7, which speaks of the Lord "sitting as King," (Revised Version), which He will never do in the case of this earth till then. The thought is corroborated by verses 9 to 14, where the Lord is seen judging and comforting the oppressed, and the latter putting their trust in Him and singing His praises.

I would suggest that a study be made of the following psalms in this connection, 46, 47, 52, 67, 72. In the first mentioned Israel is seen to be in great trouble, but firmly trusting in God (1-5). The cause of the trouble is the gathering of the nations against

her (6). But God is with her and overcomes the nations, visiting them with judgment (7, 8). Following these judgments there is peace over all the earth (9-11). This is clearly Millennial in its ultimate application. Psalm 47 is of the same general character. The 52d Psalm can hardly be read by any one familiar with the later revelations of the Bible concerning the Anti-Christ without thinking of that archdespot. He is seen to be overcome by the Lord (5), and exalted over by the righteous (6, 7), whose trust in the mercy of God has not been in vain (8, 9).

The 67th Psalm is exceptionally interesting as showing the time when the original promise to Abraham shall have been completely fulfilled, and through him all the nations of the earth blessed. How is the faith of Israel expressed, verse 1? Why do they ask that God shall cause His face to shine upon them, (2)? What will be the character and consequences of the "saving health" of God among the nations (4)? What will be the extent of this blessing to the nations (7)? The 72d Psalm is very clearly and entirely Millennial, showing the King reigning in His kingdom.

CHAPTER XX.

The Book of Proverbs.

Following the book of Psalms of which David was the principal author, come the three books usually ascribed to his son Solomon. Of these, Proverbs is the first. That Solomon was the principal author is indicated therein by chapters 1:1, and 25:1, compared with 1 Kings 4:29-32. The last two chapters, however, seem to be the work of other authors to whom reference is made in the text. Perhaps it is not necessary to suppose that Solomon collected and edited the whole book, indeed, it contains a plain statement that this was not true of a portion of it. See chapters 25-29.

A proverb is a short sentence conveying moral truth in a concise and pointed form, instruction by which means was common in the early history of nations in the East. It is the view of some that in Solomon's day there was a new and distinct class of leaders in the nation known as "teachers of wisdom," of which he, the king himself, was the

most conspicuous; a supposition which gives countenance to the further thought that the usual form of address in Proverbs, "My son," is not that of a father to a child, but a teacher to a pupil. (See Lange's Introduction). It is remarkable that most of the proverbs seem based merely on considerations of worldly prudence, which was quite like Solomon; but considering the Holy Spirit as the real Author of the book, we must believe that faith is the underlying motive productive of the conduct to which the reader is exhorted. Indeed, this is expressed in several instances, and to be presupposed when not expressed. The instances are 1:7, 5:21, 15:11, 23:17-19, 26:10.

Outline of the Book.—It is not easy to speak of the divisions of this book as, in the nature of the case, it does not lend itself to any very orderly or logical classification. The following has been suggested;

1. The superscription, 1:1-6.
2. The introduction; proverbs on the nature and advantage of wisdom, with the dangers that threaten it, 1:7, 9.
3. A group of proverbs illustrating wisdom and the fear of God in contrast with folly and sin, 10-24.
4. A group of proverbs selected by the men of Hezekiah's reign, chiefly comparisons and antitheses, 25-29. Both of these groups are of proverbs very loosely connected, whose principle of unity is not very clearly defined.
5. A group of supplemental proverbs of Agur and Lemuel, 30-31.

Particular attention is called to the personification of wisdom in the 8th chapter of the book, where the spiritually-minded reader will have little difficulty in identifying the voice of his Lord.

CHAPTER XXI.

The Book of Ecclesiastes.

The ground for ascribing Ecclesiastes to Solomon is four-fold: (1) The indirect claim of the book itself as gathered from chapter 1, verses 1 and 12; (2) the general opinion of Jews and Christians from the earliest times; (3) the fitness of Solomon to write it; (4) the lack of agreement among critics as to any other author or period.

The design of the book seems to be to show the insufficiency of all earthly objects to confer happiness, and thus prepare man to receive the true happiness in Christ when presented to him. It is not affirmed that this was the design present in the mind of the human writer, but that it was the design of the Holy Spirit who inspired the writing.

There are many different plans or theories of the book. In the first place, there are those who conceive of it as a formal treatise on the vanity of human affairs. There are others who think it merely a collection of disconnected thoughts and maxims. A third class speak of it as a kind of sustained dialogue between a teacher and his pupils, as suggested in the introduction to the Book of Proverbs in our last lesson. A fourth regard it as a biography of Solomon's own life, and a fifth, as an ideal book of the experience of the natural as distinguished from the spiritual man. This last does not necessarily exclude any of the others, but rather explains, perhaps, why any one of them may be taken as the correct view.

They who hold to the first idea of a formal treatise recognize four distinct discourses, e. g., chapters 1-2; 3-5; 6:8-15; 8:16-12:7. They who hold to the fourth idea think that the book not only records, but re-acts the scenes of Solomon's own search for happiness, making of it a kind of dramatic biography. In other words, Solomon becomes again in the writings of the book, the various phases of his former self, having fits of study, luxury, misanthropy, etc., all ending in disappointment. In this case it is important to note that the word "wisdom" as used in Ecclesiastes means "science," while as used in Proverbs it means "piety."

They who hold to the last-named conception of the book are best represented as far as I know, by Rev. W. J. Erdman, whose concise work, entitled Ecclesiastes, cannot be too highly commended.

The Book of the Natural Man.—By "the book of the natural man" is meant man as he is "under the sun," compared with the man spoken of by Paul whose "citizenship is in Heaven." The first proof presented is that the only divine name used in the book is the "natural" name, God (Elohim), the significance of which all will recognize from our reference to it in the study of Genesis. Jehovah, the name associated with the Covenant of Redemption, is not once employed in the book of Ecclesiastes; hence man is seeking what is best 'under the sun," but not seeking Him who is above the sun.

A second proof is the frequent use of that phrase just referred to, "under the sun." As Mr. Erdman says, "Man is looking up but not knowing what is beyond, except judgment." A third proof is this, viz.: that all the experiences and observations of the book are bound together by the one question: "What is the chief good?" "Is life worth living?" While the answer is sought amidst general failure, contradictions, and half-truths, because man is out of Christ, and yet face to face with the mysteries of God and nature.

A fourth proof is what the book itself styles "the conclusion of the whole matter" (12:13, 14), which, the more you think about it, the more you perceive to be that of the natural man only. "To fear God and keep His commandments," is right, but the author of Ecclesiastes confessedly has not done so, and yet he sees judgment in the distance and has not preparation to meet it. "Where man ends therefore, God begins." The book of the natural man concludes where that of the spiritual man begins. The all-in-all of man under the sun, the first Adam, convicts him of failure and guilt in order to lead him to the all-in-all of the man about the sun, the second Adam, who bare our guilt in His own body on the tree.

This conception of the book easily explains why some of its conclusions are only partially true and others altogether false, such as 2:16, 3:19, 9:2, etc. And if it be asked, How then can the book be inspired? the answer is that in contending for the inspiration of the Bible we do not claim the inspiration of the men, but the writings; while in the latter case it is not meant that every word thus written is true, and in that sense God's Word, but that the record of it is true. That is, God caused it to be written that this or that man felt this or that way, and said thus and so, and hence the record of how he felt and what he said is God's record, and in that sense true and in that sense inspired.

CHATTER XXII.

The Song of Solomon.

Of all the books of the Old Testament I feel myself least competent to speak of the Canticles, or the Song of Solomon. I am not ignorant of what others have thought and written about the book, but personally I have not grasped its contents as in the case of some of the other books. Under the circumstances, therefore, the best I can do just now is to give in substance what other teachers have said. I think Angus' Bible Hand-Book is a good guide, and I will draw chiefly from that source.

Internal evidence seems to confirm the voice of antiquity that Solomon wrote the book, see 1 Kings 4:32. As it is called the Song of Songs, the title carries with it the idea that it is the best of all his songs. Moreover, although it is not quoted in the New Testament, yet it always formed part of the Old as far as we have record, and was in the canon of sacred Scripture which Jesus and His apostles recognized as such.

When it was written is not known, but its imagery seems to be drawn from the marriage of Solomon either with Pharoah's daughter or some native of Palestine, espoused some years later, of noble birth, though inferior to her husband. For the first idea compare such places as 1 Kings 3:1, 7:8, 9:24, with chapters 1:9, and 6:12 of the song, and for the second, look at the language of the Song, 2:1, 7:1, 1:6.

There are two characters who speak and act throughout, Shelomoh, a masculine name, meaning "peaceful," and Shulamith, a feminine form of the same name. See 1:6, 3:11, 6:13, 8:12. There is also a chorus of virgins, daughters of Jerusalem, 2:7, 3:5, 5:8, 9. Towards the close two brothers of Shulamith appear, 8:8, 9, see also 1:6. As in most of the Hebrew poetry, and indeed all ancient poems, there are no breaks to indicate change of scene or speakers, which is to be determined partly by the sense, but chiefly by the use of the original of the feminine and masculine pronouns.

The whole book, as our author and many others believe, is to be regarded as a description of wedded love; and yet, of course, it has a higher aim. It is noticeable that there is a sudden change from the singular to the plural pronoun in 1:4, which seems to indicate that Shulamith must be taken collectively; a fact which, put together with some other things gives credence to the idea both of Jews and Christians that the story should be applied to the history of God's chosen people and their relation to Him. Every reader of the Bible knows that the union of Jehovah with Israel, and that of Christ and His church are represented under the same figure of marriage. See such passages as Psalm 45, Isaiah 54:5, 6, Jeremiah 2:2, Hosea 2:14-23, Matthew 9:15, John 3:29, Ephesians 5:23-27, etc.

Outline of the Book.—The following is Angus' outline of the Song of Songs:

1. Shulamith speaks, 1:2-6; then in dialogue with Shelamoh; Shul. 1:7; Shel. 1:8-11; Shul. 1:12-14; Shel. 1:15; Shul. 1:16-2:1; Shel. 2:2; Shul. 2:3.

2. Shulamith now rests, sleeps and dreams (Shelomoh addressing the daughters of Jerusalem, and charging them not to wake her, 2:7; 3:5;) 2:4-6, 8-3:4.

3. The daughters of Jerusalem see a nuptial procession approaching 3:6-11.

4. Dialogue between Shelomoh and Shulamith. Shelomoh speaks 4:1-16

(as far as "flow out"), Shul. 4:16; Shel. 5:1.

5. A night scene; Shulamith seeking for Shelomoh; meets and converses with the daughters of Jerusalem; Shul. 5:2-8; daughters of Jerusalem, 5-9; Shul. 5:10-16; daughters of Jerusalem, 6:1; Shul. 6:2, 3.

6. Morning scene; Shelomoh visits his garden early, and meets Shulamith; Shel. 6:4-10; Shul. 6:11, 12; the dialogue continuing to 8:8.

7. The brothers of Shulamith are introduced; the brothers speak; 8:8, 9; Shulamith answers them, 8:10-12; Shelomoh speaks, 8:13; and Shulamith answers, closing the scene, 8:14.

CHAPTER XXIII.

Introduction to the Prophetic Scriptures.

Dr. Samuel J. Andrews in "God's Revelation of Himself to Man," remarks upon the fact which every student of the Bible has observed, that none of the prophets in Judah or Israel from the time of Solomon down to the time when they began to write their prophecies, i. e., for two centuries, make any mention of the Messiah or His kingdom. And he accounts for this on the ground that at no time after the division of the kingdom could the coming of the Messiah have been to the nation at large an object of true spiritual desire or hope, for the reason that the moral conditions were wanting. The promises respecting Him appealed to faith, and it was "only as the people were faithfully fulfilling their duties to Jehovah as the theocratic king that they could understand the nature of the higher blessings of the future kingdom and truly desire them." In other words, the prophets could not speak of future spiritual blessings to those who had no ear to hear. It was their immediate duty, therefore, to convince the people of their sins and seek to bring them to repentance: see for example the character of the utterances of Elijah and Elisha in the Northern kingdom. As the sin had been national, so the repentance must be national, which was never the case. The Psalms, many of which were written at this period, bear witness to the fact that there were individuals who appreciated the Messianic hope, and longed for its fulfillment, but this was not the case of the nation at large.

Why Written Prophecy?—Written prophecy, which does not become a factor in revelation until about the eighth or ninth century B. C., was not really in accord with the true idea of the theocracy, as our author states, and its first appearance at about the date indicated marks an epoch in God's dealings with His people. "His presence among them theretofore, assured them of the continued communications of His will as there might be need (Exodus 25:22)," and one way in which those communications were conveyed was through the words spoken by the prophets (Deuteronomy 18:18-22), whose utterances were for their own day and generation, and hence were not necessary to be written down. When their utterances, however, came to be written down, and the transient word took on a permanent form, the change was very significant and ominous. It spoke of a future withdrawal of Jehovah's presence, a consequent cessation of prophetic utterances, and hence a delay or postponement respecting the setting up of the Messianic kingdom. Compare Amos 8:11, 12, and Lamentations 2:9. The prophet's words now were preserved for future generations, for it had become evident that both kingdoms, Judah and Israel, "though with unequal steps" would go steadily downward. The kingdom of Israel was overthrown and carried into captivity by the Assyrians about 722 B. C., not to return again as yet to their former land in any national capacity. The crisis in the kingdom of

Judah approached less rapidly, but 140 years later she too was carried away by the Babylonians. It is true that members of the tribe of Judah did after 70 years again return to the Holy Land, and with them, as well, representatives of the other tribes, and that Judah in that sense was restored to something like her former national life. But it must be remembered that it was only "something" like it and not the thing itself, inasmuch as she was always thereafter a vassal of one or the other of the ruling Gentile powers down until the day when, because of her crucifixion of the Messiah, she was at length scattered again, this time among all the nations of the earth, awaiting the consummation of those things spoken concerning her future in the prophets which we are soon to study.

The prophets, it will be seen, had a two-fold mission, i. e., one for the immediate present, and the other for the remote future, their messages revolving around three points, viz: (1), "the blessings temporal and spiritual given by God to His covenant people if faithful; (2), the judgments coming upon them if unfaithful; (3), the renewed grace to them when repentant." There is, moreover, great variety in the detail with which they speak, but their chief points of agreement are (1), that a day of righteous retribution is impending, the end of which will bring repentance, and prepare the way for the Messianic kingdom; these judgments affect Israel chiefly, but also the Gentile nations throughout the whole earth. (2), The tribes of Israel will be regathered, and a remnant purified by discipline shall form the nucleus of the

reconstituted nation, among whom Jehovah will again dwell with blessings, temporal and spiritual. (3), This reconstituted nation of Israel will be the germ, so to speak, of the Messianic kingdom and extend over the whole earth.

Why Address the Gentiles?—"But written prophecy embraces God's words addressed to many heathen i. e., Gentiles, peoples also. These words could not in the nature of the case always have been spoken to them, and even so, they have long since ceased to exist as peoples. Why, then, written down and preserved? Not simply that we of these latter days may see their fulfillment, and thus have our faith confirmed, for this fulfillment cannot in many cases be proved because of our historical ignorance. They were written rather because the purpose of God in the Jews as a people, both as wanderers and when restored and dwelling in their own land, brings them into continued relations to other peoples, and especially to those dwelling immediately around them; and although the earlier peoples, as Edom and Moab, Syria and Egypt, may cease to exist, yet other peoples arise, and the same relations in substance continue. As His own chosen nation, through whom He will reveal Himself to the nations, the Jews hold through all historical time an official position, and have a sacred character, and in the day of their restoration and of the judgment of the nations, the great question will be, how far have the other nations regarded them as His people, and so treated them."

CHAPTER XXIV.

The Prophecy of Joel.

Joel was probably the earliest of all the prophets whose writings have descended to us. His personal history is unknown further than the bare statement, chapter one, verse one. His field of labor, however, was presumably Judah rather than Israel, the southern rather than the northern kingdom, because of allusions to the center of public worship which was at Jerusalem, 1:9, 13, 14, 2:15, and because of non-allusions to Israel distinctively. Such places as 2:27, and 3:16, which you may have noticed, are

thought by most expositors to mean Israel as inclusive of Judah, i. e., the whole united nation. Although it is assumed, that Joel was the earliest of the prophets, yet the evidence therefor is inferential rather than direct. He is presumably earlier than Amos who is known to have prophesied somewhere about the close of the eighth century B. C., because he seems to be quoted by Amos v. 16-18. He also refers to the same heathen nations as Amos 3: 4-6, and to the same physical scourges as prevalent in the land, 1:4, 17, 20.

All the foregoing references are to Joel, a comparison of whose marginal notes will show the corresponding passages in Amos.

General Outline of the Book.—As to the book itself we might outline the contents of its chapters thus:

This chapter recurs to the future blessing spoken of in the preceding chapter, for the purpose of amplifying some of its features, a peculiarity of all the prophets, as was indicated in one of our earliest lessons:

CHAPTER XXV.

The Prophecy of Jonah.

The reason for placing the study of Jonah next to Joel is simply, that as near as we can gather the two were probably contemporary, the one in Judah as we have seen, but the other in Israel. There is, indeed, however, only a single reference to any prophesying of Jonah in connection with his own people, and that is found in 11 Kings 14: 25. A prediction he had made concerning the restoration of the coasts of Israel had been fulfilled in the reign of Jeroboam II, somewhere about 800 B. C., showing that Jonah must have flourished at an earlier date, though how much earlier, no one knows. Of his personal history nothing more can be told than that recorded in the same verse with the exception of what we find in his written book.

That book contains the record of his special mission to the great Gentile city of Nineveh, the Assyrian capital, a story as familiar as that of any of the old patriarchs. Every one knows how Jonah refused to comply with the divine command, the punishment which befell him in being swallowed by the great fish, the repentance which followed, his subsequent obedience and the result of his commission both on Ninevah and on himself.

Of course, the question will not down. Is this historic? The evidence for the actuality of the whole transaction is found (1), in the way in which it is recorded, there being not the slightest intimation in the book itself, or anywhere else in the Bible, that it is a parable. (2). In the almost unbroken evidence of tradition, the whole of the Jewish nation practically, accepting it as historic. (3). But especially in the testimony of Christ as recorded in Matthew 12: 38, and parallel places. There are those who are able to read these words of the Saviour in the light of the argument of which they form a part, and say that they allude only to what He knew to be a parable, or an allegory, or a myth, but I am not of their number. Jesus would not have used such an illustration in such a connection, in my judgment, if it were not that of a historic fact.

Before leaving this part of our subject, however, there are two or three other points which it might be well to speak of. In the first place, we might note as a reason for Jonah's indisposition to obey the divine command, though not as an excuse for it, that he was moved by patriotic motives. As a prophet, and a student of the Word of God, he knew what was to befall his nation sooner or later at the cruel hands of Assyria, and we can readily understand how he must have shrunk from going on an errand to that people which might result in sparing them to be the scourge of Israel, as it did.

Another thing to notice is that great and astounding as was the physical miracle of Jonah's preservation in the fish's belly, it was as nothing in comparison with the moral miracle of sparing a whole nation of confessed sinners simply on their repentance and giving heed to the message of the prophet!

Nor let us conclude our meditations either without observing how the history of Nineveh in this case illustrates the principle of God's dealings with all the heathen nations as laid down in Acts 10 : 34, 35.

Jonah a Type of Israel.—A dispensational significance in the book of Jonah and one which itself is a contribution to its historicity, is found in its allegorical or typical relationship to the history of Israel as a nation. To illustrate:

1. Jonah was called to a world mission and so was Israel.

2. Jonah at first refused compliance with the divine purpose and plan, and so did Israel.

3. Jonah was punished by being cast into the sea, and so was Israel by being dispersed among the nations.

4. Jonah was not lost, but rather especially preserved during this part /of his experience, and Israel is not being assimilated by the nations, but being kept for God.

5. Jonah repentant and cast out by the fish, is restored to full life and action again, and Israel repentant and cast out by the nations shall be restored to her former national position.

6. Jonah, obedient, goes upon his mission to Nineveh, and Israel, obedient, shall ultimately engage in her original mission to the world.

7. Jonah is succecssful in that his message is acted upon to the salvation of Nineveh, so Israel shall be blessed in that she shall be used to the conversion of the whole world.

CHAPTER XXVI.

The Prophecy of Amos.

Read verse 1 of chapter 1, and gather out what it teaches of the personal history of the prophet. In what town did he dwell? What was his original occupation? To which kingdom was he commissioned as a prophet? Who was the king of Israel at the time?

Now turn back to the time of that king (Jeroboam II), as recorded, 11 Kings 14 : 23-29. You will recall what was said in an earlier lesson about its being a golden age of Israel. What made it so? In the first place, the long reign of the king, the longest of any in the annals of the kingdom. How long was it? In the second place, the victories and gains on the battlefield. How are they alluded to? In the third place, the evidence of God's interest in their affairs as shown in the fulfillment of prophecy. Whose prophecy is referred to?

But though it was a golden age in one sense, it was leaden in another. As the study of Amos reveals, their outward or political prosperity was associated with a gross inward or moral corruption, as has been the case with many another nation down to our own time.

Discourses Concerning the Nations, 1:3; 2: 3.—Returning to the book of Amos, observe that its first natural division (after the introduction in verses 1 and 2), consists of discourses concerning the Gentile nations. While the Old Testament is concerned chiefly with God's peculiar people, the Jews, and for the reasons already outlined more than once, it must not be forgotten that He never left Himself without witness to the other nations as well. In this connection read Acts 10 : 34, 35. Sometimes these Gentile nations were used of God as scourges upon Israel for her sins, but when they in their wickedness and greed followed out their own bent, and went further in that affliction than He desired, the rod sooner or later was laid upon their own backs. Read Zechariah 1 : 14, 15. These discourses in Amos we are now considering carry our thoughts in this line. How many such nations are addressed? Of what nation was Damascus the capital? And Gaza? Examine the map, and locate the different nations geographically, as a quickener to your interest. What peculiar phrase introduces each discourse? This does not mean that the given nation had sinned only three or four times, but is a Hebraism indicating that the transgression had been innumerably often.

There are one or two observations of a general character that apply not only to these discourses, but to all in this book, and for that matter to all the books of the prophets. We are not to suppose, for example, that these are all the discourses concerning the nations which the prophet ever delivered, or that we have the whole of any one discourse in these records; but only so much of the given matter as the Holy Spirit deemed necessary to transmit to later generations. It is not affirmed that this is absolutely the case, but only that there is no obligation upon us to believe otherwise.

Discourse Concerning Judah, 2:4, 5. —Tekoa, where Amos lived, and where probably he was born, was a city of the kingdom of Judah, as the map or the Bible dictionary will disclose; but notwithstanding that, he was not commissioned to his own people, as we have seen, but to the sister kingdom of Israel. An interesting allusion to that fact will be considered again when we reach chapter 7:12, 13, which please examine in connection with the context. This is the only discourse to Judah (2:4, 5) contained in the whole book, and need not arrest our attention now, as so much of the other books of the prophets deals with that kingdom.

Discourses Concerning Israel, 2:6, 9: 15.—You will have noticed that from verse 6 of chapter 2, till the end of the book Amos is dealing only with Israel. Here are doubtless the synopses of several discourses, and it will be seen that they are built up and put together on as regular a plan as any of the orderly discourses of our own time. We will outline one or two of them as samples of the whole. Most of the commentators regard the first discourse as ending with the chapter, since the following chapter begins abruptly with another command to "Hear." This first discourse, therefore, is composed of three divisions:

1. Their sins are charged against them, 6-8.

2. Their mercies and blessings are recalled, 9-12.

3. Their punishment is announced, 13-16.

Notice that their sins were in the nature of oppression of the poor, lust, idolatry, and greed. The obscurity of verse 8 is removed somewhat by the Revised Version. The mercies and ben-

efits referred to should be fresh in our minds after the recent study of the Pentateuch, but the marginal references will refresh the memory where anything has been forgotten. Verse 13 should be read as it is in the Revised Version. The punishment spoken of may be said to have reached a climax in the vicissitudes coming upon them through Assyria, and their final captivity, as we have seen. Re-examine 11 Kings 15-17.

One more discourse may be selected for analysis before we proceed, because of its reference to

The Prophet's Call, 3:1-8.—You will remember the circumstances of the Divine call of Moses, Samuel, Elisha and other of the prophets; and how, in one way or another they were afterwards obliged to demonstrate their authority to the people. Moses' rod turned into a serpent is in point. Read also 1 Samuel 3:19, 20, and Matthew 21:23. All the prophets more or less, were thus obliged to give an account of themselves, and no wonder, when we consider the serious and startling nature of their messages at times. Amos is no exception to this rule, and in the chapter before us proceeds to give an account of his call, only he does so in oriental fashion and in a very round-about way. In the realm of nature a certain effect always follows a given cause, and his point is that God's command was the cause in this case, and his prophesying the effect. In a word, he prophesied because he could not help himself, he could not do otherwise under the circumstances. Read especially verse 8, but in connection with the preceding verses 3-7, where each interrogation assumes a negative reply.

This introduces us to the second of the discourses concerning Israel, of which the first division may be designated as the prophet's call. The second division, verses 9 and 10, is an indictment against them on account of sin, and the third, 11-14, their punishment is announced as in the former instance.

Read verse 12 carefully, and observe the figure of a shepherd engaged in a personal encounter with a wild beast in order to rescue a sheep of his flock, an experience evidently not uncommon in the East (compare 1 Samuel 16:34-37). But in this instance the destroyer gets almost the whole; almost, but not quite. How much does the valiant shepherd secure in either case? Very little indeed, but something. There would no significance attach to this of a prophetic character, were it not for the plain statements in other places that, although Israel would be severely punished, yet she would not as a nation be utterly and forever exterminated. A remnant would be saved, and this rather graphic figure, suggested by what Amos had himself seen or experienced as a care-taker of a flock, seems intended to foreshadow it. The purpose of calling attention to it just now is to prepare the class for similar allusions later on, which finally, in the aggregate, assume the proportions of a demonstration of the fact referred to—Israel's preservation and restoration in the latter days.

The Prophetic Visions, 7-9.—It is hardly necessary to continue the analysis of subsequent discourses, which are all of the same general character until we come to the last three chapters of the book. Here we have a series of visions which in the estimation of some were each expanded into a discourse. You will observe three of these visions in chapter 7, at the beginning of the chapter, one in chapter 8, and another in chapter 9. In the case of the first two, the judgments of the grasshopper and the fire, (the meaning of which is very apparent to the prophet as signifying chastisement for his people), his intercessions on their behalf are represented as successful, (verses 3 and 6), but in the following instances such is not the case (7-9, also 8 : 3, 9 : 1-4). Bear in mind the time of Amos' prophecy, 70 or 80 years prior to the Assyrian captivity, in which sad event these predictions had their fulfillment, approximately at least, however Israel's present condition may be regarded as a farther and more complete fulfillment.

Opposition Expressed, 7: 10-17.—At the risk of breaking into the continuity of our thought just here, let us follow the course of the sacred record itself in noticing the opposition presented to the prophet's ministry. Who is the official opponent here? What was the object of worship at Bethel (1 Kings 12)? What language indicates the effect of Amos' messages? How bold and direct were his utterances (11)? What shows his personal courage (13)? What further details of his history does the incident bring to light (14, 15)? What special punishment is now predicted upon the wicked and God-defying priest (16, 17)?

Your particular attention is called to verses 14 and 15, referring more at length to the prophet's early occupation and circumstances of his call. In the second book of Kings, allusion

now and again is made to the "schools of the prophets," and the "sons of the prophets," of whom Elijah, and afterwards Elisha were at the head. Nothing definitely is known of the origin or history of these schools, though it is supposed they were instituted by Samuel (1 Samuel 7 : 15, 16), something on the idea of our theological seminaries, for the training of consecrated youth in the knowledge of the law and the prophets. It is evident that the religious teachers of Israel at this time were largely drawn from these sources, but it is also evident that then, as now, God was pleased to go outside of the regular order occasionally in the calling and equipping of His servants, in order, doubtless, that the cause might not be lost sight of in the result, and that His glory might not be given to another (Zechariah 4 : 6). There are some who will read this to whom it may be a comfort, even if to others it should be a rebuke.

The Promises for Israel, 9: 11-15.—It is the characteristic of all the books of the prophets that no matter how much rebuke and threatened punishment they contain as against Israel or Judah, they always see a better time ahead, when the people shall have learnt their severe lessons and profited by them, and God can be glorified in them. We have already seen a reason for this in the fact earlier discussed, that Israel was, is, and is to be, the channel of blessing to the whole earth.

To begin with, look at verses 8 and 9 of the last chapter. God will destroy the sinful kingdom, but will it be utterly destroyed? He will sift Israel among all the nations, as He is surely doing now, but will there be nothing left in the sieve? How do these two verses agree with our conception of chapter 3 : 12?

But to come now to the plainer and more specific declaration of verses 11-15 of the last chapter. What are these promises?

The restoration of the kingdom, 11.
The possession of the nations, 12.
The prosperity of the land, 13-14.
The perpetuity of the possession, 15.

Is the kingdom of Israel some day to be restored? Is that people to bear sway on the earth? Will the land be fruitful as of old, and even more so, and the cities be built up and inhabited by them again? Will it be a time of rest for them from enemies and war? Such seems to be the literal construction of these verses. To be sure, James' words in Acts 15 : 13-17 are to be reckoned with, which seem to imply a spiritual fulfillment of these promises in the history of the Christian church. But at the risk of stepping aside for a moment from our prescribed path of synthetic teaching to that of interpretation, let us look carefully at those two words, "After this," in verse 16 of Acts 15. James has just said that God was now visiting the Gentiles "to take out of them a people for His name," i. e., (as many understood it), God is calling out the church from the world to become the body of Christ; and when this is done, when the church or body of Christ is completed and caught up to meet Him in the air (1 Thessalonians 4 : 16, 17), then "agree the words of the prophets, as it is written. After this, I will return, and will build again the tabernacle of David, etc." The thought is that Israel's restoration will be literal as Amos prophesies, but that its time will be after the second coming of Christ and what is called the "rapture" of the church. The reader will please not understand me to be dogmatizing on this point, or insisting upon any particular theory of interpretation. But there is so much of this kind of teaching found in the prophets to follow, that it seemed necessary at the beginning, and in order to clear the atmosphere somewhat, to present both sides of the case. As we proceed in the other instances you will thus be the better able to form your own intelligent conclusion. May we all be much in prayer for the enlightenment of the Holy Spirit, without which our own wisdom at the best is but foolishness.

CHAPTER XXVII.

Phe Prophecy of Hosea.

Read chapter 1, verse 1 for something of the personal history of the prophet Hosea. Whose son was he? In whose reigns did he prophesy? The allusion to four kings of Judah, and but one of Israel, might lead us to suppose that Hosea was a prophet of the first-named kingdom; but the contents of the book show differently, and the four kings of Judah are doubtless referred to for other reasons. If, however, Hosea began to prophesy when Jeroboam 11 was king of Israel, and continued till Hezekiah was on the throne of Judah, it is evident that his ministry covered a period of 60 or 70 years, ending only with the captivity of his people. Compare your diagram of 11 Kings for corroboration of this.

The Character of the Times, II Kings 15-17.—It is always well to acquaint oneself with the history of the period of a given prophet when one can do so, for obvious reasons. Read afresh, therefore, the three chapters in Kings mentioned above, and observe the unsettled and iniquitous condition of Israel at this time. It was a golden age no longer, and their sun was setting under a dark and heavy cloud. Zachariah is slain, but the regicide rules only a month in his place until he too is slain. Menahem becomes a vassal to Assyria, and levies exacting taxes on the people to meet the tribute necessary to be paid. His son reigns but two years until he is murdered by one of his own military officers who usurps the authority of the throne. Now the king of Assyria begins to foreclose his mortgage on the land and the people, and the first installment of the captivity takes place. Another murderer comes on the throne, and finally, after a siege of three years, Samaria succumbs to her stronger mistress, and the whole nation is removed far away. Please do not be satisfied with this limited sketch of the period, but by your own diligent reading master the facts for yourselves. If you do so, you will be impressed anew with the wonderful patience and love of God as illustrated by His message to such a people through the lips of our prophet. Hosea is pre-eminently a prophet of love and tenderness, whose characteristics in that respect are simply the reflection of the Divine mind, the pulsation of the Divine heart; but to be appreciated must be seen and weighed in comparison with the environment in which he lived.

An Example of Object Teaching, 14. —We hear much in these days about object teaching and the kindergarten system, but it is not so modern or so strictly mundane a method of instruction as might be supposed. God taught His people Israel in that way, of which we have already seen many illustrations in type and symbol But we come now to one of a different kind from anything yet met with. For example, God would sometimes call upon His prophets to do strange things, to act in a manner out of the ordinary. But as they were conspicuous and important personages in the land, such conduct would naturally excite inquiry, and this, in turn, would open the way for the prophet to give the particular instruction to the people which his action or conduct symbolized or figuratively portrayed.

In the present instance what strange thing is Hosea commanded to do (1:2)? Of course, though strange, it was not wrong for him to do. God's command to do it removes any thought of that character. Moreover, the prophet's motive in marrying the woman was a pure and lofty one. He was to give her his name, and his protection, and lift her out of her former life of moral degradation unto the same high plane as that on which he lived. But why was he to do this? That is, what great historical fact in His own relationship to Israel did God intend to set before them in this domestic history of His prophet? What does the last clause of verse 2 say? Is it not clear that Hosea's marriage with this unchaste woman illustrates Jehovah's marriage with an unchaste people? Where in this book does God call Himself the husband of Israel? But did Israel have anything more to recommend her to God's love and care when He took her to Himself, than this woman had when Hosea married her? Compare Deuteronomy 9:4-6, and Isaiah 51:1, 2.

Observe farther the object teaching in the very names of the children born of this union (3-9). The meaning of these names will be found in the margin.

Observe a peculiarity of prophetic teaching illustrated in verse 4. There are two distinct prophecies there, but at the first glance it reads like only one. You would think that the avengement of the blood of Jezreel on the house of Jehu and the cessation of the house of Israel were one and the same thing, and took place at one and the same time. But look back at II Kings 14:8-12, for the fulfillment of the first, and II Kings 17, for the second. How long a period elapsed between the two, represented by that punctuation mark after "Jehu," in verse 4? This offers a fitting opportunity to remark that the prophets saw the future in space rather than in time. The perspective is regarded rather than the actual distance. As another expresses it, "They speak of things future as a common observer would describe the stars, grouping them as they appear, but not according to their true position." Other illustrations of this principle will be noted further on, but let us fasten the fact on our minds now for future use.

While Hosea is speaking of Israel especially, what side reference is made to Judah in verse 7? See the application or fulfillment of these words as recorded in Judah's history sometime after Israel has been led into captivity (2 Kings 19, especially verse 35). In all such cases, form the habit of examining the marginal references in your Bible, which are a commentary and concordance in one. The above-named reference will be found there.

But is there no hope at all for Israel? Read verse 10. What is the blessing spoken of? In what place will it be realized? Will there be two kingdoms then, or only one (verse 11)? What other prophet has held out a like prospect, with whom Hosea thus agrees?

An Unfaithful Wife, 2.—We now reach a second chapter in the book, and a second in the domestic experience of the prophet. It is a very bitter one. It would appear that nothwithstanding the love of Hosea for his wife, as evidenced among other ways in his bountiful provision for her needs; and notwithstanding she had become the mother of his children, yet she turned her back upon him and them; went after her former lovers and companions in sin, and from an unchaste woman became now a faithless, an adulteress wife.

The chapter containing this story is like a dissolving picture, making it difficult to determine just where the record ceases to speak of Hosea's wife and begins to speak directly of Israel's unfaithfulness to God. We will dismiss the first idea, therefore, and confine ourselves to the second, where the intention is very plain. The teaching clearly is that notwithstanding God's goodness to Israel, calling them to be His people, providing for and protecting them when they had no more claim on His bounty than that unchaste woman had on Hosea's love, yet they had abused His kindness and committed spiritual adultery with idols, especially in Baalim worship.

What command is laid on the prophet, verses 1 and 2? What charge is laid at the door of Israel (5)? What is predicted as the outcome of her iniquity (6, 7)? What was the ground or origin of her sin (8)? What shows her culpability for this ignorance (8-13)? How do these verses indicate her punishment? To what particular period do verses 11-13 refer? May they also, according to the law of double reference, find an application in her history at the present time? What allusion to the extent of her punishment (in time) is found in verse 13? With what verse does the usual vision of hope appear? Does verse 18 apply to the present or the coming millennial age? What language agrees with the idea already expressed of Jehovah's (marriage) union with Israel? How does that language show that a great moral change must precede or accompany Israel's restoration? What language in verse 19 agrees with the last promise in Amos?

A Faithful Husband, 3.—Perhaps the third chapter in this interesting history is the most impressive of all. The prophet's wife has deserted him, but he is commanded still to love her, notwithstanding her conduct. And he is to enter into an arrangement with her, by which a certain provision is to be given her by him for her necessities, on condition that for the time being she shall no longer live adulterously with other men. He, too, will keep himself from becoming husband to another woman. It does not seem that they were to live together in their former relationship, but to be kept one for another in this separated state (see verses 1-3).

And now how plain is the application made by the Holy Spirit in the two following verses! To what period in Israel's history can verse 4 apply any more truly than the present? And on such a conclusion what inference may be drawn from verse 5? It might be well to read this verse in connection again with Amos 9:11-15.

A Sermonic Hint.—Preachers and others looking for themes and texts of discourses along deeply spiritual lines, will not neglect the precious opportunity here presented. What an analogy we have here to our own standing before God in Christ! When we were first called of God, were we not spiritually just what this woman was morally, when Hosea married her? Had we anything to commend us to Him? Was not His acceptance of us an act of pure grace on His part? And since that time, with so much more to praise Him for as His benefits have been bestowed on us, how often have we treated Him like this unfaithful wife! Is not every act of disobedience on our part a kind of spiritual adultery? Yet has God discarded us? Has He cast us away? Are not His gifts and calling without repentance? Does He not bear patiently with us? Does He not still supply our need? Does He not call us back to Him again? Does not His Spirit work in us repentance not to be repented of? And shall we not be His forever? Thus we see that although primarily, or historically, the application of these chapters is to Israel in the flesh, yet in an accommodated and spiritual sense it belongs to us. If we are thus always careful to distinguish between these two things, the historical and the spiritual, there is no reason why we may not employ much of the Old Testament in this way. Indeed doubtless, it is so intended to be employed.

General Discourses, 4-13.—The first three chapters of the book, already considered, form its first natural division, which may be distinguished by the term "Historico-prophetic." They are historic as alluding to the personal life of the prophet, but prophetic, as prefiguring God's relations to and dealings with Israel. The second division of the book may be described as at the head of this paragraph. By "General Discourses," is meant such as we have already studied in Amos, and which it will not be necessary to especially consider here. They give in detail what the first three chapters give in outline, so to speak. That is, they speak of Israel's departure from God, and describe more particularly the forms it took, viz.: falsehood (4:1), licentiousness, (4:11), murder, (5:2), robbery, (7:1), oppression, (12:7), etc. Unlike the book of Amos, however, the discourses in Hosea are not very distinctly defined one from another. The chapters have more the form of one continuous prophecy, and it is thought by some that the prophet himself probably gathered into one discourse the substance of what he had delivered in the whole course of his ministry. The name "Ephraim" so commonly used in the book, taken from one of the chief tribes, is synonymous, or used almost interchangeably, with "Israel." As "Judah" is the title given to the other kingdom, though composed of Judah and Benjamin, so Ephraim is used here as including the other nine tribes.

Your attention was called to the fact that in each of the first three chapters, after rebuke, and warning and prediction of coming suffering, the discourse ended with the promise of future blessing. So now at the close of these "General Discourses," the last chapter (14) concludes in the same way. This further illustrates the law of recurrence which was defined at the beginning of our lessons, and which is a marked peculiarity of much of the prophetic writings. For example, the ground covered in the first chapter of this book, is practically gone over again in chapter two, or chapters two and three taken together. The Holy Spirit thus "recurs" to the subject for the purpose of bringing out certain details, or calling attention to certain features not mentioned before, or if so, in only a very general or incidental way. And so it is with reference to the rest of the book. From chapters 4 to 14, the Holy Spirit is simply "recurring" to the main theme of the earlier chapters. He is not going over new ground, and the matter does not represent what we call progress of thought. The last chapter of the book now to be considered is speaking of the same circumstances, and the same period of time practically, as the last verses of chapters 1, 2 and 3, and all that has intervened has been in the nature of amplification of the other verses of those chapters. The importance of seizing upon such a simple principle as this in interpreting the prophets is too apparent to require emphasis.

The Future Hope, 14.—Let us remember, therefore, that the view-point of this chapter is about the same as that of verses 10 and 11 of chapter 1, verses 14-23 of chapter 2, and verse 5 of chapter 3. With that understanding, let us divide it into its several parts, finding in it material for another discourse or Bible reading.

The gracious appeal, 1-3.

The promised blessing, 4-8.

The practical application, 9.

Observe in the appeal that the very words are put on Israel's lips with which they are to return to God. Observe the freeness of God's blessing to them on the ground of repentance and faith (4). Observe the figurative allusions to the source and character of these blessings in that day, fully agreeing again with Amos 9 : 11-15, (5-7). Verse 8 might be considered as a future dialogue between Ephraim and Jehovah. Verse 9 justifies us, as was said before, in employing the whole subject in a spiritual sense and applying it to the present church period in which we dwell.

CHAPTER XXVIII.

The Prophecy of Micah.

There are three prophets who now form a group by themselves, Micah, Nahum and Isaiah. These all lived and prophesied at about the same time, the first of whom will be considered in this chapter.

The little known of the prophet Micah is briefly stated. From what town did he originate as gathered from from chapter 1, verse 1? Calling himself a Morasthite probably indicates Moresheth, or Mareshah, as his birthplace in the southwestern part of Judah, near Gath. The time of his prophesying is shown in the same verse by the reference to the kings of Judah, as between 758 to 700 B. C. He seems to have been the writer of his own book, if we may judge from the personal allusions in chapter 3 : 1, 8, and to have finally died in peace, judging by Jeremiah 26 : 18, 19. He is frequently referred to as a prophet, and his utterances quoted, not only in the instances above given, but in Isaiah 2 : 2-4, and 41 : 15, Ezekiel 22 : 27, Zephaniah 3 : 19, Matthew 2 : 5, and John 7 : 42. Jesus quotes him in Matthew 10 : 35, 36. For

further references to his period, see the following chapter on Isaiah.

I. A Description of Judgment.—The book of Micah, which contains but seven chapters, might be conveniently divided into three parts:

Chapters 1-3 contain a description of the approaching judgment on both kingdoms—Israel and Judah. How do verses 1 and 5 of chapter 1 indicate that both kingdoms are under consideration? Which of the two receives the earlier attention (6-9)? What towns of Judah are particularly mentioned in the conclusion of that chapter? Please look upon the map and observe that these are all in the neighborhood of the prophet's home town, thus suggesting a reason for their specialization.

Pursuing the analysis of this division further, notice the order in which the three classes of the prophet's hearers are address:

(1). He rebukes and threatens the people at large, this in chapter 2.

(2). After rebuking and warning the

people, he addresses the princes in the same way, see chapter 3 : 1-4.

(3). He now addresses himself to the false prophets, 5-8.

Unfortunately the nation or the church ruled over by unjust and unfaithful men is usually obliged to share their punishment. This idea is brought out by what follows. The prophet recapitulates his charges against the people, the princes and the priests in verses 9-11, concluding this part of his prophecy with a further and particular announcement of the judgment about to fall on the whole nation. According to verse 11 what seems to have been the most crying and general sin of all? And yet notwithstanding their covetousness and greed, how did they show either their gross hypocrisy or gross ignorance of God (same verse, last part)? It is at this point that the declaration of judgment is expressed, and in language which has been most literally fulfilled, verse 12.

II. A Vision of Hope.—Chapters 4 and 5 unfold the future and happier, because holier, experience of the nation. I ought to say just here that the first four verses of chapter 4 are quoted almost verbatim in Isaiah 2, unless we shall reverse the order and say that Micah quoted Isaiah, which may indeed be the case, though probably it is not.

At what time are these better things to come to pass according to the beginning of this chapter? That expression "the last, (or latter), days," we shall come to recognize more and more clearly as pointing to the end of the present Christian age, which is to be followed by the Millennial age. How are these better things figuratively expressed in verse 1? It is not difficult to recognize in these figures of speech the exaltation of Jerusalem and Judah over all the nations in that day. But how does verse 2 show that that exaltation will not be exacting and tyrannous over the nations, but the opposite? What language in the verse shows beyond peradventure that the Millenial age is referred to, and no period which has yet appeared in the history of the world? How do verses 3 and 4 strengthen this conviction? What expression in verse 7 almost directly states this to be the case? In the prophet Joel we saw that prior to Israel's deliverance, and, indeed, as incident thereto, the Gentile nations of the earth will be besieging Jerusalem and desirous of seizing her, and that Jehovah will interpose on her behalf;

how do the closing verses of this chapter parallel that prophecy?

Addressing ourselves to chapter 5, we discover what in a greater or less degree is the common teaching of all the prophets that this deliverance, and these good times coming for Israel and Judah are connected with the Person and work of the Messiah. For example, how is that fact led up to in verse 2? To be sure, these words are so quoted in Matthew 2, as to apply to the first coming of Christ, but that does not exclude the fact of His second coming. Indeed, His second coming may be said to be conditioned on His first coming. Moreover, all the succeeding verses in this chapter point to events which did not occur at His first coming, but will be found to be uniformly predicated of His second coming.

Let us look at some of them: Verse 3 refers to the time when "she which travaileth hath brought forth," i. e., the time when Israel shall be delivered out of her great tribulation at the end of this age. Verse 4 speaks of the Lord as feeding His flock and being "great unto the ends of the earth." Verse 5 speaks of Him as the "peace" of Israel, "when the Assyrians shall come into our land," an allusion not to the invasions of the prophet's own time but that of the latter days as is clearly seen from a comparison of verse 6. In this verse Israel is seen to be delivered from the Assyrians by the power of God, which was not true at the time of the invasions past, but shall only be true at the time of the invasion yet to come. It it be objected that Assyria as a nation has passed away, the answer is either that it shall experience some kind of a revival in the future, or else it stands as a type of that Gentile power which shall rise up as the last enemy of Israel before her final deliverance into the place of power and triumph during the Millenial age. If this proposition, or either of them, seems strange or unlikely to any of us just now, let us possess our souls in patience till the constant repetition of it in the prophets convinces us of its truth.

We need not pursue the analysis of these verses further, as even the cursory reading of them indicates that the period in mind is that when Israel shall have a place of power among the nations, her enemies overcome, and her own sins and idolatries forever put away.

III. A Contrast Drawn.—Chapters 6 and 7 have been described as presenting a "contrast between the reasonableness, purity and justice of the divine requirements, and the ingratitude, injustice and superstition of the people which caused their ruin." The conclusion of the book is in the spirit of encouragement based on the unchanging truth and mercy of God.

The closing chapter is peculiarly affecting, presenting us with a kind of soliloquy of repentance on Israel's part. The better element, the right-spirited ones among the people, are shown as confessing and lamenting their sinful condition in verses 1-6, but expressing the utmost confidence in God's returning favor (7-8). Putting all the circumstances together, there are few verses in the whole Bible more expressive of profound and quiet hope and

trust than these. It is beautiful indeed to see the spirit of humble confession and submission in verse 9, and the certainty of triumph over every foe, verse 10. Observe particularly how Jehovah Himself speaks through the prophet in verses 11-13. Revised Version. See the promise of supernatural interposition on Israel's behalf in that day, verse 15; and the confusion of the Gentile nations at their triumph, and their own discomfiture, 16, 17. Of course, the temporal blessings thus coming upon Israel are all predicated of their return to the Lord and His forgiveness of their sins (18, 19). Nevertheless these things will all take place on the ground of the original promise to Abraham (20).

CHAPTER XXIX.

The Prophecy of Isaiah.

Read Isaiah 1:1, to learn something of the prophet's personal history. Whose son was he? To which kingdom was he commissioned as a prophet? In whose reigns did he prophesy? Compare Hosea 1:1, and observe that the two prophets were contemporary.

History of the Period.—Turn again to II Kings 15-20 and refresh your recollection of the history of the period. Little attention need be given to Uzziah's reign because the prophet began his work near its close (Isa. 6:1). The chief event in Jotham's reign was the military combination of Syria and Israel against Judah. The reign of Ahaz is chiefly notable for his confederacy with Assyria against these combined enemies. This confederacy proved nearly as fatal to Judah in the end as it had to Israel formerly in the time of Menahem. From a friend Assyria soon turned to be an enemy, destroying many cities of Judah, and prevented from capturing Jerusalem itself in the reign of Hezekiah, only by the supernatural interposition of God. See II Kings 18-19. In the reign of Hezekiah the political situation is precisely reversed, and through the faith and piety of that good monarch, Jehovah is honored and Assyria is overcome. An acquaintance with these facts, especially those in the time of Ahaz, is necessary to the elucidation of certain discourses of the prophet, especially in his earlier chapters.

Discourses Concerning Judah, 1-5.—The discourses in this division of the book are similar in character to those already considered in the previous prophets. If we analyze one it will answer for all. The first discourse is generally thought to be comprehended in chapter 1. Observe the indictment against the people, verses 2-9, the threat, 10-15, the exhortation, 17-20, and the customary promise of purification and blessing, 25-27. The second discourse seems to cover chapters 2-4 inclusive, while the third in this section is in the nature of a parabolic song, chapter 5. Your attention is called again to the law of recurrence. For example, the space of time covered by the first discourse is inclusive of all the discourses following. The point of view of its beginning is the prophet's own time, and that of its ending is the millenium. Within this same cycle the thought of all the subsequent discourses revolves. The Holy Spirit simply recurs to it again and again, in other connections, and for the purpose of emphasizing particular incidents or events intervening.

The Prophet's Call, 6.—We have spoken previously of the demand made on the prophets to announce their authority, and dwelt somewhat at length on the call of Amos. We now reach the similar circumstance in the history of Isaiah as described in chapter 6. When did he receive his call (verse 1)? Describe the vision in connection

74 Synthetic Bible Studies

with it (1-4). What was the immediate effect upon the prophet (5)? What symbolizes the removal of his iniquity (6, 7)? What is the particular language of his Divine call (8, first part)? In what words does he give utterance to his consecration (8, last part)? What is his commission (9, 10)? Is it encouraging or discouraging at first? Is it discouraging or encouraging in the end (11, 13)? It will thus be seen that the prophet's commission ends as the discourses usually end, in hope for the people. It will be desirable to read these concluding verses in the Revised Version. It is hardly necessary to suggest that this chapter offers a good opportunity for a Bible reading on the individual spiritual life. We have here the conviction of the sinner, his repentance and confession of sin, his forgiveness and cleansing, his call into the Master's service, his consecration of himself, and the character of the work he is expected to do.

Judah and Assyria, 7-9.—We here reach one of the most interesting discourses in the book, not only because of its historical features, but the one or two illustrations it affords of the law of double reference hitherto explained. Observe that the cause giving rise to it, 7:1, 2, is the war against Judah, and the latter's confederacy with Assyria, recorded more at length in 11 Kings 16. Observe the gracious and encouraging commission of the prophet to King Ahaz (3-9). Observe in connection with that commission another illustration of that object-teaching spoken of in Hosea. For example, the name of the prophet's son whom he takes with him is a synonym of hope (see definition in the margin). Observe further, the sign granted to Ahaz (10-16). It is here we have the first illustration of the law of double reference (14). The virgin here referred to may in the first instance mean any ordinary maiden of Judah, subsequently to be married and give birth to a child. But it is evident from Matthew 1-:23, that in the mind of the Holy Spirit it applied ultimately and completely only to Christ.

The prophet forsees the purpose of Ahaz to disregard Jehovah and pursue his own plans with Assyria, and in this connection gives utterance to a forecast of the punishment coming upon Judah in consequence (7:7-8:22). Observe that the nation on which they now leaned would become the means of their punishment (7:17-20). Observe the extent of that punishment (8:7, 8). Observe that nothing but the head, that is, the capitol of Judah would prac-

tically be left, and compare this with the fulfillment of the prophecy in Hezekiah's day when the Assyrians were defeated in their attack on Jerusalem. It is probable that the period of sorrow and darkness further predicted of the nation in the last verse of the chapter, may cover a long time subsequent to the Assyrian assault, including the Babylonian captivity, and the later afflictions of the Grecian period. This opinion seems justified by the continuation of the discourse in the next chapter.

The Promised Redeemer.—In the midst of this darkness for Judah, what is it the prophet sees in the distance 9:2? How does he explain this figure of speech (3)? Read verse 3 as translated in the Revised Version. What would be the cause of this joy (4)? How does verse 5 (Revised Version) indicate that the reference is to the millenium? Through whom is this deliverance to be brought about (6, 7)? To whom do these verses apply (Luke 2:11)? It is proper to add that the fulfillment of this prophecy is generally applied in a spiritual sense to the growth and development of the Christian church, but that does not necessarily exclude the more literal fulfillment in an earthly kingdom yet to be set up with Judah as its center, and Christ on the throne.

Punishment of Assyria, 10-12.—Practically the next 17 chapters are taken up with discourses concerning the nations, predictive of coming judgments upon them for their sins, and especially their treatment of Judah. But the first of these discourses, that against Assyria, is so full and typical of the rest as to warrant consideration by itself.

The story is like this:—In the first place, God used Assyria to punish Judah (10:5, 6). In the second place, Assyria's own wicked motive in the matter is revealed in verses 7-11. Then comes the threatened punishment on Assyria for her pride (verses 12, 19). Following this we have the customary promise of deliverance, victory, and glory for Israel in the latter time, (chapter 10, verse 20, to chapter 12, verse 6). It should be noted that the names Israel, Judah, and house of Jacob in these chapters, are used interchangeably for the whole twelve tribes except where indicated otherwise.

Let us analyze this last part of the prophecy concerning the future of Israel. Observe their promised conversion (10:20-23); the punishment of their enemies (24-34); and the connection of both with the coming of the

Messiah (chapter 11). Observe that the reference to the Messiah is millennial, and points to His second coming. Read the first nine verses of chapter 11. Observe further in corroboration of this, that the time synchronizes with a future restoration of the people to their land, and the union again of the two kingdoms in one (verses 10-13). Observe also the miraculous intervention of God in bringing this about (verses 15, 16), and the joyful thanksgiving of the redeemed people in that day (chapter 12).

This prophecy furnishes a striking illustration of the peculiarity of the prophetic writings spoken of in an earlier chapter, namely, that they saw the future in space rather than in time. To quote another's language, "When you look from a height on a landscape, hills seem close together which are really wide apart; so in the foretelling of events, the order, succession and grouping are presented, but the intervals of time are overlooked." In the present instance the prophet covers a period of already more than 2,600 years, mentioning two or three great events, some fulfilled and some unfulfilled, with great lapses of time between them of which no mention is is made, and yet the whole appears like a continuous and unbroken sequence.

Discourses Concerning the Nations, 13-27).—The discourse against Assyria is followed by a series of similar ones against all the representative Gentile nations that had come into like relations to Israel. Please scan chapters 13-23 for the names of these nations. It is proper to say, that in the judgment of some scholars, these predictions have not yet been completely fulfilled. This consideration involves the conclusion that some of these nations at least are to experience a historical revival before the end of the present age. This is thought to be true especially of Babylon, which one school of prophecy regards as the future seat of the anti-Christ. The perusal of the prophecy concerning Babylon, chapters 13-14, is worthy of the closest attention even as literature. The scope and grandeur of its imagery is unequalled. Dante's "Divine Comedy," and Goethe's "Faust" are the nearest suggestion of an approach to it, but were inspired by and copied from it. Special interest attaches to the description of Lucifer in chapter 14, which some regard as a description of the future anti-Christ. Attention is called to the fact that, as in all the other instances, after the prophet has concluded his denunciation of the enemies

of Israel he brings his discourse or discourses to a grand climax by predicting the ultimate triumph and blessing of the people of God. In this instance the discourses against the nations are grouped together in the chapters already indicated, and in like manner the promises for Israel (or Judah) are grouped together at the end, like the finale of an oratorio. Read from chapter 24, verse 21, to the close of chapter 27.

The Relations of Judah and Egypt, Chapters 28-35.—This section of the book, as to its principal features, is not unlike that previously considered under the head of Judah and Assyria. I cannot place the first part of chapter 28 as satisfactorily as I could wish, but at verses 14-18 there is an illusion to a false covenant and the true in terms which seems to point to the end of the age. When we reach the study of Daniel this will appear plainer. In that book Israel is seen in her own land again in covenant with Anti-Christ, and it is doubtless this coming event which is forshadowed here in Isaiah as well.

As harmonizing with this, chaper 29 of our present lesson brings before us the siege of Jerusalem by her enemies of the Roman world at the end of the age, when these enemies shall have at their head the anti-Christ who shall have broken his covenant with Israel. The prophet Joel was the first who prepared us to understand this. In the further analyzation of this chapter observe these four divisions, (1), the siege itself, 1-4; (2), the overthrow of the enemy, 5-8; (3), the cause of Judah's punishment, 9-16; (4), Judah's ultimate redemption, 17-24. The data which positively determine that no past siege of Jerusalem, but one yet to come, is here outlined are found in the overthrow of Judah's enemies and her own triumph, which have never yet taken place. The third division of the chapter—the cause of Judah's punishment, may be said to explain why the conditions of divisions two and four are not yet experienced in Judah's history.

Chapters 30 and 31 of this section deal more particularly with Judah's relationship to Egypt, but those who have been following these studies closely will not be unprepared to learn that while the Egypt of the prophet's own time is now in mind, yet it is evident also that according to the law of double reference, the Egypt of the latter days is being dealt with as well. This appears in the sequel, for example:—

The theme opens with a warning to Judah against trusting in Egypt, chapter 30: 1-17. As a matter of fact, in the siege of Jerusalem by the Babylonians, which followed in the next century, Judah did fix her trust on Egypt with the result here fortold by the prophet, as we shall gather bye-and-bye from the study of Jeremiah. But notwithstanding this approximate fulfillment of his words, a remoter one is yet to come, and nothing could more strongly substantiate it than what follows. For example, verses 18-30 of the chapter show the ultimate redemption of Judah, verses 31-33, the overthrow of her enemy, both of which events are still future. In chapter 31, the warning against trusting in Egypt is repeated, verses 1-3, while immediately following is foreshadowed the interposition of Jehovah on behalf of His people. We seem also shut up to the conclusion, therefore, that in the end of the age, Judah, hard pressed by her enemies, shall once more look for help from the South instead of waiting on Jehovah, but the latter shall have mercy upon her, and when the arm of flesh fails, interpose His own.

All this is still further confirmed by the contents of chapters 32-35, which gives us a magnificent picture of the reign of the Messiah. In chapter 32, the king is reigning, in chapters 33-34 the judgments are falling on Judah's enemies, and in chapter 35 that nation is redeemed.

Part six of the book, as we divide it, Chapter XXXVI—XXXIX, it is practically a review of the story of Hezekiah's reign as given in 11 Kings 18-20, and need not be dwelt upon at length.

Discourses Chiefly Millenial, 40-66.— In the judgment of some that part of Isaiah now entered upon is so different in style from the former part, as to justify the thought of another author, a second Isaiah. But it is not within the scope of these lessons to go into that question. Jesus seems to have known but one Isaiah, and His example is sufficiently satisfying for us. However, the difference in style may be explained by the difference in subject, for while the first part of the book deals chiefly with the prophet's own time, the last part is almost entirely millenial. Nor is the difference in style so very radical after all. Those who have now read the whole book synthetically, will recognize the same style in the earlier millenial chapters like 11, 25, and 35, as in these later ones. This is certainly true in the English translation, and all scholars are agreed that it is a faithful transcript of the Hebrew.

Read carefully the first two verses of chapter 40, and observe that the prophet's thought is resting far into the future. He sees Jerusalem restored, purified, comforted and at rest. This has not yet taken place, and in the light of what we have already learned as to the scope of the prophet's vision there can be no doubt that it refers to the millenial period, coincident, as shown in the earlier chapters, (especially 11), with the second coming of Christ.

From this point to the end of the book the prophet seems to be dwelling very largely upon the intervening events which, in a sense, move forward toward the millenium. He mentions what must come to pass before the millenium appears. Or, to change the thought somewhat, let us imagine that the whole of these last 27 chapters were simply one discourse; the text, chapter 40: 1, 2; the theme, comfort; the remainder, the several divisions of that theme. This, I think, will be the simplest and easiest way of studying the lesson, and bring about as good results as any. If we had not gone pretty thoroughly into the study of the first part of the book, such a plan might be venturesome in taking too much for granted; but as it is, it will doubtless be found interesting and spiritually quickening, and also leave on the mind a very good impression of the contents and character of the whole book. Please understand, it is not affirmed that these 27 chapters did constitute one discourse originally, but we are only accomodating them to such an idea for present purposes. Our theme then is "Comfort," comfort for Jerusalem, for Judah, for the people of God in the latter days; and the question arises, What are the elements of that comfort, what is it that God commissions His prophet to say to the people calculated to awaken hope, and quicken their expectation of that promised time?

Elements of Comfort.—1. The first of these "elements of comfort" is the Divine care over scattered Israel at the present time. Let us imagine Israel doubting the glowing prognostication of the prophet on the ground of their weak, scattered and persecuted condition, and saying that God had forgotten them and His promise would not be fulfilled. Now read chapter 40: 9-26, in which the prophet enlarges upon the greatness and omnipotence of God, applying it to show that under the circumstances Israel could not be forgotten by Him, verses 27-31. The same thought is expressed in other places, notably chapter 43.

2. The second of these 'elements of

comfort" may be described as the ultimate triumph of Israel over their enemies. The nation might be represented as still questioning the possibility of the prophet's words on the ground of the vastness and strength of their enemies. Look now at chapter 41, beginning at about verse 10, for the evidence that these would be overcome by them through the power of God. The same thought is repeated in other chapters, particularly 51-52.

3. A third element is the ministry of the Messiah. If doubt still existed in their minds, as to the ground on which this care for and defence of them might be predicated, it is now shown to arise through the Person and work of that Anointed One to whom gave all the prophets witness. Read chapter 42, specially the opening verses, and compare them with chapters 49: 1-12, 50:4-11, and most particularly 52:13-53:12. It is the suffering Substitute who would bring it about and make it to be possible, in the bearing away of their sin.

4. A fourth element is the outpouring of the Holy Spirit upon them. They might still be perplexed in the acceptance of these promises on the ground of their own inward unworthiness and indifference toward God as a nation. To meet this the office of the Holy Spirit is referred to, chapter 44, verses 1-8. These verses should be read in connection with the last part of the preceding chapter to appreciate their full significance and value. It will be seen that as a result of this freshening grace the nation will revive, and there will be an eagerness to turn to the Lord and confess His name. The same thought is expressed in chapter chapter 32, verses 14-20.

5. A fifth element is the particularization of their return from Babylon, chapters 44, 45. This event, though far in advance of the millenium, might be regarded as a pledge of the fulfillment of the prophecies bearing upon that time; and awaken hope and minister comfort in the later and darker days of the present time for example, on the basis of the principle in Romans 5:3, 4.

6. A sixth element is the ultimate punishment of that strong and ancient enemy Babylon, type of every other enemy, chapters 46-48. Sufficient space has been given to the consideration of this topic in the first part of the book.

7. The seventh and culminating element is the picture drawn by the prophet of their final restoration to the land, and the increased prosperity and

blessing forever resting upon them. See 49:13-26; 54; 55; 60; 62; 65; 66. It will require but a cursory examination of these chapters to discover such facts as the following, which are referred to again and again in different connections, for example:

(a.) The restoration is to be brought about by the aid of the Gentiles (49:22).

(b.) The nation's boundaries are to be greatly enlarged as well as its population (49:18-21).

(c.) It is in some way to have dominion over the other nations (60:12).

(d.) Its possession of the land is to be perpetual (60-21).

(e.) It is to be an object not only glorifying to God, but in which He Himself shall find joy (65:19).

The Messianic Prophecies.—In our study of the earlier historical books of the Bible, very particular attention was drawn to the prophecies of Christ contained in each one of them. This it is impossible to do with all the later books because of the multiplicity of such prophecies—some hundreds of them indeed. Only the principal ones, and those coming in the direct course of our synthetic outline can be noted. But one feature of them should be again mentioned, and that is, not only the way in which they increase in number, but develop in details.

The lines of the portrait are becoming more and more clearly defined with every touch of the Divine Artist's pencil. The seed of the woman became the seed of Abraham, and the line of Judah, in Genesis. Deuteronomy spoke Him as a prophet like unto Moses; Samuel described Him as a King sitting on the throne of His father David. And now Isaiah pictures Him in so many ways! He gives His virgin birth, His two-fold nature, His many names, human and Divine, His mission to Gentiles as well as Jews, His humiliation and His glory. It is hoped that the individual student, and especially the teacher of classes will fix earnest attention on this matter as so essential to the knowledge of the Savior's Person and work, an acquaintance with the teachings of the New Testament to follow, and as an armory from which to draw ammunition for the defense of the truth of the Bible and Christianity. If these things were spoken before they came to pass they must be Divine in their origin. If they meet and find fulfillment in Jesus of Nazareth and in Him only, He must be the Son of God and the Redeemer of the world.

CHAPTER XXX.

The Prophecies of Nahum and Zephaniah.

1. The Prophecy of Nahum.—I have done little original work on the four Minor prophets to follow in this and the next chapter, and acknowledge my indebtedness to The Bible Hand-book by Dr. Angus.

Isaiah concludes his work at about the end of Hezekiah's reign, which synchronizes with the captivity of the ten tribes of Israel by the Assyrians. At this period of perplexity, to quote Dr. Angus, "When the overthrow of Samaria (the capital of Israel), must have suggested to Judah many fears for her own safety, when Jerusalem (the capital of Judah), had been drained of its treasure by Hezekiah in the vain hope of turning away the fury of the Assyrians from her border, and when distant rumors of the conquest of a part of Egypt by the same great power added still more to the general dismay, the prophet Nahum was raised up by the loving-kindness of Jehovah to reveal His tenderness and power (1:1-8), to foretell the subversion of the Assyrians (1:9-12), the death of Sennacherib the Assyrian king and the deliverance of Hezekiah from his toils (1:10-15)." "The book," to quote the same authority, "thus becomes a striking illustration of the moral use of prophecy as seen in its fitness to console the saint of God and strengthen him for present duties." The name of the prophet, by the way, means consolation.

After the consolatory introduction referred to above and which covers practically the whole of chapter 1, the prophet proceeds to predict in detail, and in most glowing colors, the destruction of Nineveh, the capital of the Assyrian empire. Properly to grasp Nahum, therefore, one needs to compare it with Jonah already considered, of which it is a continuation and supplement in a sense. "The two prophecies form connected parts of the same moral history; the remission of God's judgments being illustrated in Jonah, and the execution of them in Nahum. The devoted city had one denunciation more given a few years later, by Zephaniah (2:13), and shortly afterwards (606 B. C.), the whole were fulfilled."

2. The Prophecy of Zephaniah.—As in the case of Nahum little is known of the personal history of Zephaniah beyond the two facts stated in the first verse of his prophecy, the first bearing very briefly on his ancestry and the second on the period of his ministry. About fifty years, more or less, have elapsed since the prophecy of Nahum, and Hezekiah has been succeeded by three of his descendants (see 11 Kings, chapters 20-21). Manasseh and Amon were very idolatrous and wicked, but Josiah who is now upon the throne, is righteous and God-fearing. The story of his zealous reign is given in the succeeding chapters of 11 Kings and should be read as preparatory to the study of this book, for Zephaniah, who prophesied doubtless in the earlier part of his reign must have assisted him very greatly in his efforts to restore the worship of the true God. To quote Angus:—

"The first chapter contains a general denunciation of vengeance against Judah and those who practised idolatrous rites; Baal, his black-robed priests (Chemarims), and Malcham (Moloch), being all condemned, and declares 'the great day of trouble and distress' to be at hand, (1-2:3). The second chapter predicts the judgments about to fall on the Philistines, those especially of the sea-coasts (Cherethites), the Moabites, Ammonites, and Ethiopians; and describes in terms wonderfully accurate the desolation of Nineveh; prophecies which began to be accomplished in the conquests of Nebuchadnezzar.

"In the third chapter, the prophet arraigns Jerusalem, rebukes her sins, and concludes with the most animating promises of her future restoration, and of the happy state of the people of God in the latter days (3:1-7, 8-20).

"Coincidence of expression between Isaiah and Zephaniah are frequent, and still more between Zephaniah and Jeremiah. It may be added that the predictions of Jeremiah complete the view here given of the devastation to be effected by Chaldaea in Philistia and Judah."

I cannot refrain from calling attention very particularly to the promises for the future as contained in chapter 3:8-20, and which show that although these minor prophets, so-called, refer but briefly to that period, (and yet perhaps in proportion after all, to the length of their discourses), still their deliverances thereupon are all in harmony with the teachings of the whole school of the prophets. For example, in verse 8, observe the agreement with Joel concerning the gathering of the Gentile nations to judgment at the end of the present age. In verse 9, we seem to see these nations, or the spared and sifted remnant of them, at length converted to God and serving Him with a ready will. In verse 10 they are bringing the sons of Israel back to their own land, the second gathering of them, so to speak, as was explained in Isaiah. In verses 11 to 18, the cleansed, humble, trustful, rejoicing, nation of Israel appears, dwelling in their own land. In verses 19, 20, we find the restored and beloved people a praise and a blessing in the whole earth as foretold in the original promise to Abraham, and again and again pictured before us in the Millennial psalms. Verse 17 of this chapter will well repay careful meditation. The old marriage covenant between Jehovah and Israel is there depicted as gloriously restored anew (Isaiah 62:5; Hosea 2:19); the Husband is rejoicing in His wife, resting in His love and joying over her with singing. The word for "rest" is translated in the margin "be silent," and this silence of Jehovah towards His people is no longer the silence arising from forbearance in order to punish at last (Psalm 50:21), but because He has nothing more to reprehend.

CHAPTER XXXI.

The Prophecies of Habbakuk and Obadiah.

I. The Burden of Habakkuk.—Absolutely nothing is known of the personal history of Habakkuk, and but little definitely as to the time when he prophesied. He is placed by some, however, as successive to Zephaniah, for he seems to make no mention of Assyria and yet refers to what would appear to be the approach of the Babylonian invasion. See such passages as 1:6, 2:3, 3:2, 16-19. The book seems undoubtedly to have been written by himself, as we may judge from 1:2, and 2:1, 2.

His "burden" begins by lamenting the iniquity of his people 1:1-4. He then declares God's purpose of raising up the Chaldean nation as a scourge against them, 5-10. The probability is that at this time the Chaldeans (or Babylonians) were still a friendly nation (see II Kings 20:12-19), but they were soon to march through the breadth of the land as a ravaging enemy. There were really three invasions by the Babylonians, as the second book of Kings showed us, in the reigns of Jehoiakim, Jehoiadchin and Zedekiah, and it is thought that in his description Habakkuk alludes to all three. Verse 11 of chapter 1 might be taken as a prophecy of the disease that came over Nebuchadnezzar when, as a punishment for his pride, his reason was taken from him for a season. The chapter concludes with an expostulation to the Holy One for inflicting such judgment, and especially for using a nation to inflict them less righteous, as the prophet thinks, than themselves.

In chapter 2, he awaits God's answer to this expostulation (verse 1), and receives it (verses 2 to 4). This answer is encouraging. "The vision shall surely come and the just shall live by faith and wait for it." The continuation of the chapter is a prediction of the judgments that shall fall on the Babylonians for their cruelty and idolatry.

"The prophet, hearing these promises and threatenings, concludes his book with a sublime song, both of praise and of prayer (chapter 3). He celebrates past displays of the power and grace of Jehovah, supplicates God for the speedy deliverance of His people and closes by expressing a confidence in God which no change can destroy."—Angus.

Particular attention is called to the words of the prophet in chapter 2, verse 3, which the inspired writer of the epistle to the Hebrews, according to the law of double reference, applies evidently to the second coming of Christ. See Hebrews 10:37, 38.

In the same manner notice the expression in verse 4 of the same chapter, "The just shall live by faith," and the application of it in such New Testament passages as Romans 1:17, 5:1, and Galations 3:24.

2. The Vision of Obadiah.—Obadiah, in all probability, received and delivered his vision at a much later period than the other seers grouped together in this lesson, but for convenience sake he is classed with them. Some think his period is shortly after the conquest of Judah by the Babylonians, and just before the conquest of Edom by the same world-power.

"Of all the nations who afflicted the Jews, the chief were the Assyrians, the Chaldeans and the Edomites; and three of the prophets were commissioned specially to pronounce their destruction. Nahum foretells the destruction of the Assyrians; Habakkuk, that of the Chaldeans, and Obadiah the destruction of Edom."

As Dr. Angus remarks, Israel had no greater enemy than the Edomites, though they were then close relatives.

"They were proud of their wisdom, verse 8, and of their rocky and impregnable position, verse 3. But the prophet foretells the uncovering of their treasures, and rebukes their unkind treatment of the Jews, their kinsmen, in rejoicing over their calamities, and encouraging Nebuchadnezzar utterly to exterminate them (Psalm 137:7); for all which an early day of retribution was to come; 'As thou hast done it shall be done unto thee," verse 15.

"But the chosen race themselves had just been carried into captivity; the holy Land was deserted; and the chastisement denounced against the Edomites might therefore appear not to differ from that which had already inflicted upon the seed of Jacob. The prophet, therefore, goes on to declare that Edom should be as though it had never been, and should be swallowed up forever, while Israel should rise again from her present fall; should repossess not only her own land, but also Philistia and Edom; and finally rejoice in the holy reign of the promised Messiah."

CHAPTER XXXII.

The Prophecy of Jeremiah.

The next of the major prophets after Isaiah is Jeremiah, for the history of whose times we must refer to II Kings 21-25. The last of the kings of Judah in Isaiah's time was Hezekiah, one of the very best kings Judah ever had, but he was succeeded by his son Manasseh and his grandson Amon, both of whom were men of a different stamp and in whose reigns idolatry flourished. The great world-power Assyria, which had just subjugated the sister kingdom of Israel and carried the people away into captivity, had menaced Judah for a long while, depriving her of many of her cities, and is only prevented from destroying Jerusalem itself, as we have seen, by the intercession of Hezekiah before the Lord. When Josiah, who succeeded Amon, came to the throne, and who was a faithful and righteous monarch, Judah was already tributary to Assyria and remained so practically, until Assyria herself succumbed to her rival Babylon, when her rights in Judah reverted to her great successor.

In the meantime, Josiah, who reigned thirty-one years, and whose period was marked by a great revival of religion, was succeeded by his son Jehoahaz, and later by another son, Jehoiakim, the first reigning but three months and the latter eleven years. The brief reign of the former is accounted for by the fact that at the close of Josiah's reign the nation of Judah had temporarily, and through the fortunes of war, slipped out of the hands of Assyria into those of Egypt, to which latter power Jehoahaz was not acceptable for some reason. It was during the time of Jehoiakim that the suzerainty returned to Assyria, and that the final transfer of power from Assyria to Babylon was made. While Jehoiakim was king, therefore, the nation paid tribute first to one foreign power and then another. At length, however, Jehoiakim refused to wear the yoke of Babylon, when the latter executed punishment upon her recalcitrant vassal by carrying some of her people into captivity, and among the young princes thus dealt with at the time was Daniel of whom we shall learn more later. Jehoiachin succeeded his father in the kingdom, but was set aside by Babylon in favor of his uncle Zedekiah, who reigned eleven years, but who was always restless under the yoke of Babylon, and whose schemes and conspiracies against his master finally led to the overthrow of himself and his kingdom, and what we have come to call distinctively the captivity. This was about 588 B. C.

Jeremiah was called to the prophetic office in the days of Josiah, and continued to prophesy down to the captivity, and indeed for some little time thereafter. His particular mission to Judah was to notify that nation of her rejection on the part of Jehovah (for the present at least), and of the divine purpose to transfer earthly dominion into the hands of the Gentiles. Now was to begin what is commonly known afterwards as "the times of the Gentiles," the meaning and significance of which will be treated of in the study of Daniel. Suffice for the present to say, that God's will for Judah was to submit to her enemy, in which event it would go well with her, but otherwise ill. Jeremiah was commissioned to make this will known, but in doing so was obliged to face a nation angrily opposed to such a conception. Kings, princes, priests and people were opposed to it. And there were false prophets among them that taught the very contrary to Jeremiah. As he pleaded with them to submit that they might abide in peace, or warned them that conspiracy against Babylon meant certain destruction and captivity, these others said, "Nay, enter into confederacy with Egypt and other nations, and you will overcome Babylon and break her yoke from off your neck." To the false prophets they hearkened with the results we know. But the hatred thus engendered against Jeremiah was intense in the extreme, and made his life the unhappiest of all the prophets.

The Personal History of the Prophet. —From the first chapter of the book we learn not a little of the personal history of the prophet. His father, Hilkiah, was a priest, hence he himself was in the order of Aaron and of the tribe of Levi, though he seems never to have exercised the office of the priesthood. His birthplace was the small town of Anathoth in the land of Benjamin, and his call seems to have been settled upon him even before his birth. He entered upon his life work at a very tender age, suggesting the history of Samuel, but reminding us that youth reached the period of maturity in the far East much earlier than with us. He was never married, for reasons given in chapter 16. His general experience was one of persecution and trial, but he remained among his countrymen until the blow fell, and even then stayed in Jerusalem with the remnant left by the hand of Nebuchadnezzar, until, for reasons clearly stated in chapters 40-45, he was forcibly carried away by them into the land of Egypt where, presumably, he died.

Jeremiah appears to have been naturally diffident and weak. God is several times obliged to stimulate him, not more with comfort than with sharpened threatening. But Jeremiah is loyal. He is thus kept loyal. No matter how weak and pleading he appears when in the presence of God alone, nevertheless, standing before the leaders of the nation, for the time his enemies as well as the enemies of God, he is brave as a lion, and commanding as a general in the field. It is the study of these changing conditions in the prophet's life that to many gives the keenest interest in the book. Jeremiah is very human, very much like one of us, and God's gracious and kindly dealings with him are a wonderful revelation of His love and power to us that believe.

The Outline of the Book.—You will have discovered by your reading of Jeremiah that the chapters are not arranged chronologically, some of the earlier ones chronicling events which transpired years after other events which are referred to in later chapters, so that it will be difficult to make an orderly classification of the book unless we take the chapters just as they come, ignoring the time feature except as it is mentioned in each case.

Chapter 1 gives us the prophet's genealogy and call, upon which we have dwelt sufficiently in the introduction.

Chapters 2-10, inclusive, are composed of discourses of the usual character illustrative of Judah's degeneracy and God's loving-kindness, in terms as vivid in the one case and tender in the other as are to be found in any part of the prophetic writings.

Chapters 11-12 are interesting as revealing an inner page of the prophet's own life in the persecution he underwent at the hands of his neighbors and kinsmen doubtless, in his native town. There is reason to believe also that the occasion marked a crisis not only in the life of the prophet, but in that of the nation as well.

Chapter 13 affords an illustration of prophecies in symbol with which Jeremiah's writings abound, and which usually tell their own story and explain themselves, as in this case. We have given an exposition of this use of symbolism in our lesson on Hosea.

Chapters 14-15 reveal the prophet as interceding for his people, suggesting the supplications of Abraham for Lot, Moses for Israel at Mount Sinai, Nehemiah for suffering Jerusalem and Daniel for his captive countrymen.

Chapters 16-17 refer to the prophet's separation from the people for the Lord's sake and for their sake as well, if only they will be influenced by his example to eschew sin and follow after righteousness. The attention of the class is called to the fact that throughout all these discourses, long or short, there is every now and then intimation of Jehovah's purpose to have mercy upon His people, Judah, in the end, and after they have learned the lessons of their suffering to awaken repentance in them and restore them to Himself. See, for example, in the present case, chapter 16, verses 14, 15.

Chapters 18-20 lead up to another trying and critical episode in the prophet's life where we find him as a consequence, sitting in the stocks at Jerusalem. It is not his neighbors and kinsfolk who are plotting against him now, but those who have the highest power in the kingdom. The provincial town of Anathoth is exchanged for the court city of Jerusalem, the rustics of his native village for the priests and the princes of the capital. But he is as brave and uncompromising in the latter situation as the former, and meets the harder trial here as it had been met there with the same fortitude and the same faith in God. But when he has been discharged by the court officers, and in turn has discharged his own commission to them from the throne of God, behold the reaction which comes upon his spirits as indicated in the language of his private closet recorded in the latter half of chapter 20! To quote our language on another occasion, we have here a striking illustration of the way in which God maintained Jeremiah's faithfulness. He placed him between two "Can-nots," or, if you please, between two fires. There was the fire of persecution without, and that of the Holy Spirit within, the latter being the hotter of the two. To avoid being consumed by the one, he was more than willing to walk through the other. "I can not speak any more in God's name," he says at one time, and follows it by adding, "I can not refrain from speaking." How many prophets in our own day have known a similar experience to that in verse 9! We have to thank God, however, that He did not leave His servant in this gloomy despair, and that Jeremiah was able to testify of his deliverance (11-13).

Discourses in Zedekiah's Reign, 21-24.—The first of these is that of the siege, or preferably, the Chaldean supremacy, 21: 1-10, in which it will be noticed the prophet urges submission to Babylon on the part of Judah in compliance with God's will, but as the sequel shows, without effect (8-10). The second is in the nature of judgments upon the disobedient kings of Judah, alive and dead, 21: 11-22: 30.

The third is on the theme so dear to the prophets, rather should I say so dear to God, the future redemption of Judah through the work of the Messiah, 23. This is very beautiful. Observe the charge against the false shepherds, the priests and prophets of Jeremiah's day, and yet one can not hesitate to class with them the scribes and pharisees of Christ's day, verses 1, 2. Observe the two distinct promises in verses 4 and 5, that of the restoration and that of the faithful shepherds, the true teachers of the coming age. Observe how the allusion to the faithful shepherds in general, leads up to the specification of the One True Shepherd in particular, Jesus Christ, verses 5 and 6. Observe the name here given Him. Observe how verses 7 and 8 establish the point that it is not an immediate return from Babylon that is here referred to, but an ultimate return from all countries, hence the restoration at the beginning of the Millennial age.

The fourth and last of this series of discourses is based upon the type of the good figs and the bad, and seems to apply particularly to the prophet's own time. Those who were carried away by Babylon in the earlier reign would return to their own land after the seventy years spoken of in a later prophecy, while those who would be taken in Zedekiah's time would not so return. Chapter 24. The language of verses 6 and 7 indicates, however, that this prophecy was only partially fulfilled in the restoration from Babylon, and antitypically and fully to be fufilled hereafter.

Discourses in Jehoiakim's Reign, 25-26.—The next division of chapters illustrates what was said at the beginning about the lack of chronological sequence in the book, as we are now to deal with events preceding those in our last division, since, as you know, Jehioakim reigned prior to Zedekiah.

The first discourse of importance here is that of the seventy years' captivity, chapter 24: 1-14, which is the first time in which that memorable period is distinctly stated. Then follows a discourse on the Gentile nations, chapter 25: 15-38, in which the point is again emphasized that God has given the dominion of the world for the time being into the hands of one of them, Babylon, to whom not only Judah but all the other nations of the earth must submit.

This division concludes (chapter 26), with an account of the prophet's second arrest followed happily, by his subsequent release. A few questions may be judicially employed here in the analysis or exposition of this interesting chapter.

In whose reign did the events in this chapter occur? In what public place was the prophecy delivered? What effect did it produce (8, 9)? Who were the instigators against Jeremiah at this time (11)? Who were his defenders (16)? What precedent was quoted in his favor (17-19)? What contemporaneous event emphasizes his narrow escape (20-23)? Who was raised up of God as his deliverer (24)? How does this escape of Jeremiah bear out the promise in chapter 1:18, 19?

Second Series of Discourses in Zedekiah's Reign, 27-34.—The first discourse in that which we call the second series in Zedekiah's reign may be entitled the Babylonian supremacy, chapter 27. The theme has been dealt with before but never at the length, or perhaps with the plainness it here receives. You will observe that it involves the subjugation of all the nations, Gentile as well as Jew. You will observe further that the prophecy seems to have been delivered at a time when these nations were in conference with Judah looking towards a coalition against Babylon probably, verses 1-3. God is exercising His absolute sovereignty in the matter and not giving account of His ways, verses 4-6. It is noticeable, too, that while He is using Babylon for His purposes at this time, her own time of punishment will come when the situation for her will in a great degree be reversed, verse 7. The command is absolute, and has a penalty attached to it, verse 8. It is to the advantage of Judah to submit, but she has false teachers who are persuading her against that policy, verses 9-11.

The second discourse in this series is really more of a personal controversy, chapter 28.

It has been evident as you read this book that one of the most trying experiences of Jeremiah was the contentions engendered by false prophets. What is the name of the false prophet mentioned in this case? How did he seek to make the most of his opportunity? Does he attack God's servant privately or publicly? How does he contradict his teaching (2-4)? How does Jeremiah reply (5-9)? How does Hananiah seek to further emphasize his false prophecy (10-11)? How does

God assure Jeremiah (12-14)? In what way does Jeremiah, thus assured, return to the battle (15)? What infliction upon the false prophet (16-17)?

The third discourse should more properly be characterized as a letter dictated to those who had already been taken captive, the occasion for and nature of which are plainly stated in the text. It covers chapter 29.

The fourth discourse is on the ever blessed theme of Judah's future redemption through Christ, chapters 30-31.

What is the first fact which distinguishes it from some other discourses (30:2)? Why is its Divine Author so particular about its form (3)? What experience for Israel must precede the restoration spoken of (5-9)? How is Israel distinguished from the Gentile nations in this respect (11)? Have we met with similar declarations to this in the former prophets? Name those prophets? The words of what other prophet especially are brought to mind by verses 18-22? When is this event to take place (24)?

Does this glad promise apply only to Judah, or the twelve tribes generally (31:1)? What is the ground of this promised goodness (3)? What will again be the center of worship in that day (6)? What indicates that it is more than the return from Babylon that is referred to (8)? What further substantiates the opinion that the time is still future (12-14)? What shows that it shall be preceded by the repentance of the people (18-20)? What shows that it will usher in a new dispensation (31-34)? With what oath does God confirm this promise (35-37)? How is the promise for the people identified with the land (38-40)?

All these facts are further impressed upon us by the proceeding recorded in the following chapter. I do not say that this chapter is a continuation of the preceding in matter of time, but it assuredly is in thought. Observe the introductory incident in verses 6-15, paying particular attention to the care shown by the prophet in witnessing the transaction referred to (12), and the reason for it all. It might, at first, be thought that this "reason" had a bearing only on what took place after the return from Babylon, but the sequel points very markedly to the future.

Jeremiah, for example, does not comprehend what he has been called upon to do in this case. Observe the surprise he expresses that, under all the circumstances, he should have been asked by God to purchase the field, and the inquiry he advances (16-25). Study God's reply to His servant (26-44). What significant question does He raise, verse 27? Has He changed His purpose about punishing Judah (28-35)? Nevertheless, what will be the ultimate outcome of that purpose (36-38)? What language (verse 37) shows that more than a re-gathering from Babylon is contemplated? What shows their conversion previous to the later blessing (39)? What shows the perpetuity of their final return to God (40)? What shows that the blessing is associated with the land (41)? What shows the pertinency of the purchase of the field as a prefiguration of that blessed day (43-44)?

The Closing Events of the Siege, 37-39.

—We must pass over the discourses in Jehoiakim's reign recorded in chapters 35-36, which, although deeply interesting in themselves, and revealing still more of the prophet's personal history, do not carry us forward any distance in our present plan of study. We come next, therefore, to the closing events of the siege, which, beginning at chapter 27, present us with the distressing spectacle of the prophet's imprisonment in the dungeon; chapter 28 is interesting as describing the anxiety of the king for counsel from the imprisoned prophet which, however, he has no intention of acting upon. "Whom the gods would destroy they first make mad," a proverb which Zedekiah illustrates to the full. At length in chapter 39 the city is overthrown, and the king himself and practically the whole of his people are carried away. The same chapter reveals the consideration granted to the prophet by the king of Babylon and his representatives, who are well aware of the character of his preaching and regard him as an ally and not an enemy.

Of course, however, his influence has been thrown in favor of the Babylonians or Chaldeans, not because of his interest in them, for he is a loyal and patriotic Israelite, but because of his desire to execute the will of God, sad as its immediate outcome for his nation may be.

The History of the Remnant, 40-45.

—After the assassination of Gedaliah, (whom the king of Babylon had made governor of Judea following the captivity), the remnant of the Jews through fear, desired to flee into Egypt, and consulted the prophet about it (chapters 40-41). What was the revealed will of God in the matter (42: 7-18)? Were the people disposed to obedience or disobedience (43: 1-7)? How did their conduct in Egypt compare with their previous history in Judah (44: 1-10)? What affliction is now pronounced against them (11-14)? Does this result in penitence (15-19)? What is Jehovah's final word to them by the prophet (20-30)?

The Discourses Against the Nations, 46-51:

—In the discourses concerning the Gentile nations with which the book closes, your attention is especially called to the prediction of the revival of Moab in the latter days (48: 47). And also Ammon (49: 6). Do you recall the origin of these peoples, and their relation to Israel? If forgotten, bring your concordance or Bible dictionary into use. Note also that a similar prediction holds good for Elam (Persia), (49: 39). It is remarkable, however, that while these old nations are to be revived, nothing is said as to their forgiveness and future blessing as in the case of Israel. The allusion to their revival brings to mind the teaching of Isaiah about Babylon. Note the particular attention Jeremiah gives to that city, chapters 50 and 51.

CHAPTER XXXIII.

The Prophecy of Ezekiel.

While Jeremiah was preaching and prophesying in Judah, Ezekiel was engaged in the same service among the Jews who had been carried into captivity by the Babylonians in the siege of Jehoiachin, see chapter 1:1-3. Like Jeremiah, he seems to have been in the priestly line, although never officiating in that capacity as far we know;

unlike Jeremiah, however, he was a married man, and one of his most solemn and affecting symbol-prophecies was in connection with his wife's death, 24: 14-18.

Ezekiel's name means "God is strong," or "hard," and there is a difference of opinion as to whether it represents the prophet's natural or official character, perhaps both. Chapter 3 : 8, 9, seems to favor the latter view, although in temperament also Ezekiel is apparently influenced more by zeal for God than sympathy for the suffering people, as was true of Jeremiah.

He began to prophesy in the period of Jehoiachin, as it would seem, and continued for several years after the final and complete captivity of his people, 40 : 1. The place of his earliest labors, the neighborhood of the river Chebar (1 : 1), was in upper Mesopotamia.

Introduction to the Book.—The following transcribed from "Our Hope," a monthly magazine devoted to Bible study, especially the prophetic word, will serve as an introduction to minuter analysis of the book to follow :

"The book of Ezekiel, like every other book, has perfect order in it. It is divided into three parts. The first part, chapters 1 : 24 ; the second part, chapters 25-32 ; and the third part, chapters 33-48.

The first twenty-four chapters contain prophecies which were delivered by him before the destruction of Jerusalem. The sins of Judah and Samaria are vividly described and the threatening judgment announced.

The second part contains the announcement of the judgment of seven nations and cities. These are : Ammon, Moab, Edom, Philistia, Tyre, Zidon and Egypt. These prophecies were given after the destruction of Jerusalem. The judgments upon these nations are prophecies of the judgment of nations in the day of the Lord. Read chapters 27, 28, and compare them with Revelation 18. Yet while Israel's enemies are destroyed and their destruction is announced, Israel's hope shines bright upon the dark background of divine judgment.

The third part is the richest of all. It concerns the future. God will regather His scattered people. Again and again He says, I will, I will. The vision of the dry bones in the thirty-seventh chapter is most instructive. Israel's grave will be opened, the dry bones will come together and live; as a great army they will return to the land. The last enemy is Gog and Magog, in finest harmony with all prophecy, the one coming from the North. The judgment of God and his associates is described in chapters 38 and 39. The book closes with the grand description of the millennial temple, when Jerusalem's name will be "The Lord Is There !""

I would change the above "introduction" only so far as to make four divisions of the book instead of three, ending the third part at chapter 39, and making a separate section of the description of the millennial temple. The latter doubtless belongs organically to the chapters immediately preceding, but for convenience of study perhaps it had better stand out by itself.

Analysis of Part One, Chapters 1-24. —The amount of attention given to some of the preceding prophets may warrant, even if it does not make desirable, a briefer treatment of the present one, especially since the drift of the discourses and their principles of interpretation in all the prophets, are the same. In the chapters now under consideration, therefore, we have :

1. The prophet's call and commission set before us in a series of four visions, chapters 1-3. Compare in this case, Isaiah 6.

2. Four symbols of coming judgment, chapters 4-5. The strangeness of this mode of teaching has worn off somewhat as the result of studying Jeremiah.

3. Two discourses containing rebuke, 6-7.

4. A vision of idolatry in Judah and Jerusalem together with a prediction of their punishment, 8-14. In this case it is especially significant that each class in the community is singled out for its own peculiar share of the coming judgments, as follows: the city itself, chapter 10 ; the princes, 11 ; the king, 12 ; the false prophets, 13 ; the followers generally of the false prophets, 14. In the study of these chapters observe particularly the discrimination between the innocent and the guilty in chapter 9. There is much "food for reflection" in this. It reveals God's justice in such a way as to bring terror to the heart of the impenitent, but comfort to the humble. Particular attention is called to the departure of "The Glory," the symbol of Jehovah's Presence from the temple and then from the city, in chapters 10 and 11, to which reference will be made again in a subsequent lesson.

5. Two symbols of iniquity, 15-16.

6. The riddle of the eagles and the vine, 17. Our previous study of Isaiah and Jeremiah has prepared us to understand and appreciate the application here to Egypt and Babylon on the one hand, and Judah on the other.

7. Six general discourses, 18-22.

8. The siege of Jerusalem, 24. During this period of three years, more or less, the prophet's lips seem to have been sealed with reference to his own pople, not to be opened again until the results of the siege had been attained

and his people had, as a whole, been carried to Babylon. It is during this period that we find him prophesying with reference to the Gentile nations. Verses 15-27 refer to this silence.

Part Two, Chapters 25-32.—Perhaps enough has been said, in general terms, on the subject of these judgments on the Gentiles when we have met with it in the former prophets, to warrant our passing very cursorily over this division.

But your attention should be called very particularly to chapter 28: 11-19, which under a reference to the Prince of Tyre, seems to point ultimately to Satan or his fleshly embodiment or representative, the anti-Christ. (Compare Daniel 7:25; 11:36, 37; II Thessalonions 2:4; Revelation 13:6). This is the judgment of the authors of the Bible Commentary and many other expositors, and is strongly corroborated by the similar language found in Isaiah 14, which we dwelt on at the time, and where the name of the King of Babylon was substituted for that of the Prince of Tyre. Those who would like a fuller consideration of the mysterious theme are directed to a lucid and interesting discussion in chapter 3 of Pember's "Earth's Earliest Ages." He makes a distinction, very properly, doubtless, between the Prince of Tyre in the first ten verses, and the King of Tyre lamented in the following ones. In the address to the prince there is nothing which could not be said to a human potentate; but the king is manifestly superhuman. You will have noticed, and will notice again, more particularly in Daniel, similar blendings of the description of two persons or two events in one, where it is difficult to determine where the allusion to the first ends and that to the second begins, i. e., the precise point of departure. With regard to the first ten verses, therefore, there is no reason, says our author, why we should not apply them to then reigning Prince of Tyre, whose name, as we learn from Josephus, was Ittiobalus, but the lamentation upon the King of Tyre does not so readily yield its meaning. "There are assertions in the latter which could be true of no mortal, not even of Adam, of whom we are not told that precious stones were his covering, and who was not called the Anointed Cherub, and of whom we do not hear that he was upon the Holy Mountain of God, and walked up and down in the midst of the Stones of Fire. Indeed, so far as we can see, there is but one being of whom some of these expressions could be used,

viz: Satan, although the remainder may be explained of the anti-Christ." That is his opinion, indeed, that part of this prophecy in verses 11-19 is to be understood as spoken to the human, and part to the Satanic part of the anti-Christ. Satan is a great counterfeiter. He has counterfeited the works of God, the wonders and signs He has wrought from the beginning, that, if possible, he might deceive the very elect. But his masterpiece is yet to come, when, at the end of this present age, he will rise to the alpine height of wickedness in counterfeiting the very Person of the Son of Man. There are more than mere intimations to show that the anti-Christ, when he appears at the summit of his power, will be Satan himself, incarnated for the time in a human being.

Part Three, Chapters 33-39.—The discourses in this division as outlined previously were delivered subsequent to the destruction of the city of Jerusalem by the Chaldeans, and, as growing out of that fact, chiefly announce its restoration. As in the case of all the other prophets, however, while this restoration may have a kind of foreshadowing fulfillment in the events of the return of Judah after the seventy years' captivity in Babylon, yet the text will not permit us to believe that it found its full and complete fulfillment then, but that it points forward to the Millennial Age. A brief outline of this division might be given thus:—

1. The prophet's lips are opened after their long silence concerning Judah and Jerusalem, 33:21.

2. This event is followed by a discourse on the Shepherd and His flock, 34, which suggests a similar one in Jeremiah already considered, and points us, beyond any manner of doubt, to the times of Jesus Christ, past and future.

Taking up this discourse more in detail, observe (1), the charge against the false shepherds, 1-6. However this may have applied to the false teachers in the earlier history of Israel, every reader of the Gospel will observe its perfect fit to the scribes and Pharisees of a later period; nor is it any strain upon the fancy to say that it applies to false teachers of Israel now, and that it will continue so to apply in an increasing ratio of intensity down (or up) until the time of the crisis, which may be near at hand.

But following the charge against the false shepherds comes (2), the prediction of their punishment, 7-10; and (3), the promise of blessing for the flock, 11-22; and (4), the promise of the advent of the Good Shepherd, 23-

31. No one can mistake the application of these last-named verses to Jesus Christ, nor can he mistake their application so far as the people of Israel are concerned, to a time not yet appearing in their history, but assuredly to come.

3. The discourse on the Shepherd and His flock is followed by another in which the blessing coming upon them is set forth by contrast with the judgments to fall upon Edom, 35. We have already seen who the Edomites are, and dwelt on some of the reasons why they should be singled out for special punishment on the ground of their treatment of the covenant people.

4. We have next a discourse on the moral restoration of the nation of Judah, 36. Study especially verses 25-38.

5. We have next, a discourse on their corporate or national restoration, 37. It is the consistent declaration of all the prophets as we have thus far seen, that the national restoration of Judah depends upon their moral or spiritual restoration which must come first. They will look on Him whom they pierced, and mourn because of Him. A fountain for sin and for uncleanness shall be opened in the house of David. A new heart will be given and a new spirit put within them. Then the prediction of this chapter, which is the prediction of a good many other chapters in this and in other prophets, shall come to pass.

Note that the resurrection spoken of here is not a resurrection of individual Jews, physically dead and buried, but a resurrection corporately, politically, so to speak, of the whole nation as a nation.

Note also that in that day, as we saw in Hosea, Isaiah and elsewhere, there will be a re-union of the ten tribes and the two, Israel and Judah, as one nation with the one King, the Messiah, who is sometimes called by the very name of David, verses 15-25.

The Place of Russia in Prophecy.—
6. We next reach an account of the destruction of the last Gentile power that shall come against Israel prior to her entrance upon perfect millennial blessing, 38, 39. This Gentile power is thought by many expositors to refer to Russia and her allies at the time spoken of, that time being coincident with the end of the present age and the introduction of the age to come. Perhaps the events referred to here may take place after the destruction of the anti-Christ and the nations of the Roman Empire, at whose head he will appear. This is anticipating a little what we are to learn from Daniel, but it seems necessary in order to introduce the present theme.

The arguments leaned upon to interpret these chapters of Russia are chiefly philological, as follows: The "chief prince" is translated in the Revised Version "the prince of Rosh," and in the Latin Version, I believe, "the prince of Russ," the similarity of which to the first syllable of Russia is apparent. "Meschech," in the same way, is taken to mean Moscow, and "Tubal," Tobolsk, capital cities of Russia. "Gomer" stands for Crimea, "Togarmah" for Turkey; "Gog" is the name of the highest peak of the Caucasus, and, indeed, the first syllable of the original word "Gogases."

It is out of the question to suppose that the prophecy has been fulfilled in any event which has yet happened to Israel because (1), of the reference to the "last days" or the "latter years" (38:8); (2), because of the military combination spoken of which the history of the world has not yet seen (4-7); (3), because of the conditions existing in Israel at the time, when the people will be dwelling in their own land quiet and secure (8-12).

The result of the conflict is the defeat and almost entire annihilation of the attacking force, see 38:18-23 and 39:9, 10, 13, 22, etc.

To say that there are no difficulties in the way of this interpretation or application would be very foolish; but there is so much to favor it not only in the text itself, but in the history and spirit of Russia as compared with the Western nations of Europe, and in the trend of current affairs as to seriously commend it to every thoughtful student of prophecy.

Part Four, The Vision of the Temple, 40-48.—To quote Dr. Andrews, "While all the prophets speak of the ultimate return of the remnant, and of the glory and blessedness of the Messianic kingdom, Ezekiel alone describes in detail the new order to be established. He was bidden to show the people the pattern of a new temple and of its ritual, and also to speak of a new division of the land. But the point to be especially noted is, that as he saw the departure of the visible glory of God from the first temple (9:3, 10:4, 18, 11:22), so he sees its return to this, the last temple, i. e., the temple of the millennium (43:2-7). Sometimes objections are made to this literal application of Ezekiel's vision, on the ground of the size of the building spoken of, the references to sacrifices and feasts as if incompatible with millennial conditions and worship and access to God, and certain topographical features of the city and surroundings. But these difficulties will not seem so great if it be remembered that neither Judaism nor Christianity as such is

being spoken of, but a new dispensation, dealing with restored Israel on this earth, and involving changes of immense magnitude and of various kinds."

CHAPTER XXXIV.

Summing up the Ante-Captivity Prophets.

In the reading of Andrews' valuable book already referred to, I have come across one or two chapters from which a few sentences or paragraphs might be culled and pieced together to make an interesting and instructive summary of the teachings of the prophets thus far considered, before we enter upon the epoch of the captivity in the study of Daniel.

Dr. Andrews points out that even Moses distinctly taught that there was a point in national transgression beyond which Divine forbearance would not go, and that the time might come when, through unfaithfulness to their covenant, the Jews would cease to exist as a nation and be scattered over the earth (Lev. 26, Deut. 28). This declaration of Moses we have seen repeatedly and distinctly announced by all the prophets with even increasing fulness as the time drew near.

While the judgment referred to in these prophecies was the deportation of the Jews from their land and their subjection to the heathen nations, yet it has a larger meaning. In establishing the theocracy, for example, Jehovah entered into two relations, first, that of King of the people, and second, that of Proprietor to the land. These relations were co-existent, and so long as He was their King. He dwelt in the land as His own, and His presence was their national preservation. Even if, for a time, He permitted their enemies to invade the land, it was for their punishment and reformation; but to permit them to be carried away to another land and His temple to be destroyed, was not compatible with His honor as their King dwelling among them. Therefore, when their sins had reached that degree that He must cast them out from their land, He Himself must first depart.

This departure of Jehovah from the holy city and temple as symbolized in Ezek. 10 and 11, was the determining condition of the captivity marking, as it did, a change in His theocratic rela-

tion to the people that continues even to this day. While they did not cease to be His covenant people (Lev. 26: 44), and His promises respecting the Messiah were not withdrawn and He continued to accept their worship, yet He was no more reigning at Jerusalem. Though the people returned from Babylon by and by and rebuilt the temple, still the change continued. They were never again an independent nation under His immediate rule. For a brief period under the Maccabees there was an assertion of freedom, yet the "eagles of Rome were already hovering over Jerusalem, and failing to discern Jesus as their Messiah, they ceased to be a people among the peoples of the earth." It is thus plain that the return of a part from Babylonian exile was not the end of the captivity, or in any full sense the restoration, which cannot be until Jehovah again dwells among them, ruling them through His King of the house of David.

Their partial restoration from Babylon had its purpose in affording an opportunity for the bringing of the Redeemer into the world by His birth of a virgin, and giving Him the opportunity to present Himself to them as their promised Messiah. Had they received Him He would have gathered them under His wings, but rejecting Him, they must again be visited with chastisement, and scattered among the nations till there should be found at last that remnant which should cry "Blessed is he that cometh in the name of the Lord." (Matt. 23: 39).

Our author quotes Prof. Alexander, who says that "however frequent the people seem to be destroyed there will always be a surviving remnant, and however frequent the remnant may appear to perish, there will still be a remnant of the remnant left, and this indestructible residue shall be the holy seed which God will plant in the land to be no more rooted out."

When this time shall come no one definitely knows, for the moral element overrules the chronological. In other words, God respects the free will of men, and though His purpose is sure to be accomplished, it must be through their voluntary co-operation. When, therefore, Israel repents and submits to the will of God this time shall come. What a stimulus, therefore, is there in such a thought for our prayers on behalf of Israel, that she may repent and receive Jesus, since so much of the glory of the church and the peace of the whole world are dependent thereupon!

The Period of the Exile.—Ezekiel and Daniel were the prophets of the exile. Among those who were carried captive with the former, there were many who did not believe that Jerusalem would be destroyed by the Babylonians and cease to be the dwelling place of Jehovah, and it was necessary, therefore, for the prophet to show them how unfounded their expectations were. We have seen him do this in the vision which shadowed forth the departure of the Visible Glory of God from the temple and the city before its overthrow (chapters 9, 10 and 11). This glory was the symbol of the Divine Presence on Mount Sinai, and wherever it abode there God dwelt. For example, when the tabernacle was set up in the wilderness His glory filled it (Exodus 40:34), where He continued to manifest Himself from between the cherubim until the temple was built. At the dedication of the latter, it also was filled with His glory (1 Kings 8:10), and notwithstanding all their subsequent idolatry and wickedness, He thus continued to dwell with the people until the captivity. At this time, when He was about to permit the destruction of the temple, His glory ascended first from the cherubim in the most holy place to the threshold of the house, and thence to the cherubim at the door of the east gate, finally leaving the city altogether and standing upon the Mount of Olives.

Ezekiel, as we have seen, tells us much of the religious condition of the exiles in Babylon, from which we learn that upon the larger part of them the captivity produced no effect. The evil influences around them infected them, and if they were repelled from idolatry in the grosser forms, yet their faith in their own covenant standing and in the promises of Jehovah was weakened. There were a few, however, animated with holy zeal whose feelings are well described in such psalms as the 137th, and it was those of this stamp who were returned at the close of the seventy years, and by whom the temple and city were rebuilt. Although Ezekiel refers to this return, yet, as we have already learned, his words looked beyond them and that event to the final remnant in the latter days, in whom the Messianic kingdom is to be set up and God's purposes fully realized. A holy and obedient people shall at last be found and God will dwell among them.

It was the prophet Daniel whose prophecies most influenced the popular mind during the captivity, and gave more definite form to their Messianic conceptions. It was he, as we shall discover in our next chapter, who first set forth the Messianic kingdom in its temporal relations to the successive great kingdom of the world. The earlier prophets had spoken of the relation of the Jews to the smaller states round about them, but Daniel was to teach them the place which the Messianic kingdom should hold in the series of the great monarchies. Four should precede it, while it should constitute the fifth and last. It should not be established until the counsel of God respecting the four world monarchies had been accomplished, and until that time the theocratic people must take a position of subjection. Moreover, their national deliverance was inseparably connected with the coming of the Messiah, and until He came, they would be exposed to great oppression and affliction from these successive monarchies.

This leads us, by the way of introdution, to the consideration of the contents of the book of Daniel itself.

CHAPTER XXXV.

The Prophecy of Daniel.

The last chapter or lesson contained as much of an introduction to the study of Daniel as may be necessary under the circumstances. Chapter 1 of the book known by his name gives his early history, and relates the facts of his captivity and his training for service in the court of Babylon. The story is very familiar even to children, and requires no special explanation. It is at the second chapter, and particularly beginning at verse 36, that the interest of these lessons begins. The interpretation of Nebuchadnezzar's dream teaches us several things about the history of the world from that date to the end of the present age which it is important for every student of the Bible and of God's providences to know:

1. It teaches that God, having cast aside His own people Israel for a time, has in the meantime committed all the power and dominion of the earth into the hands of the Gentiles, who, for the time being, were represented by the Babylonians, verses 36-38.

2. It teaches that after the decay of the Babylonion monarchy this power and dominion should be entailed to three other kingdoms in successive order, which subsequent chapters of the book, supplemented somewhat perhaps by secular history, show to apply to Persia, Greece and Rome respectively, 39-43.

3. It teaches that during the period of the fourth kingdom, Rome, God Himself would set up a kingdom, which would destroy earthly or human dominion altogether and in its turn last forever, 44, 45.

It is this kingdom of God which all the other prophets have been speaking of, which shall be set up in Israel again, penitent and restored, and over which the Messiah shall reign. A difficulty suggests itself in that the fourth kingdom, Rome, is not now in existence, but this difficulty is only apparent and not real. In the first place, the territory covered by that kingdom or empire, still exists, being identical with the nations of Eastern and Western Europe bordering on the Mediterranean sea; and in the second place, the subsequent teachings of our prophet show that these nations are to be gathered together again, federated under one head, the anti-Christ, at the close of the present age.

In the meantime, the terms of the prophecy before us, verses 40-43, very fittingly represent that fourth kingdom in its present condition. (1), It is strong, for assuredly no power, or powers, of the earth could stand against the united purpose of those nations which now exist within the former compass of the Roman Empire. (2), It is divided, the two legs of the image are symbolical of the Eastern and Western divisions, while the toes suggest the ten nations of which it is apparent the federation will be composed at the end. (3), It is partly brittle,

part of iron, and part of clay, in the sense that while these nations have in them the forms of monarchical government, they have also to a greater or less degree the spirit of democracy.

The Vision of the Four Beasts.— We may pass over chapters 3 to 6, inclusive, very briefly, since they are historical rather than prophetical in character, and carry their explanation on their face. In chapter 3 we have a manifestation of Nebuchadnezzar's pride in consequence of the revelation of his greatness just made to him, with the result of it to the faithful Hebrews. In chapter 4 there follows an account of Nebuchadnezzar's abasement by the hand of God in punishment of his pride, together with the salutary lessons it taught him. In chapter 5 the kingdom, or rather the world-dominion, has passed out of the hands of Babylon altogether into those of Persia. In chapter 6 Daniel, who has been pushed out of sight for a while, "turned down," as we would say in these days, comes into power against as the premier under Darius, and the president in almost supreme control, it would appear, of that part of the Persian domain formerly known as Babylon. In chapter 7, we have his vision which constitutes the next advance in the march of prophetic truth.

In the interpretation of this vision let the law of recurrence be kept in mind, for the ground covered is the same as that of Nebuchadnezzar's dream, except that here certain details are to be brought out or certain features emphasized which were not noticed before:

1. We have a hint as to the geographical location of these four world-empires, i. e., "the great sea" is referred to, verse 2. The Mediterranean in the historico-prophetic sense is the center of the world, and the ruler of its waters is the ruler of the world. The empires before us, each in its turn, had the possession of 'the great sea" as its goal, and when it reached that it reached world-dominion.

2. We have a hint as to the moral character of these empires in succession, inasmuch as they are represented by ferocious and voracious beasts, 3-10. The idea is that cruelty, and oppression, and selfishness in one form or another will prevail in these world-powers, and in increasing ratio, to the very end of the age. Particular attention should be called here to the third of these powers, Greece, represented by the leopard with the four wings and four heads (verse 6). The number four in this case points to the subsequent

division of the Grecian empire after Alexander's death, to which further reference is made in a later vision. The similarity of the symbolism in the fourth beast to the iron part of Nebuchadnezzar's image also, is emphasized very sharply both in its super-abounding strength and its ten horns.

3. We have a hint as to the reason for the destruction of these world-powers at the end, and the necessity for the setting-up of the kingdom of God on their ruins, verse 8. This necessity grows out of the fact that their iniquity and God-defiant attitude as concentrated in the "little horn," becomes at length intolerable.

4. We have a hint as to the circumstances attending the investiture of Christ with the earthly kingdom, 9-14. (1), There is a heavenly scene revealed, the thrones placed, God the Father seated, the books opened (verses 9, 10). (2), There is an earthly scene revealed, wickedness culminated, the world-powers (or power) destroyed (verses 11, 12). (3), A heavenly scene again, the glorified Son of Man in the presence of the Father receiving the kingdom (13, 14).

5. We have a hint as to the application of the whole in detail, 15-28. For example, we see (1), who are meant by the beasts (17); (2), the ten horns of the fourth beast (24); (3), we have a fuller description of the nature and history of the "little horn," including an allusion to the period covered by his personal power (24-26); (4), the saints of God are brought into prominence as fellow-possessors of the coming kingdom of Christ with Himself (27). Touching the period covered by the personal reign of the "little horn," "time" is thought to mean a year, "times" two years, and the "dividing" or half a time, six months, in all, three and a half years.

The Grecian Supremacy.—It will be seen that the second vision of Daniel now to be considered (chapter 8), was revealed to him two years after the previous one, although both date during the Babylonian period, and while Belshazzar was on the throne. It will be seen, too, that while in this case the law of recurrence applies as usual, yet there are only two kingdoms whose history is set before us out of the four. These two are the two middle ones, Persia and Greece, the most attention being given to Greece, verses 20, 21.

Two-thirds of the chapter about, are taken up with the description of the vision, the other third, especially verses 19-26, being devoted to its explanation and application by the angel.

1. Notice first, the time of its fulfillment, " in the last end of the indignation," "at the time appointed the end shall be." The Revised Version is, if anything, still plainer, "the latter time," "it belongeth to the appointed time of the end." This does not mean the end of the Babylonion period, or the Persian or the Grecian in the sense in which as world-monarchies they are now all past, but it means what we have come to understand those phrases, or that phrase, to mean in the other prophets we have studied, viz: the end of the present age or dispensation. And, if it be asked how the end of the age can be intended when the record of events mentioned seems to be continuous, and those monarchies as such have long since disappeared, the answer must be sought in what has been said on that point in this and in other studies which have preceded it. The Roman Empire in a very practical sense exists to-day in the nations bordering on the Mediterranean, of which empire the Grecian was, and still is and must continue to be, an integral part. It has been stated that, (according to prophecy to be considered still further when it is reached in these lessons), the Roman Empire, or the ten kingdoms of which it shall be constituted, shall at the end be federated under a single head, "the little horn," (the anti-Christ). But the federation of the Roman Empire carries with it and includes that part of it which was formerly known as the Grecian. This vision is to teach us, I think, that in the startling events of the end of the age, the Grecian division of the old Roman Empire shall bear a most conspicuous part.

2. Notice, secondly, that it is the history of the Grecian rather than the Persian monarchy which is dwelt on more at length in this case. The great horn between the eyes of the rough goat is identified by all historians and Biblical expositors as Alexander the Great (verse 21). The four kingdoms following his personal rule, and foreshadowed in the earlier vision by the four heads and wings of the leopard, are the four divisions of his kingdom consequent upon his death, and which were taken by his four leading generals (22). Attention is now released from the four to be concentrated upon one, and this one particularly "in the latter time," "when the transgressors are come to the full" (23). It is the king in this case who particularly commands attention.

3. Notice thirdly, that the description of this king here tallies very re-

markably with that of the "little horn" of the preceding vision, and suggests that the two may be identical. Observe his satanic vision, his intellectual acumen, his military power, his destructive and persecuting spirit, and especially his hypocrisy and deceit (23-25).

There was a king in the line of the Grecian monarchy, Antiochus Epiphanes, of Syria, B. C. 170, who in many particulars seemed to satisfy this description. So like was he, in his character and works, the picture drawn by the prophet in this book, that the destructive critics have even gone so far as to suggest not only that he was the man, but that these prophecies concerning him were written after the event. But it is not a very hard task to disprove this late date for the book of Daniel, while on the other hand, there are certain features in the text itself which go to show that Antiochus is not the fulfillment of the prophecy, however he may be regarded as a foreshadow or a type of the one who will fulfill it. These textual features are the period of time already spoken of, and the fact that he shall "stand up against the Prince of princes," when "he shall be broken without hand" (verse 25).

These observations may lead some to the conclusion that since this "king of fierce countenance" is apparently identified with the "little horn" of the former vision, the anti-Christ in other words, that therefore we may expect that archdeceiver to arise out of that part of the Roman Empire which was previously known as the Grecian? And such is my own opinion, given, however, only for what it is worth. Personally, I am of those who look somewhere in the region of Constantinople for the rise of the Antichrist, though I may be mistaken and have to change my mind on further observation and study. But in any event, the thing for us to do now is not to become entangled with the spirit of Anti-christ, but keep ourselves very loyal to our Head, the Lord Jesus Christ, by obeying His Word through the Spirit in all things.

The Restoration of Israel.—Thus far the visions recorded in the book of Daniel have dealt chiefly with the prophetic history of the Gentile nations, the four world-monarchies, but at chapter 9 Israel comes into view again, and in this way :—

Daniel had been searching the books of the earlier prophets, especially Jeremiah, and had become impressed with the fact that the time of the Babylonian

captivity for his people of Judah, the seventy years, was about accomplished. He then began to pray to God about it (1-3), with the result that an angel from Heaven was sent to reveal to him not only the circumstances of their immediate return, but their whole history in outline, down to the end of the age (20-23). This prophetic outline is found in verses 24-27 :

1. We are told in the first place, that a certain period of time is set off for these dealings of God with Israel. "Seventy weeks are determined upon thy people and upon thy holy city." The word for "weeks" in this case is "heptads," or "hebdomads," which means simply "sevens." "Seventy sevens" are determined, whether of weeks, or months or years is not definitely stated, but the context compels the last-named conclusion. Seventy sevens of years are 490 years.

2. The dealings of God are enumerated, and included in six particulars (verse 24), all of which point to a period not yet realized in Israel's history, and synchronizing with the incoming of the Millennial age. It is only then that their sins will be made an end of or hidden out of sight, that the visions of the prophets will be confirmed by their complete fulfillment, and a normal relationship between them and God be brought about through everlasting righteousness.

3. This period of 490 years is divided again into three periods of uneven years, (1), seven *weeks,* or 49 years, (2), sixty-two *weeks,* or 434 years, (3). one *week,* or seven years (verses 25-27). It begins to be reckoned at the time of the "going forth of the commandment to restore and to build Jerusalem." This may mean the seventh year of the reign of Artaxerxes, King of Persia, when Ezra returned to Jerusalem (457 B. C.), or it may mean the twentieth year of his reign, when Nehemiah was granted authority to rebuild the walls, probably the latter.

The first seven *weeks,* or 49 years, are usually regarded as the time during which Jerusalem was restored under Ezra and Nehemiah. "The second sixty-two *weeks,* or 434 years, begins at the close of Nehemiah's period, and leads us to that of Christ, who was "cut off" crucified, "but not for Himself." This last phrase is in the Revised Version rendered, "and shall have nothing." That is, the earthly kingdom anticipated by the Jews would at that time not be realized, it would come to' nought. Moreover, the city and sanctuary should themselves be destroyed, as was fulfilled at the time of the Roman siege, under Titus, A. D. 70.

The last one week of years has not yet come into sight, but shall be coincident with the culmination of the age. To understand this we should keep in mind that Israel has no history as a nation except as the people are in their own land in a national capacity of some sort, and in fellowship with God. Time ceased to be counted or recognized towards them as a nation from the day Jerusalem was destroyed by the Romans, and their national life dissipated, down to this day. Nor will it begin to be reckoned again until they are once more restored to Jerusalem and take up their national life somewhat as before. This time is coming, as all the prophets testify, and it is with reference to this time particularly that Daniel speaks in verses 26 and 27.

4. The last week, or the closing seven years of the period, is marked by the actings of the Antichrist. He is first referred to in verse 26, in the allusion to 'the people of the prince that shall come." These "people" were the Roman people who destroyed "the city and the sanctuary" A. D. 70; but "the prince that shall come" is the Antichrist who has been frequently described in the earlier chapters of this book, and whose people shall be the Roman people, i. e., the federated nations of the old Roman Empire at whose head he shall appear. He "shall come" in the God-appointed time for him to come.

We are confirmed in applying this designation to the "prince" here named, by the translation given in the Revised Version of the words following. Where the King James' says, "And the end thereof shall be with a flood," as if applying to the catastrophe of the destruction of Jerusalem, the Revised puts it "And his end shall be with a flood," referring not to the end of the city but the end of the prince. This shows very clearly that the word "prince" applies neither to Christ nor Titus, but to the Antichrist.

He, i. e., "the prince that shall come," the Antichrist, "shall confirm the covenant with many for one week," i. e., seven years (verse 27). The "many" spoken of applies to Israel. This people are now supposed to be returned to their own land, and established in some sort of national position, perhaps under the suzerainty of the Sultan of Turkey, as at present hinted at by the leaders of the Zionist movement so-called. They have re-built their temple and are worshipping Jehovah somewhat after the pattern of their fathers, but as yet unconverted so far as the acceptance of the Messiahship of Jesus is concerned. This is the moment when the words of Jesus shall be fulfilled, "I am come in My Father's Name, and we receive me not; if another shall come in his own name, him ye will receive" (John 5 : 43). They are getting ready to receive him, i. e., the Antichrist who is coming in his own name. Now are they about to make that "covenant with death," and 'agreement with hell" of which Isaiah spoke (28 : 15). The Antichrist, whoever he may be, in power and authority in the East, will make a covenant with them, a political understanding doubtless, leaving them at liberty to continue their outward allegiance at least to Jehovah. This covenant shall be confirmed with "many." The majority in the nation will favor it, but there will be a minority who will be suspicious of it and protest against it. The terms of this covenant are to maintain for seven years, but in the midst of that period, or within three and a half years, the tyrant will break the bonds thus entered into, denying to Israel freedom of worship, causing "the sacrifice and oblation to cease;" and "upon the wing of abominations shall come one that maketh desolate (i. e., the Antichrist himself), and even unto the end, and that determined, shall wrath be poured out upon the desolator." This last quotation will be seen to have been taken from the Revised Version. It tallies with the utterance of Jesus, where, in referring to the tribulation of Israel in the last days, coming from the hands of this great deceiver, He employs the language of Matthew 24 : 15, and the following verses.

The King of the North.—The closing chapters of Daniel, 10-12, bring us back again to the history of the Gentile kingdoms, and especially that of Greece. We have seen in the vision of the ram and the goat, chapter 8, that the last-named kingdom, on the death of Alexander, was divided into four parts among his four generals. The history of one of these parts, or one of these four kingdoms, was then pursued through the line of its kings until one was reached who was notoriously wicked and God-defiant. This was in the prototype, Antiochus Epiphanes, king of Syria, who oppressed the Jews in Jerusalem and polluted their temple about B. C. 170, or near the period of the Maccabees. But in the antitype this wicked king was seen to be the Antichrist himself who at the last shall stand up against the Prince of princes and be broken without hand.

Now, in the chapters under present consideration, we have this ground again covered on the principle of recurrence, giving us further details of the history both of the prototype and antitype, down to the period of crisis already touched upon several times, and elaborated somewhat in the prophecy of the seventy weeks. Chapter 10, which, while very interesting and important in itself, is nevertheless introductory, may be passed over for the present. The outline of chapters 11 and 12 is about as follows:

1. We have a brief account of the Persian and Greek supremacies from Daniel's own time, down to the period of the Greek division, 11 : 1-4.

2. We find that in this Greek division there are two of the four kingdoms which come in for all the prophetic treatment, the other two being unmentioned. These two which are emphasized are the Southern kingdom, Egypt, and the Northern, Syria. War is almost continuous between these two with varying fortunes. At first the king of the south is pre-eminent (11 : 5-8), but finally the king of the north prevails (9-20). It is perhaps hardly necessary to say that this brief prophetic outline found a most literal fulfillment in the history of these kingdoms down to the time of Antiochus Epiphanes.

3. We have the history of Antiochus set before us in some detail, especially as to his actings towards the Jews and Jerusalem B. C. 170 (verses 21-35). But at the very moment when we reach a kind of climax in his affairs our thoughts are carried off to another king (verse 36), who is neither the king of the north or the south (verse 40), but who seems to have been foreshadowed by the former. This, person, it is believed, is the Antichrist again, whose last campaign is outlined for us in verses 40-45, and who "shall come to his end, and none shall help him," just as we have seen in all the preceding prophecies concerning him.

As a further confirmation of the fact that we are here dealing with this person and the events at the end of the age, attention is called to the opening verses of chapter 12. Michael, the archangelic defender of Israel, is seen; the latter is passing through the tribulation, but the remnant is being delivered, thank God. A resurrection scene is brought before us (verse 2), which seems to coincide with that of the saints, the first resurrection, mentioned in Revelation 20, and the Millennium has begun.

CHAPTER XXXVI.

The Book of Ezra.

We have already seen that the Babylonian captivity did not bring the Jews to national repentance, and so lead to national restoration. As the reading of Ezra will disclose, when Cyrus, king of Persia, gave permission to the captives to return to Jerusalem and re-build the temple, scarcely 50,000 availed themselves of the privilege, a considerable proportion of whom were priests and Levites and of the humbler and poorer class. And although the number and influence of these vastly increased in time, yet at no period, with a single brief exception, did they ever regain their political independence. They were always thereafter a subject people, and under the government of heathen rulers of one kind or another. This accounts for the rising influence of the priesthood, the only possible office under the Mosaic institutions. To quote Andrews, we are to remember that this restoration did not carry with it a re-establishment of the original theocratic relation. Jehovah was no longer their King as of old, nor did He return to dwell among them. They had a continuation of national existence, but on a lower plane than before. By faithful obedience they might have hastened the return of Jehovah and the establishment of the Messianic kingdom, but this, as we know, was not true of them. "Zerubbabel, who led up the first company of returning exiles from Persia, or Babylon, was the last prince of the house of David, and the royal family then sank into obscurity. The High Priesthood continued for a time in the line of Joshua, the contemporary of Zerubbabel, but afterwards passed into the hands of strangers; and the spirit of prophecy, as well, quenched by disobedience, was silent for centuries." These remarks lead to the consideration of the book of Ezra which gives the account of the return and the events immediate following.

Word Outline of Ezra.—The proclamation of Cyrus, 1.

The company of Zerubbabel, 2.
The re-building of the temple, 3.
The opposition of the adversaries, 4.
The renewal of the work, 5-6.
The company of Ezra, 7-8.
The national reforms, 9-10.

It is unnecessary to dwell at length on this book, as it tells its story so very plainly. Let us notice, however, that the chief national purpose accomplished at this time was the re-building of the temple, and this amid strong opposition from their heathen environment. It was because of this opposition, plus a coldness and selfishness on the part of the people themselves, that the cessation of the work lasted for fourteen years. This coldness and selfishness gave occasion to the pungent discourses of the prophets Haggai and Zechariah, whose books are next to be considered in this course as contemporary with the period of Ezra.

It should be observed also in passing that the Jews on their first return showed that they were not so entirely cured of idolatry by their Babylonian experience, but that they again dallied with temptation in the form of intermarriages. This was the motive of Ezra's reform movement. "Gradually, however, they became more and more strictly monotheistic, as in Jesus' day, looking with increasing abhorrence upon idols and idolatrous worship."

CHAPTER XXXVII.

The Prophecy of Haggai.

When the handful of Israelites returned from Babylon, or the land of Persia, as it might now be called because that people were now in power there, the great task set before them was the re-building of the temple to restore the worship of Jehovah. We have seen the difficulties that confronted them, fewness of number, scantiness of means, boldness of opposition from external enemies, and above all perhaps, an inward conviction of sin concerning the past which robbed them of that joy of the Lord which is our strength (Nehemiah 8:10). Under these conditions the work flagged. The people lost heart through lack of faith in God, and sin and selfishness began to creep over them. They gradually grew careless concerning the Lord's House, and correspondingly interested in their own houses. God's love for them could not permit this to continue, and hence chastisements followed. Finally, when repentance began to take hold of their hearts, the prophets Haggai and Zechariah are sent to them, whose words of instruction and cheer, accompanied by the power of the Holy Ghost, awakened a revival that results in the happy accomplishment of the work.

It is evident, however, that these instructions and encouragements have ultimate reference and application, not to the period then present, but as in the case of the earlier prophets, to the period yet to come when God shall "create Jerusalem a rejoicing and his people a joy" (Isaiah 65:18). This will appear as we proceed in the exposition of the books, more particularly Zechariah.

The Book of Haggai.—The book of Haggai consists of four discourses the time of whose delivery is stated in each case. The first is co-terminus with the first chapter. What was its date (1:1)? To whom, directly, was it addressed? What charge does it lay upon the people (2)? While neglecting the Lord's house on the ground that a propitious time had not arrived for its completion, of what had they not been neglectful (3)? What word in that verse indicates that they had been taking exceptionally good care of themselves? What solemn adjuration is used in verse 5? What chastisements had fallen on them (6)? What simple and practical remedy for the situation is laid before them (8)? How is their affliction shown to be a direct judgment from the Lord (9-11). What was the effect of the message upon the leaders and the people generally (12)? How did the Lord respond to this repentance in blessing (13)? What explanation of this ready obedience on the part of the people is given (14)? How far did the repentance of the people extend (14)? About how much time was covered by these incidents (verses 1 and 15 compared)?

The second discourse is included in verses 1-9 of chapter 2. How long after the first discourse did it follow (1)? To whom addressed (2)? For the historical point of contact in this discourse examine the record in Ezra 3:8-13. When the foundation of the temple was laid very painful emotions were excited in the breasts of the older men by the sad contrast between the prosperous circumstances in which the foundations of the first temple had been laid under Solomon, and the desolate reduced condition of things at this time. How inferior the size and costliness of the stones in this instance, how much smaller the extent of the foundation itself, how limited their means! And then this second temple would be destitute of those things which formed the great and distinguishing glory of the first, viz: the Ark, the Shechinah, or visible glory of God, and the Urim and Thummim through which communication was had with the high priest on the part of Jehovah. Not that this second temple was not a very grand and beautiful structure, but only that howsoever great its material splendor, it was still inferior to that of Solomon. In what language does the prophet refer to the emotions caused by this contrast (3) In what language does he encourage the leaders and the people generally under the circumstances (4-9)? They hesitated about going on with the work through dread of the world-power of that period, Persia, influenced by the craft of Samaria. But it would not be long before that world-power, and for that matter, all other world-powers would fall before the might of God.

"The Desire of All Nations Shall Come."—The expression at the head of this paragraph has usually been taken as a personal reference to the Messiah. He came subsequently into the house they were now building, and that fulfilled the prophecy, "I will fill this house with glory, saith the Lord," as well as the other words in verse 9.

This prophecy, however, takes on still more importance if we consider the reference to it in Hebrews 12:26. At that place the inspired writer is comparing the heavier punishment awaiting the disobedient under the New Testament with that of the Old Testament. At the establishment of the Sinaitic covenant only the earth was shaken to introduce it, but now Heaven and earth and all things are to be shaken that stand in the way of the Messiah's kingdom that "can not be shaken." In the judgment of some, the two parts of this chapter of Haggai are here brought together, verses 6 and 7 with verses 21 and 22, implying that it was one and the same shaking, of which the former verses denote the beginning, and the latter the end. The shaking began introductory to the first advent, and will be finished at the second. Concerning the former, see Matthew 3:17; 27:51, 28:2, Acts 2:2, 4:31 and concerning the latter Matthew 24:7, Revelation 16:20, 18:20, 20:11. As Sir Isaac Newton said, "There is scarcely a prophecy of the Messiah in the Old Testament which does not, to some extent at least, refer to His second coming."

But we hasten to the third discourse, verses 10:19. How long after the second was this revealed? What question is the prophet to ask, and to whom (11, 12)? What was the answer received? "Holy flesh" here refers to the flesh of sacrifices which, while it made ceremonially "holy" the "skirt" in which it was carried, could not impart that holiness to anything beyond. This is used to illustrate that the sacrifices which the nation was offering at this time, while "holy" in the sense that they had been appointed by God and represented divine truths, could not, nevertheless, make them who offered them holy while they were living in disobedience. There was no inherent grace that could be communicated by them through the mere act of their presentation. For these sacrifices to be the means of spiritual blessing to the people just now the latter must cease their neglect with reference to the building of God's house.

What second question was the prophet to ask (13) And the answer in this case? The interpretaion follows in verse 14. "Legal sanctity is not so readily communicated as legal impurity. The paths to sin are many, the path to holiness, one. One drop of filth will defile a vase of water, but many drops will not purify a vase of filth." The offerings of the people, being diligently presented on the altar erected in the open air before the temple was built, could not make them acceptable to God, because of their disobedience in failing to complete that temple. In fact, those offerings were themselves being made unclean through the uncleanness, disobedience, of the people. But how does verse 15 show that a change had taken place in their spirit and actions? The people had now begun to build on the foundations previously reared and God had begun to bless them (verse 19, last clause).

They could see no visible signs of the blessing as yet, but it was in operation in the earth in their fields, and vines, and trees, and when harvest-time came they would know that God had done it. In days gone by, while living in disobedience, they had often, in harvest-time, expected to gather a heap of twenty measures in a field where they got no more than half of it; and fifty vessels of wine were looked for out of the press, and they only got two-fifths of the quantity. Everything was against them in those days, and yet they did not see the cause of it all to be their own sin (16, 17). But it would be different now. Let them remember the date well (18). It was the date when they really began to serve God in earnest, and showed their faith by their works. Harvest-time had not yet come, the seed was in the ground and not in the barn, the trees and vines had not yet blossomed, nevertheless, "From this day will I bless you" (19). God begins when we begin. There is a great lesson here for ourselves and for the people we teach.

Zerubbabel's Resurrection. — The fourth discourse concludes the book, and seems to have been given on the same day as the preceding one (verse 20). To whom is it particularly addressed (21)? What indicates that however the prophecy may have applied approximately to Zerubbabel's own time, its ultimate application is yet to come (22)? Reference having already been made to these verses they need not be dwelt upon again. But what about Zerubbabel personally, "in that day" (verse 23)? That he will be raised from the dead we all know, but is he to stand in that day in some representative capacity before Israel literally as a witness and testimony to this promise? There are those who believe this, but I am inclined to think with another, that he is here alluded to as the representative of the Davidic family and type of the true David to come, i. e., Jesus Christ our Lord. He was chief of that family at this time, as we saw previously, and this promise was to assure him that God remembered his covenant with his forefather, and that it would be fulfilled.

CHAPTER XXXVIII.

The Prophecy of Zechariah.

The introduction of Haggai, in the last chapter, will serve sufficiently for Zechariah who was contemporary with him. Zechariah, like Haggai, had really a two-fold mission, to strengthen the hands of Israel in the time being for the rebuilding of the temple, and to quicken their hope as the earlier prophets had done, by painting in glowing colors the coming time of perpetual blessing and triumph over every foe.

This two-fold mission of the prophet is set before us in a two-fold division of the book. Chapters 1-8 give us a series of prophetic visions bearing primarily, though not entirely, upon the prophet's own time, while chapters 9-14 deal chiefly with the events culminating at the end of the age and the opening of the millennium.

Part one, after the introduction, chapter 1 : 1-6, might be outlined thus:
1. The prophetic visions, 1-6.
    The man among the myrtle trees.
    The four horns.
    The four smiths.
    The measuring line.

The high-priest in the temple.
The golden candlestick.
The flying roll.
The woman in the ephah.
The four chariots.
2. The symbolic crowning of the high priest, 6.
3. The instruction about fasting, 7-8.

The First Four Visions, 1-2.—To understand the first vision is to get the key to all the rest. When was it received by the prophet? Chapter 1 : 7. Describe what he saw (8). Observe that two persons are referred to here, the man upon the red horse, and the angel that talked with Zechariah, sometimes called the "interpreting angel." The man on the horse seems afterward identified with "the angel of the Lord," verses 11, 12, which is one of the Old Testament names for Christ. It is presumable, of course, and indeed the context makes it necessary to suppose that the other horses had angelic riders also. Who are these described to be (10)? What report gave they of the earth (11)? Prosperity and peace, in other words, seems to have been characteristic of all the peoples of the earth, while Jerusalem, however, was distressed, the temple unfinished, and the remnant of the Jews there persecuted by enemies. Who now intercedes on behalf of Jerusalem and Judah (12)? Is the answer of Jehovah encouraging or the opposite (13)? What was His answer in detail (14-17)? Was the peace and prosperity of the Gentile nations an evidence necessarily of the Divine blessing upon them (15)? Jehovah had used them to chastise and discipline His people, but what shows their own selfish and wicked intent in the premises (same verse)? What does Jehovah promise shall be accomplished by the little remnant at this time (16)? What of the future (17)? I need not pause to point out how this was fulfilled in the history of God's people at the time, in a measure at least. The temple was built, the cities were restored, and Jerusalem and Judah were comforted. And yet I am quite in accord with those who believe that there is to be a complete and grander fulfillment in the days to come. The two following visions , if we shall call them two—the four horns and four smiths (Revised Version), are closely connected with the one just considered. The four horns are identified as the four world-powers (Babylonian,Persian, Greek and Roman) who are to scatter Israel, but the four smiths are four corresponding powers of some sort, not necessarily nations, which shall overcome them at the last and bring deliverance. We are almost necessarily shut up to the conclusion that this prophecy extends to the latter days by reason of its reference to the whole of the four powers. The next vision, that of the measuring line, presents no serious difficulty. Its significance explained (chapter 2 : 4, 5), is seen to be the same practically as that of the man among the myrtles. However it may have had an approximate fulfillment in the prophet's own time, verses 10-13 indicate that it looks toward the future. What declaration in those verses seem to prove that?

The High Priest and Satan, 3.—To understand and appreciate the meaning of the vision now reached, one should keep in mind that a cause of dejection on the part of the Jews at this time was their consciousness and conviction of past sin. They felt, as was previously stated, that God had forsaken them, and that their present sorrow and numerous calamities were the result of that fact. We see herein a parallel to the spiritual condition of many a true believer in our own day, whom Satan torments with the belief that he is not saved, and cannot be saved on account of his many and black sins. Indeed this very thing is now set before us in symbol, only that there is a nation in the case here, and not merely an individual, for Joshua the high priest represents the whole of Israel.

Where is the high priest seen to be (3 : 1)? It is thought by some that he was represented as in the holy place ministering at the altar. Who is seen to be with him, and for what malign purpose? We have here in symbol, the idea of Satan's temptation of the saint to doubt God's goodness and power to forgive and save. How is this goodness and power shown, however, in the next verse? On what ground is Jerusalem to be saved, on that of merit or of the Divine choice? What does verse 3 teach as to the truth of Satan's insinuation against Israel as represented by the high priest? Does the imagery indicate the holiness or sinfulness of the people? Yet how is Divine grace illustrated in the next recorded command of Jehovah (4)? What did the removal of his filthy garments signify? What did the changed raiment signify? Compare Romans 3 :22. What next was done (5)? By this act the clothing of the high priest was completed and he was fitted for his official service, as before he was not. Who is represented as "standing by" all this time as if interceding for Joshua (and through him for the nation), and to see that these commands were carried out and these benefits conferred? With whom have we identified "the Angel of the Lord?" What charge is now laid upon Joshua, and what privilege is connected with it (7)? I quote here in part from a commentary on Zechariah, by A. C. Gaebelein. He applies the prophecy mainly to the last times, and says: "In analyzing this charge, we see clearly what Israel's earthly calling is and wherein her millenial glory and work will consist. (1) Judging in the house of the Lord, and from there ruling and judging the nations. (2) Keeping the Lord's courts. In the new millenial temple there will be ordinances, and that temple will be a house of prayer for all nations. (3) She will have places to walk among the ministering angels." In explanation of this last remark the author reminds us that Israel's cleansing will take place in that day not in Heaven, but on the earth. The church will be above occupying the many mansions, sitting with Christ on the throne, the glorified Head over all. The angels will be ascending and descending upon Him in service both earthly and Heavenly (John 1 : 51), and among these Israel may have a place. Her place being that of ministry to the nations.

What language in verse 8 would seem to indicate that the restoration and blessing of Israel in that day will be regarded as miraculous? What language in the same verse connects it with the manifestation of the glory of Christ? What other prophet in particular speaks of Him by the name of the Branch? What would lead us to suppose that the following verse (9) also refers to Christ? Can you name any other passages in either Testament that speaks of Him under the figure of a Stone? The commentary above referred to, however, regards this verse as meaning "Israel restored, and as such, the nucleus of the kingdom of God and His Christ on this earth." This is so judged because of the closing words "I will remove the iniquity of that land in one day." This whole story of Joshua standing before the Angel of the Lord affords material for a precious Bible-reading or Gospel sermon. As. Rev. W. J. Erdman puts it, it gives us a picture of the sinner;—chosen, cleansed, clothed and crowned.

The Golden Candlestick, 4.—

The Christian church is doubtless more familiar with the symbol of the golden candlestick than any other in this book, for which reason it will require but little consideration here. The candlestick was evidently a copy of that in the early tabernacle, but with what difference (verse 2)? From what source was its oil supplied (3)? What did this supply of oil from the trees symbolize (6)? The candlestick itself may be said to represent the temple which the Jews were now essaying to build, or for that matter, the Jewish nation as a whole which was now sought to be re-established on its former basis and thus become a light in the world. The difficulties in the way of accomplishing these things seemed insuperable, and were so indeed if the strength of man only should be considered, but God would interpose, and His Spirit would do what human agencies could not do. How is this difficulty and its removal figuratively expressed (7)? How is the figure explained (8-10)? On what particular point did the prophet desire further light (12)? What reply was made to him (14)? By these "two anointed ones" is sometimes understood Zerubbabel and Joshua, the leaders of Israel at this time on whom, and

through whom in a sense, the Holy Spirit would be poured out for the successful termination of the work.

Of course it is quite proper to use this symbol in an accommodated sense as applying to the church of the present day in its testimony and work; in which case the "two anointed ones" may be taken to represent any who especially "filled with the Spirit" are executing the Lord's will in power. At the same time also it is to be steadily kept in mind that the whole thing applies primarily to Israel, not only in the time of Zechariah, but in the last times when through the blessing of the Spirit, as we have seen, she shall be restored, cleansed, forgiven, and become a joy and rejoicing in the earth. It is proper to add as well that the deeper meaning of verse 14 is probably Christ Himself, "The Priest upon His throne," who will supply Israel as He now supplies the church with His own Holy Spirit!

The Flying Roll and the Ephah, 5.—

The two visions in chapter 5 are perhaps as mysterious as any in the book, and like that of the four chariots which follows in chapter 6, they seem to express the idea of judgment. That the "flying roll" has that significance would seem plain by a comparison with Ezekiel 2 : 9, 10, and Revelation, chapters 5 and 10, where similar figures have such meaning. We have seen hitherto that judgment is certainly coming upon the Gentile nations, and that Israel also is to be purified before she is finally restored, and it may be that to both these facts the present vision applies.

What is now seen (6)? An ephah or measure may fairly be taken as an emblem of trade or commerce. What was seen sitting in the ephah? What is the woman said to symbolize (8)? The whole figure then represents wickedness in commerce. What is now done with the ephah and whither is it carried? The land of Shinar at once suggests Babylon again, of whose revival in the latter days mention has already been made. Every one knows that commercialism is very prominent in Revelation 18 as the climax of ungodliness. It will be well to read that chapter in connection with Habakkuk 2 : 12, and James 5. Babylon is real, and the woman is the commercial spirit that will reign there at the end. The same spirit of self that prevailed in the early Babylon of Genesis 11, will build up and prevail in the last Babylon of Revelation 18. The description day will in the one to come, Israel of the Babylon of Nebuchadnezzar's

14:4, 17:5, 47:12; Jeremiah 50; 38, 51:7, 13. It will be the city of "the prince of this world," the seat of the Antichrist. Rome is the offspring of Babylon, but Babylon is the mother of Rome. It is noticeable that certain prophecies concerning Babylon in Isaiah and Jeremiah have not yet been fulfilled, while at the same time these prophecies are closely identified with those in Revelation 17 and 18. The drift of things in our day is in the direction of such a commercial center in the East.

Eastward the course of empire takes its way. Our possession of the Philippines, the awakening of Japan, the "open-door" in China, the railroad planned to India, the quickened interest in the Jews' return to Palestine, known as "Zionism," and many other things point that way. At the same time we must not be too hasty in forming our opinions with reference to unfulfilled prophecy, or uncharitable and dogmatic in asserting them. Let our attitude be that of prayerful searching of God's Word, humble attendance upon those who, taught of the Spirit, are in their turn able to teach us, and only kind and gentle expression of that which we believe to be truth when it is opposed by others who may seem to have as good a right to be heard.

The ninth and closing vision, chapter 6:1-8, furnishes another spectacle of judgment on the nations and the quieting of the divine Spirit with the result. Space prevents an enlargement upon it, nor is it absolutely necessary in the light of the foregoing.

The Crowning of the High Priests, 6.

—The prophet is now called upon, however, to do something in the nature of an object-lesson, which would seem to symbolize that great future event which will follow the judgments referred to, viz.: the manifested reign of Christ over the millennial earth. Who have now come from Babylon on an embassage of some kind (10)? Whose guests are they (same verse)? What precious articles do they seem to have brought with them as gifts for the temple (11)? What is the prophet to do with some of this silver and gold? What is he to say in connection with this transaction (12-13)? What then shall be done with the crowns, and why (14-15)?

That this whole transaction is symbolic is plain from two or three points of view. In the first place, the royal crown did not belong to the high priest or any other son of Levi, but to the tribe of Judah in the line of David. In the second place, there is the expression "Behold the Man whose name is the Branch!" To whom, as we have already seen, does that name belong? Then in the third place, we have the declaration, "He shall build the temple of the Lord." To whom in the fullest sense can this apply, save to Christ? And then, "He shall bear the glory," and "He shall be a priest upon His throne." Of none other than Christ has this ever been predicted. He only is the priestly King. Compare Psalm 110, and Hebrews 7. What language in verse 15 bears a possible reference to the Gentiles in that day? On what condition is all this to be fulfilled (same verse)?

We shall be obliged to pass over, for want of space, any particular consideration of the two next ensuing chapters, 7 and 8, which are in a sense parenthetical, although in perfect accord as to their teaching with the general drift of the whole book. Certain men of Bethel sent messengers to Jerusalem to inquire on the subject of ritual or ceremonial fasting. Had their fasting on certain occasions hitherto been acceptable to God and were they to continue it in the new regime? They are shown what a hollow and hypocritical thing that service had been hitherto; how it was just such formalism and hypocrisy as that which had brought the late punishment upon their fathers; how that the kind of fasting Jehovah desired was of a different nature altogether; and finally, that in the blessed time coming feasting will take the place of fasting altogether. These brief hints, I trust, will enable the readers to reach a fair understanding of the chapters under consideration in their present connection.

Part Second of the Book, 9-14.

—It was stated previously that the first part of the book, chapters 1-8, referred chiefly, though not entirely, to the prophet's own time. It is now seen in what sense that is true. The basis of all the prophecies in that part had a historical relation to the period then present. They were uttered, so to speak, to cheer and encourage the people in the work of re-building the temple. And yet, after all, there is not one of them that did not take cognizance of the far future. Indeed, some would say that they had little bearing on the prophet's own time in comparison with the remoter and completer application. However that may be, one thing is quite clear, viz: that the discourses of this, the second part, deal almost entirely with the future.

It will aid in the understanding of these chapters if we recall a few historical facts. At the date of this book the Medo-Persian was the great world-power to which the Jews were subject. It was followed by the Greeks, and the Greeks by the Romans. During the Roman regime our Lord was crucified and Jerusalem destroyed. The present (i. e. our own time), is an interregnum so far as Jewish national history is concerned, which will continue till Israel is once more in Jerusalem, in covenant with Anti-christ, and about to pass through the tribulation of that period prior to her final deliverance and blessing. Here then are three distinct periods in Jewish history which we may call, the Grecian, the Roman and the final periods. I think Zechariah treats of each of these periods in the chapters following, and while I confess to great difficulty in the explanation of them, yet I will do what I can to approach their meaning:

1. The Grecian Period, 9-10.—You will recall from the study of Daniel that this period begins with Alexander the Great, the notable horn between the eyes of the he-goat. When he crossed from Greece into Asia he swept down the Phoenician and Palestinian coast of the Mediterranean, besieging and capturing Damascus, Sidon, Tyre, Gaza and other cities in the south Philistine country. But strange to say, he passed by Jerusalem more than once without doing it harm. The Jewish historian Josephus explains this by a dream which the great monarch had, and which was remarkably fulfilled by the appearance to him at Jerusalem of the high priest and his train. However this may be, the opening verses of chapter 9 give us the prophetic outline of his career at this time. Read verses 1-7. For the deliverance of Jerusalem which actually occurred, read verse 8.

But now we come to a further illustration of the law of double reference, for the same verse which speaks of the deliverance of Jerusalem from Alexander, speaks evidently of another and more lasting deliverance which can only find fulfillment in the latter times. What shows that this ultimate deliverance, thus foreshadowed, is connected with the coming of Christ (9)? When were these words fulfilled at least in part? Matthew 21:5. What shows that their complete fulfillment, according to the law just mentioned, is reserved for the latter times, or Christ's second coming (10-11)?

Verses 13-17 are particularly obscure, but thought by some to refer to the period of the Maccabees who delivered their people for a while from the yoke of the tyrant Antiochus Epiphanes B. C. 170, or thereabouts, while the Grecians represented by him were still in power. However this may be, it is evident from what follows that, as in so many other instances previously discovered, this deliverance foreshadowed and pointed forward to a greater and final one to come.

The Roman Period, 11.—The period of Greek supremacy is at an end, and we have reached the events in the Roman period culminating in the rejection by the Jews of the Son of God. The eleventh chapter opens with a scene of judgment (verses 1-6). Then follows the cause of it (verses 7-14). It will be noticed in verse 4 that the prophet is commanded to do a symbolic act, and in verse 7 he is seen in the performance of it. What was this act? There will be little doubt in any mind after reading the complete context, that in this act he is the type of the Good Shepherd, Jesus Christ. Compare Matthew 9:36, and John 10. What does the Shepherd carry with Him to guide and protect His flock? There is difficulty in explaining the meaning of these staves unless we adopt that hinted at in verses 10 and 14, where "Beauty" seems to refer to the divine covenant, and "Bands" to the union between the ten tribes and the two.

Who are seen to be "cut off" in verse 8? It is generally supposed that these "three shepherds" "stand for the three classes of rulers that governed Israel," priests, prophets and lawyers, Jeremiah 2:8, Matthew 16:21. Our Lord pronounced woes against them (Matthew 23), and when the city was destroyed their rule came to an end. What portion of the flock paid attention to and were fed by the shepherd (11)? Compare Matthew 5:3, 11:25, 1 Corinthians 1:26-29. How does verse 12 point to the rejection of the Shepherd by the flock? What incident is foreshadowed in the next verse? Who is the prophet now commanded to impersonate (15)? What person yet to come will answer the description in verses 16 and 17? Can this be any other ultimately than the Anti-christ? Read the sad words in John 5:43.

The Final Period, 12-14.—I believe all the prophecies in this section of the book, are yet to be fulfilled, and that the fulfillment takes place at the period hitherto so frequently referred to. It is the time when Israel is once more in Jerusalem in the national sense, though at first in an unconverted condition.

We saw in the book of Daniel that the Anti-christ would at this time enter into covenant with Israel, and afterwards (in the middle of the last period of seven years), break that covenant. Then "the time of Jacob's trouble" begins, the nature of which will in part be the combination of the Gentile nations, i. e., the Roman world, against it. Antichrist himself will be at the head of this combination doubtless, if we may judge from a comparison of Daniel with Revelation. It is at this point, when the nations are beseiging the Holy City, that the present "burden of the word of the LORD" begins (12: 1, 2).

We can not pause to outline these chapters in detail, nor is it necessary for those who have carefully perused

the earlier books of the prophets in connection with these lessons. A hint here and there will suffice. For example, in this siege Jerusalem will for the first time be victorious (12: 2, 3); the victory, however, will be of a supernatural character (4-8, R. V.); the conversion of the nation will accompany it (10), also 13: 1, and it will take place coincidentally with their great tribulation (13: 8, 9, 14: 1-3); Christ shall appear to them (14: 4); the earth will rejoice (9); as will also Judah and Jerusalem (10. 11); their enemies will be punished, and the Millennium will have begun (16, and the following verses).

CHAPTER XXXIX.

The Book of Nehemiah.

In the chronological order Nehemiah follows Ezra and perhaps one ought to say Haggai and Zachariah also, after a period of about ten years, and although a Jew, he is an official of influence in the court of Persia, and one of those who did not return with either the company of Zerubbabel or the later one under the leadership of Ezra. Some of the returned captives, among them his brother Hanani, are revisiting Persia at the time when the book opens, from whom he learns that the condition of the people in the Holy Land is one of "affliction and reproach." (1: 1-3). His heart is moved by the intelligence, and like a true Israelite and true child of God he brings the matter before Him. The prayer that follows and which is the substance of the remainder of chapter one, is one of the many supplications of saints in the Old Testament which will repay the closest attention from both the historical and devotional point of view. The prayer was very definite and pointed and met with an early and favorable answer, one which it may be said Nehemiah himself helped to bring about (see chapter 2: 1-8).

Arrived on the site of Jerusalem with his commission and authority as governor and repairer of the breaches, Nehemiah makes a quiet and personal investigation of the condition of the walls before he reports his plans and purposes to the leaders of the people; but when he does so they are ready to engage in the work (2: 9-18).

This work, let it be remembered, was the rebuilding of the walls of Jerusalem, not the rebuilding of the temple, which, as you recall, was undertaken and carried through successfully in the days of Zerubbabel, who was aided by the prophesying of Zechariah and Haggai. But though the temple was rebuilt, yet the defenceless condition of the city in consequence of the broken walls, left the Jews at the mercy of every enemy, not a few of whom were adjacent to them and ready to take every advantage of injuring them. The rebuilding of the walls, therefore, was important as resulting in that re-establishment of their national autonomy which up until Nehemiah's time they had never really been able to enjoy. Of course when we speak of "national autonomy" the phrase is always qualified by the understanding that they were subject nevertheless at this time to Persia, although with a large measure of political freedom.

Some of these enemies spoken of above did everything in their power to frustrate the plans of Nehemiah and the people, by ridicule, by craft, by conspiracy as well as in other ways, but without avail. Nehemiah was a most remarkable man. One of the rarest discretion, courage, patriotism, pertinacity and leadership. But he was above all a man of God, knowing God, thoroughly consecrated to God, and of course specially equipped not only intellectually, but spiritually, for the great task before him. It was simply impossible under the circumstances for him to be overcome, and there is a sense in which his career entitles him to be ranked with the chiefest men of Israel, with Moses, David, Elijah, Daniel and others that might be named. There is a picturesqueness also about his personal history which gives it a rare charm to the student of sacred biography. Chapter 2: 19, 20, chapter 4, and chapter 6 are particularly interesting as covering the subjects above named. Chapter 3 gives us the names and order of those that builded the wall under his leadership, and chapter 5 furnishes us with a picture of the inner life of the people at this time, which is as dishonoring to those whom we might call the rich men and capitalists, as it is honoring to both the head and the heart of the great man who was the responsible chief of affairs.

Chapter 7 indicates that after the completion of the walls, Nehemiah returned to his former position at the court of Persia from which apparently he merely had a leave of absence (7: 1-4). This return, however, was not undertaken until other things besides the walls had been set in order. The law against usury spoken of in chapter 5 was not the only important piece of legislation established on a sure footing. The renewal of the genealogical records (chapter 7) was of vital moment as pertaining to the redistribution of the land and the succession of the high priest, as well as looking forward to the identification of the Messiah as the King of Israel when He should come. The revival of something of the old-time religion through the reading of the law and the formal renewal of the covenant was another event of magnitude due to Nehemiah's

authority and influence (chapter 8). The succeeding chapters down to and including chapter 12 refer to these events.

But at chapter 13 (especially verse 6), we perceive that after an interval Nehemiah returns again to Jerusalem. Verse 6 of that chapter indicates that about twelve years more or less were consumed in the execution of his first commission, but just how long a period elapsed between his report to the King of Persia and his later visit to Jerusalem is not stated. Nevertheless on his return he finds a condition of affairs to some extent not unlike that Ezra was obliged to rebuke on his earlier entrance upon the governorship. In the first place the worship of Jehovah had been sadly neglected and the temple polluted by the heathen through the wilful and selfish connivance even of the high priest. The service was not maintained because the Levites were not supported by the tithes and offerings. The Sabbath day was desecrated most outrageously, and the earlier sin of intermarrying with the heathen had been fallen into again notwithstanding the previous solemn covenant against it. Nehemiah's conduct in dealing with these sins and bringing about reforms as narrated in this chapter is about the raciest reading in the Old Testament, and while I am not an enthusiastic admirer of "political preaching" in the pulpit, yet any minister who wants good texts and stirring illustrations for use against dereliction in public office and the encouragement of fidelity and boldness on the part of public servants, will find a rich feast in this the last chapter of Nehemiah.

CHAPTER XL.

The Prophecy of Malachi.

The book of the prophet Malachi is a continuous discourse, so that, properly speaking, there are no intervening events. The prophet is usually regarded as a contemporary of Nehemiah, following closely in the wake of the former prophets Zechariah and Haggai. The evidence of this, however, is chiefly internal and gathered from two facts (1), that the second temple was very evidently in existence at the time, and (2), that the evils condemned by Nehemiah and singled out above, are those

which he also condemns. This will appear more particularly as we proceed, but those who care to do so at this time may compare the language in Malachi 1:7, 8; 2:11-16; 3:8-10 with the last chapter of Nehemiah, especially verses 10-14, 23-29.

Following an outline suggested by Professor Willis J. Beecher, D.D., we have:

The Introduction to the Book, 1: 1:5. What word in verse 1 indicates that the message, or messages, to follow are in the nature of rebuke rather than comfort or encouragement? With what touching and all-comprehensive declaration does verse 3 begin? While Jehovah thus declares Himself towards His people Israel, how do they receive it? This skeptical insinuation in the interrogation "Wherein hast thou loved us?" is a marked peculiarity of the book, and shows the people to have been in a very bad spiritual frame, and one well calculated to give birth to the practical sins enumerated later on. It is so hard for man in his natural state to believe that in the midst of trials and discipline of one kind and another it is possible for him to be the object of divine love. For example, how blind were these Israelites concerning it, and with what historic circumstances, which it would seem impossible to have been forgotten by them, does Jehovah seek to bring them to a saner mind (2-5)?

Let us be careful not to read a wrong meaning or intention into that reference to Esau, as though God caused him to be born simply to have an object on which He might exercise His hate, or as if that hate condemned the individual Esau to misery in this life and eternal torment beyond. The hate of Esau as an individual is simply set over against the special choice of Jacob as the heir to the promised seed of Abraham. Esau did not inherit that promise, the blessing to the world did not come down in his line, but that of his brother Jacob, and yet Esau himself had a prosperous and doubtless enjoyable life, nor are we driven to the conclusion by anything the Bible says that he was eternally lost any more than Jacob. Moreover, the particular reference in this case is not so much to Esau as a man as to the national descendants of Esau, the Edomites, who had not only been carried into captivity as Israel had been, but whose efforts to rebuild their waste places would not be successful as in the case of Israel, because the divine purposes of grace lay in another direction.

The Second Division of the Book, 1:6-3:4, consists of an address to the priests and Levites, more especially the former, in which they are charged with three kinds of offenses. The first offense is neglect of their temple duties, see chapter 1:6-2:9. Circumstances prevent our enlarging on the subject, but the real character of the offense is seen in verses 7 and 8, and 12 and 13 of chapter 1, while the punishment to fall upon the offenders in the event of impenitence is indicated in chapter 2:1-9. The second offense

concerns unholy marriages, covering verses 10-16 of chapter 2. It was for this sin as well as the preceding one that Jehovah had refused to accept their offerings (13, 14). Notice, in this connection, the strong argument against divorce found in verse 15. God made one wife for one man at the beginning though He had the power to make more, and He did this because of the godly seed He desired. The third offense is that of skepticism, and as Professor Beecher calls it, a bad skepticism, for there is a species of doubt which only deserves very tender and compassionate treatment and which cannot be called evil in its spirit and motive. This, however, is hardly the kind of doubt now under consideration (see chapter 2:17). This division of the book closes, as does indeed the division following, by a prediction "concerning a day in which the obedient and disobedient shall be differentiated and rewarded." This "day" we have often recognized as the "day of the Lord" still in the future both for Israel and the Gentile nations (3:1-4).

Notice the partial or introductory fulfillment of verse 1 in the career of John the Baptist, as indicated in the words and context of Matthew 11:10, Mark 1:2, Luke 1:76. But the concluding verses of the prediction show very clearly to those familiar with prophetic teaching, that a complete fulfillment must be ahead. The offering of Judah and Jerusalem has not yet been so purified by divine judgments as to be pleasant unto the Lord as in the days of old, but it shall yet so come to pass.

The Third Division of the Book, 3:5-4:3, consists of an address to the people as a whole, who like the priests, are charged with three kinds of offenses. The first offense is certain public wrongs in which are grouped false swearing, adultery, oppression and injustice (3:5-7). The second is the sin of failure to support the temple and its ministers (3:8-12), in which case please notice the solemn charge of divine robbery, and the overflowing blessing promised to faithfulness in the matter of tithes. The third is the same kind of skepticism as with the priests (3:13-15). The prediction concluding this section covers verses 3:16-4:3, and is rather more comforting in character than the preceding one.

The Fourth Division of the Book, 4:4-6, is in the nature of a grand conclusion to the whole in which the great day of the Lord is once more referred to, and Elijah the prophet named as His forerunner. We learn from the New Testament (Matthew 11:14, Mark 9:11 and Luke 1:17) that John the Baptist is to be considered at least as the type of this forerunner, but that Elijah is himself to come again to this earth is the opinion of very many, to do the work here predicted of him. There are those who believe that he and Moses are the two witnesses spoken of in Revelation 11 that shall appear and do wonders in Jerusalem during the period of the reign of the Antichrist. It is particularly to be noted in this day when false Elijahs are boasting of themselves, that the true Elijah, when he comes, will be a Jew, that his mission will be entirely to Jews, and that his place of operations will not be in the United States, for example, but in Jerusalem and Judea. He will be a prophet, moreover, and not engaged in business transactions either commercial or industrial. Neither will he be interested in the purchase or sale of real estate. There is only one Zion and that is in Jerusalem, and Jehovah will never commission any of His people to purchase that with earthly gold from the hand of His enemies. It belongs to Him and by Him was given in trust to Israel long ago. Through their disobedience they have lost its possession temporarily, but when on their repentance they shall be prepared to receive it again at His hands, He will wrest it from the nations now trampling it under foot, and give it back to them again.

CHAPTER XLI.

The Gospel of Matthew.

About four hundred years, more or less, have elapsed since the period of Malachi with whose book we have just finished, during which time no prophet had arisen in Israel. The people had remained in their land with varying fortunes, as the world would say, but with God's purposes being carried out in them as foretold in their Scriptures. We left them under the dominion of the Persians, which was soon followed by that of the Grecians including the Syrian period in which Antiochus Epiphanes flourished as their chief enemy and the Maccabees as their deliverers, somewhere about one hundred and fifty to one hundred and seventy years before Christ. Then came the Roman regime in which period it was that the Messiah appeared.

At the outset let us remember that the Old Testament promised an earthly kingdom to Israel to be set up on this earth when the Messiah came, and for which the faithful were ever looking. Jesus was the Messiah though they knew Him not, and He had come to set up that kingdom. Moreover, from the beginning of His public ministry down to a certain point to be named later, He proceeds on the assumption that the kingdom has come in Him if the nation will receive Him. He is not received, however, but rejected, whereupon He changes the character of His teaching and begins to speak of the church instead of the kingdom, and to lay plans, humanly speaking, for the formation of a new body of people altogether, Gentiles as well as Jews, who shall sustain a peculiar relation to Him while the kingdom is in abeyance, and indeed forevermore.

That phrase, "the kingdom in abeyance" I would emphasize, as meaning that the kingdom promised in the Old Testament is yet to come, and to be set up on this earth in Israel, with Jesus, the recognized Messiah, at its head. This will be when Israel, punished and repentant, shall receive Him by faith as all the prophets have spoken. In the meantime the church comes into view, with a unique origin, history and destiny, concerning which the New Testament treats almost exclusively. "Almost exclusively" and yet not quite exclusively. The Gospels have something to say about the kingdom, especially Matthew, and when we reach the book of Revelation it seems to be dealing with that theme almost altogether; but throughout the epistles, especially those of Paul, scarcely any mention of it, i. e., the kingdom, is made at all. The reason for all this will appear as we proceed, but I ask only that you note it now and so be ready to think about it further when it comes before us.

How then shall we place Matthew's Gospel which we now begin to study? Can we do better than to speak of it as covering the transition period, i. e., the period including the rejection of the kingdom by Israel and the coming into view of the church after the crucifixion and resurrection of our Lord? Please keep in mind, therefore, that Matthew is writing distinctively for the Jewish people, and is all the time seeking, under the inspiration of the Holy Spirit, to present Jesus to them as the One who fulfills the Old Testament features of the Messiah. It is for this reason that the first Gospel is sometimes called the Gospel of the Kingdom, because more than any other of the four, it dwells upon that aspect of the truth. But this suggests that each of the four Gospels has its own distinctive viewpoint of the history and work of the blessed Savior, to appreciate which is most important in the study of that Gospel. In the Old Testament the Coming One is described or alluded to in many different ways, but they have all been reduced to four, as for example: He is the King of Israel, He is the Servant of Jehovah, He is the Son of Man, and He is the Son of God. This division or classification thus re-appears in the Gospels, and as we shall see, Matthew reveals Him in the first particular, Mark in the second, Luke in the third and John in the fourth.

I. The Advent of the Messiah, 1-4.

—The first division of the Gospel of Matthew covers what may be denominated the advent of the Messiah, including chapters 1-3, and the first eleven verses of chapter 4. We shall follow Dr. Gregory's excellent analysis to a certain extent, as found in "Why Four Gospels," and thus classify this introductory section of the Gospel into four parts:—

His natural descent, 1 : 1-17.
His two-fold nature, 1 : 18-25.
His earthly location, 2 : 1-23.
His official preparation, 3 : 1-4 : 11.

Always remembering that Matthew is writing distinctively for the Jew, and that his particular mission is to convince the Jew that Jesus of Nazareth is the Messiah and the King of Israel promised in the Old Testament, it will add interest to the study of his Gospel if we observe how continually he quotes the Old Testament, and explains that all this was said or done by Jesus or to Jesus that the word of the Old Testament might be fufilled. In this respect Matthew differs very radically from the other Gospels, especially Mark and Luke as we shall see, and for reasons that will appear also.

For instance, take the natural descent of the Messiah: The Jews expected Him to come in the line of Abraham, and through David, and would not have listened to any Messianic claim of one who would not qualify in that particular. Therefore Matthew takes the greatest pains to trace the genealogy of Jesus through David to Abraham, and stops there. The Jews did not care to go back of that. The marginal references in your Bible will indicate the Old Testament passages fulfilled in the genealogy of Jesus as given by Matthew.

II. The Ministry of the Messiah, 4: 12-16: 12.

—Under this head notice (1), the place and character of its beginning (4 : 12-25), keeping in mind always Matthew's particular purpose to reach the Jews by proving Jesus to be the Messiah foretold in the Old Testament prophets. The place, for example, was Galilee of the Gentiles, and this Isaiah said would be the case (see that book, 9 : 1, 2), the character of its beginning is well exhibited in verses 23 and 24 of the lesson, which fulfill Isaiah 51 : 1-3.

Notice, (2), the constitution of His kingdom, chapters 5-7 inclusive. When the Messiah came the Jews were expecting Him to set up His kingdom, and Jesus accordingly, at the very beginning of His ministry, goes about that work. He does so by proclaiming these things:

The character of the members of His kingdom, (5 : 1-16).

The laws governing in His kingdom, (5 : 17-7 : 6).

The requirements for entering His kingdom, (7 : 7-29).

This division of the Gospel is sometimes called the Sermon on the Mount, and has suffered more perhaps from false exegesis, and application than any other portion of the New Testament corresponding in length, except perhaps in the book of Revelation. The cause of these mistakes is the common one frequently pointed out in these studies, of confounding the kingdom with the church, and applying indiscriminately to the latter what belongs almost exclusively to the former. In the present instance, these sublime teachings of Jesus are often substituted for the Gospel of salvation through faith in His blood. Nothing is said on that subject in this discourse, and therefore some would have it that the only thing for one to do in order to be saved is to "live up to the Sermon on the Mount" as the saying is, or to keep the "Golden Rule" which that sermon sets forth. As if any unregenerated man ever did or ever could live up to that standard or keep that rule! Others again, while steering clear of that error, fall into an opposite one. Instead of applying it to the unsaved as the way of salvation, they apply it to the saved as the rule of daily living, and hence come under what is known as legalism. I do not say that it has no reference to Christian believers at all, but only that the source and spring of their heavenly walk with their Lord is not found in any such series of commandments holy and beautiful as they are, but in a right apprehension of what their standing and position are in Him as members of His body.

The Sermon on the Mount is distinctively Jewish, and describes, as has been said, the character of the citizens of the earthly kingdom which the Messiah came to set up. It assumes a class of people already saved, regenerated and in fellowship with their King. This the Jews were not in Christ's time, and are not to-day, and will not be till they pass through the terrible fires of tribulation spoken of by the prophets, whence the "remnant" will come forth purified. (See the last chapter of Malachi again.) It was because Jesus laid down and insisted upon such a holy standard as this that His people rejected and crucified Him. They were looking for a political restoration of their kingdom, but refused submission to the moral restoration which must precede it. And yet the moral character of the kingdom as Jesus proclaimed it, was that of the Old Testament prophets very clearly. Matthew's Gospel is here consistent as elsewhere with its governing plan to present Jesus as the Messiah of the Jewish prophets; in proof of which consider with this division of our lesson such passages speaking of the kingdom as Psalm 72: 15, Isaiah 5: 18-25, 28: 16, 17, Jeremiah 29: 10-14, and countless more.

Notice (3). The manifestation of the Messiah's power, 8-9: 35. It was quite in keeping that after the proclamation of His kingdom had been made as in the chapter preceding, He who claimed to be the King should now present His credentials to that fact, hence the three groups of miracles which follow. And before we go further, let me at this point call attention to a peculiarity in Matthew, as seen in the way in which he groups things that have a common likeness to each other, or which may be used to illustrate or emphasize a point without reference to the precise chronological order in which they may have occurred. For example, an examination of the other Gospels will disclose the fact that these nine miracles did not all occur at about the same time or in the precise relation

to each other, indicated here; but only that Matthew uses them at this particular time under the inspiration of the Holy Spirit, in the execution of his plan to present Jesus as the promised Messiah of the Jews. He has proclaimed His kingdom and now He establishes His rights as its King. Hence, behold His mighty works, thus gathered up and brought into one general view.

Notice (4), the opposition shown to the Messianic power (9: 36-16: 12). This opposition already begins to show itself in chapter 8: 34, indeed, where the leaders of the nation, jealous of the rising influence of Jesus seek to offset His hold upon the common people by the insinuation there mentioned; but it becomes very much increased and intensified by the occasion furnished in chapter 10—the commission of the twelve disciples; through the power thus conferred upon them as He sent them forth to "the lost sheep of the house of Israel" to proclaim the kingdom in His name, He may be said to have multiplied Himself that many times. It may be noticed in passing that this, too, the sending out of the twelve, is in part at least a fulfillment of the prophets (see Ezekiel 34).

Let us observe that this commission of the twelve disciples is not the same as the "Great Commission" in chapter 28: 19, 20. That concerns the proclamation of the Gospel of grace, but this the kingdom of Israel, hence the peculiarity of the instruction in this case. These disciples were not to go outside of Israel, their sphere was limited to the twelve tribes. Their theme was not the Gospel, but the kingdom which we have now come to identify pretty clearly. They were to go without money, or change of raiment, etc., which was quite practicable under the circumstances, but which does not rest as an obligation upon Christian missionaries in our day. This is not to say that God can not or does not supply the need of some who now go forth in that way, but only that the express command does not apply to them in the same way.

This opposition to Jesus, as has been said, was intensified by this sending out of the twelve disciples, but its development is seen all along in the chapters that follow down practically, till the close of chapter 12. It begins, indeed, in the doubts of John the Baptist (11: 1-30), although it can not be said that they were expressed in a spirit only hostile. They were representative doubts, however, and on the part of others decidedly antagonistic to the Messiah. It is noticeable that in replying to John, the Savior presents His credentials as the Messiah, verses 4-6, and thereupon asserts His authority is indicated in verses 27-30. This is the peculiarity of Matthew's treatment of this whole period of the Savior's life. He describes the opposition, then emphasizes the credentials of Him who was thus opposed, and finally records a definite assertion of His authority. These features of the story do not always appear in this order precisely, but nevertheless they are never altogether absent.

Following the doubts of John comes what Dr. Gregory describes as the unorganized opposition of the Pharisees as indicated in chapter 12:1 13, and where again the assertion of authority is emphasized, verses 6-9, and in connection with it the credentials on which that authority rests, verses 10-13. The unorganized is in turn followed by an organized opposition, 12:14-45. See the reference to the council, verse 14, and Jesus' withdrawal for a while in consequence of it as indicated in verses 15-21. Immediately, however, lest the Jews, for whom he wrote, should misconstrue this action on the part of Jesus and stumble at it, Matthew presents his credentials again as illustrated in verses 22, 23 and records the assertion of His authority which follows in verses 24-45. For evidence of the fulfillment of the Old Testament prophecy in all this, as throughout in Matthew, compare the marginal references.

The effect of this opposition to the Messiah's ministry is very marked in the changed character that ministry now assumes as set before us in chapter 13. The parabolic teaching of the kingdom is now substituted for its plain teaching which had maintained hitherto. Jesus foresees His rejection and with it the rejection of the kingdom for the time being. He foresees the interregnum of this the period of the church, and begins to tell His disciples the mystery of the intervening events between His going away bye and bye and His returning again when Israel shall have learned the lesson of her rejection. Notice in this connection especially, verses 10, 17 of this chapter. Notice also that none of the seven parables in this group contains any intimation of a time when the Gospel shall prevail over the earth before the Son of man returns again, but all alike affirm that truth and error and good and evil will continue side by side until the end of the present age (R. V.). The parable of the leaven even, is no exception to this declaration, but rather confirmatory of it. Leaven is the Bible type of evil, and the parable teaches that so far as the human aspect of the kingdom is concerned error rather than truth will prevail in the present age.

What is Meant by the Kingdom of Heaven.—But some may be puzzled as to the meaning of the phrase, "The kingdom of heaven is like unto" so and so. How can the kingdom of heaven be "like unto" anything evil? The explanation is found in the definition of the kingdom, and perhaps the following taken from the Appendix of Dr. Tregelles' work on "Christ's Second Coming," may throw some light on the subject. According to the author of that appendix (Cecil Yates Biss, London,) the kingdom of God is viewed in Scripture under five different aspects, as follows:

1. As introduced into the world in the person of the Lord Jesus Christ, its King and Head. See Mark 1:14, 15, where "is at hand" should be rendered "hath drawn nigh."

2. As rejected by Israel, and therefore restricted during this dispensation to a body of men whose relationship to it is invisible, and only manifested by their subjection to its laws and principles. This body of men forms what we know as the church, the body of Christ. Now as the Gospel brings into this relationship those who believe, it follows that "to testify the Gospel of the grace of God" is equivalent to "preaching the kingdom of God." (See Acts 20:24, 25.)

3. In that outward visible aspect, in which, during this dispensation, it includes all who profess to belong to the Lord Jesus Christ—some truly, some falsely. It is in this aspect, exactly equivalent to what is commonly described by the word "Christendom," (i. e., Christ's kingdom), that it is spoken of in Matthew 13.

4. In the future, or millennial aspect, when the government of the Lord Jesus Christ will be manifested in power. The kingdom will then include (a) a heavenly department, the risen "church of the first-born ones" (Heb. 12); and (b) an earthly department, consisting of Israel as a converted people, and also the converted Gentiles throughout the earth. It is in this aspect that we pray "Thy kingdom come: Thy will be done on earth as in Heaven."

5. In the eternal aspect, as in the words, "Then cometh the end, when He (the Son) shall deliver up the kingdom to God, even the Father," etc. (1 Cor. 15:24.)

This writer, it will be seen, makes the two expressions "kingdom of God."

and "kingdom of Heaven," equivalent, but we need not contend about that just now if what he has written makes any clearer to us the sense in which the kingdom of Heaven, as used in Matthew 13, may be said to be connected with evil. It is Christendom that Christ is speaking of there, that outward visible aspect in which, during this dispensation, it includes all who profess to belong to Him whether the confession be true or false.

Let us now return to the consideration of the opposition to the Messiah which begins to culminate as illustrated in chapter 13:54 to the end of this main division (16:12). See, for example, the opposition from Jesus' townsmen (13:54-58), and the withdrawal on His part for a while in which it resulted. Then comes opposition on the part of Herod and another withdrawal (14:1-36). Observe how Matthew again emphasizes the credentials which Jesus presented in the latter half of this chapter. The opposition of Herod is followed by that of the leaders in Judea, chapter 15, in which connection observe a further withdrawal (21), and then the presentation of credentials once more (22-39), Finally, there comes the opposition from the leaders in Galilee (16:1-12), and another withdrawal of Jesus which leads up to the next great division of the Gospel.

III. The Formal Claim of the Messiah, 16:13-23:39.

—This claim is first made privately before His disciples in a section of this division covered by chapters 16:13-20:28. It will be observed that no sooner is this claim made and formally acknowledged by His disciples than He follows it with the revelation of His death. This is the first time He mentions that, and presumably because His disciples were not prepared to receive it until they had come to know and recognize Him for whom He really was. And even now how ill-prepared were they and how necessary it was for their faith and hope to be reassured by the Transfiguration which takes place in this connection! It is interesting to observe further that according to our present evangel this revelation of His death is repeated three times, each time a new feature being added until the full details are before the minds of the twelve. For instance, in chapter 16:21 His death is connected with the work of the Sanhedrin, the highest Jewish court, in 17:22, the betrayer comes into view in connection with it, and in 20:17, the Gentiles appear. It is interesting to observe still further, that in connection

with each of the three revelations of His death our Lord supplements that revelation with an appropriate discourse or some other action confirmatory to His disciples' faith, as in the case of the Transfiguration already specified.

The claim made before the disciples, however, is soon repeated, as was necessary, before the nation (chapters 20:29-23:39). In the first place He claimed to be the Son of David, at Jericho, as will be seen by a study of chapter 20, verses 29-34, and later on He claimed to be the King of Israel, as will be seen by chapter 21:1-16. This doubly-asserted claim is further supported, if one may so say, by His formal rejection of the nation which now followed. To illustrate this, let it be noted that Jesus' claim to be the King of Israel as set forth in His entry into Jerusalem in fulfillment of Zechariah's prophecy, (21:1-16), was disputed on the part of the leaders of the nation. In fact He was formally rejected by them as indicated in that same chapter, especially at verses 15 and 23. Whereupon He now as formally rejects the nation; first, in the type of the barren fig-tree, 21:17-19; secondly, in the series of three parables which follow (21:28-22:14), viz, those of the two sons, the wicked husbandmen, and the marriage of the king's son; and thirdly, in formal speech (23:38, 39). Is it not stirring to our faith and hope to notice in connection with this rejection that He refers, inferentially at least, to His second coming to set up the kingdom, when Israel will be ready to receive Him as the prophets have spoken, and when at last they shall say, "Blessed is he that cometh in the name of the Lord."

IV, The Sacrifice of the Messiah, 24-27:66.

—This division of the Gospel begins with our Lord's discourse concerning His second coming. His nation having rejected Him, and He having rejected His nation, at least for the time being, He now addresses Himself to His disciples, turning their faces as well as His own to the future, and, what the event has proven to be, a far future. The discourse on His second coming covers practically chapters 24 and 25, and while it is confessedly somewhat hard to understand in every point, yet our study of the Old Testament prophecies should enable us to grasp its main outlines.

It begins with His desire to answer the disciples' question, or questions, in the opening verses of chapter 24, after they had left the temple with Him for the last time. He does this in several parts. In the first place, He apparently describes, in outline, the intervening events between His departure and His second coming, which will culminate with the end of the Age (24: 1-14). In the next place, He describes in outline, the culminating events in the city of Jerusalem at the time of His coming (15-28). Then follows a description of the actual event itself, His second coming (29-31).

Perhaps more obscurity pervades the rest of His answer than what precedes it, obscurity that is, as to the precise place in time which it fits. And yet it may prove a fairly good "working hypothesis" for the present, if we regard it as giving us an outline exhibit of the condition of the world and of Christendom at the period of His coming. For example, we have the condition of the world set before us very clearly in chapter 24: 36-41, and as some think, the condition of the Christian ministry in verses 42-51. The parable of the virgins following (25: 1-13), is a picture of the church perhaps, though of this I am not certain, while the parable of the talents succeeding it exhibits very clearly the principle on which rewards will be adjudicated to the faithful in that day. Whether these "rewards" are to be regarded as applying to the faithful in Israel or the church, I cannot say with definiteness, but in either event the same principle doubtless applies. The judgment of the nations under the figure of the sheep and the goats, which concludes the discourse (25: 31-46), coincides, I believe, with the teachings of the Old Testament prophets with which we are familiar. These prophets taught us that at the close of this age Jerusalem would again be occupied by Israel though at first in an unconverted state, and that the nations of the Roman Empire would again besiege her federated under the lead of the Antichrist, and at this time the Messiah would interpose on her behalf, destroying her enemies and delivering her. I feel persuaded that the judgment here referred to as falling on the living nations is that judgment. That it is not the judgment at the end of the world, for example, and mentioned in Revelation 20, but the judgment at the end of the present age when Jesus comes to set up His earthly kingdom with Israel as its center. The nations thus judged are not necessarily the heathen nations, but the nations of Christendom, the Roman world, which are judged, it will

be perceived, not on the ground of individual belief or unbelief in the Savior, but on their national treatment of "these my brethren," i. e., Israel, the brethren of Christ after the flesh. Israel with all her faults and blemishes is the apple of God's eye, and woe must befall the nation which lays a hand upon her.

Thus far we have been dwelling especially on Christ's discourse on His second coming, which was in a sense necessary to be revealed to His disciples before His sacrifice was really consummated. This discourse closes with chapter 25, and the offering of Himself as a sacrifice takes place in chapters 26-27. The events of these chapters, deeply important as they are in themselves, do not call for extended notice. They include the story of the last Passover, the agony in Gethsemane, the betrayal of Judas, the trial, the crucifixion, death and burial; but attention is particularly called to the number of instances in which Matthew, true to his distinctive mission to the Jew, emphasizes the fulfillment of Old Testament prophecy at every step of the way, either in his own words or by recording those of the Savior bearing upon the subject.

Part V, The Triumph of the Messiah, 28.—The triumph of the Messiah is usually employed to describe the last great division of Matthew's Gospel. The two great facts under this head are His resurrection from the dead and His commission to the disciples to disciple all nations. As to the last-named fact, there are those who think it was practically a commission to make a further offer of the kingdom to Israel, rather than a commission to call the church into being. The calling of the church, they would maintain, did not take place until the beginning of Paul's ministry, to whom the revelation of the church was especially made known. They would maintain that up until that time, or to speak more particularly, the era of the martyrdom of Stephen, Israel had another chance to receive the kingdom by receiving the King now testified to as risen from the dead, but their continued obstinacy closed the door of opportunity against them at the crisis referred to, and the new regime of the church, or the body of Christ, then began in earnest. I am not prepared to endorse this teaching without qualification, and yet a reference to it should not be omitted.

CHAPTER XLII.

The Gospel of Mark.

As Matthew wrote for the Jews distinctively, so it is thought Mark wrote for the Gentile. The internal evidence of this is as follows: For example, unlike Matthew, he omits practically all reference to the Old Testament prophets. With the exception of the one such reference at the beginning of his gospel, I do not think he refers to them again except as he quotes Christ's references to them. This is remarkable as showing that he is addressing a people to whom such references were not necessary even if intelligible, for the Gentiles knew nothing of the sacred oracles and were not in expectation of any Great One of whom they spake. To the same purport, observe that Mark omits any genealogical table, it is not necessary for him to prove the Abrahamic descent of Jesus. All allusion to His birth and infancy is also omitted doubtless for the same reason, and so on through the whole gospel. It will be found on careful examination, I think, that all the omissions in Mark as compared with Matthew are of a specially Jewish character. Furthermore, it will be discovered that Mark feels a necessity to explain certain Jewish words and customs which he would pass over unnoticed if addressing Jews. Illustrations in point are found in chapter 5 : 41, 7 : 34, and especially 7 : 1-4.

But it may be further surmised that Mark is not only addressing a Gentile people, but of the two great Gentile peoples of that day, the Romans and the Greeks, he is addressing the first-named. The Romans, as others have pointed out, represented the idea of active power in the world. Their ideal was military glory. They were the people who, most of all, did things. Moreover, their highest conception of power, and might, and authority was themselves, i. e., the Roman state. Although they worshiped the Emperor yet they were really worshiping the state considered as represented in him. And, indeed, their spiritual need as a people grew out of this fact; it grew out of their failure to attain their ideal in the state; for with all their power, and might, and authority they saw that injustice, cruelty and suffering still prevailed, and would inevitably continue to do so. Those who have not access to larger books on this subject will find the thought sufficiently wrought out in Gregory's "Why Four Gospels?" previously referred to.

Now the Gospel of Mark will be found on close examination to peculiarly fit this condition of things, and to suggest that it was written distinctively to meet the Roman need. For example, it very noticeably sets forth Jesus from the point of view spoken of in our first lesson on the Gospels, i. e., as the active servant of Jehovah. The whole trend of the Gospel vibrates with energy, power, movement, conquest, as attractive to such a people as the Romans. To begin with, it is the briefest Gospel, 16 chapters only as compared with 28 in Matthew, evidently it was intended for a people not given to thought as much as action. And then, that which it omits is chiefly the discourses rather than the deeds of Jesus, there is no Sermon on the Mount, no charge to the twelve disciples, no discourse on the second coming. Moreover, the things which Mark adds, as distinguished from Matthew, are those calculated to arrest the attention of men of affairs and action. Speaking further of the energetic movement of the Gospel, it is interesting to note the frequent employment of the word "straightway," which, as rendered in the Revised Version, occurs something like 40 times.

And yet what has been said does not quite exhaust, or better yet, does not quite express, what is found in Mark as distinct from Matthew, and indeed from all the gospels. It represents Jesus, indeed, as the man of mighty energy and power—a servant in that sense, and yet it represents Him in the lowly and patient sense of service as well. To quote Jukes on the Differences of the Four Gospels, the early church fathers employed the four cherubim or "living creatures" as emblematic of the four gospels—the lion, the ox, the man, the eagle (Revelation 4 : 7.) It is under the first figure, "the lion of the tribe of Judah," that Jesus is presented in Matthew, but under the second, the figure for service, that He is presented in Mark. He is here the patient laborer for others, if need be offering Himself in His service as a perfect sacrifice. And the same writer points out a fitness in Mark for presenting Jesus from that point of view, for he himself was the minister, the servant of the apostles, Acts, 12:11, 12, 11 Timothy 4:11, etc.

Let us bear in mind them, in studying Mark, that side by side with the thought of Christ's energy and power we are to keep the other thought of His humility and patience. Nor does this latter conception militate against the idea of applying the gospel especially to the needs of the Romin mand. Indeed, it strengthens such application, since the more the humility and patience of Jesus are dwelt upon in the light of His mighty works, the mightier they appear.

The Outline of the Gospel.—The outline of Mark's Gospel might be made in connection with the same general periods suggested in the study of Matthew:

I. The Period of the Advent, 1:1-2:12.—It might be well to study this period in connection with the corresponding division in Matthew, to discover what Mark omits and what, if anything, he adds, and the bearing of these omissions and additions on the distinctive character of Mark's record as compared with that of Matthew. How abruptly he approaches the period of Jesus' active ministry, how he even hastens over the preaching of John the Baptist, and the details of the wilderness temptation, to speak of the call of the disciples, and the mighty works which Jesus at once began to do! The study of this period will be helped by the following analysis:

The introduction, 1:1.
The testimony of John, 2-8.
The testimony of God, 9-11.
The wilderness victory, 12, 13.
The call of the disciples, 14-20.
The works of power, 1:21-2:12.

Notice in the reading of this section how the wilderness victory of the conqueror manifests His authority over Satan and the wild beasts not only, but also the holy angels as well. Moreover, in analyzing the sphere of the manifestation of His miraculous works, it will be seen that beginning in the synagogue at Capernaum, He next makes a circuit of Galilee, returning to Capernaum again. A map would be of great value, of course, in fixing these important details in mind, and surrounding them with the force and power of reality.

II. The Period of the Conflict, 2:13-8:26, a period covering about the same ground as that designated in Matthew as "the ministry of the Messiah."

The subjects and laws of His kingdom, 2:13-3; 35.
The growth of His kingdom, 4:1-34.
The power of the king, 4:35-5:43.
The conflicts and withdrawals of the king, 6:1-8; 46.

In reading this division one will be impressed by the quiet growth of the kingdom, its entire independence of human will, and its complete conquest of the earth. This last is true no matter which view we take of the interpretation of 4:32, for whether that refers to a true or a false Christendom (see our study of Matthew), it is a demonstration of Christ's power likely to rivet the attention and command the respect of a people of power like the Romans. In the same connection notice His power as especially portrayed in sub-division (3). See how it is exhibited over the elements of nature, over Satan, over human disease, and even over death itself. Finally, under the head of His conflicts and withdrawals we will recall the similar feature of this part of Jesus' earthly life as given in the first gospel. But notice here the four localities in which these experiences took place, at Nazareth (6:1-6), in Galilee at large (6-32), at Gennesaret (53-8:9), and at Dalmanutha (8:10-26). Examine the map carefully.

III. The Period of the Claim, 8:27-13:37.—As Preliminary to a direct claim to be the king of the kingdom on the part of Jesus, Mark sets forth His teachings as to the way in which the kingdom was to be won, viz: through suffering and rejection. This is revealed in chapters 8:27-10:45, which show the sufferings to include:

(a) Rejection by the Sanhedrin, 8:17-9:29.

(b) Treachery of His followers, 9:30-10:31.

(c) Death by the Romans, 10:32-45.

The kingdom, however, was claimed by Jesus, as we saw in Matthew's Gospel, by His public entry into Jerusalem as the heir of David, 10:46-13.37. The subject is divided again into:

(a) The public advent, 10:46-11:26.

(b) The triumph over the leaders, 11:27-12:44.

(c) The revelation of the future, 13:1-37.

IV. The Period of the Sacrifice, 14:1-15:47. Under this division we perceive the preliminary preparations for His death, 14:1-41, and, secondly, the actual circumstances under which that death was brought about, 14:42-15:47.

V. The Period of the Triumph, 16:

1-20, is not essentially different in its character from the similar record given by Matthew, except as to the promised co-operation of power in the execution of the Great Commission, so-called.

This, too, is fitting and appropriate as harmonizing with the distinctive purpose of Mark in presenting Jesus to the Romans—the people whose ideal was power, power to accomplish things.

CHAPTER XLIII.

The Gospel of Luke.

Luke, like Mark, wrote for the Gentiles as is evident from a careful and comparative reading of his gospel; but for a different class of Gentiles than Mark. The writers of the first three centuries of our era testify, almost without exception, that he wrote for the Greeks, presenting Jesus from the point of view of the Son of Man, the perfect, the ideal man. This testimony is corroborated by the internal evidence of the book itself.

Who were the Greeks? What were their characteristics or ideals as distinguished from the Romans, for example? As the latter represented the idea of activity or power, so the former represented that of reason and culture. As the ideal of the Roman was military glory and governmental authority, so that of the Greek was wisdom and beauty. As the Romans felt it to be their mission to govern, to give laws to man, so the Greeks felt it to be theirs to educate, elevate and perfect man. Their thought did not include man considered as a race, but man as an individual. It was the man of genius in whom they were interested, not man as found in the common herd. As illustrating their conception of man or of humanity in this sense, it may be remarked that, unlike the less intellectual nations round about them, they made their gods in the likeness of men. Of course, it should also be borne in mind that the ideal man, the human god they had before them, was always of a worldly character, one in whom there was ever a mingling of virtue and vice, for as heathen they knew nothing better or higher.

The Gospel of Luke, therefore, meets this need on the part of the Greek in presenting Jesus as the perfect, the ideal, the universal man. He is not here the Jewish man, the Roman man, or the Grecian man as such, but all men at their best are summed up in Him—The Man.

Following Dr. Gregory here, the third gospel meets this need of the Greek in several ways:

(1), In its authorship. Luke, it is thought, was himself a Greek and a proselyte to the Jewish religion; moreover, he was a cultivated man, more so than any other of the four evangelists. His cultivation is indicated in the profession he followed, that of a physician, and also in the general style of his composition. Then, too, he was the traveling companion of Paul, himself a cultivated man, and the great apostle to the Gentiles especially the Greeks. All these things go to show the adaptability of the third gospel in its authorship to that representative class of people.

(2), In its plan. It is usually considered the most orderly history of the sayings and doings of Jesus among the four gospels. It was evidently prepared for a thoughtful and philosophic people. A careful reading of such passages as 1:1-4, also 1:5, 2:1, 3:1, etc., will show what is meant by this remark.

(3. In its style. Allusion has already been made to this fact, but it may be well to further observe that it is remarkable for its poetry, song and eloquence. Also for the depth and sublimity of its thought. Notice how many songs are recorded in its opening chapters, and consider their attractiveness to the people of the land of Homer. Close attention also will make clear even to the English reader that there is a flow to the speech of Luke, and a rounding off of his sentences that marks a higher grade of rhetoric than the other gospels. And speaking of the depth and philosophic nature of his work, observe how he abounds in the discourses of Jesus, so different from Mark. The people for whom he writes are those who think and meditate, hence he alone of the synoptics records such wonderful utterances of the Savior as the parables of the Prodigal Son and the Rich Man and Lazarus, and His teachings on prayer, and worship, and the Holy Spirit.

(4), In its omissions. Luke omits

the distinctively Jewish portions of the gospel, saying little or nothing about the Old Testament prophets, or the Abrahamic lineage of Jesus; neither does he quote the parables condemnatory of Israel. He also omits distinctively Roman features, the vivid pictures and activity associated with Mark, and affects conciseness of description rather than scenic effect.

(5), In its additions. This gospel gives those incidents in the life of Jesus which more especially demonstrate His interest in the whole race. The genealogy recorded is that through Adam from God. The sending out of the seventy disciples as well as that of the twelve is mentioned, especially as the former were not limited in their work to·"the lost sheep of the house of Israel." Likewise is a great deal of space, nine chapters (9 : 51-18 : 30), given up to the ministry of Jesus among the Gentile beyond the Jordan. The parable of the Good Samaritan and the healing of the ten lepers, whose records are confined to Luke's Gospel, are especially cheering to the same class.

(6), In its presentation of Jesus Himself. The third gospel contains peculiar marks of His humanity, as notice 10 : 21, 22 : 43, 44; 23 : 46, 24 : 39. It emphasizes His affectionate regard for women and children, 8 : 42; 9 : 38; 7 : 46; 8 : 3; 11 : 27; 10 : 38-42; 23 : 27. And also His sympathy with the despised and outcast, 6 : 20-22. Compare His discourse in the Pharisee's house, chapter 14, and the parables already noted as well as that of the publican (18). Some one has said that this gospel more than any other has given birth to the philanthropic and reformatory movements of our day, a singular and interesting illustration of which is found in the numerous inscriptions from this gospel found on the facades of public buildings devoted to such purposes.

(7). And yet Luke emphasizes also the divinity of His Person as do all the evangelists.

Outline of the Gospel.—I. The Preface, I: I-4. Notice the reference in the first verse to other gospels, perhaps only the other two synoptics are meant, and yet the word "many" indicates more than these. Of the whole number, however, the Holy Spirit has chosen to preserve only these which are bound up in our Bible and have come down to us through the channel of the church. Observe further, that according to verse 2, they who had set forth these things were eye-witnesses of what they recorded. Moreover, Luke himself possessed practically the same qualification, verse 3. The expression thus referred to has a different turn in the Revised Version and suggests an important peculiarity of Luke's Gospel, viz: its historical character. According to the Revised Version he had traced the course of all things accurately and was about to write them out "in order." There is more of the feature of sustained history in this gospel than in any of the others. Finally observe that it is addressed to an individual, possessing a Greek name, meaning a lover of God, and addressed to him for the purpose of working in him assurance of faith concerning the Gospel which he had previously heard by word of "mouth," according to the margin of the Revised Version.

II. The Period of the Infancy, I: 5-II. Under this division we have ten leading facts: announcement to Zacharias, 5-25; announcement to Mary, 26-38; visit of Mary to Elizabeth, 39-56; birth of John the Baptist, 57-80; birth of Jesus, 2 : 1-7; announcement to the shepherds, 8-20; circumcision of Jesus, 21; presentation in the temple, 22-38; residence in Nazareth, 39, 40; visit to Jerusalem, 41-52.

III. The Period of Preparation, 3-4: 13. The facts of this period may be outlined thus: ministry of John, 1-20; baptism of Jesus, 21, 22; genealogy of Jesus, 23-38; temptation of Jesus, 4 : 1-13.

IV. The Period of the Galilean Ministry, 4: 14-9: 50. Ministry in Nazareth, 14-30; ministry in Capernaum, 3--44; call of Peter, James and John, 5 : 1-11; spread of Jesus' fame, 12-26; call of Levi, 27-39; opposition of the Pharisees, 6 : 1-11; choice of the apostles, 12-16; discourse to the disciples, 17-49; miracles in Capernaum and Nain, 7 : 1-17; discourse on John the Baptist, 18-35; on the Two Debtors, 36-50; ministry of the women, 8 : 1-3; parable of the Sower, 4-18; discourse on His relatives, 19-21; stilling of the tempest, 22-25; healing of the Gadarene, 26-40; of the woman with the issue of blood, 41-48; raising of Jairus' daughter, 49-56; commission of the Twelve, 9 : 1-9, withdrawal to the desert, 10-17; transfiguration, 18-36; healing of the lunatic, 37-42; counsel to the disciples, 43-56.

V. The Period of the Judean Ministry, 9: 51-19: 27. Journey toward Jerusalem, 51-62; commission of the seventy, 10 : 1-24; discourse on Love to One's Neighbor, 25-37; visit to Martha and Mary, 38-42; discourse on Prayer,

11:1-13; on Seeking a Sign, 14-36; dinner with the Pharisee, 37-54; discourse on the Pharisee, 12:1-12; on Covetousness, 13-59; on Repentance, 13:1-9; on the Kingdom of Heaven, 10-24; on the Strait Gate, 23-30; challenge to Herod, 31-35; discourse on Hospitality, 14:1-24; on Self-Denial, 25-35; on the Lost, 15:1-32; on Earthly Riches, 16:1-30; visit at Jericho, 31-19:27.

VI. The Period of the Jerusalem Ministry, 19:28-21. Entry into Jerusalem, 19:28-48; controversy with the leaders, 20:1-21:4; discourse on the Future, 5:38; last Passover, 22:1-38; betrayal, 39-53; trial before the high priest, 54-71; before Pilate, 23:1-26; crucifixion, 27-49; burial, 50-56; resurrection, 24:1-48; ascension, 49-53.

CHAPTER XLIV.

The Gospel of John.

The first three gospels already considered are sometimes called the synoptics, from two Greek words which mean "a view together," the idea being that they set forth the same general view of the story of Jesus Christ, and contain pretty much the same material although variously arranged. They were the earliest gospels published probably within twenty-five or thirty years of the date of the Ascension, and did the work of an evangelist in carrying the knowledge of Jesus to peoples theretofore ignorant of Him. From among these peoples thus converted to Jesus, Jews, Romans and Greeks, the Christian church was founded, and to this latter body, composed of all three classes, the Gospel of John was addressed.

Thirty years, more or less, had elapsed, and with the growth and development of the church had come up certain questions for investigation and settlement that the fourth gospel was particularly designed to meet. These questions touched especially on the Person and work of Jesus, as the Messiah, His nature and the character and significance of His death, so that in answering them John necessarily reveals to us the deepest and profoundest truth found anywhere in the gospels. For the same reason John's Gospel is nearly altogether new in its facts as compared with the Synoptics. This is not to say that John invented what he wrote, or that the substance of his Gospel was unknown to the other writers, but only that in the wisdom of God the relation of such things as he records was held back until the period when it was particularly needed and could best be understood and appreciated. John was the last survivor of the twelve, dying somewhere near the

close of the first century, kept on the earth by divine Providence, until, like his Master, he, too, had finished the work given him to do.

The proof of the later date of John's Gospel is found in such references as 1:32, and 3:24, which assume a previous knowledge of the facts on the part of his readers. It is found also in the omissions of all the material of the Synoptics down to the passion. There is only one exception to this, the feeding of the 5,000, which was retained in John probably in order to introduce and show the occasion for the discourse following on the Bread of Life (chapter 6).

Further illustration of its profundity, if desired, could be found in the nature of the miracles it records, every one of which seems to show a higher decree of power, for example, than those in the Synoptics, and thus testifying all the more emphatically to the divine origin of Jesus' message, and by inference to the deity of the Messenger. Witness the turning of the water into wine (chapter 2), the healing of the nobleman's son in the same chapter, and that of the impotent man in chapter 5. Also the man born blind (9), and the raising of Lazarus (11).

The nature of the discourses in John's Gospel illustrates the same thing. They are the profoundest themes which fell from the lips of our Lord: The New Birth 3, the Living Water 4, the Honor of the Son 5, the Living Bread, 6, the Good Shepherd, 10, the Farewell Discourse 13-16.

Consider, also, in this connection the character of the doctrines emphasized in John's record. For example, those related to the Godhead alone: Observe how he speaks of God in the abstract, 1:18, 4:24, 5:37. No such teaching

about the nature of God is found anywhere in the Bible outside of the
epistles of this same evangelist and
those of Paul. Observe how he speaks
of God as Father, 3 : 16, 5 : 36, 6 : 37,
8 : 18, 10 : 30, 17 : 11. Observe how he
speaks of the person of Jesus Christ
as related to the Father, 1 : 1, 14, 18,
5 : 17, 18, 26, 14 : 9, 10 ; and as related
to man, 1 : 4, 6 : 46, 8 :40-46, etc. Observe finally how he speaks of the Holy
Spirit, 3 : 5, 4 : 14, 7 : 38, 14 : 12, 16, 26,
15 : 26, 16 : 7. Of course, in these instances, it is frequently Christ Himself
who is speaking and John simply re-
porting or quoting Him, but the point
is, it was left for John of all the evangelists to do this, to report Him in
these deeper and profounder utterances concerning the Godhead which
are so important for the church to
know :

Outline of the Gospel.—The following
outline of John's Gospel following the
general lines of the preceding ones may
be helpful :

I. The Preface, 1 : 1-14:—In the preface observe the earliest illustration of
the depth and profundity of John's presentation of Jesus as the Son of God.
Nothing quite corresponding to these
opening verses is found in any of the
Synoptics. John positively asserts the
deity of Jesus, and shows Him to be the
Creator of all things and the source
of all life (verses 1-5). He empha-
hizes the point very definitely, moreover, by comparing Jesus with John the
Baptist (6-9). He is careful, too, at
the beginning, to proclaim Jesus as the
source of the renewed spiritual life of
man, the eternal life which is co-incident with salvation (10-13). And yet
side by side with these declarations of
and testimonies to Jesus' Godhead, see
how he demonstrates His perfect humanity as well (14).

**II. The Testimony of John the Bap-
tist, 1 : 15-34:**—Every student will be
impressed with the originality of the
record in this Gospel concerning the
testimony of John the Baptist. Nothing corresponding to it is found in the
Synoptics. Observe his testimony to
the pre-existence and deity of Jesus
Christ (15-18), and to the sacrificial
nature of His death (29). These words
as well as those of the preface stamp
this Gospel as that which especially reveals the "deep things of God" concerning the person and work of the
Messiah. It was questions of this
character which arose for settlement
in the early church and which John
was retained on the earth to answer.
Was Jesus God as well as man? Was

His death a sacrifice for human guilt?
How clearly the Baptist's witness bears
upon these points.

**III. The First Visit to Judea, 1 : 35-
2 : 12:**—It is a peculiarity of the fourth
Gospel that it dwells at length upon the
ministry of Jesus in Judea while the
others mention more especially His
ministry in Galilee. In Matthew, for
example, after the narrative of the baptism which took place there, there is
scarcely any allusion to Jesus visiting
Judea until that of the nineteenth chapter, which was evidently His last visit,
coincident with His betrayal and crucifixion. Perhaps a convenient division
of the present Gospel will be along the
line of these different visits to Judea.

This first division really includes
the event of the baptism, overlapping
what we have described as the testimony of John, and might be said to
begin at verse 29 instead of 35. Besides the baptism it includes the call
of the first four disciples (35-51), a
call preliminary or introductory to the
later or more formal call referred to
in the other gospels.

This first visit to Judea at the opening of Jesus' ministry, in connection
with His baptism and the calling of
His disciples, ended with His return
to Capernaum in Galilee, on which
journey was wrought the marvelous
work of creation in the turning of the
water into wine at the wedding feast.
The nature of this miracle and the
bearing of its record upon the peculiar
position of John's Gospel has been already alluded to.

**IV. The Second Visit to Judea, 2 :
13-4:**—With reference to what occasion, and hence at what period of the
year, did this visit take place (2 : 13)?
With what display of Jesus' authority
and power is it associated (14-17)?
Comparing this with Matthew 21 : 12,
13, it would seem that this transaction
was repeated at the last Passover. In
what manner did He refer at this time
to His death and resurrection (18-22)?
What great discourse of Jesus is associated with this second visit to Judea
(3 : 1-21)? Where did this discourse
occur presumably (2 : 23)? How does
the theme of this discourse demonstrate
the profundity of the thought of this
gospel, and bear out the theory that it
was written for the church? How further does John the Baptist bear testimony to Jesus on this visit (3 : 25-36)?
An analysis of this testimony, like that
also in the first chapter, would make
an excellent sermon, or Bible-reading
outline. He testifies (1) to Jesus' relationship to His people (verse 29) ;

(2), His growing influence and authority (30); (3), His exaltation (31); (4) His truth (32, 34); (5), His supreme power and grace (35, 36).

What reason is assigned for Jesus' departure from Judea at this time (4: 1-3)? Whence did He journey, and what route did He take (3, 4)? What exhibition of loving grace was associated with this journey (5-42)? How long did Jesus remain in Samaria, and where did He next go (43)? What miracle is connected with this return journey to Galilee, and how does it bear on the general purpose of John's Gospel (46-54) An allusion to this miracle was made in the introduction to our study of John.

V. The Third Visit to Judea, 5-6 :— This visit like the second was occasioned by the Passover, and hence seems to have been a year later (6). What miracle was wrought on this occasion (2-9)? With what effect on the unbelieving Jews (10-16) How does Jesus justify such labor on the Sabbath day (17)? On what two-fold ground did His enemies seek to kill Him (18)? The latter of these two grounds, because He said "God was His Father," is peculiar and deeply important. The Revised Version translates it because "He also called God His OWN Father." The Jews understood Him to declare God to be His Father in a unique sense, a sense in which He was not the Father of other men. This is why they said He made "himself equal with God." The importance of this is seen in that it contains a direct claim on Jesus' part to be equal with God, i. e., a claim of absolute deity.

The Jews whom He addressed so regarded His words, and Jesus took no pains to correct that impression, on the contrary, His words that follow are an argument, and the only one from His lips which I know, to establish the truth of that opinion, to prove that He was God. Almost all the verses following down to verse 31 prove this, but especially and directly verse 23. This discourse on the Honor of the Son concludes with a kind of supplementary one on the Four Witnesses (32-47). We have here cited by Jesus Himself, the witness of John the Baptist (32-35), the witness of His own marvelous works (36), the witness of the Father (37, 38), and the witness of the Holy Scriptures (39), but how utterly vain so far as moving the wills of His unbelieving countryment was concerned (40)!

Leaving Judea again, where do we next find Jesus (6:: 1-3)? What miracle is associated therewith (5-13)?

This is the only miracle found in the other gospels which is also recorded by John, and this for the reason doubtless of leading up to the important discourse following on the Living Bread. What effect had this miracle on those who saw it (14)? What did they propose to do with Jesus in consequence of their opinion (15)? What did the knowledge of their purpose lead Jesus to do? What bearing has His action at this time to the incident in chapter 18: 10, 11, and His words before Pilate in the same chapter, verse 36? To what place did Jesus depart? What miracle took place during the night (16-21)? Where next do we find Jesus (22-24)? It is at this point the great discourse is given to which reference has been made, and which is one of those which, like the others already referred to, gives to the gospel its distinctively spiritual character. At what place was this discourse given (59)? How does it seem to have been received by the people generally (41, 52)? How by the disciples (60, 66)? What foreshadowing of His death does He reveal at this time (66-71)? Why did He confine His ministry to Galilee just now (7:1)?

VI. The Fourth Visit to Judea, 7-19 :— We now reach in John's Gospel what I believe is the record of the last visit of Jesus to Judea (i. e., I do not believe He returned into Galilee after this prior to His crucifixion), but as the period covered is long, and the events many, we will, for convenience, sub-divide the whole section as follows:

(1) At the Feast of Tabernacles, (7-10:21). How did the brethren of Jesus regard Him at this time (7:2-5)? What hesitancy did He exhibit in going up to this fest (6-9)? This feast, it will be recalled, took place not in the spring, like the Passover, but in the fall, corresponding to our October. This chapter and the next I have always identified as those of the Controversies in the Temple. They represent periods of sustained contention with enemies, and of nervous excitement. (though the latter expression will not be regarded as applicable to Jesus personally), such as are described nowhere else in the gospels. The crisis so clearly indicated in each of the Synoptics is now rapidly approaching. Examine in this connection verses 12, 13, 20, 26, 27, 30, 32, 43, of chapter 7. What effect had Jesus' answers to His opponents upon the officials (45, 46)? What authoritative person speaks on His behalf at this critical moment (50-52)?

Where did Jesus pass the night after this trying and exhausting day (8:1)? How, do we imagine, was He resting, by sleep or in prayer? Where is He found again the next morning (2)? With what work of courage and grace does the day begin (3-11)? Who came off victor in that contest of light and darkness, Jesus or His adversaries (6)? The controversy now begins again by Jesus' bold declaration of Himself as "the Light of the World," a declaration which, if unsupported by the truth, makes Him to be an insane imposter, but otherwise establishes His right to be all that this gospel claims for Him —even that He is God Himself. Observe the features of the controversy all through this chapter, but especially at verses 13, 19, 25, 37, 48, 52, 59. Observe, too, the repeated declarations of Jesus bearing upon the dignity of His person, as in verses 16, 18, 19, 23, 28, 36, 42, 46, 51, 56, 58. It is comforting also to note that His testimony during the day was not fruitless in the increase of discipleship (30).

As Jesus passed through and away from this murderous crowd, what miracle is wrought (chapter 9)? What explanation does Jesus afford as to why this man was born blind (3)? How does this work of power and mercy effect the enemies of Jesus, does it soften or harden their opposition (16, 28, 29)? What did they finally do to the man (34)? What does "cast him out" probably mean? Compare verse 22, last clause. How does Jesus make a further claim of deity in subsequently addressing this man (35-37)? It is to be observed in this connection that the sublime discourse on the Good Shepherd, following in chapter 10, grew out of this circumstance of the casting out of this healed man from the synagogue because of his confession of Jesus. The scribes and Pharisees are the "hirelings" Jesus has in mind in that discourse, who showed themselves to be such unmistakably in their treatment of this man. Notice how this discourse also falls into harmony with the distinctive purpose of John's Gospel throughout to present the highest, or if you please, the deepest aspect of Christ's person and work, for example, compare His utterances in verses 10, 11, 15, 17, 18. His work is clearly that of a substitute Savior, and yet none other than God could speak of Himself thus. What opposite results were produced by this discourse (19-21)?

(2) At the Feast of the Dedication, 10:22-42:—The Feast of the Dedication took place midway between that of Tabernacles just dealt with, and that of the Passover, or some time corresponding to our December or January. Where Jesus had been in the meantime is not revealed except that it is not stated that He returned to Galilee. We need not dwell on this period further than to call attention to the same features as prevailed in the previous one, viz., the putting forth of the boldest claims on Jesus' part, followed in every instance by intensest conflict with His opponents. For the claims consult such passages as verses 28 and 30, and the conflict, 31 and 39. What was the sequel of this appearance so far as Jesus was concerned (40, 41)? Notice that in the face of all the criticism and opposition, and in spite of all the efforts of the leaders of the nation to the contrary, the number of the disciples continually increased (42).

(3) At Bethany. Here occurs the great miracle of the raising of Lazarus. In the Synoptics we read of the raising of Jairus' daughter and the son of the widow of Nain. In the first case death had just ensued, and in the second but a single day had intervened. Here, however, Lazarus had been four days dead. Of course, with God it is no harder to restore life in the one case than in either of the others, and yet all must be impressed with the gradation of difficulty illustrated in the three, and that the most difficult, humanly speaking, should be recorded only in John's Gospel. This, like so many other features alluded to, shows us with the distinctive purpose of this gospel to set forth Jesus in the highest aspect of all, that of the Son of God— the Son of God giving life to the world. What a wonderful declaration that in verse 25!

Let us not pass from this incident in Bethany without observing its effect on the leaders of the nation (47, 48), and the nature of that prophecy, all unwittingly uttered, by Caiaphas, which so clearly set forth the precise character of the work Jesus came into the world to do (49-52). Nor let us fail to be impressed by the fact that the crisis is now rapidly drawing to a head (53), in consequence of which Jesus withdraws Himself again (54).

(4) At the last Passover, 12-17. The note of time suggesting this sub-division of our lesson is found at the close of chapter 11, verses 55-57. The last-named indicates the state of feeling towards Jesus prevailing at this time among the leaders of the people, and explains the conditions which made this the last Passover He ever attended. Where do we find Jesus at the begin-

ning of chapter 12? What is the incident emphasized on that occasion (3-8)? What events on the day following hastened the plot of His enemies (12-19)? The succeeding incident recorded is that of the visit of the Greeks, which some regard as the second great temptation in Jesus' life. The considerations justifying such a view are found in the effect which the request of these Greeks to see Him made upon Jesus Himself: "Now is my soul troubled," "Except a corn of wheat fall into the ground and die," "Father, save me from this hour." Also in the heavenly testimony to His Sonship which was again afforded Him.

We should not pass to the consideration of the next leading topic, without observing in passing, the additionally strong testimony John bears as his manner is to the deity of Jesus. See, for example, the argument to be drawn from his words in verses 37-41, especially the last-named. Look up the quotation in Isaiah 6, and ask yourself the question whether John's testimony must not be utterly dishonored unless Jesus is to be regarded as God incarnate. How corroborative of this are Jesus' own words, moreover, in verses 44, 45.

Following the visit of the Greeks the next leading event is how described in chapter 13? What is the ostensible lesson taught in this transaction (12-16) And yet is there not more than a lesson in humility here? What of the deep and mysterious teaching in verses 8, 9? Many expositors think we have here a symbolic representation of Christ's intercessory work for His people. They are already "clean" as far as their salvation is concerned, because of their faith in Him, and on the ground of His finished work on the Cross; but passing through the world brings daily defilement which requires daily cleansing, for which provision is made by His all-prevailing intercession as our High-priest. Compare 1 John 1 : 9.

What singular omission is found in this gospel with reference to the events of this last Passover night as compared with the Synoptics? What additional details of the betrayal are given here (18-30)?

The washing of the disciples' feet and the departure of Judas on his wicked errand, are followed by what is frequently designated the Farewell discourse, covering chapters 13-16, and which, like almost the whole of this gospel, is quite original in comparison with the others. These chapters are described by Canon Bernard as "The Central Teaching of Jesus Christ," and others call them the heart of the heart of the Gospel. Observe the themes treated of : The preparation for the second coming (14 : 1-3), the identity of the Father and the Son (6-11), the office of the Holy Spirit in the church (15-31), the source and the responsibility of fruit-bearing (15 : 1-17), the attitude of the world to the church (18-16 : 4), the office of the Holy Spirit toward the world (5-15), the personal comfort of the disciples (16-33). Perhaps there is nothing in the whole of this precious and sublime discourse of more practical value to us than what it teaches the disciple about prayer. See 14 : 13, 14, 15 : 16, 16 : 23-27. To ask the Father in Christ's name is something in advance of asking for his sake even. To ask in His name is the same as though He asked Himself with all the assurance of answer which such a fact implies. This is the privilege of the true believer who is thus a member of Christ's body, and it is a revelation of truth which Christ had at no time made known to His followers until now, doubtless, because they were not prepared to receive it.

This wonderful discourse is followed in turn by the equally wonderful prayer in chapter 17, its scope including His own glory and work (1-5), His disciples (6-19), and believers generally 20-26). It seems almost sacriligious to hasten over these so solemn and loving words, but we have time only to call attention to the four petitions offered on our behalf, (1), our preservation, verse 11, (2), our sanctification, verse 17, (3), our unification, verse 21, and (4), our glorification, verse 24.

(5) At man's judgment seat, 18-19 : 16. It would be interesting and suggestive to read this chapter in comparison with the corresponding ones in the Synoptics, in order to notice particularly what John omits and what he emphasizes. What illustration of Jesus' dignity and power is here mentioned in connection with the arrest (4-7)? What illustration of His tenderness and consideration for His disciples (8, 9)? What additional information is given by John in the story of Peter's rashness (10)? Who presumably was that "another disciple" mentioned in verse 15? What is original with John in the report of Jesus' trial before Pilate (28-40)?

(6) On the Cross, 19 : 17-37. While the different evangelists give different translations or versions of the three-fold inscription on the Cross, in what particular expression are they a unit? How do the malevolent Jews seek to

avoid the bearing of this expression (21)? What is original with John as to the events occurring while Jesus was upon the Cross (23-37)? How many distinct Old Testament prophecies does he refer to as fulfilled thereby?

(7) After the Resurrection, 20-21. What is original with John as to the burial of Jesus (19 : 38-42)? As to the details of the resurrection (20 : 1-18)? As to the first meeting of Jesus with His disciples (19-25)? What additional proof of the reality of the resurrection does this gospel afford in verses 26-29? What is stated as the object for the writing of the gospel (30,

31)? Why, do you suppose, was the addendum given in chapter 21? What apparently, was the particular object in recording that appearance of Jesus to His disciples in detail? Do you suppose the transaction of verses 15-17 explains it? Was it not just like our Savior to give Peter who denied Him thrice an opportunity to become restored in a triple confession of Him again? What prophecy of Peter's manner of death follows (18, 19)? Compare this with II Peter 1 : 14. What rumor subsequently became current about John, and why (20-23)?

CHAPTER XLV.

The Acts of the Apostles.

We shall divide the book of the Acts along historical lines, following the growth and development of the church from Jerusalem to Judea, Syria, Asia Minor and the Continent of Europe,

I. The Jerusalem Period, Chapters 1-7.—(1) Under this head we treat first, of the preface or introduction to the book covered by verses 1 and 2 of chapter one. In this preface we notice a reference to a former treatise which the writer has made, addressed to a person named Theophilus, and purporting to contain a record of the sayings and doings of Jesus up until the time of His ascension—declarations of fact which at once bring to mind the Gospel of Luke, suggesting, if not altogether proving, that he, as well, was the author of the Acts of the Apostles.

(2) We have secondly, the account of the ascertain of Christ, 1 : 2-11. The facts associated with this event and leading up to it are, first of all, the testimony of Luke to His resurrection (verse 3). Then follows the allusion of Christ to the forthcoming baptism of His disciples by the Holy Spirit (verses 4, 5). The inquiry of the disciples concerning the kingdom and our Lord's reply thereto, (verses 6-8), substantiates the teachings heretofore insisted on, that the kingdom expected by the former, and promised by the latter, was a literal kingdom to be set up on this earth. If they had been mistaken as to this, or if our Lord's rejection and crucifixion had changed the divine purpose, this would have been the opportunity, one would think, for our Lord to have indicated that

fact. But instead of doing so, He permits His disciples to continue in their expectation, only premising that the time for its realization was not to be made known. In further corroboration of this the circumstances of the ascension itself bear witness (verses 9-11). Especially observe the carefully chosen language of the angels to the disciples, verse 11. Who shall come again? How shall He come? Where is He in the meantime? Let us take every opportunity to emphasize the fact to others that our Savior is alive, not dead ; and that He is now existing as a glorified God-man in the Heavens, whence He is coming again in flaming fire taking vengeance on them that know not God and obey not His Gospel, but to be admired in all them that believe in that day (II Thessalonians 1).

(3) We have thirdly, the choice of Matthias by the disciples to succeed Judas, 1 : 12-26.

(4) We have fourthly, the baptism with the Holy Ghost, on the day of Pentecost, 2 : 1-47. As we learned in our studies in Leviticus this feast of the Jews came on the fiftieth day after the Passover, which would make it in this case about ten days after our Lord's ascension. The event it now signalizes was the fulfillment of the promise in the first chapter, verse 5— a baptism of the church which, in my judgment, was once and for all time. I think it is to this baptism Paul refers in 1 Corinthians 12 : 13, and possibly, in Ephesians 4 : 5. It seems to me that every true believer in Jesus Christ partakes of this baptism the

moment he so believes, and that it is this which constitutes him a member of the body of Christ. See 1 Corinthians 3:16, 6:19, 11 Corinthians 6:16, Ephesians 1:13. This is not to say that the believer may *not* from time to time require and obtain a renewed infilling of the Holy Spirit—(later Scriptures will be found to teach this), but only that so far as the baptism with the Holy Spirit is concerned it would seem to be extra-Scriptural to be seeking for it after it has thus once been obtained. It is a comfort to learn from Peter's words, verses 37-39, on what simple conditions this baptism becomes ours, and how extensive is the promise of grace concerning it.

(5) We are now brought face to face with the early conflicts of the church 3-7. There are three such conflicts recorded in these chapters. The first grew out of the miracle on the lame man at the Beautiful Gate of the temple, and the anger of the leaders of the nation that the apostles, Peter and John, should in that connection have "preached through Jesus the resurrection from the dead." (Chapters 3-4.) Let particular attention be given to verses 25 and 26 of chapter 3, the closing part of Peter's discourse, which afford some reason for the opinion alluded to in an earlier study that a second offer of the kingdom was made to the Jews after the ascension of Jesus, had they been ready even then to receive it by receiving Him as their Messiah. In this instance, however, as previously, the leaders were averse to His claims, as witness their action against the apostles, chapter 4. Why were they unable to gainsay the utterances of the apostles (14)? What was the outcome of this first conflict between the church and the Jewish nation (18-21)? What was the effect upon the church (23-31)?

The second conflict seems to have grown out of the apostolic persistence in preaching the Word notwithstanding the prohibition against it. The story is found in chapter 5:12-42, and it will be seen that in this case as in the previous one the Sadducces were foremost in the opposition. They were the religious party in the nation which denied the future life, and who were in consequence, particularly incensed at the preaching of the resurrection (5:17). What supernatural interposition was made on behalf of the prisoners in this case (18-20)? What shows the popularity of the preaching at this time (26)? Is there any indication that the apostles were intimidated (29-32)? Who appears on their behalf, and with what plea (33-39)? What

different treatment was given the apostles in this case (40)? What effect did it produce (41, 42)?

The third conflict arose around Stephen, the history of which is found in chapters 6 and 7, and which marked a crisis in the affairs of the church as we shall see in our next lesson.

(6) In our study of these conflicts of the church we have discovered also certain marks of progress. For example, study the picture given us of the church, chapter 2:41-47, the loyalty, the power, the love, the gladness, the increase. Also that given likewise at the close of chapter 4. Note in this connection the sharp contrast between the spirit and disposition of the many and that of the two who through pride were led into hypocrisy and falsehood (chapter 5). And note the signal and swift judgment that fell upon them and its immediate result in the discipline of the church generally. A further mark of progress is seen in the appointment of the deacons (chapter 6).

.II. The Palestinian Period, 8-12.—
This period has to do chiefly with the work of

Philip in Samaria, ... 8
Paul in Damascus, ... 9
Peter in Cæsarea, ...10-12

What explains the outspreading of the work into Samaria (8:1)? Who were excepted from the general exodus? Was the evangelistic work of the early church limited to the apostles, or even to them and the deacons (7, 8)? What are we to understand then, by the word "preaching" in this case, sermonizing, or the simple testimony to the Person and work of Christ? Has the church, have we, individual believers, anything to learn from this circumstance? Who was the divinely-chosen leader of the work in Samaria (5)? What have we learned of his character in a previous chapter? With what blessing did his labors meet (6-8)? How did Satan seek to withstand him (9-11)? How does Satan's emissary himself become a witness to the superior power of God (13)? What proves the insincerity of his professions (18-23)? Is there any evidence of deeper conviction on his part (24)? What transaction in the history of the church in Samaria shows a distinction of some kind between believing on Christ for salvation and receiving the Holy Ghost (14-17)? I am of the opinion that every believer on Christ receives the Holy Spirit in some sense the moment he so believes, and that this is equivalent to the baptism of the Holy Spirit spoken of above, and which makes us a member of Christ's body.

But I believe there is such a thing as a deeper or fuller work of the Spirit in the believer which some receive after they believe, and that this is what is referred to in the present case.

What was the next mission on which Philip was sent (26-40)? The interest in this mission gathers around the supernatural features connected with it (verses 26, 29, 39), and the additional fact that it resulted in the introduction of the Gospel to the great continent of Ethiopia.

With whom is the history chiefly connected in chapter 9? What keynote to the nature of Paul's ministry is afforded in the Lord's words to Ananias (verse 15)? To what people was he particularly sent? In what city did his ministry begin? (While Damascus is not? strictly speaking, in Palestine, but Syria, yet the proximity of the two countries seems to warrant us in classifying what was done in Damascus, as well as later in Antioch, in the Palestinian period.) Who interests himself especially in Paul at this time, and for what reason (26, 27)? Where, finally, is Paul obliged to be sent (30)?

With whose ministry are we now once more concerned (32-43)? It would be well to familiarize one's self with these locations on the map—Lydda, Joppa, Cæsarea. Whose conversion is narrated at length in chapter 10? Was he a Jew or a Gentile? Observe the method God employed to assure Peter of His purpose to have the Gospel preached to the Gentiles (9-21).

Nevertheless, while these transactions were going on in Cæsarea and Jerusalem, certain religious experiments of the same kind were being tried elsewhere. For example, where, and by whom (19-21)? Who again come into prominence together in connection with this work (23-26)? How long did they remain there? For what is Antioch memorable at this time (26)? What shows that the same Spirit of love Who dwelt in the Jewish Christians dwelt also in the Gentiles (27-30)?

We have seen that Stephen was the first martyr of the church; who was the second, according to chapter 12? What seems to have been a meeting-place for the Jerusalem church at this time (12)? How did persecution effect the growth of the church (24)? What "ministry" of Barnabas and Saul is referred to in verse 25? Compare 11:29, 30. Who now comes into prominence as a Christian worker (25)? This was doubtless him whom we know as the author of the second Gospel.

III. The Asia Minor Period, 13-15.—

At this point begins the account of Paul's first missionary journey. Whence did it originate, and under what circumstances (13:1-3)? What shows the presence of the Lord by His Spirit in the administration of the affairs of the church at this time? The query arises as to whether He does not still guide and direct as He did then, when He is permitted by the church so to do? May not the absence of His direction and guidance explain a great many things in the subsequent history of the church which are not to her credit, and which have made her a hindrance instead of a help to the world?

Trace the course of this first missionary journey on the map from Antioch to Paphos. What interest did Barnabas have in this direction? Compare 4:36. Who accompanied the two missionaries on this journey (5)? In what way did Satan seek to frustrate their work at Paphos? Who was their first notable convert? In what special manner was the power of God manifested in their ministry?

Trace the course of their journey from Paphos to Iconium (51). In what manner did John Mark signalize himself (13)? How do you distinguish the Antioch of this chapter from that in the previous one? Where and among what class of persons did Paul begin his ministry in this place (14)? In what spirit did they receive his message (45)? How do verses 46, 47, illustrate the special mission intrusted to Paul? What success was met with at Iconium (14:1-3)? How was the experience of Antioch repeated there (4-6)? What incidents, opposite in character, marked the stay at Lystra (8-19)? How did this first journey draw to a close (20-28)? What token of progress and development in the church is indicated in verse 23?

The First Church Council.—The fifteenth chapter of the Acts is one of the most important, historically and doctrinally, in the New Testament. False teachers of a Judaizing tendency, i. e., those who were ever seeking to make the Gentile Christians conform to the Mosaic law, followed Paul and Barnabas to Antioch, and indeed to other places, contradicting and undermining the Gospel of simple faith they preached (15:1). In order to silence their contention and establish the doctrine of justification by faith only, a gathering of the leaders of the church was held at Jerusalem before which Paul and Barnabas appeared. Peter also bore testimony in corroboration of their work (6-11). Finally, the decision of the council was reduced to writing and sent forth to all the Gentile churches endorsing the position of the two apostles afore-named, and settling the question of the way in which a man may be just with God for all time (24-29). Compare Peter's words in verse 11. This chapter deserves the closest study, that it may be fastened upon the memory because of its important bearing on the subsequent teaching of Paul, and, indeed, on all the later history of the church.

Some little time after the decision of the Jerusalem Council on the question of circumcision and related subjects, Paul and Barnabas purposed a second journey to the cities in Asia Minor where they had established churches. Their original plan, however, was seriously altered by the difference of opinion which arose between them on the subject of selecting John Mark, Barnabas' nephew, to accompany them. The result was four missionaries instead of two, and two missionary tours instead of one. The narrative in the Acts follows the career of Paul and Silas, beginning with what we may describe as

IV. The Greco-Macedonian Period, 15: 36-21: 17.—This period covers what is commonly known as the second and third missionary journeys of Paul. The second journey began with an excursion through what countries (15: 40, 41)? No mention is elsewhere made of churches located in these parts, except the one at Antioch in Syria, and the fact illustrates the great triumphs with which Christianity met at the first, far beyond anything which is recorded in this brief inspired account. What event of importance transpired at Lystra, and how does Paul's reception there contrast with his former experience in the same place (16: 1-3)? How does Paul exhibit his tactful disposition in this matter (3)? As this part of the journey was apparently among the churches already established, confirmatory of their faith (16: 4), what commission did the apostles execute on the way (4)? What was the effect of these apostolic visits (5)? What provinces did they next visit (6)? It appears that at this point in their travels the Holy Spirit designed to change the nature of their service from that of overseers of the flock to that for which they were originally chosen, viz: evangelists and missionaries. How is this divine purpose illustrated in verses 6-8? How farther in verses 9 and 10? Crossing the Aegean sea, what was the first place in Europe where the Gospel was preached, and with what results (11-40)? This

whole story of Paul's stay in Philippi should be read and re-read until it is known by heart. From Philippi the workers passed through Amphipolis and Apollonia to the great city of Thessalonica, the location of which should be identified on the map. In what respect did the population of this city differ from that of Philippi (17: 1)? How long was Paul permitted to remain here (2)? With what success at first (4)? Under what circumstances did he leave and where did he go (5-10). How are the Bereans distinguished (11, 12)? What is the story of Paul's visit to Athens (13-34)? What two disciples are introduced to us in chapter 18? By what means does Paul support himself in Corinth (3)? What supernatural encouragement is afforded him there (9, 10)? How long did he remain in that city (11)? Where did he next go (18, 19)? Why did he remain there so brief a time (20, 21)? To what point did he return (22)?

The third journey begins at this point with a further visit to the country of Phrygia and Galatia (23), from which point we next hear of Paul at the great metropolis of Asia (19: 1). In the meantime what other distinguished teacher has been brought upon the scene (18: 24-28)? What extraordinary marks of the Spirit's power are evidenced in Paul's ministry at Ephesus (6, 11, 12, 19, 20)? What circumstance testifies in a very practical way to the spread of Gospel truth in that neighborhood (23-41? Where did Paul go after leaving Ephesus (20: 1, 2)? Why did he return from Greece by land rather than water (3)? What word in verse 5 represents the author of the Acts as a companion of Paul and eye-witness of what he records? Contrast the two visits of Paul to Troas. Did Paul visit Ephesus again on this return trip (16)? What was the occasion of his haste? Nevertheless did he meet any representatives of the church at that place, and if so, under what circumstances (17-38)? How long had Paul remained in that city (31)? What shows the strong affection entertained for him by the brethren of that church (36-38)? It will be interesting and helpful to the memory to follow with a map the course of Paul and his companions from this point to Tyre, and thence to Cæsarea and finally Jerusalem (21: 1-17). What warning does Paul receive at Tyre (4)? We need to be careful here not to suppose that it was the Holy Spirit Himself who sought to persuade Paul against going up to Jerusalem. If such had been the case it would have been gross disobedience on the apostle's part to have done so, and the afflictions coming on him there would have been a just chastisement for his sin. The Spirit informed him through these brethren that he would be exposed there to great suffering, but it was the brethren and not the Spirit of God who urged him not to go up. It was a case of human error connecting itself with the divine truth, the flesh lusting against the Spirit, and suggests Peter's unholy dissuasion of his Lord in Matthew 16:21-23. How is this prophecy repeated, and with what additional particulars when the company reaches Cæsarea (10-12)? There was obscurity in the prediction at Tyre which is removed at Cæsarea, according to the divine principle by which revelations become clearer as the time for their fulfillment approaches.

V. The Roman Period, 21: 18-28.— Deep interest attaches to every detail leading up to Paul's visit to Rome. Our attention is called first, to his meeting with James and the other leaders at Jerusalem, where he rehearses "particularly what things God had wrought among the Gentiles by his ministry" (19). It seems to have been his habit always to stop at Jerusalem on his homeward trips, although the real end of his journey on each occasion was Antioch of Syria, the Gentile headquarters of the church. What Jewish custom was Paul prevailed upon to observe on this occasion; and on what ground (20-26)? A large number of the converted Christian Jews entertained a prejudice against Paul, because in his preaching to the Gentiles he insisted on salvation by faith without the observance of the Mosaic ceremonial law. It was the old story of Acts 15 repeated, and which, in one way or another, continues to be repeated even in our own time. In this case, to disarm prejudice, the great apostle to the Gentiles is induced to engage in one of the acts of the ceremonial law—one, the performance of which involved the violation of no Christian principle, and might do much to bring about a better feeling in the church. Into what difficulty did this lead Paul (27-30)? It is to be borne in mind that the Jews who stirred up this tumult against the apostle were not the converted Jews to conciliate whom he had taken upon himself this vow, but unconverted Jews, those who had given in no adherence to the Christian religion, and who had known of Paul and his teaching when he was in the neighborhood of Ephesus. By what providence was he delivered from the angry multitude (31-36)? In his defence before the people what circumstance in his experience does he newly dwell upon (17-21)? It would make a deeply valuable study to consider the number of such revelations of the Person of Jesus with which Paul was blessed. What was the immediate issue of this defence so far as Paul was concerned (22-29)? What second opportunity for a hearing is arranged for (30)? Into what error did Paul fall at the first (23:1-5)? By what tactful action on his part was he released from the critical situation (6-10)? What divine encouragement did he receive (11)? What conspiracy was entered into against him (12-15)? By what providence was he delivered out of their hands and into what place does he now come (16-35)? Under what circumstances is he now accused before Felix (24:1-9)? What kind of person is Felix seen to be (22-27)? Before whom is Paul now arraigned (25:1-8)? Is it not assuring to note how God moved upon the mind of a wicked governor like Festus in such a way as to frustrate the plans of Paul's adversaries? By what demand of Paul is it finally determined he shall proceed to Rome (9-12)? What circumstance intervenes (13-26)? On the sea-journey what information was divinely vouchsafed to Paul (9-11)? And later (21-27)? What indicates on the part of the soldiers an increasing respect for the words and opinions of the apostle? (Compare verse 11 with verses 31, 32, 33-36). How again, did God act upon the mind of an unbeliever to spare the life of His servant and carry out His will in bringing Him to the scene of his labors (41-43)?

Have you examined the map to locate the island of Melita or Malta (28:1)? What supernatural works were wrought on that island (7-9)? What particular consideration was shown Paul, as a prisoner, in Rome (16)? What did he improve as an early opportunity to do in the line of his divine calling (17-20)? What was the result of this first meeting (21-23)? The result of the second meeting (24-29)? How long did the apostle remain in Rome, and under what circumstances (30-31)?

There are reasons for believing that Paul had a hearing before Cæsar as the result of which he was set at liberty, pursuing his missionary journeys further to the West. Afterwards, however, as tradition holds, he was re-arrested, tried and beheaded in Rome as a martyr to the Christian faith. We shall touch upon these subjects again when we come to the study of some of his later epistles. It is presumable, by the way, that four of his epistles, and five, if we shall count Hebrews as one of his, were written during this imprisonment—Ephesians. Colossians, Philippians, Philemon, Hebrews. There is little doubt also that Luke, and other of the leading disciples who accompanied Paul to Rome, or who visited him there, labored diligently in the city at this time; but as another remarks, what almost unprecedented modesty is instanced in Luke's case, the historian of these records, who is wholly silent concerning his labors and sufferings!

CHAPTER XLVI.

The Epistle to the Romans.

In studying the epistle of Paul to the Romans we meet with:

I. The Salutation, 1:1-7.—The salutation consists of certain descriptions which may be indicated thus:

The writer, verse 1.

The Gospel to which he has been separated, (verse 2).

The Person of whom that Gospel testifies, (verses 3, 4).

The particular service to which the writer has been called, (verse 5).

The people to whom this message is now sent, (verses 6, 7).

II. The Thanksgiving, 1:8-15.—Observe that for which the thanksgiving is offered (verse 8), and how that the thanksgiving is mingled with prayer (verse 9). A special petition in this prayer is indicated (10), and the object of that petition (11). The modesty of the great apostle is beautifully illustrated in verse 12, the reason for his delay in visiting them (13), and the obligation he feels toward them (14, 15).

The terms of this thanksgiving would indicate that Paul had not yet visited Rome, and hence that the epistle antedates the events in the closing chapters of the Acts which we have so recently considered. Little did he know at this time, doubtless, how it should please his Lord and Master to gratify that longing desire to see them of which he speaks. If we inquire, therefore, how this epistle came to be written to them, we find a hint in chapter 16:1, where Phoebe, the deaconness, is mentioned as about to embark on a business journey from Cenchrea to Rome, of which advantage is taken to send a message. Cenchrea, as the map shows, is adjacent to Corinth, which gives rise to the probability that the epistle was penned, as were some others doubtless, during Paul's long residence in the last-named city. See Acts 18.

But part of the argument which goes to show that Paul had not visited Rome up until this time, shows also that no other apostle had done so. Reference is here meant to what he says in verse 11, about the impartation to them of spiritual gifts. Had he been preceded by any other apostle such gifts would have been likely to be dispensed to the church. Moreover, it seems to have been a principle with Paul not to build on another man's foundation (see chapter 15:20, and also 11 Corinthians 10:14-16). If, therefore, any other apostle had established the church in Rome before Paul, he would not have thought of going there at all. This, therefore, would seem to settle the question also, as to whether Peter founded the church at Rome? Roman Catholicism makes much of its affirmations on this point, but it would appear that they are affirmations only.

Who then, did found the church at Rome? Doubtless those we call laymen. From among the great multitudes present at Jerusalem on the day of Pentecost, who were converted and baptized with the Holy Ghost on that day there were some from Rome who, on returning to their home city, carried the seed of the Gospel with them, and it had thus borne fruit.

III. The Theme; the Gift of Righteousness, 16, 17.—The epistle to the Romans is not so much of an epistle, a letter, as it is a treatise. It has a theme, and that theme may be said to be stated in the two verses we are now considering. The apostle had expressed himself as ready to preach the Gospel to them that were at Rome, the Barbarians, as Latins were called to distinguish them from the Greeks, and he now essays a reason for his readiness to do this. He declares that he is "not ashamed of the Gospel of Christ." And why is he not ashamed of it? Because of its dynamics, because of what it can do. "It is the power of God unto salvation." But wherein consists its power? In what does its power lie? What is the essence of the Gospel? It is this, that "therein is the righteousness of God revealed from faith to faith," or as the Revised Version more properly translates it, "a righteousness of God." It is not God's own character of righteousness that is revealed, in other words, but another righteousness, a righteousness, as the epistle goes on to teach, which God gives to men, imputes to them on the exercise of their faith in Christ. To use another's words, it is "the rightness which proceeds from God, i. e., the right relation in which man is placed by a judicial act of God." It does not mean that a man is made righteous in his personal character, but declared righteous in point of law. The phrase is used seven times in the epistle, and becomes its keynote, carrying its meaning with it as it goes along. We are justified, therefore, in calling the theme of the epistle, "The Gift of Righteousness." From the human side, that which man does in order to be justified is to believe (trust) on Christ; but from the divine side, that which God does, which justifies the man who believes on Christ, is to impute unto him His own righteousness.

IV. The Necessity of the Gift, I: 18-3: 20.—No sooner does the apostle reach the declaration of his theme than he plunges into the development of it. And the first point he dwells upon is its necessity. Just as a righteousness of God is revealed from Heaven, so a wrath of God against all unrighteousness of men is revealed (verse 18); and it is this revelation of His wrath which makes necessary the revelation of His righteousness if men shall be saved. This revelation of God's wrath is in the Scriptures, but it is also in the conscience of every human being, as the context plainly shows. But we must not do God the injustice to associate this wrath with impatience on His part, or anything arbitrary or unjust. It is, as Bishop Moule says, the anger of Him who never for a moment can be untrue to Himself, who is Love and who is Light, but who is also a consuming Fire (Hebrews 10: 31, 12: 29).

The unrighteousness of men against which this holy wrath is revealed is stated in detail in the verses which follow in this chapter. And it is of the most solemn interest to note that men are without excuse in committing it (19-23). In excusing the heathen world to-day we are apt to say that they know no better, but God's Word says differently. Not only did they know better, but knowing better, they deliberately closed their eyes and turned their backs upon that knowledge, and the darkness and wickedness into which they have fallen from being the cause, has become the effect of their awful folly (24-32).

Nor is this a condition true of some men in the world and not of all, for in chapter 2, verses 1-16, the indictment is laid at the door of every one. Not that all men are guilty of all the sins enumerated in the black catalogue of chapter 1, but being guilty of some, they are without exception exposed to the wrath revealed against the whole.

And this is true not only of the Gentile, but of the Jewish world. The latter, the Jews, might be ready in their self-righteousness, to accept the dictum as applying to those whom they regarded as outside the pale of God's promises and ignorant of His revealed Word; but surely it could not be true of them who rested in the law, and made their boast of God, and knew His will, and considered themselves as guides to the blind and a light of them that were in darkness! Yes, it was true of them also, as the apostle most plainly avers in verses 17-29.

Moreover, so far as the Jews were concerned, it was hardly necessary to produce the testimony of history and experience as in the case of the blind and ignorant Gentiles, for did not their own laws in which they so much boasted teach the same? It is thus the apostle speaks in chapter 3: 1-20. Should the Jews indignantly dispute his position so far as they were concerned, on the ground that he thus put them, the chosen people, on a level with the Gentiles, he would remind them that the very oracles of God, whose commitment to them constituted one of their chief glories, were the authority for what he now said. He would recall to them the teachings of those oracles (9-18), and he would press the point upon their attention that the teachings thus quoted could not have been directed in the first place to the Gentiles, who did not have the Scriptures in which they were contained, but to the Jews distinctively, who, only, in that sense, were "under the law" (19). The result is, he would have them know, that their mouths as well as the mouths of the Gentiles, were stopped, and all the world, Jew and Gentile alike, were guilty before God. The wrath of God revealed against the unrighteousness of one class as much as against that of the other, left the one as truly as the other in need of the gift of His righteousness, which is by faith, if either class were to be saved (20).

V. The Application of the Gift, 3:21-4.

—Paul gathered up his argument under the preceding division in one concentrated sentence: "By the deeds of the law shall no flesh be justified (whether Jew or Gentile); for by the law is the knowledge, (i. e., the moral knowledge) of sin." The more, and better, a man knows the law, the more, and better, he knows what a sinner he is. The Jew thought he knew the law but he did not, as all his history proved. He is represented as surprised at the apostle's declaration that one can not be justified by keeping it. Where shall one obtain a righteousness if not by the law? Paul tells him where. He tells him of a righteousness of God entirely apart from, independent of the law altogether (verse 21). What righteousness is it? Verse 22 answers. That which comes through faith in Jesus Christ, a righteousness given unto and put "upon all them that believe," whether Jew or Gentile, "for there is no difference" between them. In this connection observe verse 25 very particularly, to see what that is concerning Jesus Christ on which saving faith rests. It is not His earthly life, character or example merely, glorious and holy as they were, but His death. Propitiation means "a price of expiation," and this price was His blood. This explains, Paul says, why God bore with sinners in the past, why He forebore them. It was because of what He had eternally purposed, and now made manifest in Christ (26).

This allusion finds illustration and emphasis in chapter 4. Go back a moment to verse 21 of chapter 3. Did some Israelite take exception that this doctrine of righteousness by faith was new? Nay, the apostle answers it is old. It is found in the Old Testament, it is "witnessed by the law and the prophets." And did they ask where or how it was so witnessed? Chapter 4 replies by pointing to the case of Abraham under the general head of the law, and David under the prophets. Both of these distinguished representatives of the Jewish nation and Jewish religion were justified by faith and not by the deeds of the law.

VI. The Effect of the Gift Upon Man

in His Relation to God, Chapter 5.—Being justified by faith, being thus declared righteous in point of law, what is the effect of this new and blessed relationship into which man is brought? It is one of "peace with God" (5:1), "Access," (verse 2), and joy or "rejoicing" (same verse). Moreover, this rejoicing is described as rejoicing "in hope of the glory of God" (2), in "tribulations" (3), and in "God" Himself (11).

The latter half of this chapter corroborates and strengthens the declaration of the former half by a comparison between the imputation of Adam's sin to the race and that of Christ's righteousness to His people (12-21). Here surely, are some of "the deep things of God," some of "the things hard to be understood" in our brother Paul's writings, but which are to be accepted as the other things have been accepted, as Christ Himself is accepted, by faith. To quote Bishop Moule again, we are to remember as another fact of the case, that this division of the chapter deals only incidentally with Adam after all. Its main theme is Christ. Adam is the illustration, Christ is the subject. We are to be shown in Adam, by contrast, some of "the unsearchable riches of Christ." So that our main attention is called not to the brief outline of the mystery of the fall (12-14), but to the assertions of the related splendor of the Redemption (15-21).

Paul closed the last division of his epistle to the Romans with a triumphant paean to the reign of grace. Where sin abounded, i. e., "in the place, the region of fallen humanity," there did grace much more abound, it was equal to the emergency, meeting and overcoming the foe in the case of them that believe.

But this might lead to a false and impious conclusion. If the more sin abounded the more grace, would it not magnify the grace to continue, even after justification, in the commission of sin? The apostle meets this objection in the next division of his treatise, where he shows that the fruit of justification by faith, in the believer's experience, is that of personal holiness. We might designate the next division, therefore, as

VII. The Effect of the Gift Upon Man in His Own Experience, 6-8.

—This truth the apostle sets before us in a gradational series of reflections. In the first place, he shows in chapter 6, that by means of justification man has been brought into a new sphere of existence altogether, where, in the sight of God, he is now dead to sin and alive unto

Synthetic Bible Studies

God (verse 2). The meaning of verse 3 seems to be, that, so closely is the believer identified with the Lord Jesus Christ in God's mind and plan, that when the Saviour died to sin, died to it in the sense that He paid its penalty and it could never again bring Him into the place of judgment, the believer died (in Him) to it in precisely the same way. Verse 4 is to be interpreted also on the same principle. When the Lord Jesus Christ rose from the dead into newness of life, especially with reference to sin and its eternal consequences, the believer is regarded as having risen with Him, and as now walking before God judicially on the plane of resurrection. It is the duty of the believer to hold to this truth by faith, whether he understands or experiences it or not (verse 11). It is the pedestal upon which he rises into an apprehension of his real power over the sins of the flesh (12-14).

But the apostle proceeding to the second stage of development in this part of his argument, shows, in chapter 7, that the justified man is not only brought into a new sphere of existence, but is also actually undergoing a new experience—an experience of conflict with sin in the flesh. The last half of the chapter, say from verse 14 onward, lays emphasis on this. Paul is doubtless giving us his own experience there at some period of his religious life, or at least the experience of some typical man, awakened to a knowledge of sin, regenerated let us say, saved by grace, and yet living on a low plane of experience and knowledge of the truth. Justified by faith is he, and because of that very fact, he is undergoing a spiritual struggle unknown to him before. While living in an unjustified state, his central choice was for self, but now, even in its failures, it is for God. Yet that mysterious other self is latent still, and asserts itself in awful reality at times when he is off his guard. It puts him to torture and shame, and he cries out in the agony of his soul, Is there no balm in Gilead? Is there no physician near! O, wretched man that I am, who shall deliver me from, or out of this body of death! He answers his own question, when he says, "Thanks be to God, who giveth us the victory through our Lord Jesus Christ."

This leads very naturally to the third and last stage in the development of this part of his theme in which he is showing the way to holiness, or, as we have described it, the effect of the gift of God's righteousness upon man in his own experience. It makes him personally holy first by bringing him into a new sphere of action or existence, chapter 6. Secondly, by awakening within him the consciousness of a new experience, that of internal conflict with sin, chapter 7; and thirdly, by putting within him a new possession, the Holy Ghost, through whom he is able to overcome in the conflict, and make that death to sin real in his life and conduct which is already real of him judicially, in the sight of God.

This third point is elaborated in chapter 8, whose relation to the preceding chapter is very clear and beautiful. Here the Holy Spirit is present everywhere as the secret of victory over sin. The chapter begins with a deep re-assertion of our justification, and then unfolds the work of the indwelling Spirit in our sanctification, and finally our glorification, bringing us back again to the point of departure in chapter 5.

How does the Holy Spirit accomplish this? First, by setting us free from the law of sin and death (verse 2), so that we willingly walk after the Spirit (3-5); secondly, by quickening our mortal bodies day by day, so that we are able to mortify (make to die) the deeds of the flesh in us (9-13); thirdly, by leading us as the sons of God (14, 15); fourthly, by witnessing within us concerning our position and heirship in Christ (16, 17); fifthly, by praying in us (26, 27), etc. We thus see that as the effect of the gift of God's righteousness upon man in his relations to God is to make him personally acceptable to God, its effect in his own experience is to make him personally holy.

VIII. The Relation of the Gift to Israel as a Nation, 9-11.

—That which follows in this epistle, in chapters 9-11, is frequently regarded as a kind of parenthesis. The apostle interrupts the flow of his main line of argument to discourse for a while of his own beloved Israel. It seems so hard that they, by their own blindness and unbelief, should be left out of the distribution of God's blessings of grace, and the Gentiles, who had never been His people in the same sense as they were, should be the recipients of them. Moreover, what was the effect of the situation on the Jews themselves? How would they regard such a Gospel? Could they believe it to be true? And if true, did it not make the God and the promises to them of the Old Testoment untrue? Before he can proceed further, therefore, the great apostle must discourse of these things. He must pour out the love of his heart for his people. He must remind them that God's promises to them still hold true, and shall be fulfilled. He must exhort them once more to believe. He must seek to arouse their holy jealousy to do so. And he must, at the same time, curb and restrain the pride and boasting of the Gentiles against them.

He begins this section with an outburst of sorrow over the situation (9: 1-5). He next defends the truth of God even though so many of Israel are left out (6-13). He next defends His righteousness in leaving them out (14-18), and His wisdom as well (19-29). In the fourth place, he defines the reason, from the human side at least, why they are left out, throwing the responsibility upon themselves (30-33).

Chapter 10 seems like a parenthesis within a parenthesis. He breaks off in the argumentative part of his discourse to once more express the sorrow of his heart for Israel (1) to acknowledge the good that is in them (2), to point out their error (3), to set before them the truth (4), to urge it upon their acceptance (5-13), and expostulate with them for turning their backs upon it (14-21).

He then returns to his main thought about Israel. The people were cast away indeed, but not all of them (11: 1-6). There was an election of grace. There were some, the believing ones, saved under the Gospel, while others were blinded (7-10). But this blindness of Israel as a nation is not a perpetual blindness, even as all the prophets foretold (11). Moreover, in the meantime, there is a blessing in it for the Gentiles, (same verse). Their restoration to God's favor (their fulness) is coming bye and bye, however, and that will mean a still greater blessing to the Gentiles (12-15). In the meantime the Gentiles are not to boast (16-22); for Israel can be taken back again into God's favor as easily as the Gentiles received that favor (23, 24); and that is, indeed, what assuredly shall come to pass (25-32). This is wonderful, indeed, but we who are familiar with the story of the Old Testament prophets are not surprised at it. Well may we say, however, as doth the apostle, "O, the depth of the riches both of the wisdom and knowledge of God!"

IX. The Effect of the Gift Upon Man in His Relation to Others, 12-15.—It is neither Jew or Gentile, as such, whom Paul has in mind in the closing section of the epistle which we have now reached, but both of these classes again as they are found in the church, and as he has been dealing with them in the first eight chapters. He has come to the practical application of his great theme, and as he has shown its bearing upon man in his relation to God, and in his own experience, it is necessary in order to round out and conclude the whole, to show its bearing upon him in his relation to his fellowmen. This he now does.

As he stands related to God, the justified man has been brought into a state of grace where before he was abiding in a state of wrath. As far as his own experience is concerned, he is now in a state of holiness, where before he was in a state of sin. And as far as his relation to others are concerned, he is now in a state of love where before he was in a state of selfishness.

How is he to show his gratitude to God for all His blessings (12: 1, 2)? You will observe it is out of this presentation of his body to God, which, in turn, is his expression of gratitude to God, that there spring all those kindly and loving relationships to his fellowmen, by which the justified man shows the effect of the gift of God's righteousness to him.

And what are some of these relationships as specified by the apostle. (1), Meekness and humility in the exercise of spiritual gifts (3-8). (2), Love and kindness in the general duties of personal conduct (13-21). (3), Subjection to human authority (13: 1-14). Consideration of the weak disciple (14: 1-15: 7).

Some would include verses 8-13 in the last-named general division of the epistle, and begin the "conclusion" at verse 14. But it seems to me that the great theme of the treatise is practically closed at verse 7, and that the first half-dozen verses following are to be regarded partly as a summing up of the preceding, and partly leading up to the conclusion with its commendations and benedictions.

CHAPTER XLVII.

The First Epistle to the Corinthians.

In Paul's first epistle to the Corinthians we have what is perhaps the most varied epistle in the New Testament. It touches not only upon two or three of the greatest doctrines of Christianity, but a number of questions of casuistry of deep practical importance, and of interest ever current. It was probably written from Ephesus, and a little earlier than the epistle to the Romans, though as to that the material for forming a judgment is not conclusive. The circumstances under which it came to be written will appear, sufficiently for our present purpose, as we proceed with the outline and analysis.

The epistle opens with the customary salutation (1-3), and thanksgiving (4-9); upon which we can not pause to dwell further than to call attention to the important allusion to the second coming of our Lord Jesus Christ in verses 7 and 8, a precious truth upon which the apostle enlarges very much in certain other of his epistles which follow.

I. Concerning Party Divisions, 1: 10-4.—The first great division of the epistle, or, if you please, the first theme on which the apostles dilates at length, is that indicated at the head of this paragraph. The general statement of the situation is contained in verses 10-17 of chapter 1. It begins with an exhortation to his readers, (10), and after relating the source of his information concerning their "contentions," (11), an expostulation follows (12, 13), the whole concluding with a general caution based upon his own example (14-17).

This general statement of the situation is followed by a particular rebuke of intellectualism as applied to the teaching and reception of the Gospel (1: 18-31), in which we begin to get a hint of the cause or origin of these party divisions. Such intellectualism makes the Cross of Christ of none effect (17: 18); it has been proven foolish by the history of the world in the past (19-25); it is in itself rather a hindrance than a help to salvation (26-29); and it is done away with in Christ (30, 31).

There is a precious substitute for intellectualism, as Paul shows in chapters 2-3 by his own example (1, 2);

it is seen in his simplicity of speech (3, 4), and his enduement of the Holy Ghost (4, 5). The absence of intellectualism, however, does not mean the absence of true wisdom (6-16), the nature of which he describes (6-8), as also its source (9-12, and means of communication (13-16). These Corinthians were really incapacitated to receive this wisdom in its richer depths for the cause which the apostle indicates (3: 1-4).

This intellectualism, thus described, was associated with a false estimate of their human teachers, as to which the apostle now seeks to set them right (3: 5-4). These teachers were simply ministers (servants) by whom they believed (5-9), and were responsible to God for the character and results of that service (10-15); hence they should not be gloried in by men (16-20). Moreover they were the possession of the church, the whole church; and one was as truly the possession of the church as another; hence the folly of divisions on account of them (21-23). They should be faithful to God (4: 1-5), and should not be regarded with partiality (6, 7). The subject is concluded with personal allusions, warnings and exhortations (8-21).

II. Concerning the Moral Disorder, 5-6.—The second theme of the epistle concerns a case of immorality in the church, covering chapters 5 and 6. The nature of it is stated in verse 1, and the sinful indifference of the church about it is referred to in verse 2. The apostle imposes a judgment upon the offender (3, 5), rebuking the church at the same time for their neglect in doing so (6-8). He also lays down a general principle to be observed in such cases (9-13).

The sixth chapter opens with a rebuke of litigation, a subject apparently very remote from that of the immorality we have just left. But as Paul recurs to that subject again at the close of the chapter, I am strongly of the opinion that the occasion for treating of litigation grew out of the immorality in some way. Notice, however, that such disputes should be settled within the church (1), which was qualified for such action (2, 3). Arbitration is recommended (4, 5), and on the whole, abnegation is to be preferred to litigation (6-8). A general warning follows (9-11).

At this point it is that the recurrence is made to the abuse of the human body, giving the inspired writer the opportunity to refer to its true dignity. First, he exposes a false general principle (12); and then refers to a special application of it (13). It was an axiomatic truth indeed, that meats were meant for the belly, and the belly adapted to the meats. But it was wrong to draw from this the easy inference that because the human body possessed other functions it was right to gratify its desires in those directions without restraint. A time was coming when there would be no meat to eat, and no physical organ to receive and digest it; and by inference, when there would be a lack of desire and capacity in other directions purely physical. Nevertheless, the soul of man would have a body, and it would be his own body raised from the dead, and glorified like unto Christ's own glorious body (14). What a shame, therefore, for this body thus dignified and exalted, and intended for the Lord to be given to fornication! Moreover, did they not know that the body of a believer was even now a member of Christ's mystical body? Would they make it a member of a harlot (15-17)? Then there was the peculiar nature of this sin to be considered (18); and the fact that the believer's body was the temple of the Holy Ghost (19); that it was redeemed by the precious blood of Christ as truly as was the soul redeemed (20); and that there rested upon each one the solemn obligation to glorify God in his body. What moving considerations these concerning the right use of the human body, and all growing out of the treatment to be accorded to the man who had been guilty of the sin and crime of incest!

III. Concerning Marriage, 7.—The heading of this division suggests the next theme with which Paul deals. It is apparent from the first verse of chapter 7, that the messengers of "the house of Chloe" (1:11), who had brought verbal reports to the apostle of the contentions and divisions in the church, had brought a written document as well containing certain questions which the brethren desired answered. One of these concerned marriage, and that of celibacy and divorce naturally arising out of it. In Paul's answers to these questions, however, we are not to suppose he has given us the whole of his views upon the subjects involved, much less the whole of the New Testament teaching thereupon, but only so much as connects itself with the particular questions put to him at the time. As Robertson says: "These are questions of casuistry which depend on the particular case, from which the word 'casuistry' comes."

There was a party in this Grecian church which held that marriage was in itself sinful in Christians and ought to be abstained from; and Paul introduces his discussion of the theme by frankly admitting that, in the abstract, the unwedded life was good (verse 1), although in the practical working of things marriage was more desirable, or even necessary as a preventative of sin (2).

If then, persons married, this meant that they were to fulfill the usual conjugal obligations of that state (3, 4); which were not to be remitted, except for a brief period possibly, and by mutual consent, lest sin should have an opportunity to creep in upon them by that means (5). Nevertheless, although he thus spoke so plainly and positively on the subject, he would not have them suppose that marriage was imposed upon all as a definite command, but only that, in opposition to the erroneous teaching, they should understand that they were permitted to marry if they chose, without committing sin in the act (6). On the other hand, his own example of unweddedness was desirable to be followed when it was possible to do so without the danger of being overcome by temptation to sin (7-9).

From the general subject of marriage the apostle is led to discuss the related one of separation and divorce. Where both parties are believers this is not permitted (10, 11); certainly re-marriage is not permitted in case such separation occurs (11). Christ, the Lord, personally taught this when here in the flesh (10). In the case also where one is an unbeliever, no separation is permitted on religious grounds (12, 13). In such a case the unbelieving one is "sanctified" by the believing one (14); the children of such an union are sanctified in the same way (14). Should the unbelieving one voluntarily separate himself, however, (on religious grounds), the believing one is not "under bondage" in that case (15). What does that mean, "under bondage?" Does it mean that the believer is not under necessity to renounce the Christian faith in order to restore his unbelieving partner, or does it mean he is not under necessity to remain without another partner? May he marry again? The first seems the safer understanding to accept and teach, but the second seems quite as near to the apostle's meaning. Great caution is needed here, and should it be assumed that Paul, as an inspired teacher, gives such liberty as this, we are to remember that it must be qualified by other teachings of the same authority, concerning our submission to "the powers that be"; governments and states pass laws on these subjects which it is the duty of the child of God to obey (see Romans 13).

Verse 16, however, is about as difficult to understand as the preceding one, i. e., it is as easily capable of two meanings. It may mean, "Hold on to your unbelieving partner for you may possibly be the means of saving him;" or it may mean, "Let him go, for how do you know you shall save him?" The first, indeed, seems more in accordance with the Christian spirit generally considered; but the second has the support of the words, "God hath called us to peace" (verse 16).

It is right to say, before passing from this immediate subject, that the "sanctification" of the unbeliever referred to in verse 14, can not mean that which is co-incident, with salvation. It must mean simply, that the unbeliever is sanctified in the sense that the believer may continue to live with him without impairing his own sanctity (compare 1 Timothy 4:5). In the case of the sanctification of the children it can only mean something of the same kind, perhaps that "the faith of the Christian parent gave the child a nearer relationship to the church than otherwise it could have." This holds good, however, only of such marriages as were contracted before the conversion of either party. Christians are, later on, forbidden to contract marriages with the unconverted (verse 39, compared with 11 Corinthians 6:14).

This law of separation, up until this point, limited in its application to the matter or marriage, is now expanded to include the separation of Jew and Gentile (17-20), and bondmen and freemen (19-24); the teaching being intended to show that Christianity does not interfere directly, but only indirectly, with existing institutions. As another expresses it, Christianity is intended to make men free in the responsibilities of their positions, and not free from those responsibilities. Christianity teaches us, in a sense, to be indifferent to external relations altogether.

The thought now recurs to the subject of marriage, or rather celibacy (25-35). First, we have the apostle's

opinion expressed (25); he next speaks of the undesirability of marriage under the existing or approaching circumstances of persecution (26-31); there is spiritual freedom in the unmarried state (32-34); nevertheless, the apostle is cautious in giving his advice (35), for he would not put an undue restraint upon them.

There are two more particulars that Paul must touch upon before his subject is concluded. One is the duty of parents to marriageable daughters (36-38), and the other the second marriage of women (39, 40). As to the first, parents, i. e., fathers, felt a sense of responsibility for the marriage of their daughters, and it was a cause of humiliation to them to have a marriageable daughter remain unmarried. But if this stricture concerning the greater desirability of the unmarried life for Christians should maintain, what were they to do? Paul indicated the circumstances under which they may permit the marriage of their daughters (36); at the same time that he assures them of the liberty they have to keep them unmarried without experiencing any shame on account of it (37); concluding this branch of his subject, as in the other instances with a statement of his own preference (38).

As to the second marriage of women, he speaks of their liberty in the premises (39), the limitation on that liberty (same verse), concluding with his own advice (40).

We now reach a new general division, which we call

IV. Concerning Social Disorders, 8-10.

The members of this church were doubtless very largely of Gentile origin, and of course, in their heathen state, worshipped idols, and participated in the social festivals to their honor in the pagan temples. Now that they had become Christians, such worship was at an end so far as they were concerned, but occasionally their heathen neighbors and friends would invite them to partake of such feasts, or of the meat offered in sacrifice thereat, in a social spirit, and out of regard to former fellowship or, as we might say, for the sake of old times. A question had arisen in the church, therefore, as to whether it were lawful for Christians to accept such invitations? There were those who answered, "Yes," and whose argument in the premises was specious. They said, "An idol is nothing in the world, there is no such thing as an idol, hence it is as lawful to eat meat offered to an 'idol' as any other kind of meat; and as lawful to eat it in an idol's 'temple', so-called, as any other place." They boasted much of their spiritual "knowledge" on these points, standing upon the principle of "Christian liberty," and reasoning, as many do in our own day quite as unjustifiably, that they were not "under law but under grace," and hence might do as they pleased.

In dealing with the subject, Paul first states the case (8: 1-3), in which he takes occasion to remark that there is something better than spiritual knowledge after all, and that is spiritual love, an occasion for the exercise of which the present question very amply afforded. He next admits the abstract truth in the argument of those who favored the liberty in question (4-6); but presents as an offset to the exercise of that liberty the claim of the weaker Christian brother (7-13). The ground of his weakness is dwelt upon (7); the injury his soul may receive (8-11); the nature of the action against him on the part of those who unduly press their Christian liberty (12); and finally, the principle that should actuate them in such a case (13).

This principle was one upon which he himself acted in all cases (9: 1-27). He had authority as an apostle (1, 2), and there were privileges connected with it (3-14); but he denied himself these privileges for the sake of the Gospel and the sake of souls (15-23); and he exhorted the church to follow his example (24-27).

Moreover, there was serious peril in their doing otherwise. Let them consider the sad chapter in the history of Israel (10: 1-14). Think of the privileges they enjoyed (1-4); but their overthrow nevertheless (5). Their example was intended as a warning (6). Their sins are enumerated (7-10). The lesson is very plain (12). Be wise, be careful (13, 14).

Lastly, there was a gross incongruity in such conduct on the part of Christians (10: 15-22). Idol feasts are compared with the Lord's Supper, and participation in both is seen to be incompatible and perilous.

The practical view of the subject is, seek first the good of others rather than your own selfish pleasures (23, 24). There is such a thing, of course, as being over-scrupulous (25-27), and yet we are to be continually on our guard for the sake of others (28-33), following the example of Paul (11: 1).

V. Concerning Ecclesiastical Disorders, 11-15.—The apostle is obliged to rebuke and censure this church in some other particulars, but before doing so, he very graciously commends them as far as he is able. Many of the instruc-

tions about church order which he had given them they had kept, but there were others of which they had become neglectful (11: 2).

I. One of these concerned the conduct of women in the religious assemblies, who, in all probability, carried their newly-found Christian liberty a little too far, over-stepping the bounds of propriety in some matters, as established by the custom of the times. In the sight of God, indeed, all are equal; i. e., in Christ Jesus, there is neither male nor female (Galatians 3: 28), but there must be distinctions in society or the latter could not exist.

Paul approaches the subject by an observation concerning the relation of the sexes (3); then treats of the particular offence of which one of them was guilty (4-6), closing the matter by an argument against the practice (7-16). In this argument he shows that in such assemblies the woman has a visible superior (7); that she was created second to man (8, 9); that she should consider the angels who are regarded as present at such gatherings (10); and that she should consider commonly understood propriety (11, 12).

II. Another of these ecclesiastical disorders concerned the administration of the Lord's Supper (17-34), their conduct of which the apostle was unable to praise (17-19). It was not conducted decorously and sacredly. The divisions or factions he refers to in this case were not doctrinal or theological, as in the case of the opening chapters of the epistle, but social cliques. The church came together in a semi-social way, and held what was called a love-feast. At the close of this the Lord's Supper was partaken of. But this love-feast is described in verses 20 and 21 as a very selfish and rather gluttonous affair. The well-to-do brought an abundance of viands with them, and gathering their "set" around them, partook without regard to the poor who were able to bring little or nothing. The apostle rebukes this spirit and conduct (22), and reminds the guilty ones of the original institution of the rite (23-26). He then warns them of the consequences of partaking of the supper thus unworthily (27-32), and tells them how they should arrange the matter in the future (33, 34).

III. A third ecclesiastical disorder touched the subject of spiritual gifts (chapters 12-14), a subject of the most practical importance for the consideration of the church in every age. In the first chapter, verse 7, the apostle had reminded them that they had "come behind in no gift." God had been very abundant in the bestowment of His benefits upon them; but these benefits were to be used for Him in the edification of the whole church. But this they had not done, however. There was an absence of true Christian love in their spiritual ministrations one to another.

Approaching the theme of spiritual gifts, the apostle (1), points to their source (4-6); (2), he describes their nature (7-11); (3), he speaks of their equality (12-31); (4), their abuse, (13: 1-13); (5), their choice; (6), their employment (26-40).

Under the head of the "equality" of the gifts we see the practical design for which they were bestowed on these believers, and we see also, in the plainest language, the wonderful unity existing among them as the one body of Christ. This is one of the deepest truths revealed in the New Testament, of which we shall have more to say, in the study of a later epistle. Suffice now to observe that all lived in the Head and for the Head, Jesus Christ, and hence their loyalty to, and love for, Him carried with it necessarily loyalty to and love for one another. How gross then, and how serious, the absence of the grace of love in the exercise of their mutually-important spiritual gifts! Chapter 13, in dealing with this, speaks first, of the supremacy of love over and above any and all of these gifts (1-3); it then describes love, tells us what its nature is, showing unmistakeably its divine and supernatural character (4-7); and finally, it dwells upon its permanency (8-13). These gifts will be done away with some day, when their need is done away with, but love, as part of the life of the renewed man in Christ shall never cease.

Under the head of the choice of the gifts (14: 1-25), the apostle emphasizes the practical value of prophesying, by which he does not mean necessarily, the foretelling of events, but rather the forthtelling of the truth. He means testifying, proclaiming, exhorting, preaching the Word of God, the commonest, simplest, and, like the air we breathe, and water we drink, the most useful and necessary gift of all. The use of the natural tongue to set forth the glory and goodness of God to the benefit of all.

This leads to a further amplification of the idea of the employment of the gifts (26-40), in which we have a picture of an apostolic prayer-meeting or church gathering, in which the different disciples come prepared to take part

(26). There is a tendency to disorder and confusion among them which the apostle corrects (27-33), and which leads him to speak especially of the contribution thereto which came from the female portion of the auditory (34, 35). In these last-indicated verses, I do not understand the apostle to contradict his position in chapter 11: 5, where, by inference at least, he grants to women the privilege of public prayer and phophesying. They were simply not to interrupt by untimely questions, which, considering the social position of women in the East, would be indecorous as well as disorderly and contributing to confusion.

VI. Concerning the Resurrection of the Body, 15.—There is nothing more vital in the whole epistle than that treated of towards the conclusion, viz: the resurrection of the body. There was a party in the church which appeared to question it. The apostle establishes the fact of the resurrection, however, on the basis of the resurrection of Jesus Christ (1-19). This was proven by the Scriptures (3, 4), and the testimony of eye-witnesses (5-11). Its denial involved the denial of everything Christian, the preaching of the Gospel (14), saving faith (same verse), the apostles' testimony (15), their salvation (17), the blessedness of the righteous dead, and all ground of hope even for the present time (18, 19).

After thus establishing the fact of the resurrection of Christ, the apostle bases thereupon the resurrection of the race (20-22). But there will be a difference in this resurrection as to time, and, inferentially, as to circumstances and character (23-28). The first division of the resurrection army is composed of the person of Christ Himself —"the first fruits;" the second will be composed of only "they that are Christ's" and will come forth "at His coming," i. e., at the beginning of the Millennium (compare 1 Thessalonians 4: 13-18); the third will be composed evidently of the rest of the dead, and come forth at "the end," i. e., the end of the world at the close of the Millennium, when Christ shall have delivered up the (Mediatorial) Kingdom to the Father (compare Revelation 20).

The next point in the discussion is the nature of this resurrection body (35-57). It will not be the same body that was buried as to its constituent particles and appearance (36, 37), and yet it will be the same as to identity (38). The superiority of the raised to the buried body is set before us, in detail, in verses 42-44. Observe the moving exhortation in which the consideration of the subject ends (58).

VII. Concluding Observations, 16.

—It is remarkable, is it not, that the inspired writer should pass so abruptly from the exposition of the transcendant doctrine of the resurrection, the very corner-stone of Christianity, to so prosaic a theme as a "collection"? But is it prosaic in the sense that it is of small account? How much it has to do with the preservation of God's witness in the earth and hence with the account we must give of ourselves in the resurrection! Notice the character or object of this collection (16:1), when it was to be made (2), and on what principle (same verse), and also the place whither it was to be sent, and the method of sending it (3). All these particulars are of importance for our government in similar matters today, and their strict observance would save scandal and heart-burnings.

Though Paul had spoken so plainly of the defects in the life of this church, what shows that it was in the spirit of love towards them (5-7)? From what place does he seem to write (8, 9)? He had spoken plainly of Apollos, but did it indicate any estrangement between those two servants of God (12)? Who especially had ministered to him of late (17, 18)? What token of validity does this epistle contain (21)? Do you know what "Maran-atha" means (22)? It means, "Our Lord Cometh." It was with this hope before him that he began his letter, and with this hope before him he laid down his pen.

CHAPTER XLVIII.

The Second Epistle to the Corinthians.

Paul's Second Epistle to the Corinthians has long been a favorite of mine, and often have I found myself turning to it for instruction and comfort; but nevertheless, I have always regarded it as one of the most difficult of all his writings to analyze, or break up into its structural parts, for the teaching of others.

Quoting Dean Alford, Paul had now left Ephesus, from which place the first epistle had been penned, and had crossed over into Macedonia (see Acts 19, 20), whence he wrote the present one (8:1-9:2). He had heard of the effect produced on the Corinthians by his first epistle (2:3-3:8), and was now on his way to visit them (7:14; 13:1). The general reception given to his letter had been favorable, but all had not quietly submitted themselves to it. He had adversaries in the church, those who opposed some of the doctrines he taught, (as we might readily gather from the argumentative tone and the spirit of rebuke of his first epistle), and these were more embittered than ever, seeking to undermine and belittle his authority as an apostle, on the ground perhaps, that he was not one of the original twelve. It was, therefore, for the double purpose, first, of comforting those who had submitted themselves to his teachings and rebukes, and secondly, of defending his personal character and apostolic authority against the impugners of both, that he wrote this second epistle. For this reason we find "consolation and rebuke, gentleness and severity, earnestness and irony succeeding one another" in his utterances, at short intervals, and without notice. Erasmus, quoted by the author before-named, says: "Such is his versatility, that you would hardly think one and the same man was speaking. At one time he wells up gently like some limpid spring, and bye-and-bye he thunders down like a torrent with a mighty crash, carrying everything with him by the way."

The epistle opens, as do all his writings, when addressed to a collective church, with words of salutation (1:1, 2). This is followed, as in other cases, by thanksgiving, or an ascription of praise to God (3), from which he glides easily and gracefully, like a craft from its moorings, into those personal matters which make the epistle at once so interesting to read and yet so difficult clearly to understand.

I. Personal Matters.—These personal matters refer first, to physical sufferings he had undergone of a very serious nature (1:4-11), the precise character and time of which are not mentioned. How precious, however, to note the purpose for which these afflictions had befallen him, and the key it affords to our own experiences and duties under similar circumstances (4-7).

Secondly, he explains the reason of his delay in visiting them (1:12-2:13). You may remember that, in his first epistle, he had promised this visit; but the fact that he had gone into Macedonia first, instead of coming directly to them (Acts 20:1-3), had disappointed his friends and given added occasion to his enemies. In explaining the cause of delay, however, he reaches the subject not directly and bluntly, but by a series of easy approaches. He is governed by a spirit of love towards them (1:12-15); and it was in no mere fickleness he had seemed to change his mind or delay his purpose (16-22); but in order to spare them (1:23-2:4). In this connection, he refers to the case of the incestuous offender dealt with in the first epistle (chapter 5), and directs his re-admission to the fold of the church on the ground of his repentance (5-11). Throughout his present journey he had been solicitous to hear from them, and grieved by disappointment in that respect (12, 13).

II. The Apostolic Office.—Next, he enlarges upon the duty and dignity of his office (2:14-7:16). Perhaps his object in this is in preparation for his later defence of himself against his adversaries. However that may be, it seems to have been suggested by his allusion to his present journey, and the occasion for it (12, 13). In speaking of the spiritual triumph and success of his ministry though (14-16), he would not have them suspect a spirit of egotism on his part, nor any necessity of commending himself to them (3:1). The latter, indeed, was not required, when they considered the manner in which He had been used in their salvation and spiritual upbuilding (2-6). This allusion leads to an allegorical contrast between the Jewish and Christian ministrations showing the superiority of the latter over the former (7-18). Attention is called to the rather obscure expressions in verses 13 and 14, which refer to the transaction in Exodus 34, and which have been commonly misunderstood because of a wrong rendering of that passage, especially verse 35. It is usually thought that Moses spoke to the Israelites with his face covered to hide the glory of God shining there; but the Revised Version indicates the opposite. His face was unveiled, the people saw the glory as he spoke; but when he had ceased speaking, the veil was put on that they might not look on the end, or the fading, of that transitory glory. "They were permitted to see it as long as it was necessary to be seen as a credential of his ministry," says Al-

ford, "but then it was withdrawn from their eyes. Thus the declaration of God's will to them was not in openness of speech, but was interrupted and broken by intervals of concealment," which is not the case in the Christian dispensation of which Paul was a minister.

Continuing his reference to his apostolate in the next chapter (4), he speaks of his spirit in its exercise (1-6), his sufferings (7-15), and his hopes (16-18). Indeed, the declaration of his hopes carries us into chapter 5, extending as far as verse 10, where, "in the midst of this highly personal matter, occurs one of those grand expositions of Christian faith and hope which are the resting-places of believing hearts in all time." Alford translates verse 3 (chapter 5) thus, "Seeing that we shall verily be found clothed, and not naked," believing it intended to substantiate and explain verse 2. "It thus asserts strongly the truth of the resurrection in a glorified body, probably in reference to the deniers of that doctrine" who are alluded to in the first epistle.

From the consideration of his hopes he passes abruptly to that of his motives in his ministry (5:10-16), in which connection I would call your attention to verse 11. As commonly understood, it refers to the thought of the perdition awaiting ungodly men as that which moves the apostle to "persuade" them, but the truth is rather, that he is referring to his own fear, his godly fear, in view of the day referred to in verse 10 when he must give account of his stewardship to Christ. He is living under the consciousness of his "appearing" there, and this keeps him faithful in warning the unsaved. See the Revised Version, where "terror," is translated "fear."

This allusion to his persuading men in the light of the judgment seat of Christ, diverts him, for the moment, from the main theme of his apostolic office, to the persuasion of these Corinthians not to receive the grace of God in vain (5:17-6:2), i. e., not to receive it without allowing it to bring forth in them the fruit of holiness, as they were in danger of doing. Immediately, however, he returns to the character of his office, with the sufferings it has entailed (3-10). His heart breaks forth in an appeal to the church at this point (11-13), and once again he exhorts them to the separated life which his earlier epistle so clearly intimates to be a necessity in their case (14-7:1). He pleads with them to receive him into their hearts, assuring

them once again of his love for them
and deep interest in them, notwithstanding the tone of severity it had
been necessary for him to use in writing to them before (2-16).

III. Contributions for the Saints.—
Leaving the subject of his apostolic
office, he begins another which seems
far enough away from it, and yet in
his own heart evidently very near, viz:
the needs of the poor saints in Jerusalem. Chapters 8 and 9 are occupied
with this. That metropolis of the
church was passing through dark and
stormy days, and its common chest
seems to have been replenished by contributions from all the daughter
churches. Macedonia, in its poverty,
had contributed very liberally it would
seem, but as yet the wealthy and flour-
ishing Corinthians had been more back-
ward, and the apostle therefore devotes
nearly one-sixth of his present letter
to arguments and pleadings for greater
generosity on their part. An outline
of these chapters would provide an invaluable store of material for preaching on this theme. For example, Paul
enjoins the duty of Christian giving
upon these Corinthians:

1. By the example of the churches in
Macedonia (8:1-4). They were poor,
yet lavish. The effect of divine grace
on their hearts.

2. By the sense of congruity in the
Christian life (8:7). They already
abounded in other gifts such as faith,
utterance and knowledge; liberality
therefore was expected. Its absence
would be a serious defect in the sym-
metry of their spiritual experience.

3. As a proof of their love and gratitude to Jesus (8:8, 9), who, though
rich, yet for their sakes had become
poor.

4. In consideration of what they had
professed to be willing to do. Regard
for their promises (8:10, 11).

5. In consideration that the offering
would be appreciated not according to
its size, but according to the spirit in
which it was given (8:12).

6. In consideration that the case of
the poor saints should not fall on a few
but that all might be equally burdened (8:13-15).

7. In consideration that the apostle's
honor was at stake (8:24, also 9:3, 4).
He had boasted of their willingness.

8. In consideration that as they sow-
ed they would reap (9:6).

9. In consideration that God was
able to reward them (9:8-11).

10. In consideration that they would
thus glorify God (9:13).

11. In consideration that they would
thus secure the prayers and love of the
saints (9:14).

IV. The Apostle's Defence.—At chapter ten, the apostle begins the direct
personal defence of himself against his
rivals and enemies, which continues
till the close of the epistle. It is in
this portion of the epistle most especially we perceive "the delicate and in-
tricate alternations of gravity and
irony, earnest pleading, and sportive
rallying, which make it very difficult
of interpretation." Chapter 10 gives
us a description of his practice, as an
apostle, not to labor in the fields of
others (14-16); but it begins with an
ironical allusion to the opinion held
concerning him by some of his enemies
in the church (1, 2). This opinion is
plainly stated in verse 10.

Chapter 11 gives a narrative of his
perils in the furtherance of his sacred
office. He feels ashamed to boast, but
he does it for their sakes (verses 1-4).
Some idea of the foolish charge made
against him may be gathered from
verses 5-10. That he had preached the
Gospel to them freely seems to have
been one of these charges! And who
were his accusers, and how does he regard them (12-15)?It is at this point
that he enlarges upon his great sufferings (16-33). But these sufferings were
not his only credentials as an apostle,
for what of that mysterious vision that
came to him, as recorded in chapter
12:1-12?

He now reminds them that he is
coming again to them—a third time
(12:14-13:1. It is a grave declaration for them under the circumstances,
and he accompanies it with exhortations and denunciations. The closing
greeting is very brief as befits the general tone of the end, and the letter
ends with the "benediction" in the
name of the Holy Trinity, which has
become the accustomed form of dismis-
sal throughout the centuries of the
Christian church.

CHAPTER XLIX.

The Epistle to the Galatians.

Our reading of the Acts showed that Paul visited the province of Galatia in Asia Minor twice, on his second and third journeys, but no mention was made of any particular city or town at which he stopped on either occasion. Acts 16 : 6, 18 : 23. It was on the third journey, and probably during his long stay at Ephesus, that this epistle was written, the evidence for which supposition is found in Conybeare & Howson's Life & Epistles of Paul, and in the introduction to any good commentary on the book. The occasion for writing it carries us back in our thought to the fifteenth chapter of Acts and the story of the first church council held at that time. The Judaizing teachers there referred to tracked Paul's footsteps everywhere, seeking to circumvent the preaching of a free Gospel and teaching the need of circumcision and other observances of the Mosaic law in order to salvation. They had good soil to work on in Galatia, for the people seem to have been of a demonstrative and fickle mind. (1 : 6, 4 : 9, 4 : 15, 16, 5 : 15). That this was the condition of things in the church, and that many had already fallen into the snare of seeking to supplement faith by works is further evident from 1 : 6-9, 3 : 3, 4 : 9-11, 5 : 3, etc., to which passages you are asked to give particular attention. The object of the epistle, therefore, is to restore these people to the faith, and in the working out of that object the epistle becomes an inspired classic on that fundamental doctrine of Christianity called Justification by Faith.

It would seem that the false teachers referred to, in order to undermine the confidence of the people in the Gospel itself, must first accomplish the same purpose, with reference to the apostolic authority of Paul. They must first destroy his authority with the people as an inspired apostle before they could weaken the foundations of the Gospel as preached. This they sought diligently to do using Peter as a sort of comparison and contrast. The last-named preached no different Gospel from Paul, but being the apostle to the circumcision, i. e., the Jews, (Galatians 2 : 6-9), presented it from the Jewish standpoint, while Paul as the apostle to the uncircumcision did the same

from the Gentile standpoint. We can readily see how there may have been some differences in the mode of presentation which gave an opportunity to these unsanctified Jewish Christians to denounce Paul as unorthodox. They had an advantage also in the fact that Paul was not not of the original twelve.

The plan of the Epistle lends itself to a three-fold division. Chapters 1 and 2 are of a personal character in which Paul defends his apostolic authority; chapters 3 and 4 are doctrinal, in which he defends the Gospel or the doctrine of justification by faith; while chapters 5 and 6 are practical in their nature and contain the application of the doctrine to the daily life of the individual Christian.

I. Paul Defends His Apostolic Authority, 1-2.—He does this on the ground of

His Divine call, 1 :1.

His Divine revelation of the Gospel, 1 : 11, 12.

His independence of the other apostles, 1 : 15-24.

His endorsement by the church, 2 : 1-10.

His rebuke of Peter, 2 : 11-14.

Speaking of his Divine call, there are those who would say that his reference to man-made apostles has an application to the choice of Matthias by Peter and the others, alluded to in Acts 1. In like manner, his reference to the way in which he received the revelation of the Gospel recalls the circumstances of his conversion in Acts 9, as well as the experience referred to in verses 17 and 18 of this chapter of our lesson. In the section treating of his endorsement by the church there is an allusion (chapter 2 :1, 2), to the journey and its results spoken of in Acts 15 at the time of the first general council of the church to settle the question of justification. Particular attention should be called to his bold and consistent attitude with reference to the circumcision of Titus (3-5), an earlier allusion to which was made in our study of the Acts. It is noticeable, too, that Paul makes as much of his final endorsement by the church as of his independence of the leaders of the church prior thereto. He would give his adversaries no advantage over him, as if they should say he were too independent and could not be acknowledged by them until he had received the acknowledgment of the accepted authorities. His rebuke of Peter shows him to have been naturally the stronger character of the two, and in consideration of the fact that Peter was doubtless being quoted by his opponents, proves a convincing argument for his own authority.

II. Paul Defends the Gospel, 3-4.—Having established his authority as an apostle, the way is now clear to defend the Gospel he preached, and this he does on the following grounds:
Their own experience of its effects, 3 : 1-5.
The history of Abraham, 6-9.
The teachings of Scripture, 10-12.
The work of Christ, 13-14.
The first might be called the *"argumentum ad hominem."* It was evident to these Galatian Christians that they had received the Holy Spirit into their lives as the fruit thereof was seen and known. But how had they come to receive Him, through observing the Mosaic ceremonials or through the simple preaching of the Gospel? The answer, of course, was foreseen. It was as the result of Paul's preaching among them, and not the observance of circumcision or anything else. Why then did they need to supplement the work of the Spirit by that of the flesh?
The second argument is well adapted to refute the Judaizing teachers, since Abraham was the founder of their faith. And yet Abraham clearly was justified by believing on God and before he was circumcised.
The argument from the teachings of Scripture requires no explanation, since the passages quoted plainly state that if one elects to be saved by the law and not by grace, he can only be so saved by keeping the whole of it. Circumcision nor ceremonialism of any kind were not enough.
The work of Christ did away with all these things which only foreshadowed Him. He hath redeemed us from the curse of the law, why then dishonor His work and put ourselves voluntarily under that curse a second time? The whole argument is very clear and convincing, and furnishes us with a sermon outline on the doctrine of justification by faith.
But at this point the apostle supplements his argument by a brief disquisition on the Relation of the Law to the Promise.
He anticipates a possible objection to his argument. It were as though some one should say: Granted that God saved Abraham or accounted him righteous on the ground of his belief in His promise; but is it not true that 430 years after that promise to Abraham He gave the law to Moses? And was not this law thus given to Moses intended to take the place of that promise as a ground of human righteousness? Paul answers, No. (Verses 15-18). His imaginary interlocutor then inquires, Why was the law given? What purpose does it serve? Paul's reply to this question discloses two points:—(1), the law was given because of transgressions, etc., verse 19. As the transgressions of men multiplied and became aggravated, God was obliged to come to His people in an entirely new way, in a more distant relation than existed in the time of the patriarchs. "The law was given, not so much in order to prevent transgressions, as to bring men under a more strict accountability for them, and a more plainly expressed curse." This brings us to the second point (2), the law was our schoolmaster to bring us to Christ, verse 24. The Greek word for schoolmaster here means a faithful slave entrusted with the care of a boy from his tender years till puberty to keep him from physical and moral evil, and accompany him to his studies and amusements. He approached his charge with commands and prohibitions, and in a sense with limitations of his freedom. All this as a means to an end, viz: that the boy might be trained for mature age and the assumption of that higher grade of life for which he was destined. (Lange's Commentary). Thus the law leads men to Christ. It restrains and rebukes us, it shows us our sin and danger, it condemns us, and thus makes us feel the need of a Redeemer and prepares us to receive Him when presented to our faith. Compare Romans 10 : 4.

Paul continues this general subject amplifying and enlarging upon it throughout chapter four, climaxing the whole matter at last in the use of the allegory of Sarah and Hagar, (21-31). This is not to say that the story of Sarah and Hagar was not a historical fact as given in Genesis, but only that the apostle here uses the fact in an accommodated or allegorical sense for purposes of illustration. The design seems to be to show the effect of being under the bondage of the Jewish law as compared with the liberty of the Gospel. Hagar and her son were treated with severity, cast out and persecuted, and became a fit representation of Jerusalem as it was in the time of Paul. Sarah and Isaac enjoyed freedom and sonship, and became correspondingly a fit representation of the New Jerusalem or the true kingdom of God. Which would these Galatian Christians choose, to remain under the freedom of the Gospel, or voluntarily put themselves into the bondage and under the yoke of Judaism?

III. Paul Applies the Doctrine, 5-6.—
In applying the doctrine Paul simply urges them to stand fast in the liberty of Christ, (5 : 1-12), but in doing so to be careful not to abuse that liberty, (5 : 13-6 : 10). He mentions at least four ways in which their Christian liberty may thus be abused:

Uncharitableness, 13-15.
Uncleanness, 16-25.
Pride, 26-6 :5.
Selfishness, 6-10.

The first-mentioned warning or exhortation speaks for itself. They were to give over contending on this matter and everything else, and seek to live in peace.

The second is very important as showing that sins of the mind (20), as well as of the body (19, 21), are to be classified as of the flesh; that the practice of such sins eternally disinherits (21), and that the Holy Spirit is given to believers for the very purpose of overcoming them (17). Read this last

verse in the Revised Version and see the different construction put upon it by the word "may" instead of "can" in the last phrase.

"The "pride" referred to in the third instance will be found to be spiritual pride; in which connection it will be profitable to note the implied contrast between verses 2 and 5 of chapter 5. The Greek word for "burden" is not the same in both cases and the statements are not contradictory. A commentary will tell you that in the first instance Paul tells them to bear with others' "burdens" of infirmity in sympathy; and in the second, that self-examination will make them feel they have enough to do with their own "load" of sin without comparing themselves boastfully with their neighbors.

What in the fourth place I have called selfishness, might be equally well described as parsimony. Verse 6 seems to refer to the care they should evince for their spiritual teachers in their temporal concerns; and the reference to "sowing and reaping" in the following verses primarily alludes to the same thing.

In closing the lesson let me call your attention to verse 11 for its bearing on what we are taught in 11 Thessalonians 3 : 17.

CHAPTER L.

The Epistle to the Ephesians.

The epistle to the Ephesians contains probably the profoundest spiritual truth revealed to man in the New Testament. The reasons why it was given through Paul to the Christians at Ephesus are also hinted at. In the epistle to the Romans we have two very noticeable statements, the first at its beginning, the second at its close. The first refers to the Gospel, which it speaks of as promised or revealed before by the prophets in the holy Scriptures, and which was never hidden. Compare Romans 1 : 1, 2, with Galatians 3 : 8. The second refers to the "mystery which was kept secret since the world began, but now is made manifest." Romans 16 : 25, 26. As it is the business of the epistle to the Romans to explain the Gospel, so is it the business of the epistle to the Ephesians to explain the mystery. Chapter 3 : 1-12. I do not say that Romans from the practical point of

view is not the more useful or important for us to master; but he who has really mastered Romans will never be satisfied till he has done the same with Ephesians. He may not know what is in Ephesians, but he will feel instinctively that somewhere in the New Testament there will be that for which his soul now yearns. A need of knowledge has been created which he feels satisfied God will supply. He has a desire to get down deep into "the whys and wherefores" of things, which the contents of Ephesians gratify.

You will recall that the Old Testament prophesied continually of the kingdom to be set up on earth with Israel as its center and the Messiah as its reigning Head. In the Gospels this kingdom was offered to Israel in the acceptance of its King, but was rejected. In the Acts of the Apostles it may be said to have been offered them again, and again rejected. Nothing more is heard or said about it till we reach the book of Revelation, where we see the kingdom actually set up, Israel converted and triumphant, and Christ on the throne. Here then is a long interval to be accounted for between the departure of Christ out of the world and His coming again. This is the Church period which is covered by the teachings of the epistles. Now the church is a distinct body from the Jews on the one hand, or the Gentiles on the other. Neither is it identical with the kingdom, but separate from it. It is something unique, something not heard of in the Old Testament, something specially given to Paul to reveal. It had its earthly beginning after Christ's ascension into glory. It will have its earthly ending when He comes again, and it is caught up to meet Him in the air (1 Thessalonians 4 : 13-18). Thenceforward it will reign with Him over the earthly kingdom then to be set up. The church is composed of a people taken out from among both Jews and Gentiles, and is called The Body of Christ.

Under this figure it is referred to in 1 Corinthians 12 : 12-27, and Colossians 1 : 18, 24, 2 : 19, etc., but the doctrine itself is amplified and enlarged upon only in Ephesians.

Let us call our theme, therefore, The Spiritual Constitution of the Church. We might define it as The Mystery of the Body of Christ, but I think the former the better title for our present purpose. Paul treats of it under four heads, to wit :—

Its origin, its standing, its design, its duty.

I, As to the Origin of the Church, its source is seen to be in the will or choice of God the Father, Chapter 1, verses 4, 5. The God and Father of our Lord Jesus Christ hath chosen us in Him before the foundation of the world. Evidently no merit or claim of ours comes into the consideration of the case at all. Indeed, the transaction is not primarily with us at all, but with Christ. We are chosen in Him before we came into existence.

But, speaking after the manner of men, it were not enough that God the Father should have chosen us, unless God the Son had done that which made His choice operative. And, therefore, we find it stated that the origin of the church is in the will of the Father through the work of the Son. Verses 7-13. "In whom," i. e., the Son, "we have redemption" (7) ; "In whom also we have obtained an inheritance," (11), or, "were made a heritage," (R. V.) : "In whom * * * ye were sealed

with the Holy Spirit of promise," (13).

Nor were this all. The last phrase of verse 13, just quoted, suggests another thought, viz : that it were not even sufficient for the Son of God by his redemptive work to have made the choice of the Father operative, had not the Holy Spirit taken of His work, so to speak, and applied it to us individually, and made it our possession, (13, 14). All these verses should be read in the Revised Version.

It is sometimes affirmed by the unevangelical that the doctrine of the Trinity is not found in the New Testament. It is indeed true that the word "Trinity" is not found there ; but the great and mysterious truth for which it stands is the very warp and woof of the New Testament. Just see how it is interlaced with, or rather forms the very foundation of the origin of the Christian church itself ! The origin of the church then, let us say, is

In the choice of the Father.

Through the work of the Son.

By the sealing of the Holy Spirit.

The next division is

II. The Standing of the Church, by which we mean the position it occupies before God in Christ. Of course, when we speak of the church as a body, we mean every individual member of that body ; and when we speak of their standing or position before God in Christ, we mean their present standing or position, not that which will be their privilege by-and-by merely, but that which is really their blessed possession now though they are yet in the flesh on the earth. The high priest in his relation to Israel in the Old Testament is a beautiful type of the truth here sought to be set forth. You will remember our studies about him and his office when we were in the Pentateuch. When he entered into the most holy place on the great day of atonement he did so representatively. He carried the names of the twelve tribes engraven on the precious stones which rested on his shoulders and composed his breastplate. They, i. e., the whole nation, entered there in him. All the exalted privileges he there enjoyed they as a nation enjoyed in him. Correspondingly, Christ now represents us in the tabernacle in the Heavens, and we are blessed with all spiritual blessings there in Him (chapter 1, verse 3). What are some of those blessings? In other words, trace along with me through the following verses some of the things which are at this moment true of every believer, and which constitute his standing or position before God in Christ.

He is for example:—
Chosen, 4. Sanctified, 4. Adopted, 5. Accepted, 6. Redeemed, 7. Forgiven, 7. Enriched, 8. Enlightened, 9. Sealed, 13. Quickened, 2:1. Exalted, 6. Consecrated, 10. Reconciled, 16. United, 21.

At the close of the first chapter, in which he dwells more particularly on what we have called the origin of the church, Paul breaks forth in a prayer that his readers may have the aid of the Holy Spirit in apprehending the wonderful things he has thus revealed to them (1:15-23). He does the same in this case, and with good reason (3:1, 14-21). These prayers will repay the most earnest and prayerful consideration. Let us make them our own.

It is at this point that the apostle enlarges somewhat upon the "mystery" referred to. At chapter 3, verse 1, he begins an allusion to his prayer on their behalf, but is shunted from his topic which he does not take up again till we reach verse 14. The intervening verses, 2-13, are really parenthetical. It is his allusion to his mission to the Gentiles that has this effect. That mission he will now speak about in passing. It was a special dispensation to him (2). How was it made known to him (3)? Had he ever referred to the matter before (3, 4)? Had it been known to men at any earlier time (5)? How does he define the secret or mystery (6)? The Revised Version omits the word "same" before "body," thus emphasizing that fact—the body of Christ, as the real mystery of which the apostle speaks. The body of Christ, of course, is synonymous with the church of Church, i. e., the true church composed of regenerated, living members united to the Head, 1:22, 4:15, also Colossians 1:18. What was one purpose of God in revealing the mystery at this time (10)?

III. The Design of the Church.—The question asked above and answered in the text quoted, leads up to the third division of our treatment of the contents of the epistle, viz: the design of the church. To simplify the matter, let us ask, Why has God manifested this grace and done all these wonderful things for us in Christ? Why has God saved sinful man? The answer in John 3:16 at once suggests itself, but it does not go deep enough. Granted that God so loved the world as to give His only begotten Son to die for it, the inquiry will not down as to why He loved it so? The answer is found only in this epistle, where at least three times in the first chapter, verses 6, 12,

and 14, it is said that these things were done to the praise of His glory or the glory of His grace. The explanation of God's wondrous love towards us, therefore, is that it terminates on Himself rather than on us. It glorifies Him to so act toward us in Christ. We instinctively feel that here is an object, a motive worthy of such acting, worthy of such a sacrifice as that of Christ. If it humbles us to think that we are not occupying the first place in God's thought concerning our salvation, it comforts us at the same time as we realize a sense of security in the fact that His own glory is involved in the perfecting of the work of grace in us. He does it for His name's sake!

But how, or in what way, is God's Glory to be manifested in the church? Compare for an answer chapter 2:7, 22, 3:10. According to the last-named passage the church is now, even at the present time, an example of God's manifold wisdom to the principalities and powers in Heavenly places. According to the first-named, it is to be an example of the riches of His grace in the ages to come. And according to 2:22, it is, and is to be this example from the point of view of His habitation in the Spirit. Compare Revelation 21:1-3.

We might, therefore, outline this third division of the theme thus:—
The Design of the church is
To be to the praise of God's glory.
a.) As an example of grace in the ages to come.
b.) As an) habitation of God in the Spirit.
c.) As an example of His wisdom now to principalities and powers in Heavenly places.

IV. The Duty of the Church.—This fourth and last division of the epistle is more easily discovered than the others and is found in the last three chapters. The duty of the church in the light of all the foregoing is simply to walk worthy of her high calling (4:1). This walk is outlined in three directions. She is to walk
In charity, 4:2. In unity, 3-16. In purity, 17-6:21.

This exhortation is then applied to the three classes of the social order, as follows:
Husbands and wives, 5:22-23. Children and parents, 6:1-4. Masters and servants, 6:5-9.

The whole concluding with very definite instruction as to the need as well as the supply of grace and power to accomplish the desired result, 6:10-20.

CHAPTER LI.

The Epistle to the Philippians.

In the treatment of this epistle, I propose an innovation, and intend to introduce it with a personal letter to myself written by a minister, at one time professor of biology in one of our older colleges, and now pastor of a church in a thriving city of the middle West. My object is to stimulate other pastors to follow his example, and obtain the spiritual blessing for themselves and their flocks which is certain to follow. In the course of his communication he says:

"I have adopted for this year instead of the usual reading of the Bible in the course of the year, a reading of a book over and over after your plan until I feel that I have secured its power and message. I write to bear testimony to the increased joy and profit to me of this method over the other way. I struggled first with Galatians and soon felt its message of Christian liberty in Christ. But when I tackled Ephesians, though so rich in phraseology, I found a task on me that did not yield its light for nearly three weeks. When, one morning, I saw its message, and in less than a half hour I secured its analysis, and I am sure that it is forever a new and still more blessed book for me. It is not only now a book of 'In Christ,' but I know just what its richness is as described by Conybeare and Howson, when they call it one of the most precious legacies to the churches of Christ that has ever been sent us.

"I took up next the book of Philippians, and had a severe struggle with it. Most commentators think that it has no special theme, but is a mere personal letter (or letters) which in the nature of the case could have not much of a sequence of thought. Usually they think the break comes at 3:2, "Beware of dogs, beware of the concision, etc." Well, I had been struggling with that beautiful book for more than two weeks when, one morning, light flashed upon me, and I caught the message and the commentators are all wrong! The book is a unity, and with a special message of joy from one end of it to the other, even at 3:2.

"In the case of Galatians I must go over the ground again and write up the skeleton, but in the cases of Ephesians and Philippians I was wise enough to

secure the skeleton at once and forever.

"As a sample I will record my work, which I used with evident profit and pleasure to others last night at a house-to-house prayer meeting. This skeleton may need revision, but it makes the book a new one to me:

THEME: The Christian life one constant joy. Keyword, Rejoice, 3:1.
1. Rejoice in the fellowship of the saints, 1:3-11.
2. Rejoice over afflictions that turn out for the furtherance of the Gospel, 1:12-30.
3. Rejoice in the ministry for the saints, 2:1-18.
4. Rejoice in the fellowship of such faithful saints as Timothy and Epaphroditus, 2:19-3:1.
5. Rejoice that our hopes are in Jesus and not in the deeds of the law and the flesh, 3:2-16.
6. Rejoice that our citizenship is in Heaven rather than on earth and in the fleshly indulgences, 3:17-4:1.
7. Rejoice even over such Christians as Euodia and Syntyche who, though at strife, have the root of the matter in them, whose names are written in the book of life, 4:2-3.
8. Rejoice always and over all things, 4:4-9.
9. Rejoice in the bounties of God's people to those in need as was Paul, 4:10-20.
Salutations and benediction."

* * * * * *

The above speaks for itself, and will be found helpful and suggestive, I feel sure.

I am now to add another view of this epistle, which I like very much, and which is suggested by E. W. Bullinger, D. D., of the Church of England.

You will recall that the great doctrinal teaching of Ephesians is that Christ is the Head of that Body of which His people on earth are the members, and that this calling of theirs implies a corresponding responsibility on their part to walk worthily of it. This worthiness is to be shown with "all lowliness and meekness, with long-suffering, forbearing one another in love," etc. (See Ephesians 4:1-16.)

Now, as Dr. Bullinger aptly says, it was in the practical exhibition of this precept that these Philippian saints failed, and it was to bring conviction to them and remedy this wrong that this epistle was chiefly written.

Hence after the Salutation, an earnest exhortation is given that they might conduct themselves "as it becometh the gospel of Christ," and "stand fast in one spirit, with one soul, laboring together for the faith of the Gospel." Then follow four examples of such a spirit which, with the exhortations, practically fill up the rest of the epistles. Example, in other words, takes the place of precept in this epistle.

The whole epistle he divides in this way:

You will have observed that the two chief examples thus indicated—Christ and Paul, are accompanied by exhortations, while the two minor examples, Timothy and Epaphroditus, are considered more briefly, each in six verses.

Moreover, Christ's example and Paul's, as our author notes, are further marked off from the other two by a statement of what each gave up, and each gained. There are seven stages in Christ's humiliation pointed out in the text, contrasted with the same number of stages in His exaltation. It will be a deeply interesting task to make an analysis of the passages referred to and ascertain these, in all, fourteen precious facts.

Following this example of the head, our attention is called to that of some of the members. Timothy had something of the mind that was in Christ. He did not act through strife or vainglory. He in lowliness of mind esteemed others better than himself. He did not look only on his own things but also on the things of others. (Compare 2 : 19-24 with the preceding allusions to Christ.)

Epaphroditus was another like Timothy—concerned about other saints more than about himself.

Then comes Paul's example He, too, enumerates his gains and losses, which were like his Master's in number, though not in nature. "Christ's glory which He laid aside, was real. Paul's gains, which he gave up, were unreal. They were no gains at all. He thought they were, but he found they were only losses, and counted them but 'dung' as compared with the glory of Christ." Counts his supposed "gains," and finds them just seven. Counts the things that took their place, and finds them seven too. And notice that these last were all "in Christ." The first five were already enjoyed by faith. The last two (resurrection and advent) were still future and to be enjoyed. The first gain bore reference to Christ as our Righteousness, the next four to Christ as our Sanctification, the last two to Christ as our "Hope of Glory." To be found in Christ, to know Him, and to be like Him, this was his all in all. Is it ours? This is Christianity. Nothing else is Christianity. Christianity is Christ.

CPAPTER LII

The Epistle to the Colossians.

Colosse was an important city of Phrygia in Asia Minor, situated to the east of Ephesus. It is not definitely known that Paul visited it, and yet it is assumed that he did so on his third journey. Chapter 2 : 1, however, would seem to point in the opposite direction. Those who believe he never visited the city suggest Epaphras as the founder of the church there (1 : 7, R. V.). The epistle seems to have been written while Paul was a prisoner at Rome, 4 : 8, about A. D. 62, and sent by Tychicus, 4 : 7, 8.

Colossians bears a somewhat similar relationship to Ephesians as that of Romans to Galatians. That is, it seems to make a pair with that epistle, and to have been written almost simultaneously therewith. It was sent by the same messenger, (compare Ephesians 6 : 21, 22). It also contains some of the same expressions. Compare 1 :4, with Ephesians 1 : 15, also 1 : 14 with Ephesians 1 : 7. Compare the prayers in the two epistles also, and the references to the Body of Christ.

The central theme of Colossians is

Christ, while that of Ephesians is the church. In the first-named we have the Head, and in the last-named the Body of the church. Both are thus seen exalted on high. (Colossians 1: 18, Ephesians 2 : 6). Perhaps it would be well to designate the theme of the epistle as, "The Headship of Christ," or "The Believers' Union or Identification with Christ."

It is quite evident from the contents that the epistle was occasioned by the fact that the spiritual life of the church was threatened by false teaching. See especially 2 : 4, 8. This false teaching seems to have been in the direction of Angelolatry, 1 : 16, 2 : 10, 15, 18. Ritualism, 2 : 16. Asceticism, 2 : 20-23.

They, i e., those influenced by the false teachings, seem in the first place to have questioned Christ's true relationship to God and to the spiritual and natural worlds. In the second place, they seem to have questioned the facts of an objective atonement, and like the Galatians, sought to supplement the Gospel by Judaism or an equivalent. While in the third place, they doubted sanctification by the Holy Spirit, accepting instead methods of a physical and dietetic character. Indeed the whole region of Phrygia roundabout is said to have been particularly prone to mystical and fanatical superstitions of one kind or another. Professor M. B. Riddle, characterizing the situation, says that while "the errors were not fully developed, they nevertheless seemed to combine Grecian philosophy, Oriental mysticism and Jewish asceticism, all three leading away from the headship of Christ."

The same authority divides the epistle into four parts:

Doctrinal, 1.
Polemical, 2.
Hortatory, 3-4 : 6.
Conclusion, 4 : 7-18.

The Doctrinal Chapter, 1.—In this first Chapter Christ is shown to be the All in All. For example: After the salutation, (1 :1-8), and the prayer (9-13), as in Ephesians, we have a declaration of His fulness (14-22), as Redeemer, 14 ; Creator, 15-16 ; Preserver, 17 ; Head of the Body (the church), 18 ; Reconciler, 20-22 ; Sanctifier of His people, 22.

This declaration is, in turn, followed by that of Paul's ministry (23-29). It is noticeable in this latter declaration that Paul speaks really of a two-fold ministry :

The first is the ministry of the Gospel itself, (23), and the second that of the mystery of the Body of Christ (24-27). Notice carefully his language in verses 25 and 26, which agrees entirely with Ephesians 3. This explains the otherwise difficult allusion in verse 24 to his filling "up that which is behind of the afflictions of Christ." "Christ" here seems to stand not only for the Head but the Body as united with the Head. Compare 1 Corinthians 12 : 12. Thus Paul was filling up on his own part that which was lacking, having his own share in the suffering of the mystical Body for that Body's sake. Notice also the marginal reading of the last phrase of verse 25. "To fulfill the Word of God," is rendered, "fully to preach the Word of God ;" from which may be gathered that such is not done save as we reveal and emphasize this secret hitherto about the Body of Christ, the mystery of the church, composed of a people called out from both Jews and Gentiles, distinct and separate from the coming manifested kingdom of Isaiah.

Before leaving this chapter let me call attention further to that description of Christ in verse 15 as "The First Born of Every Creature," which has given anxiety to some as seeming to cast a doubt on His deity or Eternal Sonship. In the light of so much else to establish that great truth we might dismiss the apparent difficulty without fear. But it may be interesting to add that certain Greek scholars, conspicuous among them S. P. Tregelles, show good reason for translating the words "First-born before all creation."

We did not find time in our study of Ephesians to analyze either of the apostolic prayers. Observe in this one however (9-13) the four needful petitions :

That they might filled with the knowledge of God's will.

That they might walk worthily of the Lord in fruit-bearing.

That they might be strengthened with power to endure temptation.

That they might be thankful.

These prayers are very suggestive as the basis of practical sermons, and Bible readings.

The Polemic Chapter, 2.—Having established the fact that Christ is the Head of the Body in whom all fulness dwells, the apostle now warns his hearers against being led away from Him (1-7). They were in danger of this through the philosophy of certain false teachers (8), and through the Judaism or asceticism of others (16-23). Perhaps we are hardly justified in making any rhetorical distinction between these false teachings, as it may be, the philosophy and vain deceit referred to in the first instance (verse 8) covers the whole. It will be seen that these Colossian Christians were in danger of putting the shadow for the substance—ordinances instead of Christ (16, 17), and a humility of the flesh, i. e., the old carnal nature, instead of one wrought by the Holy Ghost (18, 23).

Let it be carefully observed that the apostle inspired of God meets these errors with the asseveration of positive truth; and that this truth is none other than that of the believer's identification with Christ involved in the proposition about the mystical Body. The believer is circumcised, 11; buried, 12; risen, 13; quickened, 13, with Christ, and this on the basis of what Christ Himself did for him in His own death and resurrection (14, 15).

It is seemingly foolish to speak of the revelation of one truth in the New Testament as more wonderful than another where all are in a sense alike wonderful. But this one contributes to the assurance of faith in the experience of those who apprehend it as perhaps none other can. Let the illustration of our own bodily formation aid in that apprehension. If my head dies, my body dies; if my head rises from the dead, my body rises; if my head possesses quickening life, my body possessesses that life. Now Christ is the Head and the church is His Body, and we believers are individual members of that Body. Everything, therefore, which is true of the Head is true of the Body. The more we dwell upon this thought the more assurance can we draw from such familiar passages as Romans 8:1, and kindred teachings of the New Testament. Oh, the unsearchable riches of that expression "In Christ," and that other one, "Christ in you!" Let us take up this prayer of Paul upon our lips and seek that God may lead us into the understanding of them. Compare again Romans 6:1-14.

The Hortatory Chapters, 3-4:6.—The writer has just shown that in a legal or judicial sense as members of the mystical Body of Christ we, as believers in Him, have died and risen with Him, and He now exhorts us to live accordingly. On the basis of our identification with Christ in other words, we are now, first of all, to set our affections (or "our mind," R. V.), on heavenly things, i. e., on these very things he has been specially revealing to us (3:1-4).

We may, in the second place, be said to do this in the degree in which we "mortify," i. e., put to death our "members which are upon the earth" (5-11). That is, forever give up those sins of body and mind enumerated in the verses just referred to. It deserves particular notice that the renunciation of these things on the believer's part are assumed to be quite possible on the ground of his standing in Christ, however it may have been before.

But this exhortation is further carried out in a more positive form by what the believer is expected to put on, to add to his life, as well as by that he puts away (12-17). This too, it is assumed he is able to do. We have seen how he is able to do it in the study of Romans 8, i. e., through "the law of the Spirit of life in Christ Jesus," through the operation of the Holy Spirit in him giving him the victory.

It will be already seen how this applicatory part of the epistle as well as the doctrinal part agrees with Ephesians, but the similarity is rendered the more striking by the further coincidence that the three classes of the social order are again singled out for direct address, viz: Husbands and wives, 18, 19; parents and children, 20, 21; masters and servants, 22-4:1.

Much is said and written in these days about sociological topics, and chairs of sociology are being endowed in colleges and seminaries; but after all, the Bible is the best text-book on that subject to be found. If private Christians were more faithful in its perusal and preachers in its plain and simple exposition, who can tell what a solution might be found for our present problems of the family and the state?

The several topics under the head of the "Conclusion" in chapter 4:7-18, are so simple in their outline as to require no particular treatment here.

Note: For a scholarly and yet deeply spiritual treatment of Colossians, the author would commend a book edited by himself from the ms. of the late Bishop W. R. Nicholson, D.D., of Philadelphia, to be obtained through the Revell Publishing Co.

CHAPTER LIII.

The First Epistle to the Thessalonians

The first epistle to the Thessalonians was probably the earliest that Paul wrote.

You will need to look back at the seventeenth chapter of the Acts in order to get the history of the church at Thessalonica. There you will learn that it was founded by Paul in company with Silas and Timothy, and probably Luke, on the second missionary journey of the first-named. They had crossed over into Macedonia from Troas, first visiting Philippi, where Paul and Silas had been imprisoned, and then come down to Thessalonica. They were permitted to remain there but three Sabbath days when persecution drove them down to Berea. Driven out of Berea subsequently, Paul entered Athens and then later, Corinth. Here Timothy, who had evidently returned to Thessalonica for the purpose, brought to Paul a report of the situation there, whereupon the Apostle addressed this epistle, or letter, to them.

I. The Salutation, 1:1. — Whose names are associated with that of Paul therein? This, not because either of them is to be regarded as associated with him jointly in the production of the letter, of which he alone is to be considered the inspired author, but because they were equally known to the church at Thessalonica, and hence united with him in the greeting. You will notice that phrase "the 'Church' of the Thessalonians." Is it used in the case of any other body of Christians to which Paul has addressed himself? How shall we explain this peculiarity? Some think it was the only church worthy of the name, and indeed, as a matter of fact, Paul has very little to condemn or criticize in this church as compared with the others.

II. The Thanksgiving and Testimony, 1:2-10. — This gives us in a few words, verse 3, a very complete and satisfactory picture of the spiritual condition of the church. Can you name the triad of graces of which it speaks? And what further in that verse shows their absolute genuineness? What conviction touching the standing of these Christians does this spiritual fruitage awaken in Paul's mind (verse 4)? And yet, after all, may this conviction have come to him only after seeing these fruits, or may it have been borne in on his soul from the very beginning of his ministry among them? Do Christian workers now-a-days, missionaries and evangelists, ever have such a conviction in advance about any people or place? Compare Acts 18:10.

What explains this rich spiritual fruitage in Thessalonica (verse 5)? What is there in that same verse which suggests that the character of Paul and his fellow-workers had much to do, from the human side, with this unwonted spiritual power?

Following this thanksgiving, I know no better word to characterize the conclusion of this first chapter than that of Paul's testimony to the church (6-10). A testimony which, in a way, carries out the allusion to the triad of graces in verse 3. He testifies to their obedience (verse 6), their spiritual joy in the midst of affliction, (same verse), their consistency as disciples (verse 7), and their missionary spirit (8-10). I am not sure that this last reference to the way in which the Gospel sounded out from them applies so much to a direct agency in missionary work as to an indirect. Perhaps it was the report of their Christian life and character carried by travelers and others to distant parts, that constituted this missionary work they did, and yet in a vital sense it was they who did it. What is there in verse 9 to indicate that this church was composed chiefly of Gentile Christians? What in verse 10 indicates that Paul in his preaching there laid stress on the second coming of Christ?

III. The Character of Paul as a Christian Worker, 2:1-16. — Under the head of the "Thanksgiving" we saw that the power of the Spirit accompanying Paul's ministry in Thessalonica was accounted for in a measure by the "manner of man" he was among them, i. e., by his own character and life as a Christian witness. And now at the second chapter of the epistle he describes that character and life. He does this not in any spirit of boasting or self-glorying, of course, but as a further testimony to the reality of the

Gospel he preached, and for the glory of the grace of God. They had known him to be a very bold and courageous man even in the physical sense (1, 2); very faithful and impartial in his teaching, with his thought not so much on gaining favor with them as on pleasing God who had committed the gospel to him (3-6); very kind and affectionate nevertheless (7, 8); very unselfish and disinterested, working with his own hands for his temporal support as at Corinth, lest he should prejudice them against the salvation he proclaimed (9); and finally, very holy and consistent throughout, so that they could not lay a finger on anything he said or did while among them not in accordance with the standard he held up. It was for these reasons doubtless, that his gospel so recommended itself to them, and he was able to say what he does about its reception in verses 13-16, which please examine.

IV. The Origin of the Epistle, 2: 17-3. —The circumstances under which Paul came to write this letter, already outlined, are given in his own words in that part of it we are now to consider. He desired to visit them again (verse 17); but was hindered by Satan (18), doubtless through the instrumentality of the bitter persecution stirred up against him. He had, therefore, sent Timothy (from Berea) to comfort and establish them in his stead (3: 1-5); who now had returned to him (at Corinth doubtless, see Acts 18: 1-5), with a good report of their condition (3 :-6-10). This only made him pray the more earnestly that he might get to see them, and that in the meantime their love and holiness might abound and grow (11-13).

V. The Sins Rebuked, 4: 1-12.—The church at Thessalonica was not entirely "without rebuke," however, as the opening of the fourth chapter shows. Moreover, at first sight, the need of the rebuke seems to be of the gravest character, the grossest sins of the flesh being involved (1-8). How is it possible that Christians, and especially those as highly commended as these, could be guilty of such things? There is no apology to be made for them, but there is an explanation. The church was chiefly composed, not of Jewish, but Gentile Christians (compare Acts 17: 4, 1 Thessalonians 1: 9), who, prior to their conversion, had been living in heathenism, as were their forefathers for centuries, and in the commission of these sins without realizing them to be such. Indeed, the grossest licentiousness was, and is still, connected

with certain forms of pagan worship. We can readily understand, therefore, why it was difficult for them to see the blackness of such crimes, and why they were slow to renounce them. Had they been Jewish rather than Gentile believers such acts would not have been charged against them, because of their knowledge of their true character as learned from the Holy Scriptures. These the Jews possessed, but the Gentiles had no acquaintance with them. It is a relief to note that the apostolic admonition in this case was sufficient, since in the following epistle to this same people no mention is necessary to be made of the sin of fornication.

A rebuke, or at least an exhortation, touching brotherly love follows (9, 10), and especially one concerning idleness (11, 12). Some have thought the idleness to be accounted for by a misunderstanding as to what Paul had taught about the second coming of Christ. If that event were near, and the glory of the kingdom soon to be participated in, why labor so assiduously as before? Perhaps it was expected day by day, and if so, one can easily understand how those who were lacking in spiritual balance, should throw off their usual restraint and become less regardful of the proprieties and necessities of the present life.

At all events, notice for its practical value, that their idleness led to "busybodyness" as it always does. Notice also the two very practical reasons for renouncing that sin, first, that they might "walk honestly toward them that are without," and secondly, that they "might have need of nothing." "Them that are without" are, of course, their non-Christian neighbors, and it was vital they should not fall into their debt without the prospect of liquidating it. It was equally vital that their neglect of occupation should not lead them into beggary.

VI. The Doctrinal Error Corrected, 4: 13-5: 11.—We now touch upon that part of the epistle which suggests the strongest reason for its writing. We have seen that in Paul's preaching at Thessalonica he had laid much stress on the second coming of Christ, leaving the impression on the church that the event was imminent, and that they who were ready to receive Christ when He came should enter into His glory with Him. But in the meantime, as the weeks, and perhaps months, rolled by, some of their number died. Died without seeing Christ or partaking of that promised glory? They who remained sorrowed greatly on this account, feeling perhaps that their's would be a great advantage over the dead saints when Christ came. Paul proceeds to set them right on this subject, in the course of which he outlines the great and blessed hope of the church in its "Rapture" at Christ's Coming, as we meet with it in no other part of the New Testament.

Analyzing these verses, 4: 13-5: 11, in detail, he first exhorts the bereaved not to "sorrow as those that had no hope." Sorrow was permitted, but not the sorrow of the world. He next expresses the ground on which such sorrow may be removed. The departed saints will come back again to this earth when Jesus comes. We have the same reason for believing this as for believing in the death and resurrection of Jesus. Moreover, the further good news he is about to reveal to them, he has received as a special revelation from the Lord. No one else was told this, and no one else reveals it but Paul, namely: That we which are alive and remain on the earth in the flesh when Christ comes shall not precede, go before, that is, or have any advantage in the matter of time over the dead saints. The Lord Himself shall descend from Heaven with a shout, and the dead, not all the dead, but they who have died in the faith of Christ, shall rise first. Their bodies will be raised from their graves and re-united to their souls in a glorified condition. Then we Christians who are alive and remain upon the earth at that time shall be "caught up" together with them in the clouds to meet the Lord in the air. This is what is called the "Rapture." It is an experience for the whole church or Body of Christ not unlike that which came to Enoch presumably (see Hebrews 11), or Elijah. How glorious! No wonder that in the closing verse of the fourth chapter we

should be exhorted to comfort one another with these words.

Chapter 5, in continuation of the subject, speaks of the time of this event, only to rebuke that disposition on the part of some to fix dates and times for Christ's coming. So far as the situation in the world is concerned He will come "as a thief," when He is least expected, like the flood in Noah's time (see Matthew 24), with the consequences spoken of in verse 3. But true Christians will not be "overtaken" in that way. Their duty and their attitude is one of watching (6). They have no fear in the prospect of that day (9-11).

VII. Concluding Exhortations.—The epistle concludes with various exhortations, for example, for a proper regard for their spiritual rulers and guides (12, 13); for mutual carefulness of one another (14, 15); for the spirit of prayer and rejoicing (16-18), etc. They are exhorted to "quench not the Spirit," i. e., the Holy Spirit, and the direction in which they were tempted to thus thwart His purposes in and through them is indicated in the next verse, "Despise not prophesyings." Prophesying was one of the gifts much less esteemed than some others, as we saw in the first epistle to the Corinthians, and yet in the economy and for the upbuilding of the church it was, perhaps, the most important of all. It was synonymous with preaching and testifying, and could be exercised by the feeblest members of the church if endued with the Holy Spirit. To be sure, there might be erroneous teaching and false testimony, hence the admonitions which follow to "Prove all things" holding fast that which is good, but abstaining from every form of error.

The benediction follows the greeting and the charge (23-28).

CHAPTER LIV.

The Second Epistle to the Thessalonians.

Paul's second epistle to the Thessalonians was written doubtless soon after the first, and for a very important reason, which will appear in the sequel.

I. The Salutation, 1: 1-2.

II. The Thanksgiving, 1: 3-10.—The thanksgiving extends practically from verse 3 to 10, and contains some matters

of great importance to be considered. In the first place, what should you say was the spiritual condition of the church now, as compared with the earlier occasion? What does verse 3 indicate as to this? You will agree doubtless, that its spiritual condition was excellent, even better than before. But what about its outward or physical condition? What says verse 4 about it? What was God's purpose in thus calling them to suffer (5)? If it were a righteous thing for God to give them the kingdom as a result of their tribulation, observe that it was equally a righteous thing for Him to give their enemies tribulation for causing it (6). To the saints the tribulation was a "threshing," a separation of the precious from the vile, the wheat from the chaff, but to their enemies it was "a just recompense of reward." Observe further, when these discriminating judgments would be experienced by the two classes (7). It would be at the revelation of the Lord Jesus. Who would accompany Him at this time? And for what purpose would He come (8)? This raises the question as to whether Paul is here speaking of precisely the same event as that in 1 Thessalonians 4:13-18? The two events do not look alike, do they? In the former instance the Lord was coming with His saints, here He is coming with His angels. There He was coming to translate His church, here to take vengeance on His enemies. Verse 10 throws a little light on this, especially if we read "When he shall have come" instead of "When he shall come." The verb in this case is in the subjunctive mood and second aorist tense, and those who know Greek will see the justification for translating it thus. The time then when Jesus will be revealed from Heaven with His mighty angels taking vengeance on His enemies will be when He shall have come, i. e., AFTER He shall have come, to be glorified in His saints, in other words, after the rapture of the church spoken of in the earlier epistle. His coming for His church is known as His "Coming," His revelation to His enemies is known as His "Revelation," and these two events are really two aspects of but one event, or two acts in one drama separated doubtless by a certain period of time. It is during this time of separation between the two that those earthly events transpire of which we learned in the Old Testament, and which will culminate in the restoration of the Jews to their own land, the gathering of the Gentile nations against them, and the manifestation of the Antichrist. To quote Dr. Bullinger, of London, in this place: "From these passages it is clear that when the judgment on the ungodly is revealed, the Lord shall have already and previously come to be glorified in His saints, 'in that day,' and have given them the promised 'rest' of which Paul had already told them in the former epistle, and reminded them in this

chapter, verse 7. 'In that day,' at the end of verse 10, refers to that glorious day of which the apostle had spoken so fully in 1 Thessalonians 4. All hope of rest, reward, and glory is to be consummated 'in that day.'"

III. The Prayer, 1:11-12.

IV. The Cause for the Epistle, 2:1-2.

—We now reach a statement as to the reason or occasion for this second epistle, written very soon, doubtless, after the first. It seems that false teachers had followed Paul into Thessalonica, some even forging his name to a letter, who had sought to lead the church astray as to some of these important matters about the Lord's second coming. As we have just seen, that great event may be spoken of under two aspects or two acts of a single drama. One was described as His "Coming," for His saints, the other later one as His "Revelation" in judgment on His enemies. The first has been identified with His "Presence," the second with "The Day of the Lord," so frequently named in the Old Testament. To quote Dr. Bullinger again: "Paul had taught them that before 'the Day of the Lord' should come, they would be caught up to meet the Lord in the air, to be forever with the Lord. In other words, that He would come and receive them unto Himself, before that great and terrible day should set in." But these false teachers thus spoken of, had sought to reverse this teaching in a measure, and to have them believe that the day of the Lord had already come, for such is the meaning of the latter half of verse 2. This tribulation they were enduring was pointed to, no doubt, as an evidence of it. If, therefore, the day of the Lord had set in, and they had not been gathered together unto Him, they had every reason to be troubled, for then their faith and hope were vain, and Paul had deceived them. Let us see, therefore, how the Apostle offsets this false teaching, in the doing of which, by the way, he reveals matters of deep interest concerning the apostasy which is to be headed up in the Antichrist.

V. The Apostacy and Rise of the Anti-Christ, 2:3-7.—What does Paul say must come before the Day of the Lord comes (verse 3)? Remember, please, that by the Day of the Lord is not meant His coming for His saints and their translation into the air, but His revelation of Himself after that event to His enemies in flaming fire. He says there must come a "falling-away" first, that is, an apostasy from

the truth in the church. And who will then be revealed as heading up that apostacy, no doubt? How is this "man of sin," "the son of perdition," further described in verse 4? That word "above" is in the Reviseed Version translated "against." He is against all that is called God, from which fact it is that he obtains the title of "Anti" Christ. What does he himself, however, assume to be? And in what place will he set forth this assumption? This reference to his sitting in the "temple of God," recalls Daniel's prophecy quoted by our Lord in Matthew 24, about the "abomination of desolation" being established there, for the temple referred to, doubtless, is that at Jerusalem. We have seen all along that the prophets are a unit as to its re-building when the Jews shall have been returned there (still in an unconverted state so far as their acceptance of Jesus as their Messiah is concerned).

But had not Paul spoken of these matters at all during his presence in Thessalonica (5)? Yet there was some power withholding, restraining the full development of this apostacy, and the revelation of the Anti-Christ, according to verse 6. What was this power? Some would say the power was the iron rule of the Roman Empire, and by parity of reasoning the rule of the successors of the Roman Empire in our own time. But a more satisfactory answer is that the power was the Holy Spirit. He was restraining, keeping back, the full development of the apostacy until the elect Body of Christ should be called out from the world. When that is complete, and caught up to meet its Head in the air, there is a sense in which it may be said that the Holy Spirit leaves the earth with it. That is, He ceases to exercise the same restraining power over lawlessness and sin that He now does. This stands to reason, for the church is the medium He chiefly uses at the present time as the preserving salt of the earth, and when it is removed there will be little to withstand the hastening process of corruption. This idea is further strengthened by the 7th verse, which declares that the "mystery of iniquity," the apostacy, was already at work even in Paul's own day, "only He who now letteth, (i. e., restraineth), will let (or restrain) until He be taken out of the way."

In the foregoing exposition I have given my own opinion and that of expositors generally, as to the interpretation of the words, but it is only right to say that some others, take quite a different view of the meaning of verse 7. With them it is not the Holy Spirit who is holding "back" something, but Satan rather, who is holding "on" to something—holding on to his possessions in the heavenly places, in the air, until he be cast out, i. e., into the earth, as will be the case when Jesus and His church come to take possession of the regions he now occupies. (See Revelation 12:9-12, 13:1, Revised Version.) I need not dwell upon the matter further, because the opinion I have given above is not set aside in any practical sense even if Satan be the one referred to in verse 7. In other words, it still remains true that the Holy Spirit in the church is the great restraining power of iniquity, and when that power is removed, as, of course, it will be at the translation, iniquity will have an opportunity to quickly culminate.

VI. The Destruction of the Anti-Christ, 2:8-12.—To return now to the text, What shall be the end of the Anti-Christ (verse 8)? Compare here Isaiah 11:4. What shows that as the Christ when He was on the earth was energized by the Holy Spirit, His great opponent when He comes, shall be energized by Satan (verse 9)? But who, alone, will be ultimately deceived by his signs and lying wonders (10)? And who will be to blame for their credulity (same verse)? What do they fail to do that leaves them a prey to Anti-Christ's deceit? What judicial punishment now falls upon them (11)? But is this their ultimate punishment or only a step towards it (12)? What is their ultimate punishment (same verse)?

VII. Conclusion, 2:13-3.—What a blessed contrast we meet with in the verse that follows! The apostle having about completed the doctrinal or rather dispensational part of his letter now turns to matters personal and social again. But first of all, on the ground of their calling through grace (verses 13, 14), what obligation does he lay upon them in verse 15? To whom does he commend them, and for what two-fold object (16, 17)? What request does he make of them on his own behalf (3:1, 2)? What opinion does he hold of them, and what ground has he for holding it (3, 4)? What command is given them (6)? What was the nature of the "disorderliness" referred to (7-11)? To what subject of his first epistle does this bear reference? Does he address himself directly to these disorderly members of the church (12)? How was the church to treat them while they thus remained disorderly ,14, 15)? What token of validity does Paul add to this letter to offset any further forgeries of his name (17)?

CHAPTER LV.

The First Epistle to Timothy.

We now reach what are called the Pastoral Epistles of which there are three, I and II Timothy and Titus. They are so called because of their contents, which are chiefly exhortations and directions regarding the pastoral work of ministers in the church. It is quite evident that they deal with persons and things belonging to a late period in the Apostolic Age. The heretics repeatedly mentioned in them indicate this. These are of a Jewish character, for they profess to be teachers of the law (1 Timothy 1:7), and are described as of the circumcision (Tit. 1:10), and as causing men to attend to Jewish fables (3:9). And yet they are not the same kind of Judaizing teachers with which we became acquainted in our early study of the Acts (15), and the epistle to the Galatians, or even that to the Colossians. They have progressed further on the "down grade," and "are involved in a total apostasy from God and from good." They had lost all true understanding of the law (1 Tim. 1:7); had repudiated a good conscience (19); had become hypocrites and liars (4:2); were branded with immorality (4:2); of corrupt minds, using religion to better themselves in the world (1 Tim. 6:5; Tit. 1:11); subverters of the faith (II Tim. 2:17); victimizing foolish persons to their ruin (II Tim. 3:6); confessing God with their mouths, but denying Him in their works, abominable and disobedient, and for every good work reprobate (Tit. 1:16). A dark catalogue this, corroborating very strongly the teaching of Paul in II Thessalonians as to the working already of the apostasy in the church. The false doctrines attacked by Paul in his earlier epistles were now bearing fruit in laxity of life and morals.

Date of the Epistles.—It is clear from the foregoing that the date of these epistles must have been later than the period of Paul's history covered by

the record in the Acts, and that they were probably written after his liberation from Roman imprisonment at that time. There is reason to believe that Paul was imprisoned a second time, and in the interval between the two imprisonments the first epistle to Timothy and that to Titus were written, while the second to Timothy followed during the second imprisonment, as it is thought.

Following the idea of Alford, Paul, after the imprisonment mentioned in the Acts, journeyed eastward as he anticipated in his letters to Philemon (22), and the church at Philippi, 1:26; 2:24. He then visited Ephesus again, and doubtless took further journeys West occupying, it may be, three or four years. At Ephesus he left Timothy and passed into Macedonia (1 Tim. 1:3), from which country perhaps, he wrote him the first epistle. Not far from this time he must have visited Crete in company with Titus and have left him there to complete the organization of the churches in that quarter. This will appear when we come to the study of the epistle to Titus, which it is thought was written somewhere in Asia Minor, and when Paul was on his way to winter at Nicopolis in Greece. It was at this place he was arrested again probably, "as implicated in the charges made against the Christians after the fire in 64 A. D., and sent to Rome." Once more in that city, he is treated no longer with the courtesy of his former residence there but as an ordinary criminal (II Tim. 2:9). All his Asiatic friends avoided him except Onesiphorus (II Tim. 1:16). Only Luke was with him. Timothy is entreated to come to him before winter (II Tim. 4:21).. He is expecting execution (II Tim. 4:6), and in view of it he writes his second epistle to Timothy, about A. D. 67 or 68.

History of Timothy.—For the beginnings of Timothy's history you will need to recur to the sixteenth chapter of the Acts. He was converted perhaps on the occasion of Paul's first visit to Lystra, since it was on his second visit

*For the introductory part of this lesson I am indebted to Alford's, How to Study the New Testament.

he was chosen to be his traveling companion. He accompanies Paul throughout that second missionary journey, wintering with him at Corinth, and indeed seems to have been with him pretty steadily, except for the commissions on which he was occasionally sent (Acts 19:22; 1 Cor. 4:17, 16:- 10), not only throughout the second, but the third journey as well. About A. D. 62 or 63 he was with the Apostle while the latter was a prisoner at Rome (Col. 1:1; Philemon 1; Philippians 1:1).. In 66 or 67, after that imprisonment, he was left by Paul in charge of the church at Ephesus. It was while he was here that he received the first epistle or letter from Paul. A year later it may be, the second was written, when Paul was again a prisoner, and Timothy repairs to Rome to visit him, after which nothing further is heard of him.

In his character he was a very earnest and thoroughly consecrated man as we shall see, and yet he appears to have been timid and diffident, and hesitating to deal with certain difficulties of his work. Compare here 1Corinthians 16:10; 1 Tim. 4:12: 5:23; 11 Tim. 1:5, 7; 3:10.

Outline of Chapter I.

I. The Salutation, 1:1, 2. In this notice the beautiful designation of our Lord Jesus Christ as "Our Hope." He Himself is our Hope. And when we remember that these words were written by Paul in his later years, they are all the more affecting. And notice another thing, the designation given to Timothy in verse 2. What bearing has this upon the proposition that he probably owed his conversion to Paul's labors?

II. A reference to Timothy's mission at Ephesus, 3, 4. We have referred to the circumstance of his being left there by Paul, in our introduction. It seems to have necessitated some little urging on Paul's part, however, to persuade him to comply. What language indicates as much? What charge was he to lay upon the teachers at Ephesus? In what two directions (especially Jewish) were they inclined to digress from the Gospel? What would be likely to be the outcome of such digression?

III. A description of the false teachers, 5-7. In this description it will be noted that the root of the offense, as always, was in swerving from love, for such is the correct translation of the word "charity" in verse 5.

IV. A description of the true use of the law, 8-11. These false teachers pretended to discourse of the law, by which is meant what is commonly known as the law of Moses, without really knowing the subject on which they spoke. The law did not apply to those who were saved under the Gospel, but it had the same bearing as ever to the unbeliever.

V. A digression to the circumstances of his own conversion, 12-17. This digression springs from his allusion to the Gospel in verse 11, a Gospel committed to his trust as a steward to proclaim. Observe that he does not spare himself in extolling the grace of God toward him (13-15), and that he uses his own history as an example and encouragement to the worst of sinners to be saved (16).

VI. A personal charge to Timothy, 18-20. This charge is the single one to fight the good fight of faith, to which he is stimulated by two moving considerations. The first is the "prophecies which went before" on him, the supernatural predictions of his future; and the second, the failure of some who had started forth in the fight with him and fallen back. The good fight of faith in his case is perhaps not more that which was personal to himself, than that which concerned his official ministry. It is not the conflict of the Christian life in general which Paul refers to so much, as that of a leader in the church against the opponents of a pure Gospel.

Regulations Concerning Public Prayer, 2.—

The whole of chapter 2 is taken up with regulations concerning public prayer. First, he directs that intercessory prayer be made for all men (verses 1-7). What class of men is especially singled out (2)? What selfish motive on the part of the church should induce such intercessory prayer (same verse)? And yet what higher motive is suggested (4)? What does this verse suggest as to the object of such intercession so far as those in authority are concerned? On what good and sufficient ground may such intercession be made (5, 6)? It seems evident that for some reason or other such intercession was not being made in this church at Ephesus. Perhaps a time of persecution at the hands of the governmental authorities had caused it to be less earnestly conducted, or perhaps a party spirit had something to do with it; at all events the church needed to be stirred up to the doing of it, and Timothy needed to be stirred up to get them doing it. This was part of the good warfare he was to war.

Second, he refers to the way in which men should pray (8). The word "everywhere" in this verse may refer to every place where the worshippers were in the habit of assembling in Ephesus. There may have been several churches or bodies of believers there meeting regularly in different places. The fact that men without distinction of ministerial functions were to pray is significant. Not only were the deacons, or elders, or presbyters, or bishops, to pray, but the "men" were to pray. There is no priesthood in the Christian church except the common priesthood of believers including all. But how were they to pray? "Lifting up" the hands was a Jewish custom in prayer and seems to have been adopted in the Christian church.

But what kind of hands were the men to hold up? "Holy hands" are those not stained with sin of any kind (Psalm 24:4; 26:6; James 4:8). If we regard iniquity in our hearts God will not hear us. And what further direction is given? "Without wrath and doubting" might read without wrath and disputing or contention. No religious disputes, no outbreaks in daily life could be permitted where prayer was to be engaged in.

Conduct of Women in Public Prayer, verses 9-15.—All expositors are agreed that the words "I will" of verse 8 should be carried over in force to verse 9. The latter then would read thus, "In like manner, I will that the women adorn themselves," etc. What, in this case, would be the force of the expression "in like manner"? Is it meant, as another asks, that he would have the men pray in every place, and the women "in like manner" to be silent? Or would he have the men lifting up holy hands, and the women "in like manner" adorning themselves? So unlikely is either of these conclusions that many expositors further supply the word "pray" in verse 9 to complete the sense. The two verses would then harmonize like this: "I will therefore that men pray everywhere lifting up holy hands, and in like manner, I will that women pray in modest apparel," etc., to the end of verse 10. Compare 1 Corinthians 11:5.

At verse 11 there is a transition, and the Apostle passes on to something new. What is that new thing about women he now takes up? Not her relation to public prayer, but really her relation to her husband, especially in the matter of public teaching in the church. The command to silence here suggests 1 Corinthians 14:34, 35, where the context shows that there were various forms of disorder and confusion in the church assemblies. especially the making remarks and asking questions

about the words of others, from which women, who seem to have been the chief offenders, were enjoined.

But what about teaching? "I suffer not a woman to teach." To teach and to govern are the special functions of the presbyter or elder. The teacher and pastor, named in the divine gifts to the church (Ephesians 4:11), are considered by some to be the same; and the pastor is generally regarded as identical with the bishop. Now there is no instance in the New Testament of a woman's being set over a church as bishop, or teacher or ruler. What then if we say it is to this, or something corresponding, to which Paul here refers?

The reason why woman is placed in this and in other respects in subjection to man as stated by Paul in verses 13 and 14 is sufficiently plain, but there is a mystery about the statement in verse 15 I cannot explain. Certainly it does not mean that the mere act of child-bearing saves a woman, which would be to contradict the primary truth of the Gospel that we are saved by faith and not works. As a matter of fact, moreover, the word for child-bearing here includes more than the act of giving birth, and means the proper nurture and training of children. Conybeare & Howson's note on this reads: "The apostle's meaning is, that women are to be kept in the path of safety, not by taking to themselves the office of the man (taking part in the assemblies of the church), but by the performance of the peculiar functions which God has assigned to their sex." This explanation is not altogether satisfactory to me, but I give it for what it is worth.

Regulations Concerning Church Officials, 3.—Chapter 3 is taken up with a charge to Timothy concerning the selection and the duties of certain church officials. First, he treats of bishops or overseers (1-7). It is to be remembered in this connection, as stated previously, that the word for "bishop" here is the same as that for "presbyter" or "elder" elsewhere. and does not mean a higher and distinct order of the ministry. See Titus 1:5, compared with verse 7 of the same chapter. Secondly, he treats of deacons (8-13). Then, to quote Alford, he brings these directions to a close by a solemn statement of their object and glorious import (14-16).

Prediction and Description of False Teachers, 4.—Chapter 4 is occupied chiefly by instruction concerning false teachers. In verses 1-6, they are foretold and described. At what period are they to appear? Notice that this agrees fully with Paul's previous teachings to the Thessalonians about the apostasy. It also has a close bearing upon the current question as to whether the world is growing better or worse. That question is too vast for any mortal to answer, and we can only fall back upon what God says about it. In this place, and in other places, He has plainly told us what to expect as the end of the age draws near, and it is for us to square our understanding and conduct accordingly.

Notice the detail into which the Holy Spirit goes in describing these false teachers. They shall be under what kind of influence (verse 1)? What two leading tenets of their system are mentioned in verse 3? How does the inspired Apostle contradict these teachings in verses 4 and 5? Here we need to guard against the disposition to limit the application of this false teaching to Roman Catholicism. Celibacy and abstinence from meat at certain times suggest that phrase of Christianity, but a familiarity with the teachings of the occult sciences, Christian Science included, would lead us to enlarge our horizon considerably in estimating what the Holy Spirit meant in this case.

The remainder of this chapter, verses 7-16, or perhaps beginning rather at verse 6, may be regarded as an exhortation to Timothy himself to that steadfastness and growth in his Christian life and calling so imperative in view of the false teaching he was called upon to combat, the germ of which, very evidently, had already sprung up. How does verse 7 indicate that, in Paul's estimation, these heresies were mere "abstract speculations without any connection with the historical realities and practical tendencies of Christianity?" The reference to "bodily exercise" in verse 8 is interesting. According to many it had reference to the physical abstinence from certain food, from marriage, etc., referred to above, which the heretics commended, but which Paul condemned. According to others, he means the gymnastic exercises so much in vogue with the Greeks, especially the Olympic games. He would have the youth Timothy appreciate the fact that the exercise begins with the inner man.

Directions for the Government of the Church, 5.—Chapter 5 gives directions concerning Timothy's management of church affairs, first, as to his behavior towards the older and younger members of the flock, of both sexes (1, 2). Secondly, as touching widows (3-16). By "widows indeed," verse 3, Paul means those who had no near relatives to support them (see verses 4 and 5), and who were humbly and prayerfully trusting in God (verse 6). At this point the Apostle turns for a moment from the consideration of the widows themselves to that of the persons whose duty it was to support them (8), returning to the widows again, however, for the purpose of treating the subject from a somewhat different point of view, viz: that of the church deaconness, as many, if not most, recent expositors believe (9, 10). The younger widows were not to be inducted into this sacred office from the likelihood that, desiring to marry again, they should thus become unfaithful to their covenant to serve Christ in this manner (11, 12), and also for the other reason named in verse 13. Of course, Paul does not mean that it was sinful in itself for young widows to marry a second time, or else he would not have recommended it as he does in verse 14, but only that it was a breach of their faith to Christ to do so after having betrothed themselves to Him, so to speak, for this special service. In verse 16, he recurs to his command in verse 4, about the pecuniary support of widows by their near relatives that the church treasury may be relieved of the burden.

Third, he speaks of Timothy's relation to the elders, i. e., the presbyters of the church (17-22). The Greek word for elders here is the same as that in verse 1, but while in that case elder men merely were intended, here the context shows an official distinction. The directions to Timothy concern the pecuniary provision for these church ministers (17, 18), the esteem in which they should be held (19), and yet the impartiality with which they should be treated in the event of their wrongdoing (20, 21). In the same connection, Timothy receives a caution about the selection of such men for that office (22). The chapter closes with certain advice to Timothy in regard to his health. It seems to be quite irrelevant to the main subject under consideration, and yet was suggested doubtless by the command at the end of the preceding verse. Speaking of the irrelevancy, it is worth while quoting the observation of Dr. Paley that it affords a strong incidental proof of the genuineness of the epistle. It is incredible that an imposter forging an epistle in the name of Paul should give a direction like this, so remote from everything else discussed. "Nothing but reality," he says, "the real valetudinary situation of a real person, could have suggested it."

I have spoken of this verse as closing the chapter, and yet two others follow which seem quite as irrelevant in a way as it. Perhaps, however, they are intended to restrain Timothy from hasty judgments, referred to in verse 22, in the selection of men for the ministerial office. There are some men whose faults are very apparent, but others who can be known only by an after judgment. With reference to the latter great circumspection on the part of Timothy is urged. The same facts, however, apply to good works as well as evil, so that Timothy might be consoled in the thought that if he had unwittingly overlooked some of the latter class, they would sooner or later come to the light.

Regulations about Matters Civil and Social, 6.—In the final chapter of the epistle ecclesiastical or church matters give place, for the most part, to those of a different character. The "servants" mentioned in verses 1 and 2, are doubtless, bond-servants, slaves. After laying down the law in relation to them, Paul digresses into a designation and criticism of those who teach otherwise concerning them (3-5). It surprises us to learn the depth of the hypocrisy of these false teachers even in those early days of the church, since the Apostle speaks of them as using godliness for a way of gain. A show of Christian life for them was, somehow or other, a lucrative business, (compare Titus 1:11). This digression, in turn, leads to another, if one may say so, for the reference to godliness and gain brings up the whole question of earthly riches in the life of the disciple (6-10). There is a sense in which true godliness does bring gain, if it be mingled with contentment, but contentment takes wings in the case of those whose unhappy condition is outlined in the verses following. The warning against this sin associated with the love of money leads to an earnest exhortation to Timothy personally, and a doxology springing out of it, when the theme is returned to again for the purpose of registering a charge concerning the rich (17-19). The epistle then concludes with another solemn personal address to Timothy to keep the trust committed to him, avoiding the errors before enumerated.

There is much in this epistle of deep practical value to us to-day, and especially applicable to all ministers, Sunday-school teachers, Christian workers and church leaders of every kind. May the Holy Spirit Himself apply it to us!

CHAPTER LVI.

The Second Epistle to Timothy.

When Paul addressed his earlier letter to Timothy, the latter was resident in Ephesus, and there are reasons suggested by the contents of the present one to believe that was still there. And yet the point is one forbidding positive affirmation, nor is it particularly essential for our present purpose.

Paul was now a prisoner in Rome for a second time, awaiting a hearing before the Emperor, and there is reason to believe he was not being treated with the consideration shown him on the earlier occasion (Acts 28), but like a common prisoner. The immediate occasion for the sending of this letter grew out of this circumstance, for he is anxious to have Timothy and Mark as his companions (1:4, 4:9, etc.). He is conscious, however, that his death by martyrdom could not long be delayed, for these were the days of wicked Nero, and not knowing whether he should see Timothy, his "own child in the faith" again, or not, he was desirous of adding still further to the instructions and exhortations he had already given him.

There is, moreover, reason to believe that Timothy required these encouragements in a marked degree. His character, as far as it can be gathered from the few limited allusions to it, was not of the stuff that Paul's was made of. He suggests the timidity and diffidence of Jeremiah in the days of the Old Testament, without some of the redeeming qualities which he possessed. For references to the lack of courage and perseverance on the part of Timothy, see such passages as 1:5, 7, 3.10.

Outline of the Epistle.—1. Salutation, 1:1, 2.

2. Thanksgiving, 3-5. It is interesting that in this thanksgiving on Timothy's behalf, there is a reference to

his spiritual history which seems to have come down in his mother's line.

3. Exhortation, 6-14. The exhortation which now follows, and which has grown out of the remembrance of Timothy's past life and the piety of his ancestors, contains three or four natural divisions of thought:—

(a) An exhortation to firmness in the faith (6-8). This firmness can be cultivated, stirred up. It is inherent in the spiritual gift he received from God at the time he was set apart formally to the ministry, and is not consonant with the spirit of fearfulness, the moral cowardice to which he seems to have been addicted, but is evinced rather in the exercise of suitable discipline in the spirit of love (Revised Version), and in boldness of testimony even to the point of suffering and affliction.

(b) This exhortation to firmness is then enforced by a consideration of the character of the Gospel and the mercy of God (9-11). Compare this declaration of the Gospel with that previously considered in the epistle to Titus.

(c) Finally, the Apostle cites his own example (12-14). He suffers for his testimony, and is not ashamed of it; that is, he is willing to suffer, he counts it worth while, in the light of his faith. Let Timothy profit in word and deed by what he sees and knows to be in him.

4. Description of false brethren, (15-18). This exhortation to Timothy gathers force from the circumstance that some who have professed fealty to Christ have been guilty of defection, if one may judge by their desertion of Christ's faithful servant in his hour of trial (15). Their action, however, serves to bring out all the stronger the love of another brother for whom he devotedly prays (16-18).

5. Instruction (2-4:8). I feel hardly justified in making any particular distinction between the general character of the contents of the epistle which follows and those already considered, and yet perhaps there is a shade more of instruction in these chapters than in the first. And yet with the instruction is mingled exhortation throughout. Indeed the exhortation overtops the instruction, the explanation and reason for which was considered in the general introduction to these pastoral epistles.

The instruction which follows may be divided into three or four parts.

(a) He is instructed concerning his duty as a teacher of teachers (2:2), but immediately in that connection he himself is again exhorted to firmness, or rather to strength and "hardness," which are practically the same (verses 1 and 3). What figure of speech does Paul use at this point to illuminate his theme? What particular lesson would be drawn from it (verse 4)? What second figure does he use at verse 5? Here there is a reference to contending for prizes in the Olympian games. How must a man have contended in order to win the crown? What third figure is used at verse 6? What reward does the faithful husbandman receive? It is easy to see from these illustrations the direction in which this young minister or Christian worker required encouragement and warning in the execution of his office. He must separate himself from the world, strive faithfully and obediently, and work diligently in order to receive the blessing. In this connection, and for the inspiration it afforded, what particular fact was he ever to keep in mind (8)? Note here how Paul once more digresses to the consideration of his own example. He was not laying upon Timothy any burden he did not himself bear. Indeed, on behalf of the Gospel just spoken of, he suffered "hardship," (for so the word "trouble" should be translated in verse 9), and he also endured (10). For whose sake was it done? And why? Speaking of the "eternal glory" the elect were going to obtain, was it an assured experience for them (11-13)?

(b) Again, in this instruction to Timothy as a teacher of teachers, he is particularly directed to caution them about idle and foolish words (14). But no sooner is this dictum laid down than he himself is once more exhorted, as in the other case, to be the kind of teacher he would have others be. To what is he exhorted in verse 15? What do you suppose that expression means, "Rightly dividing the word of truth?" In reply to this question, note the three classes of peoples into which Paul divides mankind in 1 Corinthians 10:32. Do you not think that "rightly dividing the word of truth" must mean at least, giving to each of these their "portion of meat in due season?" But how can this be done where one is ignorant of the dispensational teaching of the Bible, which we are here trying to emphasize somewhat? What is especially to be avoided in this kind of teaching (verse 19)? To what physical disease is that kind of foolish teaching likened in the next verse? How careful we need to be not to allow our study of dispensational truth to become fanatical gangrene! How much we need the wisdom that cometh down from above, the balance of mind and heart which the Holy Spirit alone can supply!

But we need not pursue our inquiries into this chapter further. The same kind of mingled exhortation, instruction and warning continue throughout, and can be brought out by the careful student through a process of questioning and patient waiting for the answer to suggest itself as above.

(c) Proceeding to chapter third, Timothy receives instruction concerning the character of the last times, i. e., the times at the end of the present age. What kind of times does the Spirit of God, through Paul, say they will be (1)? The word "perilous" is in the Revised Version rendered "grievous." What shall constitute their grievous character (2-5)? What class of persons are particularly designated as influenced by these things, and why (6, 7)? How does the Apostle seek to strengthen Timothy against these things by his own example (10-13)? And what exhortation does he now receive (14-16)? What tribute to the Holy Scriptures is contained in verse 15? And how is their authority and infallibility affirmed in the following verse? The Revised Version renders this verse a little differently, but this is one of the places where the King James translation is to be preferred not only as the stronger, but also the more scholarly of the two. To what "charge" to Timothy does this allusion to the

Holy Scriptures lead (4:1, 2)? What consideration adds great solemnity to that charge (1)? What consideration makes that charge to be necessary (3, 4)? What office is Timothy to exercise in addition to that of an overseer and teacher in order to "make full proof" or fulfil his ministry (5)? What consideration personal to Paul, adds solemnity to this exhortation (6-8)?

6. We have now passed beyond the portion of the epistle devoted to instruction, and reached that in which the writer deals with personal matters altogether, (4:9-22). An aged prisoner in Rome, awaiting trial, and almost certain execution, he is, alas! forsaken by many who should have stood by him. Demas has left him, Crescens, and even Titus. He wishes Timothy to hasten to his side, and to bring Mark with him. It has all been made up with Mark since the sad affair in Acts 13. He needs his cloak too, and parchments. He can not at this moment forget that man Alexander. Is he the Alexander named in Acts 19? Doubtless. Timothy is warned against him, for he is still in Ephesus.

Paul has had one hearing before Caesar and another is coming. At the hearing, however, he was sadly deserted by his friends. O! the grief of defection! Nevertheless the Lord stood by him, and He will continue to do so. Friends are saluted at Ephesus. Hasten Timothy, I want you.

CHAPTER LVII.

The Epistle to Titus.

The previous chapter gives the reasons leading to the opinion that the epistle to Titus was written prior to the second to Timothy. Alford, and others, suppose that after Paul's liberation from prison (see Acts 28), he journeyed eastward as anticipated in Philemon 22 and Philippians 1:26, 2:24, and visited Ephesus again. Other journeys to the West followed, occupying three or four years, during which time, it is thought, he visited Crete in company with Titus, leaving him there to complete the organization of the church in that place and neighborhood. This church had probably been founded prior to this time, and now the same kind of heresy is beginning to show itself as in the case of the church at Ephesus over which Timothy had been set.

The epistle to Titus was probably written from some point in Asia Minor where Paul was stopping on his way to winter at Nicopolis in Greece (3:12), Crete is a small island to the west of Cyprus and where the waters of the Mediterranean and Agean Seas may be said to meet. No account is found in the Acts as to the circumstances under which the church originated there, but it is probable the seed of the Gospel was borne to the island by some of the Jewish converts at Jerusalem on the memorable Day of Pentecost.

Of Titus himself also little is known. The earliest references to him are those in Galatians, where we learn that he was a Gentile, probably one of Paul's own converts, who accompanied him and Barnabas to Jerusalem at the time

The Epistle to Titus

(Acts 15). See Galatians 1 : 1-4. He
is mentioned again several times in II
Corinthians, where he seems to have
been sent by Paul on a mission to Corinth from Ephesus (II Corinthians 8 : 6,
12 : 18). See other references to him
in the same connection in that epistle,
in chapters 2 and 7. For a number of
years he is lost sight of after this, until
we now find him at Crete. His later
career does not seem to have been all
that it might have been so far as his
loyalty to the person of the Apostle is
concerned, if we may judge from the
slight allusion to him in II Timothy
4 : 10. During Paul's second imprisonment at Rome he seems not to have remained with him.

Outline of the Epistle.—The epistle
may be outlined thus:

1. The salutation, 1 : 1-4.

2. The commission to Titus, 5-9. In
these verses it will be seen that the
duties of Titus at Crete were substan-
tially those of Timothy at Ephesus,
noted in our last lesson. Reference to
that will throw light on this.

3. The description of false teachers,
10-16. The need of the elders and
overseers just referred to, and especially the need of such as Paul had indicated, was seen in the heresies that
were rife in the church, and which were
much of the same character as those
mentioned in the previous epistle to
Timothy. The errorists, as in the other
case, were chiefly Jews (10). The language referring to them in verses 12
and 13 is particularly striking, since
Paul there quotes from one of their
own poets against them (Epimenides),
whose witness is borne out by other
ancient writers as Livy, Plutarch,
Polybius and Strabo, who speak of
the Cretan's love of gain, natural fe-
rocity, fraud, falsehood, and general
depravity. Titus did not have an easy
place to fill, and the study of his work
ought to bring comfort to a good many
Christian workers under not very different surroundings to-day.

There is a statement also in verse
15 that calls for particular attention.
"To the pure all things are pure," is
an aphorism often very greatly abused.
To understand it, turn back to I Timothy 4 : 4. The reference here in Titus
is the same as there, (and indeed also
in Romans 14 : 20), to the eating of
certain meats which the Jewish law
forbade on ceremonial grounds. The
Jewish professing Christians referred
to previously as false teachers, were
seeking to impose these customs, or
similar ones, upon the young converts
from Gentilism, and Paul was with-
standing them by saying, just as he
had contended all along, and as God
Himself had taught Peter on the house-
top in Acts 10, that there was nothing
of this kind unclean in itself. That
is, it was not sinful for a Christian to
eat such things. The "pure" in this
case means those who are sanctified by
faith, true believers on the Lord Jesus
Christ. Such are not bound by the
Jewish fables and commandments of
men in the matter of ritualistic eating
and drinking, but are at liberty to eat
all the creatures of God set apart for
their use, without sin. How monstrous
in the light of the true meaning of the
inspired Apostle's words, for people of
the world and semi-Christians to employ them as a permission to look at
obscene pictures in art galleries, and
listen to lewd stories, and read impure
books, and witness impure plays at the
theater. These very actions on their
part testify that they are not the "pure"
whom Paul has in mind at all, but the
defiled and the unbelieving rather, referred to later in the same verse.
"They profess that they know God, but
by their works they deny Him."

4. Instructions concerning church
members, 2 : 1-3 : 11. Paul now enters
upon instructions to Titus as he had
done in the case of Timothy concerning
his dealings with different classes in
the church. Aged men are first spoken
of, verses 1, 2. It is of the nature of
sound or healthful doctrine that these
be of the character herein described.
Aged women are next referred to (3),
and under cover of that exhortation
comes an allusion to the younger women (4, 5). It is noticeable that Titus
does not exhort the young women directly on the themes indicated, but indirectly through the older women. A
hint here for Christian workers in our
own time, and especially in slum dis-
tricts, where a certain discretion is to
be observed in dealings between the
sexes. The young men come in for
treatment next (6), to whom Titus,
himself evidently a young man, was to
be careful to set the right example (7,
8). Then follows an exhortation for
servants, where bond-servants or slaves
are meant (9, 10). "The duties of
these last, and indeed of all classes, are
grounded on the moral purpose of God
in the Gospel concerning us" (11, 14).
These last-named verses are full of
strong meat, and will bear close analysis. See what the Christian's hope is,
as set forth in verse 13. Observe the
two-fold object which Christ, our
Savior, had in view in the work of the
Cross, verse 14, and the obligation it

lays upon us believers, as shown in verse 12.

All these several classes are now put in mind of their duties and obligations with reference to the civil powers, and perhaps to outsiders and unbelivers generally (3 : 1-3) ; an exhortation affording the writer another opportunity, often improved, of contrasting the present state and condition of believers with that in which they were prior to their salvation. Here again we find a rich and precious declaration of Gospel truth in words which should be learned by heart (4, 7). The theme is salvation. How NOT was it effected? How was it effected? When, at what period of time? What is the result? Indeed the eighth verse might be included here also, as showing the obligation of the saved growing out of their salvation.

Titus was to constantly affirm these things, avoiding other things and subjects of discussion that might come up (9). What a lesson for the ministers and teachers of our own time? Finally, he is directed how to deal with these false teachers and their followers (10, 11).

5. Personal directions and commissions, 12-15. A messenger from Paul is shortly to be sent to Titus, perhaps a successor to relieve him in his office (12), and then he himself is to hasten to Paul at the place where he intends to spend the winter. In the meantime he is to show diligence in advancing the interests of two other brethren named who are perhaps journeying to meet Paul ahead of him (13). He breaks into these personal matters for a moment, however, in order to set forth a further exhortation to the church along practical lines (14). "Let ours, or our people, also learn to maintain good works, or profess honest occupations, for necessary uses, or necessary wants, that they be not unfruitful." It is possible that by "ours" or "our people" here, the Apostle may be referring to the leaders in the church such as the two mentioned in the previous verse; and the "honest occupations" may mean the necessary labor to provide the means for just such missionary journeys as that contemplated in the context. Here is a valuable suggestion, surely, for those among us who are contemplating similar work for the Lord. It would, if acted upon, make them very independent of societies, and mission boards. And happily, it is being acted on by not a few, and with the most blessed results, for God "is the same yesterday, to-day and forever."

CHAPTER LVIII.

The Epistle to Philemon.

We have now come to the last of the epistles which, without serious objection from any quarter, are admitted to have been written by Paul. Philemon, however, like some other of the epistles, is not located in the canon chronologically. It will be seen to have been written by the Apostle while he was a prisoner at Rome, and the supposition at first might be that the second imprisonment was meant, because it follows II Timothy. But we should be mistaken there, as it was addressed to Philemon, beyond doubt, on the earlier occasion. See verse 22 as a hint of this. In verse 23 Epaphras is named as one known to Philemon, who, according to Colossians 1 : 7, and 4 : 12, was a minister at Colossae, and perhaps therefore Philemon and his household were members of his flock. As Philemon, however, owed his salvation, under God, to the labors of Paul, (verse 19), we may believe that the latter had made his acquaintance during his long stay in Ephesus and its vicinity, (Acts 19, 20), for Colossae was in that neighborhood.

The Story of the Epistle.—The story of the epistle seems to be something like this: Philemon had a slave named Onesimus who seemed to have run away from his master, perhaps having stolen from him besides (18), and, escaping the vigilant police ever on the lookout for such, had found his way to Rome, and some way or other was thrown into the way of Paul. The world would say this, but we would rather say that a gracious God led him into the way of Paul. Perhaps he had known Paul when he had lived with Philemon at Colossae, and perhaps Paul at that time had labored with him in vain to accept the Gospel. At all events, the circumstances are changed now, and under the power of a burdened conscience, the fear of arrest and punishment, and perhaps too, the very condition in which he now finds his old friend as a prisoner, he is moved to give more earnest heed to the message, he is converted and is rejoicing in the Lord.

But one of the first duties of the converted man, and without which he cannot know very much of rejoicing, is confession and restitution of wrong done to his fellow-man, especially his fellow-Christian. Onesimus knows this and is ready to return to his master, but naturally shrinks from doing so unless he shall have some document to show the genuineness of the change that has been wrought in him, and some plea from the mutual friend of both his master and himself that may intercede for him and avert that which under other circumstances would be almost certain to fall upon him on his return. And what a loving letter Paul writes! How it exemplifies in so many ways his own exposition of what love is in the thirteenth chapter of first Corinthians.

The Outline.—The epistle begins as usual with the salutation, verse 1-3. Notice that Timothy's name is coupled with his own, a fact which lays just that much more of an obligation upon Philemon to comply with his loving request. Notice, also, that Apphia is named, and Archippus, the first perhaps the wife, and the second the son of Philemon. The last-named also seems to have become a public minister in the church. "The church in thy house," is mentioned, showing that in the primitve times the gatherings of the Christians were in private homes; each gathering, and there may have been several in the one city at the same time, being a kind of church within the church, just as we now have several churches with different names in the one city or town. The picture thus afforded of the assemblies of these early Christians is very interesting, and contributes a moving argument in favor of the "cottage" prayer-meeting of our own time.

Now comes the Thanksgiving, 4-7. Paul makes mention of Philemon in his prayers. It was his custom to do this, as we have seen, with all his converts. How far do we follow his example? How do our prayers compare with his in their range? What do we know of the experience, the joy, and the power of intercessors? We have not begun to pray until we pray thus. Paul had good reason to remember Philemon in thanksgiving and prayer, for see what kind of man he was! Es-

pecially notice the expression of his Christian faith in kindness and benevolence to other saints.

Following the thanksgiving, there is revealed the real reason for the letter, the plea for Onesimus, 8-21. He pleads though he might command (8, 9); love is more potent than force. Onesimus has been converted by him while a prisoner in Rome (10); are we equally faithful to what should be the main business of our lives, witnessing for Jesus, "in season and out of season?"

Onesimus means "profitable," but he had not been very profitable to his master theretofore, he had belied his name. He had now, however, become profitable to both Philemon and Paul (11). The fruit of the Spirit in men greatly enhances their value. Paul would like to have kept him with him in Rome, he was so profitable to him, only he had not the mind of Philemon on the subject, and did not feel at liberty to do so (12-14). He was returning now to Philemon in a new relationship (15, 16). It were well worth while to have lost him for a while to get him back forever! What a striking, though incidental, testimony to the fact that saints shall know each other in the life to come! But he was now coming back not merely as a slave, but as a beloved brother! This does not mean that the old relationship as master and slave should be dissolved (see 1 Corinthians 7 : 17-24), but only that it should now be continued under these different and more blessed circumstances. Observe how delicately Paul pleads for him on the ground that he is now his (Paul's) brother (16, 17). Paul is willing to assume whatever pecuniary responsibility might be attached to his running away, but gently and tactfully insists that if Philemon considers the premises, he will regard himself as still in the Apostle's debt (18, 19). What is his closing plea (20)? Does he believe it will be acceded to (21)?

Following the plea, the letter concludes with certain personal allusions, greetings and the benediction (22, 25). Who, only, of the brethren named in verse 24 were with Paul in his second imprisonment? Which one did he ask to come unto him? See II Timothy.

Applicatory Words.—If some persons were curiously to ask why such a personal letter as this should find a place among the inspired books of Holy Scripture, it would seem sufficient to reply that its value is found in the glimpses it affords of the social intercourse of Christians in the primitive days.

But there is something else here, already alluded to in our treatment of the text, viz: Christianity does not hastily or rashly interfere with existing institutions, even when they in the long run are found to be inimical to its principles. Philemon was not bidden to give Onesimus his freedom. Does Christianity, then, countenance or endorse human slavery? Nay, wherever Christianity has made headway, slavery has fallen. The truth makes free. The union of believers in Jesus Christ, when rightly understood, promotes love to one another, and love ministers to freedom.

There is still another beautiful Gospel lesson to be drawn from this story by way of illustration. As Paul found Onesimus wandering from his master's house and from the place of duty and love, so the Lord Jesus Christ found us wandering from God. As Paul pleaded for the restoration of Onesimus, asking that what he owed might be placed to his account, so the Lord Jesus Christ acts as our Advocate with the Father, having borne our sins. As Philemon, we may believe, received Onesimus on Paul's account, so God has received us, and made us what we never were before, "profitable" unto Him—"created in Christ Jesus unto good works which he hath before prepared for us to walk in them."

CHAPTER LIX.

The Epistle to the Hebrews.

In the case of the epistle to the Hebrews there is uncertainty as to the authorship. It may have been written by Paul, or Apollos, or some one else, we can not tell absolutely. There is also uncertainty as to the church addressed. While Jewish Christians are in the mind of the writer very evidently, yet there is no positive knowledge as to where they were located, whether at Jerusalem, Alexandria, or Rome, possibly the place last-named.

But while uncertainty exists as to these two particulars, there can be none whatever as to the reason for writing the epistle. No one can read it carefully even two or three times, without perceiving a two-fold object, viz: to comfort the Christians under persecution, and to restrain them from apostacy on account of it. And the persecution must have been very severe, judging by the nature of the temptation to which it gave rise. For the apostacy contemplated was not like that of the Galatians, the supplementing of evangelical faith by the works of the law, but the renunciation of that faith altogether and the return to Judaism. It is the assumption all the way through that the temple was still standing at this time, with its glorious history and magnificent priesthood, and that the followers of Moses were allowed to pursue their religion in quietness and peace. All this was very different from the outward meanness and poverty, the unrest and tribulation of those seeking to follow the teachings of the Nazarene.

The Theme.—There were many lines of argument open to the Apostle (for convenience, I assume the writer to be Paul), by which to counteract this tendency towards apostacy, but he chooses only one, viz: *Christianity is superior to Judaism as seen in its Founder, Christ.* The tempter is represented as urging that Judaism was introduced to the world by "the goodly fellowship of the prophets." "Christ is superior to the prophets." Judaism was ministered to Israel through angels. "Christ is superior to the angels!" Judaism owes its position to that mighty man, Moses. "But Christ is superior to Moses!" Judaism is associated with the divinely-instituted priesthood of Aaron. "Yes, but Christ is superior to Aaron!" These are, so to speak, the four points of the discourse, but the whole revolves around the single argument already indicated.

And yet the Apostle does not go straight on with his argument. He makes a digression every once in a while, sometimes at the close of one division of his theme, and sometimes in the middle of it, for the purpose of warning his hearers, for the purpose of comforting them, or exhorting them to steadfastness in the Christian faith. And this we shall see as we proceed.

The Outline.*—1. Christ is superior to the prophets, 1:1-3.
He is so in seven particulars:
He is God's Son.
He is heir of all things.
He made the worlds.

He is the express image of God.
He upholds all things.
He Himself purged our sins.
He is sat down at the right hand of God.

2. Christ is superior to the angels, 1 : 4-2 : 18.

(1) He has the more excellent name of Son, 1 : 4, 5.

(2) He is worshipped by the angels, 1 : 6.

(3) He is Himself the Eternal God, 1 : 7-12.

(4) He is (as Mediator) awaiting the possession of the kingdom, 1 : 13, 14.

(5) He is the ruler of the age to come, 2 : 5-8.

It is in this division of our theme that we meet with the first of the digressions spoken of, one occurring in the middle of the argument, chapter 2 : 1-4, and another at its close, 2 : 9-18. The first is in the way of warning, the second in the way of comfort. If the earlier dispensation, that of Judaism, punished every transgression, and disobedience, how shall we escape if we neglect this greater light, the heavenly origin of which was so unmistakably demonstrated by witnesses at once confirming and being themselves confirmed. And then, on the other hand, think of your privileges! your exaltation to the position of "brethren," and your claims upon the Lord of glory as your true High-priest, faithful, merciful, capable and sympathetic. Capable and sympathetic because He has suffered through persecution just as you are suffering, and knows all about it and how to overcome it.

The student will notice how the inspired writer naturally and easily glides form one link in the chain of reasoning to another. The testimony to Christ's superiority to the prophets brought him face to face with Christ's present position at the right hand of the Majesty on high, above the angels, and this led to a comparison with the angels. The comparison with the angels, in turn, leads to the statement about Christ's humanity and the qualification of priesthood it confers. Ready is he now to enlarge upon that thought (see chapter 3 : 1), only pausing to touch for a moment upon the third division of his argument which now begins.

3. Christ is superior to Moses, 3 : 1. 4 : 13.

The comparison in this case runs in two parallel lines of two members each:

(1) Moses a servant over God's house, 3 : 5.

(2) Christ a Son over His own house, 3 : 6.

That is an interesting phrase, "Whose house are we," (verse 6), suggesting a simple plan for a fruitful sermon. In what sense are believers' Christ's house?

He built them—"without Him was not anything made that was made."

He bought them—"Ye are not your own, for ye are bought with a price."

He occupies them—"Ye in me and I in you."

Here, as in the previous instance, we meet with a digression, first, of warning, 3 : 7-4 : 13, and then of comfort, 4 : 14-16. The warning turns on the interpretation of that "rest" denied to God's Old Testament people because of disobedience, as recorded in Psalm 45. It is not the rest of Canaan (4 : 8, R. V.), but the rest of faith in Christ (4-10 compared with 3 : 14). Under the head of the comfort in this case the writer recurs again to the theme of the priesthood of Christ from which he had been diverted for the moment, and on which he now enlarges, practically to the end of the epistle.

4. Christ is superior to Aaron, 4 : 14-10 : 39.

(1) Christ is Himself a priest, a fact very necessary to be established if any comparison with Aaron shall be made, and which the writer establishes in two ways, 5 : 1-10. He is a priest because He possesses the capacity for sympathy (1-3), and because He has received a divine appointment to that office as Aaron did (4-10).

The customary digression now follows in which the readers are exhorted (5 : 2-4 : 3), warned (6 : 4-8), and comforted (6 : 10-22).

(2) Christ is a priest after a higher order than Aaron, viz: the order of Melchisedec 7 : 1-19. This is a higher order because it is of a kingly type (verse 3), and of permanent duration (3), because Melchisedec received tithes from Aaron in the loins of Abraham (6), and because he blessed Abraham (7). Moreover, the permanency of this order implies the abrogation of the Levitical law (11-17).

(3) Christ is a priest made with an oath, 7 : 20-22.

(4) He is an unchangeable priest. 7 : 23-25.

(5) He is sinless, 7 : 26-28.

(6) He is a priest of a better covenant, 8. A better covenant because based on better promises. These promises are written on the heart, not on tables of stone (10) ; they are universal in their application and not limited to

a single people; and they bring forgiveness with them (12).

(7) He is a priest of a better tabernacle, 9. This tabernacle is not material in its structure, but spiritual (12); it is not hallowed by the blood of beasts, but by His own blood (13); and it does not stand for temporary but eternal redemption (13).

(8) He is a priest of a better sacrifice, 10. He Himself is that sacrifice, the substance of which the Old Testament sacrifices were but the shadow (1-9); a sacrifice necessary to be offered only once (10-18).

The digression in this case, as in the preceding, is in the nature, first, of exhortation (19-25); secondly, of warning (26-31); thirdly, of comfort (32-39).

Conclusion.—It may be questioned whether I am justified in placing the whole chapters 11-13 under the general heading of the "Conclusion," as the first two are very closely connected with the comforting part of the "digression" noted above. Opinions will differ as to this. At all events we have here a disssertation on the history of the Old Testament saints (chapter 11), showing what faith is and what faith can accomplish in men and through them. Of course the design of the writer is very apparent, viz: to encourage his hearers to remain steadfast under present trial in consideration of the glorious outcome of it all. And this design he expresses, indeed, in the exhortation which follows (chapter 12:1-13), and the warning (14-29). The conclusion, speaking more definitely, is confined to the last chapter with its several precepts and admonitions, the loving benediction and the personal requests and salutations.

---

*This outline in part was used by the author in the Homiletic Review.

CHAPTER LX.

The Epistle of James.

We have now reached that part of the New Testament containing the General or Catholic epistles. They are so called because they are addressed not to any particular individual or church, but to the church at large. And yet this is not true of all of them, not true of the one whose study we are entering upon, which is addressed to a particular class of Christians named in the first verse. This gives an opportunity to remark that this general title, like the headings to the chapters in our English Bible, and the superscriptions in italics at the end of some of the books are not part of the inspired text, and have no authority but that of the human printer or editor—often not to be relied upon, as in the present case.

Who was the author of this epistle? There are three persons named James mentioned in the New Testament. One was the brother of John, another the son of Alpheus, and a third the brother of our Lord. The first named was martyred at an early date in the history of the church (Acts 12), and is not likely to have been the author, because the epistle reveals a state of Christian or church development more advanced than that likely to have been true then. Nor is it likely to have been written by the son of Alpheus, for nothing is heard of him in the later history of the church, while the James who wrote this epistle is evidently well known and influential, a fact which was also true, it would seem, of James the brother of our Lord. It is he, apparently, who presided at the first council of the church in Jerusalem (Acts 15), and who is distinguished in other places as a leader, notably Acts 12:17, 21:18, Gal. 1:19, Jude 1, etc.

A peculiar interest attaches to the fact that, as the brother of our Lord, he did not believe on Him as the Messiah up until the resurrection perhaps. Compare John 7:5 with Acts 1:13, and 1 Corinthians 15:7. His conversion may have taken place at the time mentioned in the last named Scripture, which, if so, accounts for his presence with the church as shown in the reference to the Acts. Tradition teaches us that he was a particularly holy and just man, being designated indeed, "James the Just"; and that he ended his life in martyrdom, being stoned to death under one of the high priests, some time after the death of Festus mentioned in the Acts.

As to his religious character, he was a very strict Jew, a faithful observer of the law, both moral and ceremonial, without, of course, relying upon it as a ground of salvation. He gave Paul and Barnabas the right hand of fellowship in their work among and for the Gentiles, but personally he remained more firmly attached to the Jewish form or aspect of Christianity. His place in the Christian scheme was to win over the Jewish people, and no one probably was better fitted for this than he.

The Persons Addressed.—The epistle is addressed "to the twelve tribes scattered abroad," which proves its Jewish designation; but that they were Christian Jews nevertheless is shown in the further language of the salutation, where James styles himself "a servant of Jesus Christ." There are several indications in the epistle of their Jewish origin, however; for example, their place of assembly is called a "synagogue," (2:2, Revised Version), and there are several references to the law.

As to their social condition they seem to have been composed of rich and poor, the tendency of some of the former being both to oppress and despise the latter, as we shall see. Like all the other classes of Christians, they were passing through trials of various kinds, and like them, too, they were more or less under the influence of false teachers. The doctrine of justification only by faith was especially being perverted among them, and from various points of view, indeed, their condition was disclosed as quite unsatisfactory. The writer comforts them in their trials, but he sternly rebukes them for their sins, and seeks throughout to give them much needed instruction concerning the matters in which they were in error.

The style of the epistle is fresh and vivid, sententious and yet rich in graphic figure. There is not in it the logical connection found in Paul's writings, the thoughts rather arranging themselves in groups strongly marked off from one another; but yet the writer goes at once into the midst of his subject, and with the first sentence beginning a section says out at once what is in his heart. The first words of each section might almost serve as a title for it, while that which follows is the development of it, ending usually in a kind of recapitulation. (How to Study the New Testament, second section, pp. 163, 164).

The Outline.—We will now look at the contents of the epistle in outline. After the salutation, 1:1, the writer offers:

I. *Some instruction concerning trial,* chapter 1. "Temptations," in verse 2, is to be taken in the sense of trials (see Revised Version margin). Why should they be received with joy (verse 3)? In what spiritual condition will such a reception and use of trial result (4)? What will effectually aid in that direction (5, 8)? Along what lines of trial were they being exercised (9, 11)? Notice that the poor man is to find comfort in his truly high estate in Christ while the rich man is to find comfort in a truly humble spirit before God in view of the facts referred to.

But there are two kinds of testings which come upon believers, those already spoken of as "trials," whose source is divine, and whose purpose is strengthening and purifying, and those now brought into view as out and out "temptations," not from God, but from themselves. What reward comes to the disciple who successfully encounters these (12)? What is their immediate source and outcome (13, 15)? What three arguments are presented in verses 13, 17 and 18, to show that God is not the author of these temptations? On the ground, then, that we have our good from God, and our evil from ourselves, what lesson is drawn (19, 20)? Speaking of our being "swift to hear," whose words has the writer in mind (21)? What shows, however, that the "hearing" he has in mind is a very practical experience (22, 25)? Speaking of our being "slow to speak," how does he emphasize its importance (26)? In what does "pure religion" consist other than in mere talk (27)? Remember here, that James is talking to believers in Christ, to those who supposably have "religion," and he is merely instructing them how it should be manifested. Men are not saved by benevolence and kindness to the widowed and the orphaned, or even by strenuous efforts after a pure life, but by Christ, who bore their sins in His own body on the tree; yet they show that they are saved by such works as these spoken of in the text.

II. We next have *some instruction or admonition concerning respect of persons,* or the relation of the rich and the poor, 2:1, 13. This would seem to be connected in thought with the trials of the poor mentioned in chapter 1. It not infrequently happens that the very people who, in their need, complain of the over abundance of the rich, are the most obsequious in their conduct, as if they expected something from them as a result. Perhaps it was so here. Or it may be, that this instruction laps on still more closely to what had just been said about "pure religion," and visiting the fatherless and widows, and keeping one's self unspotted from the world, 1:27.

Respect of persons was really incompatible with any one of these things. Note that the Revised Version translates "have" of verse 1 by "hold." It was equivalent to saying that these two things could not be held at one and the same time. What instance or illustration is given of them holding it (2, 3)? Of what wrong would they be guilty in such a case (4)? What kind of judges would such partiality show them to be (same verse)? What would demonstrate the unwisdom as well as unkindness of such partiality (5)? What would show their meanness of spirit (6)? Their disloyalty to their Saviour (7)? On what principle rather, should they exercise themselves toward rich and poor alike (8)? How were they in danger of violating this principle (9)? What fundamental truth about sin is enunciated in this connection (10, 11)?

III. *Some instruction on the relationship of faith and works*, 2:14-26. We have seen that the subject of respect of persons probably grew out of the declaration about "pure religion" at the close of chapter 1, and there is reason to believe the same of the present subject. Certainly it has a close relation to it.

Before considering the verses at all in detail, it may be well to remark on a criticism sometimes made that James is here contradicting Paul. The latter insists upon faith without works, while the former insists upon works with faith. But there is no contradiction really, because Paul is simply laying down the principle of salvation, while James is showing the working of that principle in the life. Paul as well as James insists upon a faith that lives, and works and brings forth fruit, and was himself a fine example of it. I think the epistle of James was written at quite an early period, before Paul's epistles were very generally known at least, and possibly before the council was held at Jerusalem (Acts 15), which may account for his treatment of the subject of faith from a different standpoint to that made necessary by the admission of Gentiles into the church.

Observe in this connection the change which the Revised Version makes in the last clause of verse 14. "Can THAT faith save him?" Faith saves, James declared, but it is not the kind of faith which produces no fruit. It is not dead faith, but living faith. What illustrations of a fruitless faith are given in verse 16? And verse

19? What two illustrations of a fruitful faith are given in verses 21-25? Read carefully verse 22, which teaches us that Abraham's faith was simply shown to be faith, a perfected thing in that sense, by his obedience to God. So our faith in Jesus can hardly be called a saving faith if it works no change in our lives and produces no results.

IV. The fourth natural division of the epistle contains *instruction or rather an admonition concerning the control of the tongue*, 3:1-18. Just as the instruction in the second and third divisions grew out of something written in the first chapter, so also here. He had exhorted them on the ground of a certain premise to be "swift to hear and slow to speak;" following that he had showed them how to hear in the sense that they must be doers of what they hear; and now he would show them how to be slow of speech in the sense that they should "set a watch before their mouths and keep the door of their lips."

The word "masters" in verse 1, is really "teachers." This shows the direction of their temptation to talk too much. They affected teaching, airing their opinion about things which they did not understand, after the manner of those rebuked by Paul in his letters to Timothy and Titus. There was danger to themselves as well as others in their doing this, as verse 1 indicates. A heavier responsibility rested upon teachers than upon the taught, and there was the strong likelihood of stumbling in that capacity (verse 2).

Note now how he speaks first, of the power of the tongue (3-5). What three illustrations does he employ? Secondly, he speaks of the evil of the tongue (6). How is it described? What does it do? Whence the source of its iniquity? Thirdly, he speaks of its uncontrollableness (7, 8). With how many wild, and subtle, and strong things, does he compare it in this regard?

After speaking thus of the tongue in general terms, how does he apply the subject to the present condition of things (9, 10)? By the use of what similes does he seek to better it (11, 12)? What is the relation between wisdom and speech (13)? What does the strife of tongues indicate as to the condition of the heart (14)? What is the source of such strife (15)? Its product (16)? How does true wisdom compare with it as to its source, character, and effects (17, 18)?

V. *An admonition concerning worldly-mindedness*, 4:6. Like some of the other divisions of this epistle this one is so closely connected with the last, and grows out of it so naturally, that it is difficult to say just where the division occurs. The writer had been speaking of envying and strife in their expressions through the tongue, and now puts in his plow a little deeper to show their source in the antecedent condition of the heart. The word "lust" in this chapter is not to be taken in the limited sense of sensuality as now commonly employed, but in the broader sense of worldly pleasure or gratifications of any kind.

I confess that in this connection verse 2 presents great difficulty. Consistency makes it necessary to suppose that James is here addressing Christians as throughout the epistle, and yet how incongruous to think of Christians committing murder to gratify their desires! Luther translated the word "kill" by "hate," and doubtless expressed the real meaning by so doing, although, to quote Neander, "James used the stronger expression in order to designate with the utmost precision the nature of that evil which, whatever may be the outward form of manifestation, is still the same."

Nor let it be thought strange that such persons as these should be referred to as engaging in prayer (verse 3), for nothing is more common in our own time than for worldly-minded Christians to supplicate heaven for the gratification of desires purely and entirely selfish, giving no consideration either to God's purpose or pleasure, or the interests and well-being of their neighbors. How plainly and bluntly James reveals the cause for the non-results of such prayers!

What names does he bestow upon these worldly-minded Christians (4)? How does the language of this verse indicate that he has in mind adulterers in the moral and spiritual sense—professing loyalty to God and yet consorting with the world? What shows the incompatibility of such things? Verse 5 should be read in the Revised Version, showing as it there does, that the Holy Spirit who dwells in the believer is not a spirit of envy. What, however, was their hope under such circumstances of sin, and in what direction should they look for deliverance (6)? What pre-requisite was necessary on their part in order to obtain this grace (6-10)? How, chiefly, did the want of humility seem to show itself in the case of their prayers (11, 12)?

But this worldly-mindedness took to itself various forms, and James addresses himself to another in the verses following in this chapter. What false reliance upon the mundane is spoken of in verse 13? How is it rebuked (14)? What advice and admonition is given (15, 16)? It was not enough for them to know this truth, how does he teach them the need of acting upon it (17)?

What further application of worldly-mindedness follows in chapter 5? Who are addressed now? What warning is given them? "Ye have laid up your treasure in the last days," is the way verse 3, last sentence, should be rendered. How vividly it applies to-day!

Are we not nearing the last days, and are not treasures heaping up in the coffers of the rich as never before? What three charges are laid against the rich here (4,6)? Fraud, voluptuousness, injustice! How awful to think of these things under the cloak of Christianity! Or shall we say that James is here referring to the rich outside the Christian church altogether? It is difficult to say. Different readers will have different opinions as their experience leads them to think. Notice carefully, however, the judgments coming upon these rich people. What miseries indeed!

VI. The epistle closes, however, as it began, *with comfort for the tried and oppressed*, verses 7-20. What hope is set before the oppressed laboring men of that day (7, 8)? How different, is it not, from the principle of the strike and the boycott? If the rich of our day be at fault, are not the poor equally so, the Word of God being the standard? What examples of long-suffering patience are set before them in verses 10 and 11?

What closing recommendations and exhortations are now set before all concerning oaths (12)? Concerning heavenly-mindedness in the opposite experiences of life (13)? What specific directions are given concerning the sick (14-16)? What testimony to the efficacy of prayer is given in this last-named verse? How is it illustrated (17, 18)? With what statement of the believer's privilege and obligation does the epistle close (19, 20)?

CHAPTER LXI.

The First Epistle of Peter.

We need not devote any time to the history of Peter who writes the epistle following that of James. He is readily identified as, in some sense, the leader among the twelve disciples, the story of whose life is given with such detail in the Gospels and Acts of the apostles. The last we read of him in the Acts he was laboring in Jerusalem and its neighborhood (chapters 10-12), but subsequently he seems to have migrated further to the east and south where we now find him, at Babylon, writing this epistle (verse 13).

He is addressing it to the "strangers" scattered throughout the different provinces of Asia Minor, an introductory form of address suggesting that of James' epistle, and leading to the opinion that he wrote practically to the same class of persons, only perhaps a little later in time.

The word "strangers" must not put us off the track as if they were simply persons unknown to Peter, and hence strangers in that sense, but rather strangers in the general sense in which all the saints are strangers and pilgrims here. See other uses of the word or its equivalent in 1 : 17, 2 : 2, etc. Also Paul's words in Philippians 3 : 20, where "conversation" should be rendered "citizenship."

It is quite evident that the persons to whom he wrote were undergoing severe trial and persecution, and that his purpose was to inspire them with hope.

The Apostle of Hope.—Indeed just as Paul might be called the apostle of faith, and John the apostle of love, so Peter might be called the apostle of hope. He was the active, impetuous, springy and expectant one among the twelve, ever their inspiration and mouth piece; and the same qualities that marked his career then are seen here in his later experience and writings, only purified, trained, exalted by what he had passed through, and by what he has been taught of the Spirit. As illustrating the characteristic of hope, note the number of instances in which that word is used in this epistle, 1 : 3, 13, 21, 3 : 15, etc. But note as well another circumstance quite as illustrative, viz: that wherever he speaks of earthly suffering, either on the part of Christ Himself or His people, he always throws it in the light of the glory that shall follow. As Dr. Boardman says, "'It is not as if there were an allotment of suffering here, and an allotment of glory by-and-by, with no connection between the two; but the suffering is incidental to the glory." Peter emphasizes this continually by the juxtaposition of the two ideas. See 1 : 6, 7, 11, 4 : 12, 13, 5 : 1, 2, 4, 10, etc.

The Object of the Epistle.—There was a two-fold purpose in the mind of the apostle in writing this epistle as he tells us in the sequel, verse 12. His purpose was to exhort and to testify, and the theme of his testimony was "the true grace of God." A good text this for a sermon, the outlines of which might easily be discovered in the full text of the epistle, and indeed in its doctrinal portion only which is confined to the first few verses of chapter 1.

The Outline.—I. The epistle opens with the customary salutation, 1 : 1, 2, in this case even more interesting and instructive than usual, since some of the richest teachings of the true grace of God are found in it. See the second verse, for example. There is the grace of election in the first place, and then that election as drawing forth the operation of the three Persons of the Adorable Godhead. The opening remarks in our lesson on Ephesians might profitably be consulted here, where attention is called to the fact that the doctrine of the Trinity is not called by that technical term in the New Testament, yet it is the very warp and woof of that revelation.

II. Following the salutation we have the thanksgiving, which really extends from the third verse of the chapter to the twelfth, and offers a rich mine of precious ore for the seeker after truth.

It begins with a declaration of God's mercy towards us, expressed in what great fact of our Spiritual condition (3)? On what anterior fact in the life and work of our substitute Saviour is our new birth grounded? What is the nature of the "living hope" to which we have thus been begotten (4)? What four features of this inheritance are enumerated in that verse? Is there danger of the saints losing this inheritance (5). At what time is it to be fully revealed and enjoyed? Does it at all militate against our heirship that we are now passing through sorrow at times (6)? What is the meaning of this sorrow and what will be its outcome (7)? What does this verse teach as to the period referred to by the "last time" in verse 5? When, then, may we look for the consummation of our salvation, the end of the world or the coming of Christ? Is this revelation concerning the coming glory of Christ limited to the New Testament (10, 12)? Did the Old Testament prophets know anything of the time of His revealed glory (13)? What intelligence beside ourselves are deeply interested in the outworkings of these marvels of grace (same verse)?

III. Following the thanksgiving, which for the most part, exhausts the doctrinal portion of the epistle, we have what might be called its application, extending indeed to the very close. It is introduced by the word "Wherefore" in verse 13.. You have been chosen, regenerated, endued with a living hope, and an eternal inheritance, "Wherefore" do these things live this kind of life whose outline follows. In other words observe the obligations of conduct, 1 : 13-3 : 12.

(1) Be hopeful, 1 : 13. Having been begotten again unto a living hope, be hopeful. Hopefulness in the truest and most far-reaching sense has been made possible through Christ, now exercise it. Hope in verse 3 is a condition, in verse 13, an experience. It is our duty to hope. What preliminary is necessary to hope (same verse)? When is this hope to be changed into fruition?

(2) Be holy, 14-16. What two motives to holiness are given in these verses? Note that "conversation" here does not mean merely talking one with another, but our whole conduct or manner of living. See Revised Version.

(3) Be God-fearing, 17-21. What two motives for Godly fear on the part of the child of God are given in these verses? By what language is it seen that Peter and Paul agree perfectly as to the only ground of human redemption?

(4) Be loving, 22-25. Note a twofold use of the word "love" here parallel to that of the word "hope" in the previous verses. First, we see love as a condition into which we have been begotten by the Holy Spirit through the Gospel, and then we see it as something to be practiced in our dealings one with another. What was funda-

mental as a pre-requisite to this love (23)? With what is the word of God identified in verse 25?

(5) Be increasing, 2 : 1-3. Here is another "Wherefore", growing out of the premise in the preceding chapter and affording a third illustration of the peculiar grammatical or rhetorical construction previously alluded to. You have been born again by the Word of God. The Word of God is a living Word. Wherefore desire the Word that you may live, grow, increase in strength in the Lord. There was a pre-requisite to the exercise of hope, of holiness, and there is one to the exercise of growth. What is that pre-requisite (verse 1)? How these pre-requisites, these "puttings off" of things in order to the "putting on" of other things suggest the pruning of the husbandman that makes the vine grow, and bud and put forth fruit!

(6) Be praising, 4-10. Under what figure of speech very common to the Scripture, is the Lord referred to here (4)? Under what corresponding figure are believers referred to in relation to Him (5)? What are these "living stones" called, by apposition, in the same verse? What "sacrifices" is this priesthood to offer? On what ground have such sacrifices become acceptable? Here is a beautiful thought almost overwhelming in its revelation of divine love and grace towards us in Christ. The reason our sacrifices are acceptable to God is because of the preciousness of Christ to God through whom those sacrifices are offered, a preciousness attaching to Him as revealed in the Old Testament Scripture quoted in verse 6. But this preciousness really belongs to us; it has been made over to us in Christ, and has become ours in Him. Hence the reason our sacrifices are acceptable to God is because of our preciousness in His sight—preciousness imputed unto us in Christ. The Revised Version brings this out more clearly, since it reads (verse 7), "For you therefore which believe is the preciousness." But now what does verse 9 show to be the peculiar character of the sacrifices we are to offer up? And why, what reason have we, for thus offering them up? Read the conclusion of this section.

(7) Be self-restrained, 2 : 11, 12. The carnal appetites seem here to be referred to, and yet the expression "fleshly lusts" may have the general meaning of worldliness as suggested in the epistle of James just studied. "Conversation" (verse 12) remember, means general conduct, behavior. "Honest" means seemly, consistent. Who are

meant by the Gentiles, the church or the world? Why should they be careful and restrained in their conduct because of them?

(8) Be submissive, 2-13-3:7. The spirit of submission here inculcated is along these lines, governmental, (13-17), industrial, (18-25), conjugal, (3:1-7).

(9) Be like minded, 3:8-12. What the Spirit means by like-mindedness in this case is explained in what follows: Having compassion or sympathy, being tender-hearted, loving and meek. He enlarges upon the last-named virtue. We should not render railing for railing, but rather blessing. We were called in Christ to do this, and by this means we ourselves come into blessing (10-12).

Testimony to the Hope.—We have been dwelling upon the obligations devolving on us as Christians and growing out of the living hope into which we have been begotten through the mercy of God. Another of these obligations, introducing us to a new field of Christian activity altogether, is that of witnessing or testifying to the hope itself. The subject is easily reached through the reference just made to the need and the value of meekness under provocation or wrong. The Christians were enduring wrong; it was a time of persecution, if not general and continuous as at some later periods, nevertheless fierce while it lasted, and to be met only with faith and patience. An observance of the advice in the preceding verses (10-12), would enable them to escape much of it, (verse 13), and yet when it fell upon them in what spirit should it be received (14)? It is at this point that the obligation to testify is presented, the subject extending from 3:15 to 4:6, at least, and including one or two expressions of so mysterious a character as to have given rise to much controversy.

Observe please, the features by which this testimony should be marked as indicated in verses 15 to 17, viz: readiness, intelligence, meekness, and well-doing. Thus would they not only be delivered, but thus would they triumph over their enemies as Christ Himself was delivered and as He triumphed. This is the significance of the mysterious words following about the

Spirits in Prison.—These "spirits in prison", verse 19, are not, I think the spirits of men, but evil angels, the evil angels mentioned in connection with the days of Noah (verse 20, compared with Genesis 6), and spoken of again by Peter in the same connection

in his second epistle 2:4, 5, and by Jude 6. Christ suffered for sins, was put to death as to His flesh, but was delivered, quickened as to His spirit. He was not only delivered, however, but was caused to triumph openly over his enemies, for in His spirit He went and proclaimed His victory through the Cross before the evil angels reserved in chains and darkness unto judgment, and is now "gone into heaven and is on the right hand of God, angels and authorities and powers being made subject unto him" (22).

That word "preach" in verse 19 is not the one usually employed in connection with the Gospel, but another word having the meaning only of a herald or a proclaimer of news, not necessarily the good news of salvation. Christ did not go into Hell to preach the Gospel to the lost, and give them "another chance," so to speak, but He went into the prison-house of the condemned evil spirits of Noah's day awaiting judgment, and announced to them the results of Calvary which they had sought to frustrate.

Now observe the practical exhortation to these persecuted and suffering Christians based upon the experience of Christ (chapter 4), "Forasmuch then as Christ suffered in the flesh arm yourselves with the same mind," suffer as did He, and you will triumph as did He, especially in that day when you shall give account to Him who judges the quick and the dead. This reference to the dead brings up the thought of some of their number who had died, perhaps as a result of the persecution suffered, and Peter reminds them that the Gospel had been preached to them to this same end. They had indeed been "judged according to men in the flesh," had suffered the judgment of men while in the body, but they were living "according to God in the Spirit." Their spirits were alive before Him, for men could kill their bodies but not their souls.

This reference to the preaching of the Gospel to the dead, it will thus be seen, means a preaching which they heard and accepted, not after they had died, but while they were still alive here in the flesh. Dead though they were now as to their bodies, their spirits were alive unto God, and awaiting the triumphant resurrection of their bodies as in the case of Christ.

Concluding Exhortations.—The remainder of the epistle, 4:7 to the end, is taken up with specific exhortations naturally suggested by the foregoing. For example:

1. To sobriety, verse 7. Observe the

the working out of the proposition that fellowship with God is to be maintained by doing righteousness, the apostle speaks of three distinct things:

1. The motive for doing righteousness, viz: the hope we have through our sonship to God (3:1-10).

2. The test of doing righteousness, viz: love to the brethren, (3:11-18).

3. The reward of doing righteousness, viz: assurance of salvation, (3:19-4:6).

Referring more at length to what I have called the "motive," notice particularly that our sonship to God includes likeness to Christ in His manifested glory (2). Notice, too, that the evidence of the sonship is in a sense bound up with this expectation of His coming, and the holiness of living it begets (3). Verses 3-8 practically continue the thought of Christ's holiness, and His work on the Cross to make it possible in our experience. Verse 9, has presented difficulty to some, but it may be stated as a contribution to its consideration that the phrase "whosoever is born of God," is taken by many to refer only to the new nature in the believer which does not sin. Others again interpret the word "commit" in the sense of practice (compare Galatians 5:21), Revised Version). It is one thing to fall temporarily into sin as a consequence of sudden and strong temptation, and it is another thing to practice it, i. e., to live in the continual performance of known transgression. This no regenerated man does or can do. The teaching of this verse should always be carefully balanced with that of 1:8, where the apostle, be it remembered, is speaking to the very same persons as in the present instance.

Referring to the "test" of doing righteousness, it may impress some as peculiar that brotherly love should be insisted on again as in the case of walking in the light. But it will be found to have an equally prominent place in the third cycle of thought, thus stamping this epistle as peculiarly the epistle of love. It speaks much of God's love toward us and our love toward Him, but singularly, either side of that truth with John always runs into the corresponding one of love towards one another in Christ. What a large place this last holds in the mind of God and in the Christian life! Notice what hinders the flow of this love as indicated by verse 12. How watchful we should be over envy! Notice its importance as demonstrating our spiritual condition in verse 14. Notice the deeply spiritual application of the sixth commandment in verse 15. Notice the very practical way in which this love should be demonstrated in verses 16-18.

Referring to the "reward" of righteousness as consisting in the assurance of salvation, I would call attention to the number of times and the different relations in which that word "know" is employed by the apostle. This is the "assurance" epistle all the way through as well as the epistle of love, and it is more than a simple coincidence that these two things should go together. See how much assurance of salvation depends upon our having a good conscience and a warm heart in Christ (19-21). See, too, how that this assurance of salvation carries with it a corresponding assurance in prayer (22-24). Some Christians are ever asking how they may be sure that their prayers are heard. Here is the simple answer: Live the life of obedience to God in the faith of His Son Jesus Christ and dismiss all misgivings. See, again, that this is the evidence of the abiding life in Christ (24), and that just in the measure in which we are pleasing our Heavenly Father as Jesus did, will we receive the witness of the Holy Spirit to that fact as He did. Finally the Christian who thus lives obediently has his assurance increased in the testimony to his overcoming of temptation. He will not be carried away by false doctrines or deceived by any anti-Christ (4:1-6).

IV. The Third Cycle of Thought, 4:7-5:21.—What is the third characteristic of God which John reveals (7, 8)? If, then, God is love, How is fellowship to be maintained with Him (same verses). In the working out of the thought thus suggested, that fellowship with God is to be maintained by experiencing and exercising love let us notice (1), how His love was particularly manifested toward us (9, 10), and (2), how our love towards Him should be manifested (11, 12). In the third place, notice how such love implies fellowship (13-16). In the fourth place, notice how it effects our spiritual life, begetting assurance, (17-18). In the fifth place, notice how its absence destroys fellowship (19-21). In the sixth place, notice how that the experience and exercise of love is only another aspect of walking in the light and doing righteousness (5:1-4). In the seventh place, notice that the basis, and in a sense, the source of this love, is faith in Christ (5-12). In conclusion, notice how many things we may thus know. Verses, 13, 15, 18, 19, 20.

CHAPTER LXIV.

The Second Epistle of John.

It is generally assumed by the church that the second and third epistles of John were written by the author of the first epistle bearing that name, who was as well the author of the fourth Gospel and the book of Revelation. There have been hints of some other John known as the "Presbyter" of the second century, but his existence can not be proven. Moreover, there are strong corroborative indications of an internal character going to show identity of authorship between these two epistles and the first of the same name. But these questions of criticism, as we have said all along, hardly belong to the scope of our present work. (See the author's work, Primers of the Faith" (Revell Company).

The second epistle is addressed to whom? The word "lady" in the Greek is Kyria, which may be translated as a proper name as well as impersonally, and perhaps in this case it should be so understood. Kyria was a common name among the Greeks and refers here, it may be, to some notable saint in the church or among the churches of Asia, in the neighborhood of Ephesus, to which John especially ministered in this his old age. The letter is a brief one, for the writer is soon to make a visit to this sister in Christ and to speak with her face to face (12).

1. The Salutation, verses 1-4, is interesting for three or four things:

(a) The deep humility of the writer. He who might have called himself not only an apostle, but the last of the apostles, and even the apostle whom Jesus loved, is content to describe himself as "the elder."

(b) The tender regard for the sister in Christ to whom he writes; but it is as a sister in Christ that he addresses her, whom he loves in the truth, i. e., in Christ. A love, spiritual, holy eternal.

(c) The solicitude for the honor and majesty of Jesus Christ. The mercy and peace which come to us are not only from God the Father, so to speak, but the Second Person of the Godhead as well, Jesus the Christ. And He is the Son of the Father. Not a Son but THE Son. How like this is to John's emphasis on the same truth in his first epistle.

(d) The insight into the spiritual condition of this sister's household. He had found, come across, in his travels, certain of her children who were walking in the. truth, i. e., knowing the truth, and living in the power of it. Were all of her children doing this?

II. The burden or real message of the letter follows next, 5-11. This burden is the old one of John, the message he reiterates—love. But love in the New Testament means, as we have seen, not a passion, not an emotion, a life. An abiding and controlling principle of being influencing for righteousness, this is love, Christian love. Is not that what John says again and again in his first epistle, and is it not what he says here (6)? And see how the idea is emphasized in verse 7. Not to love is not to hold to the truth in doctrine and to practice it in life. False teachers do not love. They may be amiable and kindly in their family and social relations, but they have not love, this Gospel love. They are deceivers, wittingly or unwittingly, and love and deceit do not go together. And mark, too, what is the central fact of that truth which constitutes love— the confession that Jesus Christ is come in the flesh. This strikes at the Jew's denial of Jesus, certainly, but how can Christian Science, for example, which denies the material body confess this? But changing the language again to conform to the Revised Version, we see that they are the deceivers and the anti-Christ in spirit who fail to confess that He "cometh in the flesh." It is Christ's second coming John has in mind as truly as His first coming. How more and more important this dotrine, this hope of the church, seems to become as we advance in the study of the New Testament!

In the light of the above consider now the warning in verse 8. There is danger of Christian believers losing something which belongs to them. That something is "a full reward." Compare Luke 19 : 15-27, 1 Corinthians 3 : 11-15, 11 Peter 1 : 5-11. But when does this reward come to them? See Matthew 16 : 27, Revelation 22 : 12. Does not the comparison of these passages bear out the thought of John in verse 7 as rendered by the Revised Version? Is not that false teaching which denies the coming of Jesus again in the flesh? And will not they who are deceived by it fail of their full reward when He comes? And should they not look to themselves, guard this point, in their faith?

What is it to transgress as given in verse 9? By the "doctrine of Christ" there is not meant merely the things He taught with His own lips while here in the flesh, but the whole doctrine or teachings concerning Him, i. e., the whole of the Old and New Testaments. To deny the truth concerning Christ is to deny His first and His second coming in the flesh, and He who denies this "hath not God." He may speak much of the "Father," but he only has the Father who has the Son. To have the One you must have the Other, (9).

And observe how strenuous we should be in maintaining this doctrine (verse 10). I think the command there "receive him not into your house," is not absolute but relative. I do not think it means that we are to deny him meat and shelter altogether, if he be in need of them, but only that we are not to fellowship him as a brother. Even our personal enemies we are commanded to bless and to pray for, if they hunger we are to feed them and if they thirst give them drink. But those who are the enemies of God by being enemies of His truth, we are to have nothing to do with in the capacity of fellow-Christians we must not aid them in their plans or bid them God speed. How would such a course on our part involve us (11)?

The apostle closes this epistle with that allusion to his visit already referred to, and a greeting from Kyria's elect sister. Did this mean her sister in the flesh or only in the faith? And in this last case was it the apostle's wife?

CHAPTER LXV.

The Third Epistle of John.

To whom is the third epistle of John addressed? Gaius is a name frequently alluded to by Paul as you must have observed, but whether this were the same individual as that or any of those mentioned by him, is problematical. In any event he seems to have been a convert of John (verse 4). Another form of the name is Caius and this was a very common name indeed.

What distinction in spiritual things is ascribed to Gaius (2)? His soul was prospering even if his bodily health and his business were not, and how much more important this was. But it is of value to note that the inspired apostle is interested in other things as well. The Christian should be careful of his health, and it is perfectly compatible with a deep spiritual life that he should have a successful business.

The Christian Character of Gaius.— After this salutation in verses 1 and 2, the next division of the epistle deals with the Christian character of Gaius, and enlarges upon the directions in which his soul's prosperity displayed itself, 3-8. Here are three particulars named (1). He possessed the truth (3)., (2), He walked in the truth, i. e., his life and conduct measured up to the light he had received from God, (3, 4). (3), As walking in the truth he was "careful to maintain good works," especially in the distribution of his means (5, 6). It is noticeable that his "faithfulness" in this regard is mentioned. It was not a spasmodic or impetuous thing on his part, but a steady flow of grace through him. His breadth of disposition is also mentioned, which indeed illustrated his faithfulness from another point of view, since his giving was not limited to those he knew but extended to those he did not know (5). Some particular recipients of his bounty are referred to in verse 6, and a journey is mentioned toward the expense of which he was contributing (6). All this is very realistic, and seems to bring the life of the church in the first century "up to date" as we sometimes say.

One or two facts, however, are given concerning the recipients of Gaius' gifts equally honoring to them, (7). Look at the motive of their journey, "His Name's sake," and look at the spirit actuating them "taking nothing of the Gentiles," i. e., the heathen. Whatever the journey was, they might have been assisted in it pecuniarily by those who were not actuated by a love for and fidelity to His name, but their conscience would not permit them to receive such aid. How valuable the instruction of this example. And what a close relationship it bears to the teaching of the second epistle about fellowshipping with heretics. How should such loyal and self-denying workers as these be treated in the church, and why (8)?

The Worldly Character of Diotrephes.
—The third division of the epistle deals with another type of the professing Christian and sets before us the worldly character of Diotrephes, 9-11.

What seems to have been his besetting sin (9)? What boldness on his part to have withstood even an apostle in such a way. How this experience of John recalls that of Paul in connection with the churches of Corinth, Galatia and Thessalonica? In what manner did John intend to deal with him (10)? Does this also recall anything similar in the exercise of apostolic authority

on Paul's part? How does verse 10 further reveal the worldliness and insincerity of Diotrephes? What an awfully disagreeable, overbearing, autocratic, unholy man he must have been! How did he get into the church?

What advice is given Gaius in verse 11? How does this verse testify to the relation between a living faith and good works? What opposite kind of example is set before him in verse 12? How many kinds of witnesses testify to the Christian character of Demetrius? One can not help wondering if this were the Demetrius of Acts 19. Such trophies of grace are by no means unusual, Paul was such an one.

Note the similarities in the conclusions of this epistle and the one previously considered (13, 14), suggesting that they may have been penned at the same time.

CHAPTER LXVI.

The Epistle of Jude

The writer of the epistle of Jude was evidently not an apostle, he calls himself a "servant of Jesus Christ and brother of James." Which James? There were two whose brother he might have been, the son of Alpheus and the brother of our Lord. It would be profitless to speculate on this question here, enough to say that the general opinion is in favor of the lastnamed relationship.

I. The first division of the epistle, as usual, is the salutation, 1, 2. In what terms are the believers addressed? Notice the Revised Version in this case: "them that are called, beloved in God the Father, and kept for Jesus Christ." How comforting all this is! They who are called of God are beloved in God the Father and kept for Jesus Christ. Why kept for Him? How much this suggests as to His coming manifested glory and the part believers will take in it?

II. The object of the epistle follows, 3, 4. What is that object as stated in verse 3? To what did he find it necessary to exhort them to whom he wrote? Notice that according to the Revised Version the faith delivered to the saints was delivered "once for all." The word "faith" here is to be taken in the sense of that body of Christian doctrine which forms the sum and sub-

stance of the truth concerning "our common salvation." It is used synonymously with the word "Gospel." This was delivered to the saints, to the body of the church, at the beginning of its history as a complete revelation in itself (Revelation 22:18, 19). It is a sacred deposit not only to be preserved in its integrity, but to be defended and earnestly contended for. The necessity for this defense is seen in the substance of verse 4. The word "foreshadowed" in that verse should be "forewritten," i. e., the false teachers therein referred to had been predicted as coming in among the flock. Our Lord had spoken of them, and so had all His apostles. The nature and outcome of their teaching as suggested by that word "lasciviousness" is particularly noticeable.

II. The third division of the epistle deals in detail with the subject of these false teachers (5-16). We have first, a revelation of their condemnation or punishment (5-7), from which their position as professed disciples would not save them any more than it saved the Israelites who were brought out of Egypt, when they afterwards sinned against light (5): or the angels referred to previously in Peter's epistles and Genesis (6); or Sodom and Gomorrah (7). Do not fail to observe the special class of sins prominent in these instances, especially the two last-named, and their relationship to that word "lasciviousness" already spoken of. While the erroneous teachings of these false teachers were intellectual, of course, yet their power was terribly augmented by association with carnality of the grossest kind.

The description of these false teachers is followed by a declaration of the punishment coming upon them, (8-13). Observe in verse 8 that they not only defile the flesh but speak evil of dignitaries, by which may be meant both civil and ecclesiastical superiors. And in this connection there is a strange illustration used in verse 9, that throws a good deal of light on the mystery of the death and burial of Moses as recorded in Deuteronomy. Why that mystery? Why should God Himself have buried the body of Moses, and kept the burial place a secret? Why should Satan have desired possession of that body? Did his foreknowledge of what should take place on the Mount of Transfiguration have aught to do with it? And shall we say with some, that Moses in the flesh is to be one of the two witnesses named in Revelation 11, and did Satan seek thus to frustrate God's purposes concerning the last days? And then the contention of Michael, how that brings to mind the teaching in Daniel concerning his particular relationship as the prince that stands for Israel. What a bearing all this has on the teachings of the New Testament about the dominions, and principalities and powers of the air (see Ephesians 6).

It may be asked, Where did Jude obtain this information about the conflict between Michael and Satan? Of course, the answer is very simple, that he obtained it by inspiration of God; but is it not remarkable that it is spoken of nowhere else in the Scriptures? He refers to it as though it were a matter of tradition among the Jews, and a reference to it is found in their books; but the tradition must have had a source, and we can hardly believe an inspired writer would thus employ it if that source were not divine.

Further analysis of the character of these teachers is afforded in verse 11. With what three Old Testament individuals, each conspicuous for his self-willed and rebellious spirit, are they compared? How strange it would seem that such persons could have any standing in the Christian church were it not that we discover their successors among us at the present day. Read

verse 12 in the Revised Version for a rather clearer idea of the intent of the figurative expressions there used. "Spots in your feasts of charity," should be "hidden rocks in your love-feasts." These "love-feasts" were the Christian gatherings on the first day of the week for the "breaking of bread," and the presence of such would-be leaders and teachers in those assemblies suggested the perils of the hidden rocks to the mariners on the broad seas. What exceeding care and circumspection were required to avoid disastrous contact with them. "Feeding themselves without fear," should be, "Shepherds that without fear feed themselves." It is characteristic always of the heretical teacher that he is thinking of himself rather than the flock. "There is a rough, incisive earnestness, and yet a majesty and eloquence" in all the language the inspired writer uses here, for the probable meaning of which, however, it will be necessary to consult a commentary.

The description of these false teachers is followed by a reference to the fore-knowledge of them. And here is a quotation from Enoch in verse 14, on which we might say a word. Where are these words of Enoch found? There is an apocryphal book in which they are found, but its author probably quoted from our epistle. Doubtless their real source should be spoken of in the same way as that of the reference to Michael and the body of Moses already mentioned. How deeply interesting to learn that Enoch, away back there before the deluge, and his mind carried out in the Spirit to the day of the Second Coming of Christ! And how perfectly his words agree with those of all the later prophets down to the very last, concerning the details and the purposes of that momentous event!

Every reader of this epistle must have had his attention arrested by the fact that this whole passage, indeed from verse 3 to verse 10, is very similar to one found in 11 Peter 2: 1-10. Does it not look as though one of these inspired writers saw and used the text of the other? And would this destroy the feature of inspiration in either case? Certainly not, any more than it would destroy the same in the case of Moses, to learn that he had obtained his data for the book of Genesis from tradition or earlier written sources. Inspiration is as truly needed, and may be as truly exercised in the selection and use of such material as in that which is original in the most absolute sense. Some who have carefully examined the two passages have reached the conclusion that Jude is the earlier writer of the two and that Peter is the copyist. And yet Peter is using the words with a somewhat different object from that of Jude, and is changing and abridging them a little to suit that object. Let the two passage be read side by side and these distinctions will scarcely need to be pointed out.

IV. The detailed reference to the false teachers or ungodly leaders in the church closes with verse 16, and gives way to the fourth general division of the epistle, which contains a description of the true church or true believers in sharp contrast with the false (17-25).

It begins with a caution (17-19). To which of the apostles in particular is he here referring, do you think? How does he describe these ungodly persons who have found their way into the visible church? That word "sensual" is in the margin of the Revised Version, "natural" or "animal." It is simply a case of unregenerated Christians of whom the church is still also plentifully supplied.

The caution is followed by an exhortation (20, 21). "Build," "pray," "keep," "look," here are the four corner posts defining the possessions of the Christian life. Does the exhortation to build suggest similar instruction from any apostle recently studied? What is peculiar about the exhortation to pray in this case? In Romans 8 we have revealed the inspiring truth that the Holy Spirit prays in us, but here we are to pray in Him. Are these contradictory teachings? Is it not true that the Holy Spirit is our inner life, and that He is also our spiritual atmosphere? In what are we to keep ourselves according to this exhortation? Does this mean that we are to keep ourselves in God's love to us or in our love to Him? How better can we keep ourselves both in the experience of His love to us, and the conscious emotion of our love to Him than by building ourselves up on our most holy faith, and praying in the Holy Spirit? What do you suppose is mean by "looking for the mercy of our Lord Jesus Christ unto eternal life." In the light of all the previous teaching about the appearing of His glory, may it not refer to that?

The exhortation is followed by instruction, and instruction especially concerning soul-winning (22, 23). The Greek text here, especially in verse 23, is somewhat obscure, but the teaching in any event calls for compassion on our part, and an effort to save the sinner while hating the sin.

The benediction and ascription follow, concluding the epistle in language as well known to, and appreciated by the whole church as any in the New Testament. What two great things is God able to do for believers in His Son? No wonder, therefore, that we should ascribe unto Him through Jesus Christ "glory and majesty, dominion and power throughout all ages."

CHAPTER LXVII.

The Book of the Revelation.*

In my view, the book of Revelation is more closely related to the Old Testament than the New. It deals chiefly, especially in the apocalyptic part following the third chapter, with the events synchronizing with the Day of the Lord. The earthly judgments accompanying that Day, and the incoming of the Millennial reign of Christ are the themes of which it treats, stamping it at once as a Jewish book to a great extent, a book that deals with Israel as a nation, again carrying us back to the thoughts associated with our studies in Daniel for example, or in Matthew, particularly our Lord's discourse on the last things as found in chapters 24 and 25. Keeping always in mind that, beginning with chapter 4, we are dealing with Kingdom truth rather more than Church truth, will aid very materially in the interpretation of the book and save the student from much confusion of thought. Further explanation of its general scheme may wisely be postponed until the difficulties actually come before us.

A rough working outline of the book might be given thus:
I. Introductory, 1.

*The most recent and one of the very best treatments of the book of Revelation of which I know, is Ford C. Ottman's "The Unfolding of the Ages." Every minister at least should carefully read it.

II. Epistolary, 2, 3.
III. Apocalyptic—Pre-Millennial, 4-18.
IV. Apocalyptic—Millennial, 19-20 : 6.
V. Apocalyptic—Post-Millennial, 20 : 7-22.

I. Under the head of **"Introductory,"** it seems suitable to say that the authorship of this book is generally ascribed to John, the beloved disciple, who wrote the Gospel and three epistles bearing his name, who was at this time, about 95 A. D., banished with other Christians, by Domitian, the Roman Emperor, to the Isle of Patmos in the Agean Sea (1 : 9). The date is in dispute, some placing it as early as the rule of Nero, 64 or 65, but the preponderance of evidence is in favor of the later period.

(1). The opening chapter consists (1), of the Preface, verses 1-3. A few questions will put us in better possession of it. Whose revelation is this? Of course, the reference here is to Jesus Christ considered as to His human nature, considered as man. Whence did He receive this revelation? For whom was it given unto Him? And for what purpose with reference to them? To which one of His servants was it representatively sent? And through what agency? What did this servant do with the revelation thus committed to him (verse 2)? That expression in verse 1, "things which must shortly come to pass," has puzzled some, and given rise to the opinion that the predictions in this book have largely been fulfilled in connection with the course of history from that time. I think, however, that while some of them have been fulfilled in the particular history of the Seven Church of Asia, for example, that the bulk of them are still future in that respect. "One day is with the Lord as a thousand years." However, this matter will be considered later.

(2) The Salutation follows the preface, 4-8. The Seven Churches in Asia therein addressed and afterward named, were probably those over which John at this time had some particular charge. But, as others have been careful to say, it were a mistake to suppose that the readers of this book were limited to the members of those churches. To quote Alford, "The number seven itself can hardly have been chosen except as symbolical of universality, according to the writer's practice throughout the book." Speaking further of the numbers used in this book, it may be well just now to say that seven is that of perfection or completion. In the several series of God's judgments, each

complete in itself, seven is the number of the seals, trumpets, thunders and vials. Four is the number of terrestrial or physical extension ; four seals, four trumpets, etc., in each case complete the number of judgments consisting in physical visitations. Twelve is the number belonging to Israel, or to the church, or perhaps to both. Certainly the latter remark may be true where twice twelve are referred to as in the number of the elders. The heavenly city has twelve gates and on them the names of the twelve tribes ; it has also twelve foundations corresponding to twelve apostles. The half of the mystic seven is also a ruling number in the book. Three and a half days are mentioned, and three and a half years, but of these things more shall be said later.

Observe in the Salutation the evident allusion to the Trinity. "Him Which is, and Which was, and Which is to come," God the Father. "The Seven Spirits before His Throne," God the Holy Ghost ; "Jesus Christ the faithful witness," God the Son. Compare for the Seven Spirits, Isaiah 11 : 2-5.

(3.) The Salutation is followed by a revelation of the preparatory vision which John received, and which constituted his authority to write, 8-20. This vision was that of the Person of the glorified Christ into the details of which it is beyond our province to go, but those who would like to study the symbolism of the passage a little further may be helped by the following, taken from a little work by Rev. Mr. Wight. For the candlesticks, compare Revelation 1 : 20, Matthew 5 : 14-16 ; the clothing, Isaiah 11 : 5, 61 : 10 ; Ephesians 6 : 14 ; Revelation 19 : 8 ; the white head and hair, Daniel 7 : 9 ; Matthew 17 : 1, 2 ; Acts 22 : 6-8 ; 11 Peter 1 : 16-18 ; Revelation 22 : 5 ; the eyes of fire, 11 Timothy 1 : 7, 8 ; Hebrews 12 : 29 ; the feet of brass, Proverbs 1 : 24-28 ; Isaiah 48 : 4 ; Luke 13 : 25-27 ; the voice of many waters, Daniel 10 : 6 ; Revelation 14 : 2, 3, 19 : 6 ; the seven stars, Daniel 12 : 3 ; Malachi 2 : 7 ; Revelation 1 : 20, 12 : 1 ; the two-edged sword, Ephesians 6 : 17 ; Hebrews 4 : 12 ; the keys, Isaiah 22 : 20-22 ; Matthew 16 : 19 ; Luke 11 : 52 ; Revelation 3 : 7, 20 : 1 ; Matthew 28 : 18 ; John 20 : 22, 23 ; 1 Corinthians 12 : 4, 8.

II. Epistolary.—There are those who regard the epistolary portion of this book, chapters 2 and 3, as giving, in the form of the epistles to the seven churches, a prophetic outline of the "the decline and approaching judgment of corporate Gentile Christianity," i. e., Christendom. Those who remember the teaching of the seven parables of

Matthew 13, will need no explanation of this remark, but will recall at once the distinction between Christendom and the true Church, or Body of Christ. The apostasy set in in the apostolic days, and has been running and increasing in power ever since, and will culminate as we have seen, in the development of the anti-Christ at the end of the age. The course of this apostasy, the growth of the tares among the wheat, is supposed to be indicated in these epistles, which show a gradual decline from the fervor of the first love or the Ephesian period, to the lukewarm condition, (spued out of the mouth) of the Loadician period.

But prior to dwelling on this further, let us be very clear in the first place, that these churches were, in John's time, seven historical existences in Asia. Nevertheless, in the second place, they are doubtless to be regarded as representative churches. Representative of what? (1) Representative of the Church Universal at that period. Doubtless the church of the apostolic days in every place contained within it the various elements of decline, summed up in these seven epistles. (2) Representative of the different characteristics of the Church Universal always more or less existent in every period of her history. In other words, not only in the apostolic age, but in every age succeeding, the commendations on the one hand, and the censures on the other contained in these seven epistles have been applicable to the Church Universal. (3) Representative of the dominant characteristics of the Church Universal in seven different periods of her history. That is, in the earlier period of the Church Universal her dominant characteristic is set forth in the epistle to the church at Ephesus. The next period in her history is indicated in the state of the church at Smyrna, etc. These seven periods in the history of the Church Universal have sometimes been divided in the following manner: The epistle to the church at Ephesus represents the spiritual condition of the Church Universal in the first period of her history, or in other words, from the ascension of Christ to the close of the first century, the apostolic era. The epistle to the church at Smyrna, represents the second period, or the martyr church, so-called, from the death of the last apostle, John, to the rise of Constantine, 100-311 A. D. The third epistle, Pergamos, from the State Church under Constantine to the rise of the papacy (Pope Gregory I), 311-590. The fourth epistle, Thyatira, from the rise of the

papacy to the Reformation, 590-1517. The fifth, Sardis, the Protestant churches from the Reformation to the rise of Methodism, 1517-1755. The sixth, Philadelphia, the Missionary period, 1755, to somewhere near the present time. The seventh, Laodicea, from the present time to the Second Coming of Christ.

Little space is left to speak of the structure of the epistles themselves, but quoting Archbishop Trench at this point, it will be seen that there are certain forms fundamental to all of them, for example: (1), an order to write, (2), a glorious title of the speaker, (3), an address to the church, (4), a command to hear, (5), a promise to the faithful. Those who are desirous of material for Bible readings will find the outline thus given a very helpful one. It is further interesting to note also, that the title of the speaker, Christ, has in every instance two main features, first, it is taken for the most part from the imagery of the preceding vision, and secondly, it always seems to harmonize with the state or condition of the church addressed. Let the student carefully examine this.

III. Apocalyptic—Pre-Millennial 4-18.

—(1) Chapters 4 and 5. In these chapters we have a kind of introductory vision to those that follow, which seems to set before us a picture of the glory of the risen saints in Heaven and the going forth of the Lamb (who is at the same time the Lion of the tribe of Judah), in those judgments upon the living Gentile nations of which the prophets have informed us, and which we are prepared to learn will fall upon the earth after the church has been caught up to meet her Lord in the air. (2) Chapter 6. In this chapter we see this work of judgment actually going on upon the earth after the church, doubtless, has been caught up. In the first seal, Christ himself is the rider on the white horse, a figure symbolizing his triumphant and glorious advent. It is a kind of "preface of blessing" for that which follows in the case of the other seals, which represent the afflictions on the Roman world-war, famine, pestilence, etc., preceding it. In other words, after the church has been caught up to meet the Lord in the air, and before he actually comes to reign on the earth with His church, these purifying judgments must fall; but the revelation of His coming precedes that of the judgments, and is described as the "preface of blessing." This is the plan throughout all the visions that follow. The order of narration, in other words, is not historical but moral, that which occurs last usually being narrated first. But some one may ask, what about the fifth and sixth seals? The second, third and fourth represent the judgments just spoken of, but the fifth, it is thought, represents the faithful souls on the earth amid the prevailing error at that time. It is quite conceivable, and indeed almost necessary to believe, that after the church has been caught up to meet the Lord in the air, and before the destructive judgments on the nations shall culminate, there will be some here who will have turned to him and be serving him. We can understand how the very translation of the church itself is likely, by God's grace, to produce that effect, and these are the ones who, as the great tribulation is settling down upon the earth, are heard to cry out, "How long, O Lord, how long?" The sixth seal is the representation of the culminating judgments— literal signs in Heaven and earth just before the end, just before the fulfillment of the first seal, and synchronizing with the events forcast by Christ in the flesh, as recorded in Matthew 24-25.

(3.) Chapters 7-9. In this section, according to the law of recurrence, we have fuller details of the divine judgments which precede the millennium. The "preface of blessing" is given in chapter 7, where we have set before us "the two elect bodies preserved for blessing at that time." The first is the faithful remnant of Israel which shall be preserved through the tribulation (verses 1-8), and the second is the church caught up to meet the Lord (9-17). Now follow, in the revelation of the six trumpets, the judgments already outlined in the vision of the seals. It would appear that the judgments under the figure of the trumpets, however, are confined to the people and the land of Israel, and it will be seen that they are destructions partly resulting from the exercise of the powers of nature and partly from superhuman agencies.

(4.) Chapters 10-13. This section gives still further details of the same judgments as the preceding sections, but it is restricted apparently to the last 1260 days of this dispensation, i. e., the last "half-week," the last three and a half years referred to in Daniel 9. To quote an English writer, Cecil Yates Bliss, the plan of the section is as follows:

In chapter ten we have the "preface of blessing," viz: a vision of the Lord's coming in power and glory, the "little book" symbolizing possibly the preceding witness-bearing of the faithful ones referred to above. In chapter 11 we have Jerusalem's history during 1260 days, the chief feature being the testimony of "the two witnesses," who many regard as Moses and Elijah returned in the earth in the flesh. In chapter 12 we have Christianity cast out from the city and persecuted. This is not the church, which we are to remember is caught up with the Lord, but the Christian system under the special circumstances of that period as previously stated. The "male child" possibly represents the converts to Christianity in Jerusalem just prior to the absolute reign, the anti-Christ being some secular despot represented by the beast. The ten horns are the ten kingdoms of the Roman Empire federated under him, and the seven heads possibly the seven systems, commercial, military, educational, political, ecclesiastical, etc., which contribute to the unity or federation afore mentioned, The second beast is an ecclesiastical head subordinate to the anti-Christ.

(5.) Chapter 14. Here we have a vision enlarging again upon certain points mentioned before. The "preface of blessing" is contained in verses 1-5. The Lamb on Mt. Zion with the 144,000 seems to represent the remnant of Israel purified and delivered through the tribulation, having overcome the anti-Christ, and now reigning with Christ over the earth in the Millennium. To quote B. W. Newton, the figure represents "the earthly seat of the new and heavenly power ordering the earth during the Millennium. Verses 6 and 7 represent the previous witness-bearing of the Gospel, which shall just precede the gladsome day. Verse 8 is to be regarded, I think, as a testimony against the city of Babylon itself, which, as we saw in our study of Isaiah and Zechariah is doubtless to be restored as the center of commercial and political greatness in the world at the time of the end. Verses 9-12 are likewise a testimony against the system and the person of the anti-Christ himself at that time reigning there. Verses 14-16 forecast the judgments on the nations again, especially the nations of Christendom, while verses 18-20 may be referring perhaps to those which shall fall more particularly on Israel and what we know as the heathen nations.

(6.) Chapters 15-18. This section seems to deal particularly with the judgment on Babylon herself. The "preface of blessing" is set before us in chapter 15, where we have a vision of the Millennial glory and reign of

Christ and his saints, as depicted in the allusion to the sea of glass and what follows. The pouring out of the vials in chapter 16 represents the judgments preceding the realization of this Millennial reign. The battlefield is, I think, a literal battlefield between the Roman nations with the anti-Christ at their head, and the nations of the East and North, perhaps with Russia at their head. Christ, however, is seen as interposing on behalf on his people, i. e., the faithful remnant.

Chapter 17 gives us a picture of the fate of moral Babylon, or Babylonianism, the anti-Christian system which has made possible the anti-Christ himself, and which is represented by the harlot sitting on the scarlet beast. This woman, according to Mr. Newton, symbolizes the moral, political, commercial, and ecclesiastical systems spoken of in an earlier paragraph in this lesson. The seven heads, indeed, may be seven system forming a perfect whole, the sum and substance of Babylonianism in the last days. The ten horns are the ten kingdoms of the Roman federation which support the system. The seven kings may be the seven world-monarchies leading up to this last. Five are fallen, viz, those of Nimrod, Assyria, Babylon, Persia, and Greece. One is, viz, the Roman (of John's own day). The "other" was not yet come, i. e., the constitutional monarchies of the present time. The "eighth" is that of the anti-Christ of which we are now speaking. The system is destroyed by the ten kings who give their power to the anti-Christ for that purpose, having wearied of the restriction of their power which has been entailed upon them by the harlot or, in other words, by Babylonianism.

Chapter 18 speaks for itself, and outlines the destruction of Babylon as a city, the material Babylon, the capitol city of anti-Christ's dominion.

The necessity for brevity in the outline thus completed gives to some of the declarations it contains a fixed and dogmatic character which the writer does not intend to convey. I feel the need of caution and modesty in interpretations of prophecy, realizing my own limitations, and the fact that brethren for whom I have the profoundest respect as students of the Word differ on some points. Please understand that what is here written is simply the best I know at present, and is subject to improvement as God may bestow more light. It affords, however, a working basis for those desiring to go further.

IV. Apocalyptic—Millennial, 19-20: 6.

—In the previous division, Apocalyptic-pre-Millennial, the coming of Christ was referred to again and again, but was not particularly described. It was held in the foreview as the "preface of blessing" to each of the visions enumerated, but the visions represented judgments of different kinds to fall on the nations, and on Israel, for punitive and purifying purposes, prior to the realization or the actual experience of his coming. Remember, however, that by the Coming of Christ in this case is meant not His coming for His church which will have already taken place, but His coming with His church to inaugurate the Millennial reign.

This view is called the Futurist because it holds, as we have seen, that the fulfillment of the visions is future, synchronizing, indeed, with the close of the present age, perhaps with the first half of the last seven years of this age —Daniel's last week of the seventy. The strongest rival to this school of interpretation is the Historic which treats the chapters covered as a progressive sketch of the course of events in the world and in the church from the days of John to the end of this dispensation or age. In part they have been already fulfilled, in part they are being fulfilled, and in part they are yet to be fulfilled. This school of interpretation generally holds to the idea that Babylon means Rome, and that the anti-Christ is the papacy, and is distinguished by what is called the year-day theory, i. e., the principle that the "days" spoken of in the book mean in each case a year. The Historic interpretation is very fascinating, and holds the student at first under the spell of its conclusions; but the study of the Bible as a whole, or even such a limited study as that we have just pursued, convinces one that however the Historic school may approximate or foreshadow the events of the coming end, the teachings of Revelation have reference to them in a very special sense. We can not spend longer time on this introduction but must proceed at once with the oultine of Part IV.

1. We have first, a representation of the actual coming of Christ, 19: 1-10.

2. We have, secondly, a representation of the church coming with him, 11-14. The saints thus seen as coming with him were those previously raised ere the beginning of the end, and harmonizing with the teaching in 1 Thessalonians 4: 13-18.

3. We have thirdly, a further representation of the judgments on his enemies, 15-21. These judgments I interpret. according to the law of recur-

rence, as the same as those previously referred to several times in the book, only that now they are seen in a somewhat different connection or relationship.

4. We have, fourthly, the binding of Satan, for the Millennial season, 20: 1-3. The absolute limitation of his power over men for the time being.

5. We have fifthly, the actual Millennial reign of Christ and his church, 4-6.

V. Apocalyptic — Post - Millennial. —

The fifth and last part of the book of Revelation, covering chapters 20 : 7-22, and dealing with the age to follow the Millennium, can receive but the briefest treatment.

1. The first fact mentioned, however, is the loosing of Satan, 20 : 7, who is given another opportunity to test men in his antagonism to God.

2. The loosing of Satan is followed by the last conflict with evil in the flesh that God will ever have, 8, 9. Some people are surprised to learn that the Millennium will be followed by such a conflict, for they have supposed that all sin would be put down during that period, in fact exterminated, and forever. But such is not God's plan. Sin will be in existence during the Millennium, latent, or dormant, if you please, but still existent. It will not be able to raise its head as it does now, for righeousness will be in the ascendant, but it will be crouching at the door ready to spring into life and action as soon as an opportunity appears. And the sin appears when Satan appears. The truth is that the Millennial age will be man's last chance on this earth to decide whether he will voluntarily serve God or not. And it will be a chance under most favorable circumstances, for the earth which will then be peopled from pole, will have within its view the visible glory of Christ and his church in the air; it will have the advantage of all the experiences of past ages, and all the excellency of God's power and goodness in the Millennium itself, but it will fail as it has always failed since the garden of Eden. When Satan is loosed there will be those on the earth who, neither regenerated or united to Jesus Christ, will again yield to his seductions, and oppose God. They will even dare to compass the beloved city, the earthly Jerusalem, the citadel of the saints itself, and then it is that the last judgment begins to fall.

3. We, therefore, see next, the destruction of Satan himself, verse 10. His time has come at length, and he will deceive the nations no more. Notice who have preceded him into the lake of fire and brimstone.

4. The judgment of the dead follows, verses 11-13, by which I understand all the dead from Adam to that time— the end of the world, except, of course, the saints who were reigning with Christ throughout the Millennium. Notice that the present earth and Heaven flee away, also that a "book of life" is mentioned. I suppose this book of life to contain the record of the saved ones during the Millennial reign.

5. The destruction of death and hell, or hades, the place of the dead, 14. They are personified here as representing the enemies of Christ.

6. The new heaven and earth, 21: 1. Observe the sequence of events suggested by this verse, e. g., now, i. e., in the present time, we have the church; in the Millennium will be the kingdom (?) ; and after that the new world where God shall be all in all. To quote one of the commentaries here, "Man's soul is redeemed by regeneration through the Holy Spirit now, his body shall be redeemed at the resurrection, and his dwelling-place at the creation of the new heaven and earth." "And there shall be no more sea." The sea is the type of perpetual unrest, and its absence after the metamorphosis of the earth answers to the unruffled state of solid peace which shall then prevail. A "river," and "water" are spoken of in the next chapter, but no sea.

7. The descent of the holy city upon the earth as the tabernacle of God, 2-8. Here are revealed some wondrous and precious things. Always distinguish between this New Jerusalem out of heaven, and that earthly Jerusalem in which Israel in the flesh shall dwell during the Millennium. The two are distinct. The one will be done away with when the other comes. This new Jerusalem will be God's tabernacle, God's dwelling-place with men in the new earth. It is the antitype of the tabernacle in the wilderness, and is also the same Greek word as that used of Christ's tabernacling among us (John 1 : 14). He was then in the weakness of the flesh, but at the new creation he shall be seen in the glory of his Godhead.

8. The description of the city, 9-22 :5. All the details of this city suggest glory, beauty, security and peace. In the Millennium, literal Israel in the flesh, dwelling in Jerusalem, is the antitype to the Old Testament earthly theocracy, but in this, the eternal (?) age, the heavenly Jerusalem is the antitype of the church, composed of Jews and Gentiles. This idea seems to be sug-

pested by the names of the twelve tribes and the twelve apostles written upon the gates and the foundations. The fact that no temple is seen in this city is remarkable, and suggests that the means of grace cease when the end of grace has come. Uninterrupted, immediate, direct communion with God and the Lamb will then be enjoyed. The student will be struck by the comparison evidently intended to be drawn between the picture in chapter 22:1-4, and the story of the garden of Eden and the expulsion of our first parents.

9. Conclusion or postscript to the book, 6-21. In this conclusion there is nothing more solemn than that stated in verse 11, which emphasizes the thought that "the punishment of sin is sin, just as the reward of holiness is holiness." "Eternal punishment is not so much an arbitrary law as a result necessarily following in the very nature of things as the fruit results from the bud." In this same connection notice the allusion to the eternity of sin in verse 15. May God quicken us who know these things to do our duty in bearing witness to them, that some by all means may be saved. This duty is set before us in verse 17, and "He which testifieth these things saith, surely, I come, quickly. Amen. Even so, come, Lord Jesus!"